Social Justice, Peace, and Environmental Education

The concept of "standards" seems antithetical to the ways critical educators are dedicated to teaching, but what would "standards" look like if they were generated from social justice perspectives and through collaborative and inclusive processes? Such is the central question posed by the contributors of this groundbreaking collection on the interconnectivity of social justice, peace, and environmental preservation. Challenging education that promotes consumerism, careerism, and corporate profiteering, they boldly offer examples of a new paradigm for practicing a transformative critical pedagogy. Rather than just talking about coalition building within and across educational communities, they demonstrate how we might communicate from different vantage points and disciplinary boundaries to create a broader picture of social and eco-justice. *Social Justice, Peace, and Environmental Education* will be required reading for educators and students who want to envision and practice living, acting, and teaching for a better world.

Julie Andrzejewski is a Professor in the Department of Human Relations and Multicultural Education, St. Cloud State University, Minnesota.

Marta P. Baltodano is an Associate Professor of Education at Loyola Marymount University in Los Angeles.

Linda Symcox is a Professor in the Department of Teacher Education, California State University, Long Beach.

The Teaching/Learning Social Justice Series

Edited by Lee Anne Bell

Barnard College, Columbia University

Critical Race Counterstories along the Chicana/Chicano Educational Pipeline
Tara J. Yosso

Understanding White Privilege
Creating Pathways to Authentic Relationships Across Race
Frances E. Kendall

Elusive Justice
Wrestling with Difference and Educational Equity in Everyday Practice
Thea Renda Abu El-Haj

Revealing the Invisible
Confronting Passive Racism in Teacher Education
Sherry Marx

Telling Stories to Change the World
Global Voices on the Power of Narrative to Build Community and Make Social Justice Claims
Edited by Rickie Solinger, Madeline Fox, and Kayhan Irani

Educator Activists
Breaking Past Limits
Edited by Catherine Marshall and Amy L. Anderson

Interpreting National History
Race, Identity, and Pedagogy in Classrooms and Communities
Terrie Epstein

Social Justice, Peace, and Environmental Education
Transformative Standards
Edited by Julie Andrzejewski, Marta P. Baltodano, and Linda Symcox

Social Justice, Peace, and Environmental Education

Transformative Standards

Edited by

Julie Andrzejewski
Marta P. Baltodano
Linda Symcox

Routledge
Taylor & Francis Group
NEW YORK AND LONDON

First published 2009
by Routledge
270 Madison Ave, New York, NY 10016

Simultaneously published in the UK
by Routledge
2 Park Square, Milton Park, Abingdon, Oxon OX14 4RN

Routledge is an imprint of the Taylor & Francis Group, an informa business

Typeset in Minion by EvS Communication Networx, Inc.
Printed and bound in the United States of America on acid-free paper by Edwards Brothers, Inc.

Library of Congress Cataloging in Publication Data
Social justice, peace, and environmental education standards : a transformative framework for educators / edited by Julie Andrzejewski, Marta P. Baltodano, and Linda Symcox.
p. cm.
1. Critical pedagogy. 2. Transformative learning. 3. Social justice—Study and teaching—United States. 4. Peace—Study and teaching—United States. 5. Environmental education—United States. I. Andrzejewski, Julie, 1945– II. Baltodano, Marta. III. Symcox, Linda.
LC196.S63 2009
370.11'5—dc22
2008048418

ISBN 10: (hbk) 0-415-96556-X
ISBN 10: (pbk) 0-415-96557-8
ISBN 10: (ebk) 0-203-87942-2

ISBN 13: (hbk) 978-0-415-96556-9
ISBN 13: (pbk) 978-0-415-96557-6
ISBN 13: (ebk) 978-0-203-87942-9

Contents

Foreword

An Eco-Pedagogy in the Pursuit of Social Justice and Peace

Antonia Darder

> It is urgent that we assume the duty of fighting for the fundamental ethical principles, like respect for the life of human beings, the life of animals, the life of birds, the life of rivers and forests... Ecology takes on fundamental importance... It has to be present in any radical, critical, liberationist educational practice. For this reason, it seems to me a lamentable contradiction to engage in progressive, revolutionary discourse and have a practice that negates life. (Freire, 2004, p. 47)

> A critical [eco-pedagogy] involves the ability to articulate the myriad of ways in which cultures and societies unfold and develop ideological political systems and social structures that tend either towards ecological sustainability and biodiversity or unsustainability and extinction. (Kahn, 2008, p. 553)

Everywhere we look, we are bombarded with signs of political systems and social structures that propel us toward unsustainability and extinction. At this very moment, the planet faces some of the most horrendous devastation of natural resources ever to be experienced in the history of humankind. Hurricane Katrina and a variety of other cataclysmic "natural disasters" have sung the environmental hymns of planetary imbalance and reckless ecological practices gone awry.

The devastation that has resulted locally and globally is heavily marked by an increasing concentration of wealth within the U.S. oligarchy and its agents of capital; the loss of livelihood among working people everywhere; the gross inequality of education; the absence of health care; an unprecedented number of people living behind bars; trillions spent on fabricated wars fundamentally tied to the control of natural resources; and all this financed through the destruction of safety nets for the poor, while the wealthy enjoy corporate welfare in the United States, to the tune of $700 billion dollars.

Hence, one of the most resounding lessons, highlighted in a variety ways in *Social Justice, Peace, and Environmental Education*, is the need to embrace the fundamental relationship of interconnectedness that we share with all life on this planet. The Western ethos of mastery and supremacy over nature has, to our detriment, supported the unrelenting expansion of capitalism and its unparallel domination over all aspects of human life. This is the worldview that has been unmercifully imparted within the hidden curriculum of schools and universities.

As a consequence (and irrespective of liberal human rights rhetoric that insists "we are all created equal") racism and the political economy of globalization—once known as imperialism—has dominated the ecological exploitation of societies, creating conditions that threaten peril, if we do not reverse its direction.

Yet, despite the importance of this phenomenon to the survival of the planet and the manner it should earnestly underscore the decisions we make in our life, seldom are the questions of ecological concerns made central to the discourse of pedagogical preparation. Perhaps, it is exactly this historical "missing link" in the curriculum that is most responsible for an uncritical and inhumane response to the suffering of human beings under regimes of genocide, slavery, and colonialism. In truth, a deeper view exposes a legacy that persists today in the shrouded values and attitudes of educators from the dominant class and culture who expect the oppressed to adhere to the cultural domination of the powerful elite.

Often this veiled message translates into a need for those with power and privilege to obsessively seek some specific identification with "the other"so that they might deem those perceived as "different" worthy of love and respect. What is truly unconscionable about this process is that if satisfactory identification with the humanity of the other cannot be found, then racialized institutional policies and practices render the "untouchables" as problematic to the political project of capitalist democracy and hence, unworthy and disposable.

It is precisely such a worldview that participates in the extinction of whole species, or thinks nothing of the destruction of cultures and languages outside of a "first-world" tongue classification. Rapidly our biodiversity is slipping away, despite scientific findings which clearly warn about the loss of hardiness and vitality to human life, as a direct consequence of assimilation and homogenization. It is truly ironic that in a world that obsessively denies its participation in the oppression of life and embraces all sorts of confounded rhetorics of diversity, we find ourselves more and more pressured into a "safe" essentialized world of sameness and familiarity. There are examples of this everywhere we look, but nowhere is the oppression of it more felt than in the lives of youth, who are still far more organically present to the diversity of life. The consequence here, of course, is the manner in which the repression of the body is manifested with capitalist fervor to commodify as quickly as possible its design on the new generation. Schools are one of the most complicit institutions in the repression of the body and thus, the repression of our emotional nature, our sexuality energies, and the spiritual capacities that open us to communion with natural world.

What this heralds then is the need for a more comprehensive and complex understanding of human diversity and its multitude of legitimate expressions, beyond those made available by the academic dictates of power and capital. Here, issues of social justice and human rights within the context of schooling cannot be addressed outside of the political economy and the myriad of ways in which it orchestrates a politics of hate and fear, in the name of progress and democracy. This is to say, that without a deep willingness to interrogate the manner in which educational policies and the practice of teachers as moral leaders supports the inhumanity of capitalism in this country and abroad, it is impossible to build a new critical paradigm that supports all life as precious and worthy of love and respect.

As many of the contributors to this volume attest, the majority of the social and political problems facing us today are fundamentally rooted in competition, paternalism, arrogance, absolutism, violence, and greed. Such attitudes are predicated upon an ahistorical and uncritical view of life that enables the powerful to abdicate their collective responsibility to democratic ideals of social justice, while superimposing a technocratic and instrumental rationality, which commodifies and instrumentalizes all human existence. Through a systematic web of hierarchal meritocratic relationships, neoliberal education functions to sustain a political economy of oppression, both locally and globally. It is precisely these values that have supported the destruction of democratic conditions for the construction of knowledge and replaced it with fractured curricula and fetishized methods, even in the realm of multicultural education. Hence, it is no surprise that education for oppressed populations is reduced to teaching-to-the-test, while the heirs of the elite are provided mobility of their bodies, a wide variety of content, as well as consistent access to state-of-the-art technology.

Social Justice, Peace, and Environmental Education sends a clear message to educators who express a commitment to human rights. If they are to contend with many of the issues raised here, it will necessitate a critical ecological perspective of education that is informed by standards firmly anchored upon an emancipatory praxis. This encompasses a pedagogical refusal to adhere to artificial disconnections which falsely separate those political and economic dynamics that shape the local, global, regional, rural, urban, and so on; and instead, challenges forthrightly static views of humanity and the planet—views that inadvertently serve the commodifying interests of capital and its penchant to divide and conquer, through paternalistic discourses of expertise. In contrast, what a critical ecopedagogy must encompass is a philosophical principle that embraces ambiguity and dissonance as an ever present phenomenon within a world where human differences are both commonplace and valued for their necessary role and creative potential in the making of a truly democratic, just and peaceful world.

Moving educators beyond an orthodoxy of consumerism, careerism, and corporate profiteering, the authors here courageously pose a new paradigm for the living out of a transformative critical pedagogy that encompasses human rights, peace, and an integrative co-existence with all our fellow-species on the earth. More importantly, it points toward a re-envisioning of our work as revolutionary educators, committed to ending oppression in all its manifestations, while embracing with love and respect all life on the planet.

References

Freire, P. (2004). *Pedagogy of indignation.* Boulder, CO: Paradigm.

Kahn, R. (2008). Towards ecopedagogy: Weaving a broad-based pedagogy of liberation for animals, nature, and the oppressed people of the earth. In A. Darder, M. Baltodano, & R. D. Torres (Eds.), *Critical pedagogy reader.* New York: Routledge.

1 Social Justice, Peace, and Environmental Education

Global and Indivisible[1]

Julie Andrzejewski, Marta P. Baltodano, and Linda Symcox

This book seeks to demonstrate that social justice, peace, and environmental preservation are integrally connected, that they are of equal importance, and that educators should play a major role in teaching students how to understand global problems and take corresponding social action. Inspired by the *Alaska Standards for Culturally Responsive Schools* (Assembly of Alaska Native Educators, 1998), we present standards and guidelines to assist educators who want to integrate social justice, peace, and environmental education (SJPEE) into classrooms and schools. This introductory chapter provides an overview of the topics covered in this book, and sets the stage for how urgently educational reform is needed.

Education for Urgent Global Problems

As the first decade of the 21st century comes to a close, humanity faces problems of a magnitude unknown to previous generations. We are now living in an "epidemic of extinctions: decimation of life on earth" according to the latest Living Planet Report (Loh, 2008) which measures species extinctions. The 2008 report documents a loss of 27% of 4,000 monitored species in the last 35 years, all related to human activities: climate change, pollution, destruction of natural habitat, invasive species, and overexploitation of species. Every life system is experiencing decline or stress from human activities: oceans, rivers, lakes, forests, plains, mountains, tundra, deserts, arctic regions, and the earth's atmosphere. Global warming is finally being acknowledged and verified in spite of continued corporate campaigns to spread doubt (Dauncey 2001, Robinson, 2007).

Increasing competition for scarcer resources spawns wars and ethnic conflicts, imposing a terrible toll on humans, animals, and ecological systems. The affluence and consumption of some people continues to increase while others are born, live, and die in utmost despair and deprivation, and while millions have experienced hunger and starvation for decades with inadequate global response, the global food crisis is intensifying. Agricultural production continues to shift from grains for human consuption to crops for biofuels and feed for animals, as meat consumption increases for the affluent. Food riots erupting around the world illustrate people's desperation, while giant agribusinesses report huge profits (Lean, 2008). The world's supply of water is shrinking dangerously, raising the specter of conflict over this most vital of natural resources (Barlow, 2008).

While each of these crises may seem separate and distinct, they are interrelated in profound and complex ways. The economic and political activities of humans, which benefit some people and some species at the expense of others, now dominate the earth by maximizing short-term gains for a few without regard for the long-term survival and well-being for all. Regardless of the "reasons" manufactured to justify these inequities, all living beings are negatively affected by them, directly or indirectly, sooner or later (LaDuke, 1996; Shiva, 1995).

People are now confronted with evidence that many of the products and activities that we have been taught to associate with "the good life" actually undermine our health and the ecosystems in which we live. The problems we face locally are interrelated, and thus global. If we are to understand them, and change our lives for the better, and help to preserve the planet, we must think globally, and act locally *and* globally.

Yet despite the seriousness and urgency of these problems, preK-12 schools and higher education institutions have experienced political pressure to avoid study, discussion and action on these issues, for fear of being accused of political bias. While some exceptional educators have courageously educated students about these urgent issues, institutions have been reluctant to provide the leadership needed to prepare effective global citizens who can act to save the planet, other species, and humanity itself. To meet this need, educators can provide leadership by preparing ourselves and our communities for active global citizenship; citizenship focused more on restoring the earth and the web of life than on personal wealth, consumption, entertainment, comfort, and status.

Our Purpose: Increasing Social Justice, Peace, and Environmental Education

Inspired by the Alaska Native Knowledge Network's *Standards for Culturally Responsive Schools* (2001), a dedicated group of educators has worked for the past several years to draft social justice, peace, and environmental education standards or principles. We believe SJPEE is best understood and taught in a global context, drawing upon many intellectual traditions, ways of knowing, and social movements. A global perspective increases awareness of the interconnections between all forms of suffering and liberation, and compels us to move beyond a self-centered, single-issue, or national focus to consider what is good for all, what is necessary for survival and recovery of the planet, and how our treatment of other species matters.

Too few people are aware of the principles collaboratively distilled into international agreements such as the Universal Declaration of Human Rights, United Nations Conventions on Racial Discrimination, Discrimination Against Women, the Rights of the Child, Biological Diversity, the Rights of Persons with Disabilities, Indigenous Rights, and the Coolangatta Statement, the Earth Charter, or the Animals' Platform. Based on such documents, the authors share a single goal: to increase the quantity, quality, visibility, credibility, and accountability for social justice, peace, and environmental education in local communities and national educational agendas. We believe that central to our future well-being is our ability to foster the practice of these values in our own lives and in the lives of people around the world through education.

Unfortunately, many of today's educational agencies and policymakers are engaged in political agendas or remain uninformed or lackadaisical about the growing threats to the quality of human life and the environment. Instead, policies and curricula designed to uphold a world order grounded in a competitive, exploitative, global economy continue to be uncritically followed. The current neo-liberal educational agenda has banished democratic ideals and social justice issues from preK-12 curricula, replacing them with corporate-inspired goals and values, norm-referenced testing, and punitive bottom lines. Propelled by a sense of urgency for change, this book offers an alternative view to the prevailing corporate orthodoxy. The devastating social and ecological problems we face today stem from dominant patterns of development, production and consumption that are validated and reinforced by the current educational system. We hope, therefore, that the issues covered in this book will become integrated into curricula, institutional policies, and everyday educational practices. If education is to become a positive force helping to resolve the crises facing the world, social justice, peace, interspecies and earth education must move into the educational mainstream.

This project also strives, in multiple ways, to cut through the artificial boundaries dividing social justice education, peace education, and environmental education.

- First, we see global capitalism as the common denominator forming and/or exacerbating the conditions for: human oppression; militarism and war; and destruction of species and environment.
- Second, we move beyond essentialism within and among social justice issues toward embracing the multiplicities and complexities of oppression and emancipation.
- Third, we illustrate the necessity of an educational vision and practice that recognizes that social justice, peace, and eco-justice are indivisible.
- Fourth, we strive to bridge the mythical divides between the local, regional, national, and global. Too often educators view ourselves and our work within a certain context—a school, a community, or a nation, and we may not recognize or understand the impact of global policies on our local community. Conversely, educators may not be familiar with the proposals and actions by international bodies that can exacerbate or ameliorate these problems. We highlight the connections between the local and global, between personal well-being and the well-being of others and the earth.
- The chapters in the book follow a general format; first presenting a synthesis of the challenges being faced within a global context and their interconnections with other issues. Second, they introduce national, international or key organizational documents to provide positive goals. Finally, they present a set of standards or principles to encourage self-reflection, and generate practical ideas and actions by and for students, teachers, administrators, staff, and teacher educators. We know that writing standards for

social justice, peace, and environmental education is a new activity, and that its results must be provisional. Hence, we chose deliberately not to stipulate a single organization or language for the "standards," leaving authors to name their own with a richness of variation and detail to maximize the potential for adaptation by educators.

Benefiting Educators, Students, and Institutions

Although we hope this book can be useful to multiple constituencies, we expect it will be especially beneficial to teacher education candidates, graduate students, or other educators at all levels of elementary, secondary, and post-secondary institutions. As educators ourselves, we are products of the neo-liberal educational system previously described, so we know what it is to feel ill prepared to teach about issues of social justice, peace, and the environment. It is our hope that the practical visions, standards, and guidelines in the following chapters will help educators teach how to mitigate, alleviate, and repair some of the damage we humans have done, and even more importantly, how to inspire students to forge creative new (and old) ways of living in harmony with the natural world, other humans and other species.

An integrated and timely agenda is unfortunately still unavailable to students in most educational institutions. While students may encounter fragments of information, they rarely have more than a rudimentary sense of the problems, how their own behaviors might be contributing to them, or what organizations or social movements might be working on solutions. Many students freely admit that they do nothing to alleviate the global problems that concern them and frankly have no idea what they can do. This is not intended as a criticism of students or teachers but of the educational structures within which we find ourselves. It highlights the urgent need for committed and knowledgeable educators to make a substantial difference in the lives of students, and by extension, create a better world by facilitating new social consciousness, life changes, and action choices.

Claiming *Standards* for Justice

Education has always been the battleground for political struggles between those who want to control others for their own benefit and those who want to liberate themselves and the oppressed. Those who wished to maintain slavery made it illegal to educate slaves while those who opposed slavery educated slaves in violation of the law while organizing to change the law. As social movements challenged injustices, new ways of denying equal education to oppressed groups were continually developed through segregation, tracking, hidden curricula, and the like. Techniques were devised to create the appearance of fairness and equality while in essence replicating the same stratified system to maintain advantages for some groups at the expense of others. In the latest of these endeavors, a system of "standards" and tests with the egalitarian title of "No Child Left Behind" (NCLB) has been established to deliver an education which is just and caring in name, but which in practice proves to be neither just nor caring.

At this point we should perhaps clarify why we have chosen to use the word "standards" for this project. Through several years of work, the authors have struggled with the idea of using the language of standards, because *standards* suggests both an orthodoxy and a means of measuring deviations from prevailing norms and behaviors. In addition, the controversy that raged around the US National History Standards in 1994–95 warns us of the pitfalls and dangers inherent in any attempt to create a canonical set of standards (Symcox, 2002). However, the term, *standards,* also refers to the establishment of goals, and the identification of specific ways to reach those goals. Using standards in this way requires going beyond a critique of existing standards, toward a positive outcome for progressive educators and their students. This book represents the first steps in this direction by laying out sets of proposed standards, and inviting criticism and revision for continuing to improve SJPEE standards, guidelines, and best practices. These standards and principles are designed as starting points in the process of implementing social justice goals, and perhaps more importantly, for redirecting educational discourse about accountability to include social justice, peace, and environmental sustainability.

An inspirational example of such standards is the work of the Alaska Native Knowledge Network (ANKN). Over the last decade and more, the ANKN has been influencing educational systems in Alaska through a series of groundbreaking Standards and Guidelines for students, parents, educators, curriculum, communities, schools, libraries, and school boards (Assembly of Alaska Native Educators, 1998, 1999, 2000, 2001, 2002). Using an inclusive decision-making process, five major Native cultural regions in Alaska cooperatively developed a vision to integrate indigenous worldviews and ways of knowing into Alaskan educational systems. The cultural standards that emerged from this process established a powerful design for educating Alaskan native children while assuring the flexibility of activities and timelines needed by each distinct cultural group. Using the ANKN standards as a model, we invited progressive educators to develop similar positive *standards* for social justice, peace, and environmental education. This book is the result.

Historical and Political Context

As the debate over the U.S. National History Standards dramatically illustrated, educational standards are strenuously contested. With the mass media concentrated into ever fewer giant corporations, censorship, propaganda, and public relations campaigns serving the interests of corporate elites are on the rise (Phillips & Roth, 2007; Stauber 2002). Parallel efforts toward the corporate control of education include the promulgation of the General Agreement on Trade in Services (GATS), the voucher movement to shift public funding to private schools, and top-down standards implemented through high-stakes testing, and the growing privatization of education (Berliner & Biddle, 1995; Vinson, Gibson, & Ross, 2001). Such educational policies serve the interests of the few at the expense of the needs of people and the environment, and increase global problems rather than mitigate them. Countervailing forces are needed more than ever.

At the same time as corporate-controlled politicians are pressuring educational institutions and accrediting agencies to conform to neo-liberal policies, progressive multicultural, social justice, and environmental education movements have grown within academic, professional, and non-profit institutions. Creative spaces for questioning, investigating, and teaching new perspectives and knowledge bases have deepened and matured. Outside of the national media spotlight, parents, educators, and students have responded to the standards and testing movement in multiple ways. Some communities and professional organizations have issued statements challenging high-stakes testing and voicing their right to quality education (New Paltz Education Network, 2002; National Association of Multicultural Education, 2001). Others have made the repeal of NCLB a key part of their activism (Neill, 2006; Miner, 2007; see www.fairtesting.org and www.educatorroundtable.org).

Still other organizations are responding by developing and implementing educational standards or guidelines promoting democracy, inclusion, and social justice. On a global level, the World Indigenous People's Conference on Education (WIPCE) issued the Coolangatta Statement on Indigenous Peoples' Rights in Education (1999). It situates indigenous human and educational rights in a global colonial context and draws upon numerous international charters, conventions, and civil rights declarations to stake its claim to "systems of education which reflect, respect, and embrace Indigenous cultural values, philosophies, and ideologies..." (WIPCE, p. 3).

The ANKN standards and guidelines were created as part of this movement. They were then endorsed by governmental and non-governmental agencies, and adapted to address areas beyond schooling, including the development of Culturally Responsive Guidelines for Alaska Public Libraries, developed by the Alaska Library Association (2001). On an international level, the ANKN standards were recently incorporated into an indigenous higher education accreditation system developed by the World Indigenous Nations Higher Education Consortium, and have served as the subject of a case study on innovative practices in indigenous education prepared by UNESCO.

On the other side of the spectrum, the US National Council for Accreditation of Teacher Education (NCATE), National Board of Professional Teaching Standards (NBPTS), and the Interstate New Teacher Assessment and Support Consortium (INTASC) have failed to address SJPEE standards for teacher education. Beyerbach and Nassoiy (2004) evaluated the standards of these three organizations on the extent to which "they defined and advocated for educational equity." They concluded,

> Whereas race, class, gender, ability, language, and religion were explicitly mentioned in each set of standards with regard to diversity, these terms were rarely linked to the concepts of equity, power relations, prejudice, and oppression... Though there was some talk about stereotyping...and some language about testing bias..., an anti-bias...perspective was noticeably absent in the national standards. (p. 33)

In fact, NCATE has no commitment to address social justice, peace, or environmental education. This became clear in 2006 when NCATE quickly dropped the term *social justice* used as an *example* of a disposition in teacher education when it came under pressure from the National Association of Scholars, the American Council of Trustees and Alumni, and the Foundation for Individual Rights in Education. At the same time, "the *de facto* elimination of sexual orientation through the addition of various phrases and qualifiers" was also arranged by NCATE (Quinn & Meiners, 2007). Later, NCATE (2008) tried to appease social justice educators by reintroducing a narrow definition of social justice into its documents which does not challenge vested interests in the status quo (see chapter 5 for further discussion).

Since accrediting bodies are clearly not providing leadership for SJPEE issues, alternatives must be created by educators and organizations already dedicated to SJPEE issues, and uncompromised by dominant economic and political forces.

Teaching the Indivisibility of Peace, Justice, and Preservation

It is not uncommon for people to become passionate about a particular social or environmental justice concern (often one that they see affecting themselves most directly) and to view other problems as "not their issue." When encouraged to investigate the roots of all these problems, however, people uncover a web of power and money that spells the difference between suffering and death, or life and sustenance. Many are surprised to learn the extent to which human activities are causing the environmental crises now underway. Very few have had the opportunity to discover that coveting and stealing natural resources, land, and/or labor has been at the root of oppression, violence, and warfare for millennia. As industrial, technological, and military projects exploit human and natural resources in ways devastating to people and life on earth, the frequency of environmental conflicts will increase and the links between these factors will become more visible.

Some examples of the interwoven nature of the problems may help illustrate how seemingly disparate issues are integrally related. In 2004 and 2007 respectively, two people, Wangari Maathai and Al Gore, won the Nobel Peace Prize for environmental activism. Environmental issues are related to peace, they explained, because as resources shrink and the human population increases, conflicts and wars over limited supplies of water, oil, arable land, forests, and other resources will multiply and intensify. The current violence in Darfur is a case in point. Although usually identified as an ethnic conflict, new reports place the origins of the Darfur conflict with desert expansion and competition for water (Borger, 2007).

This relationship was further highlighted in a secret Pentagon report leaked in 2004 with the astonishing prediction that global climate change would undermine global stability far more than terrorism (Townsend & Harris, 2004). A 2007 report by the International Institute for Strategic Studies confirmed and expanded dire predictions of competition and conflict over dwindling resources (Lovell, 2007). Another United Nations report "estimates that in the next ten years desertification alone could displace some 50 million people" (Joseph, 2008, p. 301).

Because these problems are multifaceted, the solutions to them must be as well. Unidimensional efforts cannot resolve them. Social movements and activist organizations around the world are forging innovative initiatives across environmental, peace, and social justice borders. Only when people can see the complexities, will they be able to engage minds, resources, and actions for the greatest benefit. Here education offers the key.

To help educators grapple with these challenging and critical issues facing humanity, each chapter in this book seeks to answer the following questions:

1. What background knowledge will help educators empower students to create and sustain movements that link social justice, peace, and the environment?
2. What powerful and credible documents and treaties already exist to support educators who want to move in this direction?
3. What standards might assist students, educators, and schools to integrate SJPEE into curricula and institutional policies?

Making Connections Through Theory and Activism

Integrative theorists from many fields have often recognized the leadership of indigenous and peasant thought and social change movements. Since educators have always drawn upon multidisciplinary resources, work of integrative theorists and activists from around the world can provide us with a rich fund from which to draw educational expertise for social justice, peace, and environmental education. For instance, Uruguayan author Eduardo Galeano's early work presents a provocative account of the centuries of extracting South American resources to finance the industrial revolution in Europe, detailing the toll on indigenous peoples, African slaves, and the natural environment (1971). Indian physicist Vandana Shiva joined the resistance to corporate bioprospecting to chronicle movements where Indian farmers challenged the patenting of the Neem tree, and later rebelled against the imposition of genetically engineered seeds. Shiva connects the dots between the domination of women, third world peoples, and nature with the theft of indigenous knowledge through the three waves of globalization: colonialism, "development," and "free trade," demonstrating how biotechnology threatens biodiversity through the colonization of "the interior spaces of women, plants, and animals" (1993, 1995, p. 5). Winona LaDuke, Native American organizer, exposes the relationships between violence, resource extraction, and indigenous oppression (1999, 2005). Linda T. Smith, Maori educator, analyzes how imperialist science and research are deeply implicated in the violent theft of indigenous lands and knowledge (1999). Wangari Maathai, imprisoned for organizing to save the forests of Tanzania, helps women make a living by planting trees, showing that saving the environment is necessary for peace (2003). Canadian activist Maude Barlow fights free trade agreements, elucidating corporate plans to sell the earth's water (Barlow, 2008).

Another significant area of theory and research informing this project is the impact of commodification of non-human animals on the welfare of human beings, ecological systems, and on the lives of animals (Rifkin, 1991; Mason, 1998; Nibert, 2002; Robbins, 2001). Robbins documents the consequences of producing and consuming meat on humans, animals, and the environment (2001). Rifkin explains how indigenous peoples are removed from their lands for the production of cattle (1991). Such theorists cross boundaries of social justice, peace, and environmental issues to reveal previously excluded factors, relationships, and complexities. Each chapter presents some of the key theorists and activists that have influenced education, policies, and actions that are bringing together social justice, peace, and environmental education in each special arena.

Using International Documents for Credible SJPEE Standards

Since international agreements, mandates, and activist documents on behalf of human rights, social justice, and ecological sustainability have already been refined by years of discussion, revision, and ratification by multiple constituencies, they provide another rich source of integrative and applied research as well as legitimacy for the development of SJPEE standards. Yet, many educators are unaware of them. For example, many do not know that the Universal Declaration of Human Rights (UDHR) of 1948 includes a *mandate* for "every individual and every organ of society" to "strive by teaching and education to promote respect for these (*human*) rights and freedoms" (United Nations, 1948). It is not surprising, therefore, that implementation of this mandate is sporadic, at best. Thus in two reports, Banks (2001, 2003) found that 25 U.S. states include human rights education (HRE) concepts or content somewhere in their state standards, but 25 states do not. Even where HRE is included, however, it is often limited in scope and depth and does not extend to an exploration of values and action. In this climate of ignorance and neglect, SJPEE standards could help inform teachers about the UDHR mandate that provides a strong rationale upon which to include human rights in their teaching (see Jennings, chapter 6, this volume). Many other international documents have multiple constituencies that can provide significant guidance for the development of SJPEE standards. Just a few are listed here by date.

- Universal Declaration of Human Rights (UDHR), 1948
- UN Convention on the Elimination of Racial Discrimination (CERD), 1969
- International Covenant on Economic, Social, and Cultural Rights (ICESCR), 1976
- Tbilisi Declaration, 1977
- UN Convention on the Elimination of Discrimination Against Women (CEDAW), 1981
- UN Convention on the Rights of the Child (CRC), 1990
- Principles of Environment Justice (First National People of Color Environmental Leadership Summit) 1991
- Kari-Oca Declaration of Indigenous Peoples' Earth Charter, 1993

- Beijing Declaration and Platform for Action for Women (United Nations) 1995
- UN Plan of Action for the UN Decade for Human Rights Education, 1995–2004
- Coolangatta Statement on indigenous peoples' rights in education, 1999
- Hague Agenda for Peace and Justice for the 21st Century, 1999
- Earth Charter USA Campaign, 2000
- UN Convention on the Rights of People with Disabilities, 2007
- UN Declaration of Indigenous Rights, 2007

These documents and others are used to inform the SJPEE standards and the principles presented in the following chapters.

Criteria Recommended for Developing SJPEE Standards

While certain key components have been emphasized and explained above, we would like to share some general criteria to help guide educators who wish to adapt or write their own standards or guidelines. We tried to follow them ourselves in the chapters following

- Theory-based: The authors in this book sought to apply and translate available theory and research on SJPEE to the development of guidelines or principles to help students, teachers, schools, communities, teacher preparation, accreditation, and other aspects of education.
- International Agreements: Groundbreaking agreements, declarations, and laws developed through extensive research and deliberation impart credibility to the standards and justify including social justice, peace, eco-justice, and interspecies education into all levels of education.
- Integration of Social Justice, Peace, and Environmental Issues: In order to teach SJPEE effectively, it is necessary to affirm the interdependency of the factors that make up the field, and to acknowledge that all are equally important. They do not function in isolation and when multiple factors interact their effect is magnified.
- Accessible: Standards should be clear and understandable to educational practitioners at all educational levels, and by students wherever possible.
- Practical: Standards should be practical, useable, and adaptable to help foster SJPEE in any areas of education where desired and possible.
- Adaptable: Standards "are not intended to be inclusive, exclusive or conclusive, and thus should be reviewed and adapted to fit local needs" (Assembly of Alaska Native Educators, 1998, p. 3).
- Experiential: Practical activities and community-based learning are intended to advance everyday social responsibility and global citizenship (Andrzejewski & Alessio, 1999).
- Affirmative: Positive standards and principles should encourage education on social justice, global peace, human rights, and ecological preservation.

The Overview Statement

The following overview statement introduces our vision and the chapters in the book follow through, each with their own special contributions, to develop and explicate this vision.

Social Justice, Peace, and Environmental Education Standards

Overview Statement

As educators, teacher educators, activists, and scholars focusing on social justice, peace, and environmental education, we envision a world of caring, respect, compassion, and peace. We seek to encourage understanding, conservation, and celebration of differences—different species, ecologies, cultures, languages, belief systems, epistemologies, and ways of knowing.

We advocate for education, informed by the international agreements discussed in this book, that puts into practice the values of human rights, liberty, justice, dignity, democracy, freedom of body, speech, and religion, and access to adequate food, water, shelter, and health care. We draw upon the collective wisdom of many cultures around the world that value cooperation, sharing, compassion, reciprocity, equanimity, harmony, natural law, biodiversity, spirituality, non-violence, and peace. Central to the future of human beings, other species, and the natural environment is the ability to apply these values in our lives, in our institutions, and in our societies.

Mission statements of most educational institutions in the United States currently highlight key elements of these values. However, missions, philosophy statements, and institutional goals are only as good as their implementation and lived experiences. In keeping with the movement for greater accountability of social institutions, these guidelines provide a lens through which to evaluate whether the everyday actions of our educational institutions are congruent with their stated values. They further provide a mechanism for monitoring the extent to which the entire educational system embodies these values.

We encourage educational institutions at all levels to integrate and foster social justice, peace, environmental preservation, and interspecies education throughout the educational process. Toward that end, educational institutions have an obligation to prepare active, peace-oriented, democratic citizens with the commitment, motivation, knowledge, and skills to work for a better world.

Book Overview

The four parts of this book have separate but complementary purposes and foci. Each chapter culminates with standards or principles (by various names). Based on collectively created documents, they facilitate the educational vision presented therein and provide a rich resource for educators wishing to pursue these objectives. A comprehensive set of standards, drawn from the chapters, is presented in the last chapter.

Part 1, "Learning from Native Educators and Indigenous Communities: Transformative Principles and Cultural Standards," describes the inspirational work of Native educators and elders that served as a model for the SJPEE project. In chapter 2, "Mai i te Maramatanga, ki te Putanga Mai o te Tahuritanga: From Conscientization to Transformation," Graham Smith describes the liberatory, transformative educational theory (Kaupapa Maori Theory), that Maoris have created as an alternative to decades of colonial education, as a way to reclaim and sustain their sovereignty, language, and culture. Even beyond the Maori context, these principles provide a lens through which educators might examine their own institutions to determine if they are meeting the needs of the communities they serve. In chapter 3, Ray Barnhardt introduces a key inspiration for the SJPEE project, "Culturally Responsive Schools for Alaska Native Students: A Model for Social Justice, Peace, and Environmental Education." When Alaskan Native educators and elders became aware of the national standards movement, they were deeply concerned with the mismatch between the national standards and indigenous cultures. Therefore, educators and elders from various native groups in Alaska came together to identify the positive cultural attributes, knowledge, and skills they wanted their children to learn. These groundbreaking cultural standards have been endorsed by the Alaska Board of Education and used throughout the state for years. Inherent in the Alaska Standards for Culturally Responsive Schools are the values of social justice, peace, and environmental preservation.

Part 2, "Transformative Education for Human Rights, Peace, All Species, and the Earth," covers issues that are not specific to any particular region or group but are overarching and encompass everyone. Building upon chapter 1 and part 1, part 2 demonstrates the need to integrate global social justice, peace, and environmental issues with each other and into education.

Chapter 4, "From *A Nation at Risk* to No Child Left Behind: 25 Years of Neoliberal Reform in Education," by Linda Symcox frames the need for social justice, peace, and environmental education within the context of neoliberal reforms in the United States which have supported corporate economic globalization and surreptitiously shaped the national educational agenda. She shows how the movement for academic standards and high-stakes testing, the taxpayer revolt launched by Proposition 13 in California, the movement promoting charter schools and vouchers, and the No Child Left Behind Act have all evolved out of a common neoliberal framework. Todd Jennings explores the unrealized mandate and potential of the Universal Declaration for Human Rights (1948) in chapter 5, "Reclaiming Standards for a Progressive Agenda: Human Rights Education Standards for Teachers and Teacher Education." After presenting human rights standards for classroom teachers, Jennings discusses implications for teacher education, how to overcome obstacles and develop support systems, and presents examples for integrating human rights education into subject matter at all levels.

In chapter 6, "Environmental Education: From International Resolve to Local Experience and Inquiry," David Greenwood, Bob Manteaw, and Gregory Smith provide a critical analysis of international agreements on the environment and how these, combined with powerful environmental education theory, inform the queries they pose as a basis for eco-justice education. Julie Andrzejewski's "Education for Peace and Nonviolence" (chapter 7), draws upon The Hague Appeal for Peace

(1999), to illustrate how global justice and environmental issues are fundamental to peace and well-being and present educational tools and practices for teaching integrated perspectives on peace. After a compelling description of the state of the world's children, Beth Swadener and Leigh O'Brien draw upon international documents of children's rights, and grounding theories and research, to develop principles for early childhood education in chapter 8, "Social Responsibility and Teaching Young Children: An Education for Living in Ethical and Caring Ways." In chapter 9, "Interspecies Education for Humans, Animals, and the Earth," Julie Andrzejewski, Helena Pedersen, and Freeman Wicklund introduce misconceptions about animals through the lens of speciesism, and examine how the treatment of animals affects humans, the environment, global conflict, and social justice.

Part 3, "Community Struggles for Global Justice, Peace, and Environmental Education," speaks to how community challenges of racism, sexism, ableism, and heterosexism are connected to the broader global challenges of peace, justice, and the environment. In chapter 10, "(Re)imagining New Narratives of Racial, Labor, and Environmental Power: Towards a Liberatory Education for Latina/o Students," Yvette Lapayese describes how Latinas/os have traditionally been marginalized in schools and society through racism, linguistic genocide, environmental degradation, and capitalism. She proposes some "starting points" to articulate a liberatory education for Latina/os, such as breaking away from hegemonic stereotypes to focus on the subjugated epistemologies and counter-narratives of people of color. Glen Omatsu uses history, theory, and Asian activism to argue that the social construction of Asians as a racial category is an ideological invention grounded in colonialism, and proposes an alternative framework for exploring the Asian American experience in chapter 11, "Liberating Minds, Hearts, and Souls: Forging an Anti-Colonial Framework to Explore the Asian-American Experience." Omatsu explains that the histories of African Americans, Latina/os, indigenous peoples, and other minorities are connected by the transnational forces that have benefited from their oppression. In chapter 12, "'A Past is Not a Heritage': Reclaiming Indigenous Principles for Social Justice and the Education of People of African Descent," Nola Butler Byrd and Menan Jangu illustrate how colonization and re-colonization have shaped the lives of Africans in Africa and the Diaspora in parallel oppressive systems of violence, wealth extraction, and environmental destruction. They propose an African-principled education that values human rights and partnerships across borders and ethnicities, caring for the earth and other species, sharing resources equitably while reducing overconsumption, affirming indigenous knowledge, and using resources for life and peace, not violence and death.

In "Achieving Conceptual Equilibrium: Gender Justice in Education" (chapter 13), Renée Martin contextualizes gender oppression within the larger ideological framework of global capitalism and explores the benefits of the empowerment of women for health, community, economic well-being, peace, and the environment. Martin also explores new roles for men, and proposes some foundational standards to assist teachers. In chapter 14, "Disability Studies in Education: Guidelines and Ethical Practice for Educators," Robin Smith, Deborah Gallagher, Valerie Owen, and Thomas Skrtic challenge the special education clinical model, drawing upon disability activism and scholarship to propose a vision of disability as a cultural signifier in the same way that race, gender, sexual orientation, age, and religion are examined. They propose an interdisciplinary examination of disability anchored in the humanities. Finally, Darla Linville, Christopher Walsh, and David Carlson challenge the expected norms of heterosexuality to queer the curriculum and move beyond tolerance to propose experiential vows for nonviolence and sexual justice in chapter 15, "Queered Standards: Living and Working for Peace and Justice."

Part 4, "Themes, Challenges, and Potential of SJPEE Standards," suggests different approaches through which the SJPEE standards can be developed and implemented in these crucial but neglected areas and some of the expected challenges of this work. Marta Baltodano's "The Pursuit of Social Justice in the United States" (chapter 16) describes some of the obstacles and challenges to social justice and proposes a set of transformative guidelines which lay the groundwork for the potential formulation of a Declaration of Teachers' Rights. In chapter 17, "Developing Social Justice Standards: A Multicultural Perspective," Robert Crafton invokes the National Association of Multicultural Education's Criteria for Evaluating State Curriculum Standards to explore how state academic standards might be evaluated and used in positive ways to further SJPEE that respects diverse peoples, interests, and ways of knowing. In the concluding chapter, "Towards a Collective Vision of Social Justice, Peace, and Environmental Education," Julie Andrzejewski, Marta Baltodano, Ray Barnhardt, and Linda Symcox synthesize a set of six themes and five overarching standard areas that reflect the collective visions represented in the book.

The editors and authors hope this volume can help educators reclaim and focus education on issues desperately needed for survival and well-being of humans, other species, and the earth.

Note

1. Portions of this chapter have been previously published in the article, The Social Justice, Peace, and Environmental Education Standards Project, *Multicultural Perspectives*, 2005, *7*(1), 8–16.

References

Alaska Library Association. (2001). *Culturally responsive guidelines for Alaska public libraries.* Fairbanks: Alaska Native Knowledge Network. Retrieved January 15, 2008, from http://www.ankn.uaf.edu/standards/library.html

Andrzejewski, J., & Alessio, J. (1999, Spring). *Education for global citizenship and social responsibility.* Burlington: John Dewey Project for Progressive Education, University of Vermont.

Assembly of Alaska Native Educators. (1998). *Alaska standards for culturally-responsive schools.* Fairbanks: Alaska Native Knowledge Network. Retrieved January 15, 2008, from http://www.ankn.uaf.edu

Assembly of Alaska Native Educators. (1999). *Guidelines for preparing culturally responsive teachers.* Fairbanks: Alaska Native Knowledge Network. Retrieved January 15, 2008, from http://www.ankn.uaf.edu

Assembly of Alaska Native Educators. (2000). *Guidelines for respecting cultural knowl-*

edge. Fairbanks: Alaska Native Knowledge Network. Retrieved January 15, 2008, from http://www.ankn.uaf.edu

Assembly of Alaska Native Educators. (2001). *Guidelines for strengthening indigenous languages and guidelines for nurturing culturally healthy youth*. Fairbanks: Alaska Native Knowledge Network. Retrieved Jnauary 15, 2008, from http://www.ankn.uaf.edu

Assembly of Alaska Native Educators. (2002). *Guidelines for culturally-responsive school boards*. Fairbanks: Alaska Native Knowledge Network. Retrieved January 15, 2008, from http://www.ankn.uaf.edu

Barlow, M. (2008). *Blue covenant: The global water crisis and the coming battle for the right to water*. New York: The New Press.

Banks, D. (2001, April). *What is the state of human rights education in K-12 schools in the United States in 2000? A preliminary look at the national survey of human rights education*. Paper presented at AERA Conference, Seattle, WA.

Banks, D. (2003). Promises to keep: results of the national survey of human rights education 2000. Retrieved on November 28, 2003, from http://hrusa.org/education/PromisestoKeep.htm

Berliner, D., & Biddle, B. (1995). *The manufactured crisis: Myths, fraud, and the attack on America's public schools*. Reading, MN: Addison-Wesley.

Beyerbach, B., & Nassoiy, T. (2004). Where is the equity in national standards: a critical review of the INTASC, NCATE, and NBTS standards. *Scholar Practitioner Quarterly, 2*(4), 31–43.

Borger, J. (2007, June 23). Darfus conflict heralds era of wars triggered by climate change, UN report warns. *The Guardian*. Retrieved on January 15, 2008, from http://www.guardian.co.uk/environment/2007/jun/23/sudan.climatechange

Dauncey, G. (2001). *Stormy weather: 101 solutions to global climate change*. Gabriola Island, BC: New Society Publishers.

Earth Charter USA Campaign. (2000). *The earth charter*. Retrieved on July 31, 2003, from http://www.earthcharterusa.org

First National People of Color Environmental Leadership Summit. (1991, October). Principles of environmental justice. Retrieved January 23, 2004, from http://www.charity-advantage.com/summit2/EJPrinciples.asp

Galeano, E. (1971). Open veins of Latin America: Five centuries of the pillage of a continent. New York: Monthly Review Press.

Hague Appeal for Peace. (1999). *The Hague agenda for peace and justice for the 21st century*. New York: Hague Appeal for Peace.

Joseph, P. (2008, January/February). Peace, gore, and global warming. *Sierra*. 93(1), 18.

LaDuke, W. (1996). *Native American land struggles, environmentalism, and indigenous women* [video presentation St. Cloud State University, MN].

LaDuke, W. (1999). *All our relations: Native struggles for land and life*. Cambridge, MA: South End Press.

LaDuke, W. (2005). Recovering the sacred: The power of naming and claiming. Cambridge, MA: South End Press.

Lean, G. (2008, May 4). Multinationals make billions in profit out of growing global food crisis. *The Independent/UK*. Retrieved June 9, 2008, from www.commondreams.org/archive/2008/05/04/8710/

Lovell, J. (2007, September 12). Global warming impact like 'nuclear war.' *Reuters*. Retrieved June 3, 2008, from www.commondreams.org/archive/2007/009/12/3791/

Loh, J. (2008, April). *2010 and beyond: Rising to the biodiversity challenge*. Gland, Switzerland: World Wildlife Fund. Retrieved June 3, 2008, from http://www.wwf.org.uk/filelibrary/pdf/2010_and_beyond.pdf

Maathai, W. (2003). *The greenbelt movement: Sharing the approach and the experience.* New York: Lantern Books.

Mason, J. (1998). *An unnatural order: Why we are destroying the planet and each other.* New York: Continuum.

Miner, B. (2007, Spring). Can NCLB be left behind? *Rethinking schools, 21*(3). Retrieved December 18, 2008, from http://www.rethinkingschools.org/archive/21_03/nclb213.shtml

National Association of Multicultural Education. (2001). *Resolution on Standardized and State Mandated Testing.* Resolutions and Position Papers. Retrieved December 1, 2003, from http://http://hwww.nameorg.org

National Council for Accreditation in Teacher Education (NCATE). (2007, November 13). NCATE issues call for action; defines professional dispositions as used in teacher education. Retrieved January 25, 2008, from http://www.ncate.org/public/102407.asp

National Council for Accreditation in Teacher Education (NCATE). (2008). *Professional standards for the accreditation of teacher preparation institutions.* Retrieved December 19, 2008, from http://www.ncate.org/documents/standards/NCATE%20Standards%202008.pdf

Neill, M. (2006, Fall). Overhauling NCLB. *Rethinking Schools. 21*(1), 111–124.

New Paltz Education Network. (2002). Statement on testing and assessment. *Community Bulletin, 3.*

Nibert, D. (2002). *Animal rights human rights: entanglements of oppression and liberation.* Lanham, MD: Rowman & Littlefield.

Phillips, P., & Roth, A. (2007). *Censored 2008: The top censored stories of 2006–07.* New York: Seven Stories Press.

Quinn, T., & Meiners, E. (2007, Summer). Do ask, do tell. *Rethinking schools. 21*(4). Retrieved January 25, 2008, from http://www.rethinkingschools.org/archive/21_04/ask214.shtml

Rifkin, J. (1991). *Beyond beef: The rise and fall of cattle culture.* Salt Lake City, UT.

Robbins, J. (2001). *The food revolution: How your diet can help save your life and our world.* Boston: Conari Press.

Robinson, E. (2007, Spring). Exxon exposed. *Catalyst. 6*(1). Retrieved January 15, 2008, from http://www.ucsusa.org/publications/catalyst/exxon-explosed.html

Shiva, V. (1993). Colonialism and the evolution of masculinist forestry. In S. Harding (Ed.), *The racial economy of science.* Bloomington: Indiana University Press.

Shiva, V. (1995). *Biopiracy: the plunder of nature and knowledge.* Boston: SouthEnd Press.

Smith, L. T. (1999). *Decolonizing methodologies: Research and indigenous peoples.* London: Zed Books.

Stauber, J. (2002). *Toxic sludge is good for you* [Video]. Northampton, MA: Media Education Foundation.

Symcox, L. (2002). *Whose history: The struggle for national standards in American classrooms.* New York: Teachers College Press.

Townsend, M., & Harris, P. (2004, February 22). Now the Pentagon tells Bush: Climate change will destroy us. *The Observer International.* Retrieved January 4, 2008, from http://observer.guareian.co.uk/international/story/0,1153513,00.html

Vinson, K., Gibson, R., & Ross, E. W. (2001). *High-stakes testing and standardization: The threat to authenticity.* Monograph in Progressive Perspectives. Burlington: John Dewey Project on Progressive Education, University of Vermont.

World Indigenous Peoples' Conference on Education. (1999). T*he Coolangatta statement on indigenous peoples' rights in education.*

Part I

Learning from Native Educators and Indigenous Communities

Transformative Principles and Cultural Standards

Introduction

This section introduces the theory, community organizing, and educational practices that inspired the Social Justice, Peace, and Environmental Education Guidelines Project. Graham H. Smith lays the foundation with his excellent summary of Kaupapa Maori theory and transformative principles in chapter 2. He succinctly describes the historical and contemporary circumstances that the Maori find themselves as a result of centuries of colonial, neocolonial, and more recently, neoliberal domination and exploitation. He clearly delineates the role that colonial education has played in supporting and maintaining that process, especially through cultural assimilation and the introduction of free market ideologies. While the details and dates may differ, these circumstances are a common experience of many, if not most, indigenous peoples and many other colonized peoples around the globe. Though cautioning that the Kaupapa Maori theory should not be "uncritically export(ed)," since each local community must assess their own conditions and context in determining whether or how it might be helpful, he points out,

> What may be useful for other indigenous communities and groups, however, are insights into the processes, experiences, and understandings related to Maori developing indigenous theorizing as an instrument for conscientization, resistance, and transformation. (pp. 19–20, this volume)

The Kaupapa Maori theory provides a set of principles used in the development of Maori alternative education to reclaim and sustain their sovereignty, language, and culture. Even beyond the indigenous context, these principles provide a lens through which communities and/or educators might examine their own circumstances and determine if the current educational system is meeting the needs of their children or students. For example, a question generated by this theory might be: Is the educational system preparing students to acquiesce to a neoliberal globalized economy or to confront the serious problems of the world with innovative and vigorous solutions? If the answer is not satisfactory, what actions might then be taken to rectify this situation?

Smith's chapter provides an excellent context to introduce the key work that inspired this SJPEE project: the "educational restoration endeavor" of the Alaska Rural Systemic Initiative (AKRSI). Ray Barnhardt outlines the connections in chapter 3. When Alaskan Native educators and elders became aware of the national standards movement, Barnhardt explains, they "were greatly concerned by what they did not see." The ground-breaking cultural standards developed by the AKRSI, "endorsed by the State Board of Education and...used throughout the state," originated with Native educators and elders from the various cultural regions in Alaska who came together to identify the positive cultural attributes, knowledge, and skills they wanted for their children.

Leaving aside the critique of western education, they skillfully assert the importance of providing an education that prepares students for making a life for themselves and their communities, not just making a living. The meticulous articulation of the collective vision, the positive focus, the embodiment and nurturance of indigenous world views and various cultural traditions, specific enough to be meaningful yet general enough to allow flexibility, and the process of learning *through* the local culture as the foundational principle create a gentle, reasonable, yet radical document to foster transformation of the educational system for Native children and beyond. Inherent in the Alaska Standards for Culturally Responsive Schools as well as in the process of its origination and in the development of subsequent implementation guidelines described by Barnhardt, are the values of social justice, peace, and environmental preservation. The creativity of expression and vision in these documents has inspired the work in this volume.

2 Mai i te Maramatanga, ki te Putanga Mai o te Tahuritanga

From Conscientization to Transformation[1]

Graham H. Smith

Introduction

Education is considered a crucial site of struggle for the redevelopment of Maori in the face of widespread high and disproportionate levels of socioeconomic disadvantage. For the most part, such disadvantage has been both produced and reproduced within the social context by unequal power relations between dominant Pakeha (non-Maori, mainly European New Zealanders) and subordinated Maori. This paper reflects on innovative responses within Maori education in Aotearoa/New Zealand since the 1980s; in particular, it describes some of the critical circumstances that have led Maori to develop their own theorizing related to education. This particular indigenous theorizing has been labeled Kaupapa Maori theory (Smith, 1988; Smith, 1999).

It is important to understand the evolution of Kaupapa Maori theory within a process of praxis. Kaupapa Maori as an educational resistance strategy has grown out of an ongoing struggle that occurred within both Maori communities and Pakeha dominant institutional contexts. The notion of struggle is important in the overall development of Kaupapa Maori theory in that it connotes the thinking, commitment, and political conscientization of Maori with regard to the critical issues and understandings that needed to occur in order to make the theoretical components both robust and effective. This formative process of critical reflection and (re)development is very apparent within the research work of Maori scholars from the University of Auckland. More recently there has been a burgeoning of both literature and practical activity based on Kaupapa Maori theory from other University sites, Maori researchers, and community interest groups across New Zealand.

Before proceeding with this discussion on conscientization and transformative action within a Maori educational context, it must be clarified that the intent is not to uncritically export the Kaupapa Maori theory to other indigenous communities and contexts. One of the important principles argued around Kaupapa Maori theory is that the context in which it is being used is important; that is, theorizing needs to evolve from and interrelate with the specific cultural context within which it is to be applied. What may be useful for other indigenous communities and groups, however, are insights into the processes, experiences, and understandings related to Maori developing indigenous theorizing as an instrument for conscientization, resistance, and transformation.

A primary emphasis in this paper is placed on developing an understanding of the process of transformation itself. Thus, for change to occur and to be effective, there is a need to know more precisely the key transformative elements within a given strategy. We ought to know more accurately (a) how and why communities buy in to a transformative process, (b) what counts as transformation, (c) how we know that transformation has actually taken place, and (d) whether or not the transformation is truly beneficial. Thus, the significant need here is to move beyond conscientization to change through transformative praxis.

The Maori Context

The Maori are a minority population within the very land of which they are the original inhabitants. They make up approximately 15% of a total New Zealand population of around four million. Despite efforts to resist the erosion of their knowledge, language, and culture, Maori have been significantly colonized and assimilated by the dominant Pakeha society. Within education, Maori continue to experience high and disproportionate levels of crises and disadvantage. For example in 1996, 42.6% of Maori males and 35.3% of Maori females left school with no formal qualifications. This is compared with 16.9% of non-Maori males and 12.2% of non-Maori females. Furthermore, since 1992, the gap in educational success between Maori and non-Maori has been widening.

The New Zealand context is made more interesting by the fact that in the 1980s the government launched headlong into neo-liberal economic reform. Many of these free market reforms were embedded within education structures and have arguably made Maori even more vulnerable to the colonizing imperatives within the education system. Although I do not wish to go into depth on this point, there is a strong correlation between the worsening statistics related to Maori performance in education and the insertion and impact of the neo-liberal education reforms. Some of the free-market reforms have proven to be extremely problematic for Maori and have been critically described as representing "new formations of colonization" (Smith, 1997). In this view, it is argued that the economic reforms have enhanced the intersection of economic exploitation and cultural oppression.

For those unfamiliar with New Zealand, the following list of demographic features will give a quick overview of the Maori situation:

- The New Zealand population is currently about 4 million people.
- Maori people make up 15% of the total New Zealand population.
- Maori were the first people to systematically inhabit the islands of New Zealand.
- It is popularly espoused that the first European explorers to "discover" New Zealand were Abel Tasman (1642) and James Cook (1769).
- The British began to settle in New Zealand around the 1800s.

- In 1840 the Treaty of Waitangi between the Crown of England and Maori tribes of New Zealand was signed and formally established British colonial presence in New Zealand.
- Historically, Maori have been colonized and assimilated into European culture.
- The church and the education system have been significant agencies for cultural assimilation.
- Maori, as a group, have the worst crisis statistics in most social indices, including health, education, imprisonment, wealth, and the like.

The Economic Context

In coming to understand the rise of Maori political consciousness and critical developments in education, it is important to appreciate the economic context that stimulated both resistance and transformative action. In particular, it is necessary to understand the history of economic reform in New Zealand since the 1980s. This reform has been generalized as neo-liberal economic restructuring and is also referred to as free-market reform. This restructuring of the New Zealand economy is very significant as it marked a shift from a "welfare state" to a "free market" orientation. More ominously perhaps, New Zealand, once regarded as one of the leading examples of a successful welfare state economy, was moving to reposition itself as a champion of the neo-liberal approach. This economic redirection was aided by a number of factors. First, New Zealand is a relatively small-scale economy; it is an island state and is consequently geographically isolated with clearly defined ocean borders. Second, and perhaps more importantly, New Zealand had a new Labor (ostensibly socialist-oriented) government that was willing to implement the radical reforms necessary.

The Maori population of New Zealand provides a particularly interesting case study in which to observe and understand the development of a theoretically informed resistance to the new formations of colonization embedded in the neo-liberal restructuring of education. For example, a key strategy was the constructing of new hegemonies around the market notions such as "freedom of the individual," "consumer choice," "the autonomous chooser," "user pays," "increased competition," "accountability," "standards," "horizontal equity," "meritocracy," "co-opted democracy," and "economic management" (rather than economic policy). The implicit values embedded within this form of restructuring did not simply reinforce and support dominant Pakeha values, behaviors, and thinking. They went further—they provided impetus to marginalize, demean, derogate, and subjugate Maori people and their cultural preferences. Thus, Maori cultural values, which emphasize collective responsibility (rather than individual), choice, rights, ownership, wealth, and economics were constructed as the "other," "oppositional," and "contradictory." Elsewhere it has been argued that this culturally captured form of economics, with its emphasis on processes of commodification and privatization, can be interpreted as new formations of colonization (Smith, 1997).

The Rise of Alternative Forms of Maori Education

The indigenous population of New Zealand has developed some innovative educational intervention strategies following the implementation of its pre-school immersion model (Te Kohanga Reo) in 1982. The growth of the Maori education resistance initiatives since the 1980s represents a revolution within Maori education. These resistance initiatives respond to the new economic formations of colonization in that they are counter-hegemonic and are responsive to the commodification impetus of the neo-liberal economic context.

The essence of the revolution of 1982 is summarized in the following comments:

- In the 1980s, Maori took more control over the key decision-making and organization of their own education through various alternative education initiatives.
- During this time, Maori, themselves, became increasingly proactive in taking action against educational and language crises.
- These actions resulted in increased numbers of Maori becoming politically conscientized and involved in political action.
- Maori developed a vision and plan of action related to language recovery and revitalization that resulted in significant support from large sections of the Maori community.
- During the struggle for Maori language revitalization, many Maori developed critique and critical analysis of the shortcomings of the existing system, and the prevailing social context maintained by dominant Pakeha power relations.
- Maori individuals and groups developed a theoretical dimension to the struggle to reclaim language and schooling, called Kaupapa Maori.
- This reclamation lead to many Maori going outside of the existing schooling structures to have their educational needs met.
- This search for alternative schooling caused a legitimacy crisis for state schooling that eventually led to a "settlement," with the state incorporating and funding the new Maori schools.
- There are now more than 70 state funded Kura Kaupapa Maori primary schools in New Zealand that teach through the medium of Maori language.
- The Kaupapa Maori methodology and theory is now being used to bring about changes for Maori in other sectors.

Since the 1982, Maori have been engaged in a number of educational interventions that attempt, first, to revitalize Maori language, knowledge, and culture; and second, to overcome a number of social crises related to educational underachievement. As a consequence of the negative, mono-cultural experiences endured by many Maori in and through schooling, Maori communities have developed a series of Maori immersion schooling initiatives. These have been implemented at the pre-school (Te Kohanga Reo), the primary school (Kura

Kaupapa Maori), the secondary school (Te Kura Tuarua), and the tertiary levels (Waananga) in an attempt to respond to the twin concerns outlined above. These resistance initiatives grew out of many years of struggle and frustration as increased numbers of Maori withdrew from the mainstream, state schooling options. These initiatives were heavily politicized and often became embroiled in charges from disaffected Pakeha as being "separatist" and "cultural retrenchment" movements. A major development at this time was that Maori communities formed a substantial critique (in that they became politically conscientized) of the continued failure of the existing system, despite, ostensibly well-intended policy reform over the years, to change these negative outcomes for Maori. Furthermore, Maori parents became increasingly conscientized about some of the structural impediments to their education aspirations. That is, they began to penetrate the hegemonies that held dominant, Pakeha state education in place. For example, Maori critically engaged the government over such issues as control of funding and resources, manipulation of democratic processes, and mono-cultural management and administrative structures. In this process of engagement, Maori parents became more critically aware of some of the structural barriers and constraints that underpinned the system's inability and reluctance to deliver on their aspirations. These critical penetrations of prevailing hegemony gave impetus to education initiatives taken up by Maori. Paulo Freire's (1970) notion that "the oppressed must also free themselves and that the oppressor alone can not free the oppressed" has meaning here. My doctoral dissertation research on Kaupapa Maori theory and practice analyzes and discusses some of the fundamental intervention elements that are embedded across all of these Maori resistance initiatives (Smith, 1997).

Thus the new formations of colonization that are forged at the interface of cultural oppression and economic exploitation required new resistance strategies. In this sense the real revolution of the 1980s was not so much the language revitalization programs (although these are important in their own right), but the revolution in Maori critical thinking and the realization by Maori that they could make change themselves. This has been generally referred to as the Kaupapa Maori Revolution, but more recently (in recognition of its powerful ability to mobilize Maori community resistance and to develop transformation) it has been more definitively described as "Kaupapa Maori theory" and transformative praxis.

Kaupapa Maori Theory

In this next section, I examine the set of transformative elements that are common to Maori alternative education initiatives, from pre-school (Te Kohanga Reo) to tertiary institutions (Waananga), identifying them as a core set of change factors. It is hoped that in identifying these common intervention elements that we are then able to make some informed generalizations about developing successful transformative action that has the potential to be applied in other societal contexts and indigenous situations.

One of the critical elements that ought to be understood relates to the renewed commitment of Maori adults and parents to realizing the potential of education.

This shift in attitude towards schooling is a major turn around for many Maori who endured considerable suffering during their own personal experiences in the dominant state schooling system. Gradually, the misgivings, fears, and resistance of Maori towards education have been replaced by an understanding that education can be changed to serve their needs.

The following six principles are considered to be the crucial change factors in Kaupapa Maori praxis.

Six Principles of Praxis

1. The Principle of Self-Determination or Relative Autonomy

The perceived need by Maori to have increased control over their own lives and cultural well-being has made gains within the kaupapa of Maori schools given that they have been organized by Maori decision-makers, many of whom are teachers. Greater autonomy over key decision-making in schooling has been attained in areas such as administration, curriculum, pedagogy, and Maori cultural aspirations. Because Maori people have assumed leadership roles in education, they have made choices and decisions that reflect their cultural, political, economic, and social preferences. Furthermore, when Maori make decisions for themselves, the commitment by Maori participants to making the ideas work is more certain and solid.

2. The Principle of Validating and Legitimating Cultural Aspirations and Identity

In Kura Kaupapa Maori, "to be Maori" is taken for granted, so there is little need to justify one's identity, as is the case in most mainstream educational settings. In Kaupapa Maori educational settings, Maori language, knowledge, culture, and values are validated and legitimated—this is a "given," a "taken for granted" base in these schools. Maori cultural aspirations are more assured in these settings, particularly in light of the wider societal context of the struggle for Maori language and cultural survival. One of the common faults of previous schooling interventions has been the inadequate attention paid to this aspect of supporting the maintenance of Maori culture and distinctive cultural identity. By incorporating these elements, a strong emotional and spiritual factor is introduced to Kaupapa Maori settings, which gains the support and commitment of Maori. In particular, many Maori adults are now convinced that schooling—that is, Kaupapa Maori schooling, has relevance.

3. The Principle of Incorporating Culturally Preferred Pedagogy

Kaupapa Maori teaching and learning settings and practices closely and effectively connect with the cultural backgrounds and life circumstances of Maori communities—that is, teaching and learning choices are selected as being culturally preferred. But the movement is also inclusive in that other pedagogy are also utilized, including those borrowed from general Pakeha schooling methods and from other Pacific/Asian cultures. The latter is a logical development given close cultural similarities, and given the shared commonalties of the Austronesian group of languages.

4. *The Principle of Mediating Socioeconomic and Home Difficulties*

Through its *ngakau* (emotional) and *wairua* (spiritual) elements, the *kaupapa* (philosophy) of Kura Kaupapa Maori is such a powerful and all-embracing force, that it commits Maori communities to take the schooling enterprise seriously. It not only impacts schooling at the ideological level, and assists in mediating a societal context of unequal power relations; it also makes schooling a priority consideration despite debilitating social and economic circumstances. Within the collective cultural structures and practices of *whanau* (extended family), some alleviation of the impact of debilitating socioeconomic circumstances can be obtained.

5. *The Principle of Incorporating Cultural Structures which Emphasize the Collective Rather than the Individual*

The extended family structure underscores the relationship between social factors and Maori family life. This collective provides a shared support structure to alleviate and mediate social and economic difficulties, parenting difficulties, health difficulties, and others. Such difficulties are not located in individual homes but in the total *whanau* (extended family structures and networks)—the *whanau* takes collective responsibility to assist and intervene.

While the *whanau* structure implies a support network for individual members there is also a reciprocal obligation on individual members to invest in the *whanau* group. In this way, parents are culturally "contracted" to support and assist in the education of all children in the *whanau*. Perhaps the most significant aspect of *whanau* administration and management is that it brings back into the schooling setting many parents who were once extremely hostile to education given their own unhappy schooling experiences. This is a major feature of Kura Kaupapa Maori schooling intervention—it has committed parents who have reinvested in education for their children.

6. *The Principle of a Shared and Collective Vision/Philosophy*

Kura Kaupapa Maori schooling has a collective vision, which is written into a formal charter entitled Te Aho Matua. This vision provides the guidelines for excellence in Maori education. It also acknowledges Pakeha culture and skills required by Maori children to participate fully and at every level in modern New Zealand society. Te Aho Matua builds on the kaupapa of Te Kohanga Reo, and provides the parameters for the uniqueness that is Kura Kaupapa Maori. Its power is in its ability to articulate and connect with Maori aspirations—political, social, economic, and cultural.

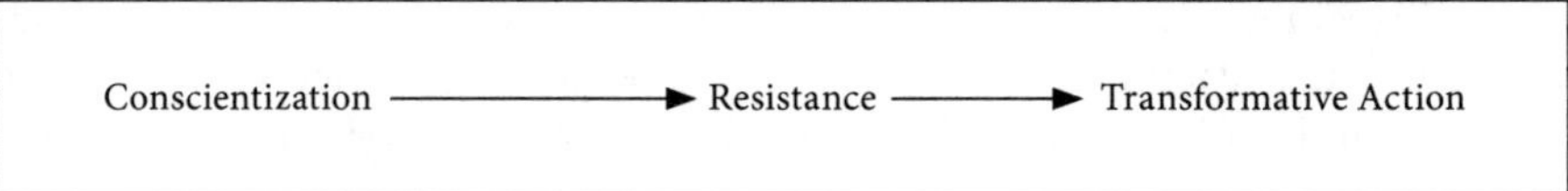

Figure 2.1 Western View of Transformative Action

Lessons in Transformative Praxis

Underpinning the Maori intervention elements are important understandings about transformative praxis and, by extension, critical pedagogy. The intervention strategies applied by Maori in New Zealand are complex and respond simultaneously to multiple formations of oppression and exploitation. The Kaupapa Maori educational interventions represent the evolving of a more sophisticated response by Maori to freeing themselves from these multiple forms of oppression and exploitation. The very emergence of Kaupapa Maori as an intervention strategy reconstitutes the Western dominant resistance notions of conscientization, resistance, and transformative praxis. In particular, Maori cultural ideology rejects the notion that each of these concepts stands individually; or that they are necessarily to be interpreted as being a lineal progression from conscientization, to resistance, to praxis. That is, one state is not necessarily a prerequisite to, or contingent on, the other states. Thus the popular representation of transformative action shown in Figure 2.1, which is based on a predominantly Western type of thinking, needs to be critically engaged.

The position implicit within the new formations of Maori intervention, and which may have wider significance for other indigenous populations, is that all of the above components are important; all need to be held simultaneously; and all stand in equal relation to each other. This representation might best be understood as a cycle.

A further point here is that individuals and groups enter the cycle from any position and do not necessarily (in reflecting on Maori experience within Kaupapa Maori interventions) have to start at the point of conscientization. In other words, individuals have been caught up in transformative praxis (e.g., taking their children to Kohanga Reo), and this has led to conscientization and participation in resistance. This is a significant critique of much of the writing on these concepts that tend to portray a lineal progression of conscientization, resistance, and transformative action. Maori experience tends to suggest that these elements may occur in any order and indeed may all occur simultaneously. It is important to note as well that the arrows in Figure 2.2 go in both directions, which reinforces the idea of simultaneous engagement with more than one element.

One of the most exciting developments with respect to the organic resistance initiatives of Maori in the 1980s and 1990s has been the discernible shift and maturing in the way resistance activities are being understood and practiced. Now, a greater emphasis is placed on attempting to take account of structural concerns (i.e., economic, ideological, and power structures) as well as cultural concerns, in particular, those related to agency. Some of the important factors

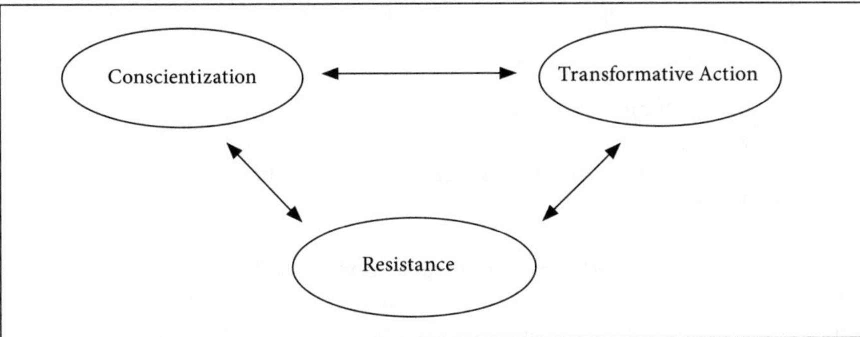

Figure 2.2 Maori View of Transformative Action

with which Maori resistance initiatives attempt to engage relate to economic, ideological, and power dimensions that are derived from a nexus of state, dominant, Pakeha cultural interests.

Where indigenous peoples are in educational crises, indigenous educators must be trained to be change agents whose primary task is the transformation of undesirable circumstances. They must develop radical pedagogy that is informed by their cultural preferences and by their own critical circumstances. They must be taught about the importance of reflecting on and questioning their work: What, for example, is transformative practice? How can it be achieved? Do indigenous people's needs and aspirations require different schooling approaches? Who benefits? Such critical questions must not only lie at the heart of indigenous teacher education approaches, they must ensure "buy in" from the communities that are purported to be served.

The Real Revolution of the 1980s

The revolution of Maori education in the 1980s was not simply about an innovative educational approach towards language revitalization and intervention in educational underachievement. The revolution was also about the development of new transformative strategies that developed both culturalist and structuralist emphases. It was also about:

- Maori being proactive in transforming education, that is, not waiting for Pakeha to make the changes, but doing it themselves.
- Maori developing critical theory on how knowledge is socially constructed within educational settings, and formulating approaches to transformative action.
- Maori developing critical theory on economic conditions, including scientific/technical rationality, and formulating approaches to transformative action.
- Maori coming to understandings about critical theories of education; about their social construction, and about their usefulness when applied by Maori in their own interests.

- Maori recognizing the need to undo Pakeha hegemony and to decolonize themselves.
- Maori understanding that given multiple sites of oppression, there must also be multiple sites of struggle and multiple strategies for change. In short, complex colonization requires complex responses (c.f., Gramsci's notion of war of position in Hoare & Nowell-Smith, 1971, as discussed by Smith, 1997).

Finally, this chapter attempts to move beyond critical analysis to transformative praxis. It is argued that indigenous peoples need to more fully understand how change is developed and actually achieved. There is a need to move beyond mere description of problems and issues to making sure that change does, in fact, occur. The status quo for most Maori is problematic and there is an urgent need for change. In the words of Tuki Nepe (personal communication, 1988):

> We are paddling our own canoe and we are heading in this direction [alternative schooling]. You [Ministry of Education officials] can either get on board and come with us or you can stay here and drown. We are going to go anyway—with or without you!

This shift in focus beyond political consciousness-raising to actually taking transformative action is encapsulated in the Nepe's quote and is the essence of the revolution which has occurred in New Zealand since the 1980s. It has been this movement beyond the ideology and rhetoric of resistance that is an important and critical learning, not just for Maori, but also for other indigenous groups.

Note

1. This chapter has been previously published in *Educational Perspectives*, 2004, *37*(1), on "Indigenous Education."

References

Freire, P. (1970). *Pedagogy of the oppressed.* New York: Seabury Press.

Hoare, Q., & Nowell-Smith, G. (Eds.). (1971). *Selections from the prison notebooks of Antonio Gramsci.* London: Lawrence & Wishart.

Smith, G. H. (1988, March). *Kaupapa Maori schooling: Implications for educational policy making.* Proceedings of the Conference by the Royal Commission on Social Policy. Wellington: New Zealand Council for Educational Research.

Smith, G. H. (1997). *Kaupapa Maori: Theory and praxis.* Unpublished doctoral dissertation, The University of Auckland, New Zealand.

Smith, L. T. (1999). *Decolonizing methodologies: Research and indigenous peoples.* London: Zed Books.

3 Culturally Responsive Schools for Alaska Native Students

A Model for Social Justice, Peace, and Environmental Education

Ray Barnhardt

This chapter will describe the context and processes that led to the development of the *Alaska Standards for Culturally Responsive Schools* and illustrate how the assertion of local initiative by Alaska Native people has served as a model for promoting social justice, ecological sustainability and peaceful coexistence as an educational outcome for all people. The original intent of this initiative was to bring the indigenous knowledge systems and ways of knowing that have sustained the Native people of Alaska for millennia to the forefront in the educational systems serving Alaska students and communities today. As part of a larger educational restoration initiative, Native people have sought to reintegrate their own knowledge systems and ways of knowing into the school curriculum as a basis for connecting what students learn in school with life out of school and thus restore a traditional sense of place while at the same time broadening and deepening the educational experience for all students (Barnhardt & Kawagley, 2005). Imbedded in the "cultural standards" is an emphasis on the role of local Elders, traditional values, experiential learning and alternative ways of knowing, all of which serve as the basis for a pedagogy of place that shifts the emphasis from teaching *about* the local culture to teaching *through* the culture as students learn about the immediate environment they inhabit and their connection to the larger world within which they will make a life for themselves.

Alaska Native Knowledge Comes Out of the Shadows

For well over a century, Alaska Native people have been subjected to an onslaught of external forces and institutional practices (including schools) that have tended to render obsolete much of the knowledge and life ways that have sustained them for millennia. In an effort to address the issues associated with converging knowledge systems in a comprehensive, in-depth way and apply new insights to address long-standing problems with schooling for Native students, in 1995 the Alaska Federation of Natives, in collaboration with the University of Alaska Fairbanks and with funding from the National Science Foundation, entered into a long-term educational restoration endeavor—the Alaska Rural Systemic Initiative (AKRSI).

The underlying purpose of the AKRSI was to implement a set of initiatives to systematically document the indigenous knowledge systems of Alaska Native people and develop school curricula and pedagogical practices that appropriately incorporate local knowledge and ways of knowing into the formal education system (Kawagley, 1995). The central focus of the AKRSI strategy has been the fostering of connectivity and symbiosis between two functionally interdependent but historically disconnected and alienated complex systems—the indigenous knowledge systems rooted in the Native cultures that inhabit rural Alaska, and the formal education systems that have been imposed to ostensibly serve the educational needs of Native communities. This effort was predicated on the notion that within each of these evolving systems is a rich body of complementary knowledge and skills that, if properly explicated and leveraged, can serve to strengthen the quality of educational experiences and improve the academic performance of students throughout Alaska (Barnhardt & Kawagley, 1999).

Given the often ineffectual and contentious history of schooling for indigenous peoples throughout the world, the issues to be addressed by the Alaska Rural Systemic Initiative were not limited to the educational context of Alaska. Nor were they limited to the experiences of indigenous people alone, but, in fact, required confronting far-reaching concerns with implications for social justice, ecological sustainability and peaceful coexistence affecting all living beings. The following account will describe how the journey of Alaska Native people unfolded as they asserted their own definition of education, and how their efforts spilled over to inspire the social justice, peace, and ecojustice education (SJPEE) project.

The Development of Local Standards and Their Link to SJPEE

Six years after the Alaska Rural Systemic Initiative had been created by the Alaska Federation of Natives, the AKRSI staff was invited to report on our work at the 2001 American Educational Research Association Annual Meeting in Seattle. In response, we organized a workshop on "Integrating Indigenous Knowledge, Ways of Knowing and World Views into the Educational System," which included a description of the epistemological basis for the project, the cultural documentation process involved, the development and implementation of cultural standards, and a summary of the impact of the project on student achievement, as well as the implications for curriculum, teaching, and support structures for village schools. One of the participants attending the workshop was Julie Andrzejewski, whose interest in social justice issues led her to organize an exploratory symposium the following year inviting representatives of all the AERA Special Interest Groups (SIGs) interested in social justice and environmental education issues. The 2002 symposium explored the possibility of developing broad social justice/environmental education standards modeled on the work that was underway in Alaska, which led to an AERA-hosted mini-course the following year around conceptual issues associated with developing such standards or guidelines.

What started out as a localized effort to address particular educational issues in a remote corner of the country was beginning to take on much broader significance that required thinking through the implications of extending the ideas behind the cultural standards to address issues far beyond village schools in Alaska. In the course of further discussions at the AERA annual meetings in the ensuing years, the notion of extending the idea of "standards" to the social/ecojustice arenas stimulated a wide range of questions and concerns, some of which have been considered in the implementation of the Alaska standards and others of which have caused us to carefully examine how indigenous educational practices were being implemented in Alaska schools.

Of particular concern in both the local and national discussions was how to make sure these standards were not used in a rigid, prescriptive way leading to a one-size-fits-all approach (as has been the tendency with existing content standards), but rather that they were seen more as open-ended protocols to stimulate and guide the development of localized interpretations and adaptations to the issues addressed by the standards. In Alaska, that meant the cultural standards had to be general enough to accommodate the wide range of potential applications across the many Native cultural groups that inhabit the state, with the details to be filled in by each school and community. In the national SJPEE process, it meant that there had to be enough flexibility for each SIG to frame the issues in a way suited to their interest area. As such, the products of this endeavor should be seen as works-in-progress rather than as definitive statements, and each set of standards/guidelines should continue to evolve to fit changing conditions over time and differences from place to place.

For example, one of the major constraints in achieving long-term improvement of any kind in rural schools in Alaska is the persistent high turnover rate among educational personnel (an average of one-third annually in rural schools), coupled with a statewide Alaska Native teaching staff of under five percent, when the Native student population constitutes 24% of the school enrollment. Therefore, one of the challenges of any significant effort to improve schooling has been the need to bring about a degree of stability and continuity in the professional personnel in the schools, particularly through the preparation of qualified Alaska Native teachers and administrators, and engaging Elders and local experts in the educational process. This led the AKRSI to focus on local capacity building through the formation of a series of regional Native educator associations to foster collaboration among and strengthen the role of those few teachers for whom the community/region/state is their home. Without active involvement of knowledgeable Native people to bring their perspectives and practices to bear in all levels of the educational system, any effort to foster social and ecological justice would be an empty promise.

Making a Life versus Making a Living: Adding Value to Western Education

As the Native educators in Alaska (including Elders) began to examine the curriculum development, staffing and policy issues impacting their schools, they became concerned about the constricting forces that were bearing down on their schools as a result of the nascent standards movement—a school reform process being driven by a national and state agenda in which they had little involvement. As they reviewed the standards that had been developed for the various content areas, they did not quarrel with what they saw, but were greatly concerned with what they did not see. From their perspective, neither the state nor the national content standards in all the subject areas added up to a well-rounded education—as one Elder put it, "The schools are more concerned about preparing our children to make a living than they are in preparing them to make a life for themselves." With guidance from the Elders, the Native educators in each cultural region began to document what they thought their children and grandchildren needed to know and be able to do as they went through school, and the strategies by which these life-affirming knowledge, skills, and values might be achieved.

A turning point in the AKRSI efforts took place when the Native educators from each of the regional associations assembled their collective insights and produced the *Alaska Standards for Culturally Responsive Schools,* which have since been endorsed by the State Board of Education and are now in use in schools throughout the state. The "cultural standards" have provided a template against which schools and communities can examine the extent to which they are attending to the educational and cultural well-being of their students, i.e., preparing them to make a life for themselves. They include standards in five areas: for students, educators, curriculum, schools, and communities. The emphasis is on fostering a strong connection between what students experience in school and their lives out of school by promoting opportunities for students to engage in in-depth experiential learning in real world contexts. The cultural standards embodied the cultural and educational restoration strategy of the AKRSI and their implementation has had ripple effects throughout Alaska, in urban as well as rural schools.

Through the *Alaska Standards for Culturally Responsive Schools*, educators and community members are directed toward preparing culturally knowledgeable students who are well grounded in the cultural heritage and traditions of their community and are able to understand and demonstrate how their local knowledge and practices relate to other knowledge systems and cultural beliefs. This includes:

- providing multiple avenues for the incorporation of locally-recognized expertise in all actions related to the use and interpretation of local cultural knowledge and practices as the basis for learning about the larger world;
- reinforcing the positive parenting and child-rearing practices from the community in all aspects of teaching and to engage in extended experiences that involve the development of observation and listening skills associated with the traditional learning ways of the respective cultural community;
- incorporating cultural and language immersion programs and the organization and implementation of extended camps and other seasonal everyday-life experiences to ground student learning naturally in the surrounding environment.

As articulated by the Native educators, the *Alaska Standards for Culturally-Responsive Schools* point to the need for educators who:

- incorporate local ways of knowing and teaching in their work.

- use the local environment and community resources on a regular basis to link what they are teaching to the everyday lives of the students.
- participate in community events and activities in an appropriate and supportive way.
- work closely with parents to achieve a high level of complementary educational expectations between home and school.
- recognize the full educational potential of each student and provide challenges necessary for them to achieve that potential. (ANKN, 1998, pp. 9–12)

Subsequently, the Native educator associations have elaborated on the cultural standards through the development of *Guidelines for the Preparation of Culturally Responsive Teachers* (which are now being put to use in pre-service and in-service programs around the state), as well as a set of *Guidelines for Respecting Cultural Knowledge, Guidelines for Nurturing Culturally Healthy Youth, Guidelines for Strengthening Indigenous Languages, Guidelines for Cross-Cultural Orientation Programs*, and *Guidelines for Culturally Responsive School Boards* (the latter have been adopted by the Alaska Association of School Boards). These cultural standards and guidelines are all designed to assist schools and communities in the appropriate integration of indigenous knowledge in all aspects of their operations, and are all rooted in the belief that a form of education grounded in the heritage language and culture indigenous to a particular place is a fundamental prerequisite for the development of culturally-healthy students and communities.

With regard to participation, the standards and guidelines themselves emphasize the importance of extensive community and parental interaction and involvement in their children's education, both in and out of school. Elders, parents, and local leaders are encouraged to be involved in all aspects of instructional planning and the design and implementation of school programs and curricula. Culturally responsive schools foster extensive on-going participation, communication and interaction between school and community personnel. Elders are accorded a central role as a primary source of knowledge throughout the standards and guidelines. An important element for building upon the traditional learning styles of local indigenous peoples is the creation and maintenance of multiple avenues for Elders to interact formally and informally with students at all times. This includes opportunities for students to engage in the documenting of Elders' cultural knowledge on a regular basis, thereby contributing to the maintenance and transmission of that knowledge. The cultural and professional expertise of Elders is essential and is to be used in appropriate and respectful ways.

Focusing on the Positive: What Schools and Communities Can Do to Improve Education

As they were being developed, all of the cultural standards and guidelines were deliberately phrased in positive and proactive terms, rather than dwelling on and delineating the negative aspects of past educational practices, i.e., the emphasis was on what schools and communities should do rather than what they should not do. Some of the multiple uses to which Native educator's envisioned the cultural standards being put are as follows:

- They may be used as a basis for reviewing school or district-level goals, policies, and practices with regard to the curriculum and pedagogy being implemented in each community or cultural area.
- They may be used by a local community to examine the kind of home/family environment and parenting support systems that are provided for the upbringing of its children.
- They may be used to devise locally appropriate ways to review student and teacher performance as it relates to nurturing and practicing culturally healthy behavior, including serving as potential graduation requirements for students.
- They may be used to strengthen the commitment to revitalizing the local language and culture and fostering the involvement of Elders as an educational resource.
- They may be used to help teachers identify teaching practices that are adaptable to the cultural context in which they are teaching.
- They may be used to guide the preparation and orientation of teachers in ways that help them attend to the cultural well-being of their students.
- They may serve as criteria against which to evaluate educational programs intended to address the cultural needs of students.
- They may be used to guide the formation of state-level policies and regulations and the allocation of resources in support of equal educational opportunities for all children in Alaska.

Since their adoption in 1998, the cultural standards have been used for all these purposes and many more, including serving as model criteria for an international accreditation system for indigenous-serving higher education programs and institutions (Barnhardt, 2006; WINHEC, 2004).

For educators new to the use of the cultural standards, a helpful resource has been the *Handbook for Culturally Responsive Science Curriculum*, which provides further insight, practical information and examples of how to incorporate traditional knowledge in science curricula and integrate it with Western science, how to relate curriculum topics to the cultural standards, and examples of culturally appropriate strategies for instruction and assessment. The *Handbook for Culturally Responsive Science Curriculum* provides useful information on how to approach and involve Elders as teachers, and highlights how traditional teaching and learning can be combined with strategies for teaching inquiry-based science. Some of the compatible strategies identified include:

- community involvement and cooperative groups;
- multiple teachers as facilitators of learning;
- investigate fundamental science questions related to life, seasons, and environment;

- investigate questions from multiple perspectives and disciplines;
- learn by active and extended inquiry;
- use of multiple sources of expert knowledge including cultural experts;
- diverse representations and communication of student ideas and work to classmates and community. (Stephens, 2000, p. 28)

In an effort to assess the impact of the strategies embodied in the cultural standards on student achievement, we turned to the results from the current regimen of norm- and criterion-referenced tests implemented by the State of Alaska. The data reported here represent results from each of those tests in the area of mathematics, comparing the performance of students in the 20 AKRSI partner school districts with that of students in 28 non-AKRSI rural school districts. The national standardized CAT-5/6 test and state benchmark exams serve as indicators of the effects of the implementation of the AKRSI initiatives over a period of 10 years. The data show a steady net gain of AKRSI partner schools over non-AKRSI rural schools in the percentage of students who are in the upper quartile on Grade 8 standardized achievement tests in mathematics, as well as a steady gain in mathematics proficiency levels on state standards-based assessments for both grades 8 and 10 students in AKRSI partner schools (AKRSI, 2005).

In addition to the state benchmark data, we also have norm-referenced test results for ninth grade students who have been taking the Terra Nova/CAT-6 since 2002. Though the differential gains for each group between 2002 and 2004 remain small, the AKRSI students do show a steady increase in performance, while the non-AKRSI students reflect a small decrease in their performance over the three years of available data. The consistent improvement in academic performance of students in AKRSI-affiliated schools over each of the past 10 years leads us to conclude that the cumulative effect of utilizing the *Alaska Standards for Culturally Responsive Schools* to promote increased connections between what students experience in school and what they experience outside school appears to have a significant positive impact on their academic performance (AKRSI, 2005).

With regard to academic achievement, the incorporation of the *Alaska Standards for Culturally Responsive Schools* in all aspects of the school curriculum and the demonstration of their applicability in providing alternative avenues to meet the state content standards is central. As indicated in the standards, culturally responsive curricula:

- reinforce the integrity of the cultural knowledge that students bring with them;
- recognize cultural knowledge as part of a living and constantly adapting system that is grounded in the past, but continues to grow through the present and into the future;
- use the local language and cultural knowledge as a foundation for the rest of the curriculum and provide opportunities for students to study all subjects starting from a base in the local knowledge systems;
- foster a complementary relationship across knowledge derived from diverse knowledge systems;

- situate local knowledge and actions in a global context: "think globally, act locally";
- unfold in a physical environment that is inviting and readily accessible for local people to enter and utilize. (ANKN, 1998, pp. 13–19)

The cumulative insights of the Native educators and Elders have recast education as a reciprocal process engaging schools in a two-way exchange with the communities they serve. If the *Alaska Standards for Culturally Responsive Schools* contribute to a more flexible and open-ended approach to education writ broadly, they will have accomplished far more than anything envisioned in the early days of their development.

The primary thrust of the Alaska Rural Systemic Initiative in its effort to create a place for indigenous knowledge in education can best be summarized by the following statement taken from the introduction to the *Alaska Standards for Culturally Responsive Schools*:

> By shifting the focus in the curriculum from teaching/learning *about* cultural heritage as another subject to teaching/learning *through* the local culture as a foundation for all education, it is intended that all forms of knowledge, ways of knowing and world views be recognized as equally valid, adaptable and complementary to one another in mutually beneficial ways. (ANKN, 1998, p. 3)

While much remains yet to be done to fully achieve the intent of Alaska Native people in seeking a place for their knowledge and ways in the education of their children, they have succeeded in demonstrating the efficacy of an educational system that is grounded in the deep knowledge associated with a particular place, upon which a broader knowledge of the rest of the world can be built. It is through a reconciliation of the local versus global nexus in the provision of a well-rounded education that issues of social justice, ecological sustainability, and peaceful coexistence can be resolved for all peoples.

References

Alaska Native Knowledge Network (ANKN). (1998). *Alaska standards for culturally responsive schools*. Fairbanks: Alaska Native Knowledge Network, University of Alaska Fairbanks. Retrieved July 1, 2007, from http://www.ankn.uaf.edu/standards/

Alaska Rural Systemic Initiative (AKRSI). (2005). *Annual Report*. Fairbanks: Alaska Native Knowledge Network, University of Alaska Fairbanks. Retrieved July 1, 2007, from http://www.ankn.uaf.edu/arsi.html

Barnhardt, R. (2006). Culture, community and place in Alaska Native education. *Democracy and Education, 16*(2), 44–51.

Barnhardt, R., & Kawagley, A. O. (1999). Education indigenous to place: Western science meets indigenous reality. In G. Smith & D. Williams (Eds.), *Ecological education in action* (pp. 117–140). New York: State University of New York Press.

Barnhardt, R., & Kawagley, A. O. (2005). Indigenous knowledge systems and Alaska native ways of knowing. *Anthropology and Education Quarterly, 36*(1), 8–23.

Kawagley, A. O. (1995). *A Yupiaq world view: A pathway to ecology and spirit*. Prospect Heights, IL: Waveland Press.

Stephens, S. (2000). *Handbook for culturally responsive science curriculum*. Fairbanks: Alaska Native Knowledge Network, University of Alaska Fairbanks. Retrieved July 1, 2007, from http://www.ankn.uaf.edu/handbook/

WINHEC. (2004). *WINHEC accreditation handbook*. Auckland, New Zealand: World Indigenous Nations Higher Education Consortium. Retrieved July 1, 2007, from http://www.ankn.uaf.edu/ihe.html

ALASKA STANDARDS FOR CULTURALLY RESPONSIVE SCHOOLS

Cultural Standards for Students
Cultural Standards for Educators
Cultural Standards for the Curriculum
Cultural Standards for Schools
Cultural Standards for Communities

Sponsored by:
Alaska Federation of Natives
Alaska Rural Systemic Initiative
Alaska Rural Challenge
Alaska Native Knowledge Network
Ciulistet Research Association
Association of Interior Native Educators
Southeast Native Educators Association
North Slope Inupiaq Educators Association
Association of Native Educators of the Lower Kuskokwim
Association of Northwest Native Educators
Alaska Native Education Student Association
Alutiiq Native Educator Association
Unangan Educator Association
Alaska Native Education Council
Alaska Native Teachers for Excellence/Anchorage

Tribal College Consortium/Ilisagvik College
Alaska First Nations Research Network
Center for Cross-Cultural Studies

Adopted by the
Assembly of Alaska Native Educators
Anchorage, Alaska
February 3, 1998

The following standards have been developed by Alaska Native educators to provide a way for schools and communities to examine the extent to which they are attending to the educational and cultural well-being of the students in their care. These "cultural standards" are predicated on the belief that a firm grounding in the heritage language and culture indigenous to a particular place is a fundamental prerequisite for the development of culturally healthy students and communities associated with that place, and thus is an essential ingredient for identifying the appropriate qualities and practices associated with culturally responsive educators, curriculum and schools.

For several years, Alaska has been developing "content standards" to define what students should know and be able to do as they go through school. In addition, "performance standards" are being developed for teachers and administrators, and a set of "quality school standards" have been put forward by the Alaska Department of Education to serve as a basis for accrediting schools in Alaska. To the extent that these state standards are written for general use throughout Alaska, they don't always address some of the special issues that are of critical importance to schools in rural Alaska, particularly those serving Alaska Native communities and students.

Through a series of regional and statewide meetings associated with the Alaska Rural Systemic Initiative (with funding provided by the National Science Foundation and the Annenberg Rural Challenge, and administrative support from the Alaska Federation of Natives in collaboration with the University of Alaska), Alaska Native educators have developed the following "Alaska Standards for Culturally Responsive Schools" for consideration by educators serving Native students around the state. Though the emphasis is on rural schools serving Native communities, many of the standards are applicable to all students and communities because they focus curricular attention on in-depth study of the surrounding physical and cultural environment in which the school is situated, while recognizing the unique contribution that indigenous people can make to such study as long-term inhabitants who have accumulated extensive specialized knowledge related to that environment.

Standards have been drawn up in five areas, including those for students, educators, curriculum, schools, and communities. These "cultural standards" provide guidelines or touchstones against which schools and communities can examine what they are doing to attend to the cultural well-being of the young people they are responsible for nurturing to adulthood. The standards included here serve as a complement to, not as a replacement for, those adopted by the

State of Alaska. While the state standards stipulate what students should know and be able to do, the cultural standards are oriented more toward providing guidance on how to get them there in such a way that they become responsible, capable and whole human beings in the process. The emphasis is on fostering a strong connection between what students experience in school and their lives out of school by providing opportunities for students to engage in in-depth experiential learning in real-world contexts. By shifting the focus in the curriculum from teaching/learning *about* cultural heritage as another subject to teaching/learning *through* the local culture as a foundation for all education, it is intended that all forms of knowledge, ways of knowing and world views be recognized as equally valid, adaptable and complementary to one another in mutually beneficial ways.

The cultural standards outlined in this document are not intended to be inclusive, exclusive or conclusive, and thus should be reviewed and adapted to fit local needs. Each school, community and related organization should consider which of these standards are appropriate and which are not, and when necessary, develop additional cultural standards to accommodate local circumstances. Terms should be interpreted to fit local conventions, especially with reference to meanings associated with the definition of Elder, tradition, spirituality, or anything relating to the use of the local language. Where differences of interpretation exist, they should be respected and accommodated to the maximum extent possible. The cultural standards are not intended to produce standardization, but rather to encourage schools to nurture and build upon the rich and varied cultural traditions that continue to be practiced in communities throughout Alaska.

Alaska Standards for Culturally Responsive Schools

Cultural Standards for Students

A. **Culturally knowledgeable students are well grounded in the cultural heritage and traditions of their community.**
   Students who meet this cultural standard are able to:
   1) assume responsibility for their role in relation to the well-being of the cultural community and their life-long obligations as a community member;
   2) recount their own genealogy and family history;
   3) acquire and pass on the traditions of their community through oral and written history;
   4) practice their traditional responsibilities to the surrounding environment;
   5) reflect through their own actions the critical role that the local heritage language plays in fostering a sense of who they are and how they understand the world around them;
   6) live a life in accordance with the cultural values and traditions of the local community and integrate them into their everyday behavior.
   7) determine the place of their cultural community in the regional, state, national and international political and economic systems;

B. **Culturally knowledgeable students are able to build on the knowledge and skills of the local cultural community as a foundation from which to achieve personal and academic success throughout life.**
Students who meet this cultural standard are able to:
   1) acquire insights from other cultures without diminishing the integrity of their own;
   2) make effective use of the knowledge, skills and ways of knowing from their own cultural traditions to learn about the larger world in which they live;
   3) make appropriate choices regarding the long-term consequences of their actions;
   4) identify appropriate forms of technology and anticipate the consequences of their use for improving the quality of life in the community.

C. **Culturally knowledgeable students are able to actively participate in various cultural environments.**
Students who meet this cultural standard are able to:
   1) perform subsistence activities in ways that are appropriate to local cultural traditions;
   2) make constructive contributions to the governance of their community and the well-being of their family;
   3) attain a healthy lifestyle through which they are able to maintain their own social, emotional, physical, intellectual and spiritual well-being;
   4) enter into and function effectively in a variety of cultural settings.

D. **Culturally knowledgeable students are able to engage effectively in learning activities that are based on traditional ways of knowing and learning.**
Students who meet this cultural standard are able to:
   1) acquire in-depth cultural knowledge through active participation and meaningful interaction with Elders;
   2) participate in and make constructive contributions to the learning activities associated with a traditional camp environment;
   3) interact with Elders in a loving and respectful way that demonstrates an appreciation of their role as culture-bearers and educators in the community;
   4) gather oral and written history information from the local community and provide an appropriate interpretation of its cultural meaning and significance;
   5) identify and utilize appropriate sources of cultural knowledge to find solutions to everyday problems;
   6) engage in a realistic self-assessment to identify strengths and needs and make appropriate decisions to enhance life skills.

E. **Culturally knowledgeable students demonstrate an awareness and appreciation of the relationships and processes of interaction of all elements in the world around them.**
Students who meet this cultural standard are able to:

1) recognize and build upon the inter-relationships that exist among the spiritual, natural and human realms in the world around them, as reflected in their own cultural traditions and beliefs as well as those of others;
2) understand the ecology and geography of the bioregion they inhabit;
3) demonstrate an understanding of the relationship between world view and the way knowledge is formed and used;
4) determine how ideas and concepts from one knowledge system relate to those derived from other knowledge systems;
5) recognize how and why cultures change over time;
6) anticipate the changes that occur when different cultural systems come in contact with one another;
7) determine how cultural values and beliefs influence the interaction of people from different cultural backgrounds;
8) identify and appreciate who they are and their place in the world.

Cultural Standards for Educators

A. **Culturally responsive educators incorporate local ways of knowing and teaching in their work.**

Educators who meet this cultural standard:

1) recognize the validity and integrity of the traditional knowledge system;
2) utilize Elders' expertise in multiple ways in their teaching;
3) provide opportunities and time for students to learn in settings where local cultural knowledge and skills are naturally relevant;
4) provide opportunities for students to learn through observation and hands-on demonstration of cultural knowledge and skills;
5) adhere to the cultural and intellectual property rights that pertain to all aspects of the local knowledge they are addressing;
6) continually involve themselves in learning about the local culture.

B. **Culturally responsive educators use the local environment and community resources on a regular basis to link what they are teaching to the everyday lives of the students.**

Educators who meet this cultural standard:

1) regularly engage students in appropriate projects and experiential learning activities in the surrounding environment;
2) utilize traditional settings such as camps as learning environments for transmitting both cultural and academic knowledge and skills;
3) provide integrated learning activities organized around themes of local significance and across subject areas;
4) are knowledgeable in all the areas of local history and cultural tradition that may have bearing on their work as a teacher, including the appropriate times for certain knowledge to be taught;
5) seek to ground all teaching in a constructive process built on a local cultural foundation.

C. **Culturally responsive educators participate in community events and activities in an appropriate and supportive way.**
   Educators who meet this cultural standard:
   1) become active members of the community in which they teach and make positive and culturally appropriate contributions to the well being of that community;
   2) exercise professional responsibilities in the context of local cultural traditions and expectations;
   3) maintain a close working relationship with and make appropriate use of the cultural and professional expertise of their co-workers from the local community.

D. **Culturally responsive educators work closely with parents to achieve a high level of complementary educational expectations between home and school.**
   Educators who meet this cultural standard:
   1) promote extensive community and parental interaction and involvement in their children's education;
   2) involve Elders, parents and local leaders in all aspects of instructional planning and implementation;
   3) seek to continually learn about and build upon the cultural knowledge that students bring with them from their homes and community;
   4) seek to learn the local heritage language and promote its use in their teaching.

E. **Culturally responsive educators recognize the full educational potential of each student and provide the challenges necessary for them to achieve that potential.**
   Educators who meet this cultural standard:
   1) recognize cultural differences as positive attributes around which to build appropriate educational experiences;
   2) provide learning opportunities that help students recognize the integrity of the knowledge they bring with them and use that knowledge as a springboard to new understandings;
   3) reinforce the student's sense of cultural identity and place in the world;
   4) acquaint students with the world beyond their home community in ways that expand their horizons while strengthening their own identities;
   5) recognize the need for all people to understand the importance of learning about other cultures and appreciating what each has to offer.

Cultural Standards for Curriculum

A. **A culturally responsive curriculum reinforces the integrity of the cultural knowledge that students bring with them.**
   A curriculum that meets this cultural standard:

1) recognizes that all knowledge is imbedded in a larger system of cultural beliefs, values and practices, each with its own integrity and interconnectedness;
2) insures that students acquire not only the surface knowledge of their culture, but are also well grounded in the deeper aspects of the associated beliefs and practices;
3) incorporates contemporary adaptations along with the historical and traditional aspects of the local culture;
4) respects and validates knowledge that has been derived from a variety of cultural traditions;
5) provides opportunities for students to study all subjects starting from a base in the local knowledge system.

B. **A culturally responsive curriculum recognizes cultural knowledge as part of a living and constantly adapting system that is grounded in the past, but continues to grow through the present and into the future.**
A curriculum that meets this cultural standard:
1) recognizes the contemporary validity of much of the traditional cultural knowledge, values and beliefs, and grounds students learning in the principles and practices associated with that knowledge;
2) provides students with an understanding of the dynamics of cultural systems as they change over time, and as they are impacted by external forces;
3) incorporates the in-depth study of unique elements of contemporary life in Native communities in Alaska, such as the Alaska Native Claims Settlement Act, subsistence, sovereignty and self-determination.

C. **A culturally responsive curriculum uses the local language and cultural knowledge as a foundation for the rest of the curriculum.**
A curriculum that meets this cultural standard:
1) utilizes the local language as a base from which to learn the deeper meanings of the local cultural knowledge, values, beliefs and practices;
2) recognizes the depth of knowledge that is associated with the long inhabitation of a particular place and utilizes the study of "place" as a basis for the comparative analysis of contemporary social, political and economic systems;
3) incorporates language and cultural immersion experiences wherever in-depth cultural understanding is necessary;
4) views all community members as potential teachers and all events in the community as potential learning opportunities;
5) treats local cultural knowledge as a means to acquire the conventional curriculum content as outlined in state standards, as well as an end in itself;
6) makes appropriate use of modern tools and technology to help document and transmit traditional cultural knowledge;
7) is sensitive to traditional cultural protocol, including the role of spirituality, as it relates to appropriate uses of local knowledge.

D. **A culturally responsive curriculum fosters a complementary relationship across knowledge derived from diverse knowledge systems.**
A curriculum that meets this cultural standard:
1) draws parallels between knowledge derived from oral tradition and that derived from books;
2) engages students in the construction of new knowledge and understandings that contribute to an ever-expanding view of the world.

E. **A culturally responsive curriculum situates local knowledge and actions in a global context.**
A curriculum that meets this cultural standard:
1) encourages students to consider the inter-relationship between their local circumstances and the global community;
2) conveys to students that every culture and community contributes to, at the same time that it receives from the global knowledge base;
3) prepares students to "think globally, act locally.

Cultural Standards for Schools

A. **A culturally responsive school fosters the on-going participation of Elders in all aspects of the schooling process.**
A school that meets this cultural standard:
1) maintains multiple avenues for Elders to interact formally and informally with students at all times;
2) provides opportunities for students to regularly engage in the documenting of Elders' cultural knowledge and produce appropriate print and multimedia materials that share this knowledge with others;
3) includes explicit statements regarding the cultural values that are fostered in the community and integrates those values in all aspects of the school program and operation;
4) utilizes educational models that are grounded in the traditional world view and ways of knowing associated with the cultural knowledge system reflected in the community.

B. **A culturally responsive school provides multiple avenues for students to access the learning that is offered, as well as multiple forms of assessment for students to demonstrate what they have learned.**
A school that meets this cultural standard:
1) utilizes a broad range of culturally appropriate performance standards to assess student knowledge and skills;
2) encourages and supports experientially oriented approaches to education that makes extensive use of community-based resources and expertise;
3) provides cultural and language immersion programs in which students acquire in-depth understanding of the culture of which they are members;
4) helps students develop the capacity to assess their own strengths and weaknesses and make appropriate decisions based on such a self-assessment.

C. **A culturally responsive school provides opportunities for students to learn in and/or about their heritage language.**

A school that meets this cultural standard:

1) provides language immersion opportunities for students who wish to learn in their heritage language;
2) offers courses that acquaint all students with the heritage language of the local community;
3) makes available reading materials and courses through which students can acquire literacy in the heritage language;
4) provides opportunities for teachers to gain familiarity with the heritage language of the students they teach through summer immersion experiences.

D. **A culturally responsive school has a high level of involvement of professional staff who are of the same cultural background as the students with whom they are working.**

A school that meets this cultural standard:

1) encourages and supports the professional development of local personnel to assume teaching and administrative roles in the school;
2) recruits and hires teachers whose background is similar to that of the students they will be teaching;
3) provides a cultural orientation camp and mentoring program for new teachers to learn about and adjust to the cultural expectations and practices of the community and school;
4) fosters and supports opportunities for teachers to participate in professional activities and associations that help them expand their repertoire of cultural knowledge and pedagogical skills.

E. **A culturally responsive school consists of facilities that are compatible with the community environment in which they are situated.**

A school that meets this cultural standard:

1) provides a physical environment that is inviting and readily accessible for local people to enter and utilize;
2) makes use of facilities throughout the community to demonstrate that education is a community-wide process involving everyone as teachers;
3) utilizes local expertise, including students, to provide culturally appropriate displays of arts, crafts and other forms of decoration and space design.

F. **A culturally responsive school fosters extensive on-going participation, communication and interaction between school and community personnel.**

A school that meets this cultural standard:

1) holds regular formal and informal events bringing together students, parents, teachers and other school and community personnel to review, evaluate and plan the educational program that is being offered;
2) provides regular opportunities for local and regional board deliberations and decision-making on policy, program and personnel issues related to the school;

3) sponsors on-going activities and events in the school and community that celebrate and provide opportunities for students to put into practice and display their knowledge of local cultural traditions.

Cultural Standards for Communities

A. A culturally supportive community incorporates the practice of local cultural traditions in its everyday affairs.

A community that meets this cultural standard:

1) provides respected Elders with a place of honor in community functions;
2) models culturally appropriate behavior in the day-to-day life of the community;
3) utilizes traditional child-rearing and parenting practices that reinforce a sense of identity and belonging;
4) organizes and encourages participation of members from all ages in regular community-wide, family-oriented events;
5) incorporates and reinforces traditional cultural values and beliefs in all formal and informal community functions.

B. A culturally supportive community nurtures the use of the local heritage language.

A community that meets this cultural standard:

1) recognizes the role that language plays in conveying the deeper aspects of cultural knowledge and traditions;
2) sponsors local heritage language immersion opportunities for young children when they are at the critical age for language learning;
3) encourages the use of the local heritage language whenever possible in the everyday affairs of the community, including meetings, cultural events, print materials and broadcast media;
4) assists in the preparation of curriculum resource materials in the local heritage language for use in the school;
5) provides simultaneous translation services for public meetings where persons unfamiliar with the local heritage language are participants.

C. A culturally supportive community takes an active role in the education of all its members.

A community that meets this cultural standard:

1) encourages broad-based participation of parents in all aspects of their children's education, both in and out of school;
2) insures active participation by community members in reviewing all local, regional and state initiatives that have bearing on the education of their children;
3) encourages and supports members of the local community who wish to pursue further education to assume teaching and administrative roles in the school;

4) engages in subsistence activities, sponsors cultural camps and hosts community events that provide an opportunity for children to actively participate in and learn appropriate cultural values and behavior;
5) provides opportunities for all community members to acquire and practice the appropriate knowledge and skills associated with local cultural traditions.

D. **A culturally supportive community nurtures family responsibility, sense of belonging and cultural identity.**

A community that meets this cultural standard:

1) fosters cross-generational sharing of parenting and child-rearing practices;
2) creates a supportive environment for youth to participate in local affairs and acquire the skills to be contributing members of the community;
3) adopts the adage, "It takes the whole village to raise a child."

E. **A culturally supportive community assists teachers in learning and utilizing local cultural traditions and practices.**

A community that meets this cultural standard:

1) sponsors a cultural orientation camp and community mentoring program for new teachers to learn about and adjust to the cultural expectations and practices of the community;
2) encourages teachers to make use of facilities and expertise in the community to demonstrate that education is a community-wide process involving everyone as teachers;
3) sponsors regular community/school potlucks to celebrate the work of students and teachers and to promote on-going interaction and communication between teachers and parents;
4) attempts to articulate the cultural knowledge, values and beliefs that it wishes teachers to incorporate into the school curriculum;
5) establishes a program to insure the availability of Elders' expertise in all aspects of the educational program in the school.

F. **A culturally supportive community contributes to all aspects of curriculum design and implementation in the local school.**

A community that meets this cultural standard:

1) takes an active part in the development of the mission, goals and content of the local educational program;
2) promotes the active involvement of students with Elders in the documentation and preservation of traditional knowledge through a variety of print and multimedia formats;
3) facilitates teacher involvement in community activities and encourages the use of the local environment as a curricular resource;
4) promotes parental involvement in all aspects of their children's educational experience.

Part II

Transforming Education for Human Rights, Peace, All Species, and the Earth

Introduction

Building upon chapter 1 that established the purpose and context of this project, and Part I that provided an introduction to the indigenous inspirational models, Part II lays out the intersecting rationales for Social Justice, Peace, and Environmental Standards from the history of the No Child Left Behind Act (NCLB) through the overarching and challenging issues of education for human rights, the environment, peace and nonviolence, children, and animals. Each chapter presents and establishes another building block for integrated educational transformation, demonstrating how these overarching issues are interconnected with one another.

Audre Lorde (1983) forcefully declared that there is no hierarchy of oppressions. In addition to the study of human oppression and liberation, this book considers the destruction of our life support system—the earth and the other beings living on the earth—as being equally worthy of consideration. Thus the chapters here address global problems where the interconnections between social justice, peace, and the environment can be easily seen and understood. While not viewed as any more or less important than the issues presented in other sections, each chapter in this section illustrates several key points that permeate this book:

1. The significance of a global perspective from which to see connections that are not always visible at the local or national levels.
2. The educational potential of internationally developed movements and documents.
3. The power of individual educators to take leadership in integrating these issues into their own courses and programs.
4. The potential of proposed standards to stimulate discussion and increase visibility of SJPEE.
5. The adaptability of SJPEE recommendations, queries, guidelines, and principles to meet local and culturally sensitive goals, not imposed as rigid benchmarks.

Linda Symcox exposes the connections between global corporate economic policies and the targeting and dismantling of public education in the United

States through privatization and heavy-handed accountability schemes. By situating the SJPEE project within the historical context of the neoliberal reform movement that has dominated the national educational agenda since the Reagan-era *A Nation at Risk* report (1983), Symcox traces the pathway that led to the current oppressive educational policy, *No Child Left Behind* (2001). Symcox also recounts how the middle classes repudiated the Great Society programs of the 1960s and 1970s through tax revolts and a mass exodus from public schools during the 1980s and 1990s. Finally she proposes a set of positive standards to point the way to a more democratic vision for public schools, a pre-condition for social justice, peace, and environmental education.

In stark contrast to the planned failure of children and schools through NCLB standards and high-stakes testing, Todd Jennings proposes a very different use of standards in his chapter 5. Jennings points out that "human rights are standards" as are "required competencies for professional practice," arguing that progressive educators should not hesitate to use the term "standards" to establish a vision and goals for urgent topics that have been ignored, censored, or neglected in education. Based on the Universal Declaration for Human Rights of 1948, he proceeds to illustrate the complexities of human rights education in several arenas: What areas does human rights encompass (civil, political, economic, social, and cultural rights)? What should professional educators know about human rights? Why should educational methodologies *embody* human rights principles? How can human rights become a focus without eliminating other important topics? Why is it important to go beyond character-based education? After presenting human rights standards for classroom teachers, Jennings discusses implications for teacher education, how to overcome obstacles and develop support systems, and examples for integrating human rights education into subject matter at all levels.

Building on the human rights chapter, David Greenwood, Bob Offei Manteaw, and Gregory A. Smith explore the integral relationship between human rights, peace, and environmental issues in chapter 6. Setting the stage for the urgent need for environmental education, they succinctly present and critique major international environmental agreements all educators should know. They explain why governmental bodies drag their feet on environmental actions and why non-governmental organizations are creating the most visionary and practical documents for education and action. Using these available resources, they legitimize the need for educators to inspire youth to take leadership in local and global actions for the survival of the planet and its inhabitants. They examine the "ideological, structural, pedagogical, and curricular practices" in schooling that create obstacles for deep environmental education, and present ideas and queries to help educators change their own classes and the larger educational agenda.

Peace is fundamental to human rights and environmental integrity as Julie Andrzejewski documents in chapter 7. Yet, she points out, "peace is rarely a topic in schools even as violence and war permeate our everyday lives, media, and world." Without formal training themselves, educators are often at a loss about what they might do to teach peace and nonviolence. This chapter is meant to help educators quickly understand a range of key aspects of war and violence as well as peace and well-being drawn from internationally recognized sources to stimulate an interest in teaching relevant topics and skills in their own courses. Andrzejewski begins by concisely describing some root causes of war, violence, and hatred and how everyday individual actions can inadvertently and unconsciously perpetrate serious brutality as illustrated in the Tower of Violence. She presents "seven foundations for a better world," and some personal and collective principles and actions for peace based on ancient wisdom and intellectual traditions. The Tower of Peace and Well-being shows how acts of individual and group courage can contribute to a larger culture of peace. Both "towers" can be used as teaching tools. She ends by identifying forceful international documents educators can use and a set of educational practices for peace and justice.

The systemic and global suffering of children from policies of neglect, poverty, slavery, war, inequitable resources, and ecological destruction continues unabated despite almost universal sentiments of concern. As Swadener and O'Brien state in chapter 8, "children often bear the brunt of the suffering in the world." After a compelling description of the state of the world's children, they draw upon international documents of children's rights and foundational theories and research to make recommendations for early childhood guiding principles and identify some innovative initiatives to inspire educators to "join a global movement to build a world fit for children." Not meant to be prescriptive, the interconnections of social justice, peace, and environmental preservation are all fundamental aspects of this vision.

Often left out of social justice and peace conversations and sometimes viewed as peripheral even in environmental discussions, Julie Andrzejewski, Helena Pedersen, and Freeman Wicklund explore the oppression of other animals and how their treatment is integrally related to social justice, peace, and environmental education in chapter 9. They presents three questions to guide the discussion for educators:

> 1) How is the well-being of humans interdependent with the well-being of other animals? This question explores why it is in human self-interest to learn about and act to protect animals of all kinds. It documents the need for greater public awareness of the human health and environmental impacts of various industries on animals. 2) What is speciesism and why should interspecies education be given the same critical examination as other ethical issues? This discussion examines beliefs, censorship, and misinformation about other animals, especially exposing how animals are treated under factory farming. 3) How is the treatment of other animals and species interrelated with social justice, peace and ecological survival? The intersection of speciesism with other social justice and peace issues is explored through sexism, racism, classism, heterosexism, and peace studies. A Practical Vision of Interspecies Education is presented through which educators can consider integrating animal perspectives.

These chapters on overarching topics provide a strong background and context for interconnecting social justice, identity, and cultural issues presented in Part III.

Reference

Lorde, A. (1983). *There is no hierarchy of oppressions. Homophobia and education*. New York: Council on Interracial Books for Children.

4 From *A Nation at Risk* to No Child Left Behind

25 Years of Neoliberal Reform in Education

Linda Symcox

This chapter frames the Social Justice, Peace, and Environmental Education (SJPEE) project within the historical context of the neoliberal reform movement that has dominated the national educational agenda since the election of Ronald Reagan in 1980 and his administration's *A Nation at Risk* report (1983). It will examine 1) the movement for academic standards and high-stakes testing, 2) the taxpayer revolt and public retreat from social justice programs, 3) the movement for charter schools, vouchers and privatization, and, 4) the No Child Left Behind Act (NCLB, 2001). Finally, the chapter will demonstrate the pressing need for a new vision for educational reform that will be genuinely democratic, for democracy is both a pre-condition and an essential concomitant of social justice. Over the past quarter century, the ideal of democratic education has been subverted by an anti-democratic "reform" project based on the ideology of neoliberalism. But this era is fading fast, for the contradictions and limitations in neoliberalism have brought it to an impasse, which opens the way to restoring the democratic purpose of education, and thus to advance the ideal of social justice.

I must start by defining what I mean by the term "neoliberalism." It can be defined as a concept of political economy based on the classical economics of the late 18th and early 19th centuries, exemplified in the work of Adam Smith (2003/1776) and David Ricardo (2004/1817). The classical economists were the founders of what was described at that time as "liberal" economics, which today we would call free market or *laissez faire* capitalism. They argued that economics operates by its own laws, and that governments should not intervene to distort or obstruct the operation of these laws. In the late 1970s, neoliberalism became increasingly influential. Theorists such as Frederick von Hayek and Milton Friedman inspired politicians like Margaret Thatcher and Ronald Reagan to advance what came to be called neoliberal policies (Friedman, 2002/1962; Hayek, 1978): slashing expenditures on social services, privatizing them as far as possible, and deregulating what was left. The aim was to minimize government intervention and allow the market to operate freely. Government's function would be reduced to maintaining order at home through an expanding prison system, and abroad, through massive armed forces, sustained by the "defense" industries, and any intervention would be in favor of the corporations. Social justice was at best an irrelevancy; at most a culpable interference in the free play of the market. Thatcher famously summed up the neoliberal program by saying that "there is no such thing as society, there are only individuals" (Keay, 1987, pp. 8–10). In America, Reagan followed the same course.

The educational policies listed above (national standards and high-stakes testing, charter schools, vouchers, and NCLB) grew directly out of this neoliberal ideology during the 1980s and 1990s. Public education was starved of funds in order to encourage privatization and so create a vast new market, setting back the cause of social justice, and widening the educational achievement gap. Democratic values were banished from the curriculum, and replaced with corporate-inspired goals, with dire results. High-stakes testing has led to curricular fragmentation instead of holistic thinking, to disjointed lessons chopped into snippets of measurable time, and to teacher-centered pedagogies that frustrate the process of open inquiry (Saltman, 2000). Neoliberal "reforms" have also promoted the idea that student achievement can and should be measured by norm-referenced tests and punitive bottom lines, rather than by a student's love of learning, ability to think critically, or capacity for global citizenship. Simply put, neoliberal educational policy conflicts with the aims of social and environmental justice; its model for education is that of corporate business, not the public good; it is thus profoundly anti-democratic. It does not inculcate critical thinking because it is designed to produce compliant workers and consumers, not responsible, autonomous citizens. Under NCLB, its impact is greatest on poor and minority students because they and their teachers are saddled with behaviorist pedagogies, a narrow, lock-step curriculum, and pervasive policing through punitive benchmarks and tests (Hillocks, Jr., 2002). Meanwhile, better-off students and their teachers benefit from inquiry-based classrooms, an enriched curriculum, and the opportunity to ask their own questions, devise their own solutions, and imagine their own futures (Anyon, 1980; Bracey, 2007; Kozol, 1991; Willis, 1981). This is the ideology that has dominated U.S. educational policy for the past 25 years, in direct opposition to any ideals of social justice. The question is how we can reverse this trend, now that it is becoming clear that neoliberal reforms have failed. The time is now ripe for a return to non-elitist, non-market-driven, democratic education, grounded in the principles of social justice in a global context, globally conceived.

A Nation at Risk and the Movement for Academic Standards and High-Stakes Testing

On April 26, 1983, the National Commission on Excellence in Education (NCEE) released a report entitled, *A Nation at Risk: The Imperative for Educational Reform* (NCEE, 1983). Seized by the Reagan administration, it gave birth to the conservative reform cycle that would last for the next quarter century. Japan and Germany were seen as overtaking the U.S. economically and *A Nation at Risk* provided a simple and compelling explanation for the perceived economic decline of the United States: it was the fault of the public schools. The report therefore issued a clarion call for educational reform, in rhetoric charged with nationalistic fervor: the failure of America's public schools was tantamount to "an act of war" (NCEE, p. 2).

Although several state governors answered this call for reform with statewide educational makeovers during the 1980s, reform on a national scale would not begin in earnest until 1989, when George Bush Sr. convoked an "education summit" attended by all 50 governors. It proposed six major reform goals, one of them being the creation of national standards in language arts, mathematics, history, and science. The development of national standards was written into law in Bush Sr.'s *America 2000* Act (1991), and in his successor Bill Clinton's *Goals 2000 Act (*1994), and was then combined with a testing regimen in the *No Child Left Behind Act* (2002). These academic goals were laudable, but to be truly effective they should have also included provisions for dealing with the root causes of educational underperformance, by improving childhood healthcare, reforming drug policy, and reducing childhood poverty. But the vision for reform was limited to improving academic performance and was therefore bound to be limited in its effects (Berliner & Biddle, 1995; Farhi, 2007).

Over the next few years the U.S. Department of Education funded the development of national standards in language arts, history, mathematics, and science. Later in the 1990s, all 50 states developed their own content standards, following guidelines set out in the federally funded national blueprints. In 2001, under the NCLB legislation, states began developing high-stakes assessments to measure student content knowledge aligned with the standards they had developed.

During the Reagan administration, as in the earlier post-Sputnik reform era, schools and sinking test scores were blamed for the current national malaise, and regardless of whether or not the statistics for declining test scores were accurate (Berliner & Biddle, 1995), the call went out for higher academic standards. However, in contrast to the post-Sputnik era, when extensive financial resources were allocated to education, the Reagan-era government relied on rhetoric rather than providing funds to carry out its reform (Bennett, 1984). In an era of fiscal restraint, the public welcomed a policy that shifted the blame for economic failure to the schools, while absolving the government of the need to provide the funding they needed to resolve the problem.

The vision motivating the 1980s standards movement was inherently undemocratic. With global economic competition now setting the agenda, a business model replaced the democratic purpose of schooling. Behind it lurked an undisclosed aim: to "weaken the nation's public schools, redistribute support for those schools so that privileged students are favored over needy students, or even abolish those schools altogether" (Berliner & Biddle, 1995, p. xii).

At this point we must examine how such a centralized reform program as nationally mandated standards and high-stakes testing could be implemented in a country with 16,000 fiercely independent school districts and a history of local decision-making. It took shape in part thanks to a masterful public relations campaign conducted by scholars working in neoliberal think tanks that popped up during 1980s and 1990s to combat the "liberal elite's" perceived dominance over the universities and government bureaucracies. Funded by large corporations and right-wing donors, private foundations such as the Heritage Foundation and the American Enterprise Institute now jumped on the "nation-at-risk" bandwagon. They attributed the nation's supposed academic and economic decline to the social programs of the 1960s and 1970s like the War on Poverty. They accordingly sought to shift the educational agenda away from issues of access and equity towards academic competition and excellence (Bennett, 1984; Cheney, 1987; Scatamburlo, 1998). These well-funded conservative scholars gained the upper hand in the debate over educational policy because of their ability to funnel hundreds of books, statistical studies, and opinion pieces directly to the increasingly corporate-controlled media, spreading alarm and fear about America's public schools (Poynor & Wolfe, 2004). Students were now seen as human capital rather than as citizens.

Taxpayer Revolt and the Retreat from Social Justice Programs: A California Case Study

One could argue that the attack on the public schools, the retreat from efforts to create social and racial equality, and the emergence of the neoliberal educational agenda began as a middle-class, grass-roots movement during the 1970s, and not simply as a top-down movement spearheaded by politicians and think-tank pundits (Symcox, 2002). In fact, the two trends were complementary. Even before desegregation and civil rights policies began to be implemented in public schools during the 1960s and 1970s, millions of middle and lower-middle class Whites had already fled to the suburbs, far from the troublesome inner cities. In the 1970s the Vietnam War, Watergate, and economic turmoil provoked cynicism about government institutions; the civil rights movement lost its cohesion and energy; and the Christian fundamentalist movement emerged as a powerful conservative force, especially in the suburbs. Suburbanites began to foment a quiet but effective middle-class revolution against past social justice policies including racial integration, the War on Poverty, affirmative action, and publicly funded education. This was especially true in California, which because of its size, economic power, and tendency towards social experimentation, became a trendsetter nationally. Conservative Californians used the state's initiative process to achieve their goal. They achieved victory with Proposition 13, the great property tax revolt that passed by a wide majority in 1978, and subsequently spread throughout the nation (Doyle, 1982; Elmore & McLaughlin, 1982; Fischel, 1989; Lekachman, 1978; Lo, 1990).

At first sight this initiative looks like a simple grass-roots response to excessive property taxes. However, for suburban homeowners in Los Angeles's San Fernando Valley, the launching pad for Proposition 13, much more was at stake (Davis, 1990). Concerns about property taxes converged with concerns about public education, and especially school busing. Californians had watched Boston go through a particularly ugly version of this social experiment in 1976. Sharply escalating tax assessments arrived in California mailboxes just as court-ordered busing was to be implemented by the Los Angeles Unified School District (LAUSD). In June 1978, the U.S. Supreme Court, in a landmark reverse discrimination case, determined that Allan Bakke had been passed over for admission to medical school at the University of California, Davis, in favor of less qualified minority applicants. Proposition 13 joined these emotionally charged issues in the headlines.

Moreover, the 1976 *Serrano v. Priest II* court decision added fuel to the fire by equalizing school funding throughout California, requiring redistribution of property tax revenues from richer to poorer districts. In 1978 the tax revolt converged with the campaign against busing, which figured alongside Proposition 13 on the ballot as Proposition 1, called BUSTOP.

The passage of Proposition 13 in November 1978, as commentators have noted for the past 30 years, was a political watershed. With it, the rollback of the Great Society's social programs began in earnest. Court-ordered busing, financially blocked by Proposition 13, would end in 1982 when the California Supreme Court refused to overturn Proposition 1. Thus by 1982 conservative activists in California had effectively reversed the landmark civil rights decision in *Brown v. Board of Education* (1954), and had halted school desegregation in Los Angeles. Writing for the *Washington Post*, journalist Thomas Edsall summed up the impact of Proposition 13.

> It split the electorate along lines that reinforced and widened the divisions that had already begun to appear over race. The tax revolt was a major turning point in American politics. It provided new muscle and new logic to the formation of a conservative coalition of taxpayers versus tax recipients dovetailed with racial divisions.... The tax revolt provided conservatism with a powerful internal coherence, shaping an anti-government ethic, and firmly establishing new grounds for the disaffection of white working- and middle-class voters from their traditional Democratic roots. (cited in Smith, 1998, p. 56)

This was only the beginning. During the 1990s, Californian voters launched a further assault on Great Society programs by passing a series of propositions dismantling affirmative action in state agencies, and social services for illegal immigrants. Some of these efforts were overturned by the courts, and others were challenged by civil servants who refused to implement them, but the shift away from Great Society programs was clear. In 1996 a 54% majority of Californians passed Proposition 209, prohibiting public institutions from using quotas on the basis of race, sex, or ethnicity. As a result, the enrollment of African Americans and Latinos decreased dramatically at the University of California and other universities. Just two years later, Proposition 227 passed, replacing bilingual education in the public schools with an English-only policy.

Meanwhile, across the nation, large numbers of better-off parents were abandoning the public schools and placing their own children in private schools. White evangelicals increasingly turned to homeschooling as a solution to the "problem." This mass exodus meant that the large majority of children remaining in public schools were poor students of color, creating a new form of class and racial segregation beyond the reach of the courts. More than five decades after the *Brown* decision, the public school system in the United States is still racially segregated, with more than 70% of African American students educated in predominantly Black schools, and an even greater percentage of Latino students educated in predominantly Hispanic schools (S. Head, 2007). In June 2007, the Supreme Court's landmark ruling in *Parents Involved in Community Schools v.*

Seattle School District No. 1 further dismantled *Brown*. Under the ruling, school districts could no longer assign students to public schools solely for the purpose of achieving racial integration. With this decision the Supreme Court effectively determined that *de facto* segregation was legal, overturning the unanimous opinion in *Brown*.

Charter School, Voucher, and Privatization Movements: The Dismantling of Public Education

Until the mid-1970s most Americans believed that their public schools were excellent, that schools were getting better all the time, and that each generation would be better educated than its predecessor. In fact, belief in the transformative power of public education had been almost universal for more than two centuries (Jefferson, 1781–1784; Du Bois, 1903; Dewey, 1916; Cremin, 1957; Hayes, 2006). However, during the 1970s this perception changed dramatically: Gallup Polls have revealed that confidence in the public schools has dropped progressively since 1975 (Tyack & Cuban, 1995, p. 53).

Amid this rising skepticism about public institutions, the campaign to privatize the schools gained ground, originally inspired by Milton Friedman, the founding father of neoliberalism (Saltman & Gabbard, 2003). Public services, including education, were to be shifted to the private sector, which would simultaneously be deregulated, opening up a vast untapped market, education, to a new breed of educational entrepreneurs. The democratic idea that education should be governed by non-market criteria was pushed into the background. Neoliberal economic theory aimed to eliminate every obstacle to the free market, whose benefits would supposedly trickle down and provide for all (Tabb, 2001).

In order to privatize public education, neoliberals created a three-pronged strategy: vouchers, charter schools, and a war against teachers' unions, according to the plan set forth in Milton Freedman's *Capitalism and Freedom* (1962). In the early 1990s, with conservatives like Chester Finn, Jr. and William Bennett leading the way, the campaign gathered momentum. They worked tirelessly to build their case for privatization, while never actually calling it that in name. Success has been mixed. While the charter school movement has taken off, vouchers have been defeated consistently in local elections. But despite these mixed results, the movement towards privatization has accelerated in recent years with government and philanthropic support. "Charter schools, private schools, Edison schools, parochial schools, and opportunity scholarships all provide healthy competition to our K-12 schools," philanthropist Eli Broad argues. "I support rapidly increasing the number of seats available outside of our public school system." He and other latter-day robber barons like Bill Gates are setting the goals for school reform, jeopardizing democratic control over public education (Miner, 2005).

A particularly egregious example of how the privatization movement has played out is the *Renaissance 2010* reform of Chicago's public schools, not coincidentally supported by the Gates Foundation and others. In 1995 the Illinois state legislature placed control of the Chicago public schools under the mayor and a five-member board, with sweeping powers to hold schools accountable for performance. The goal was to open 100 new schools in "underperforming" communities by 2010. By 2007 the mayor had already closed 60 "underperforming" schools and established a process by which private groups could compete for the right to operate charter schools employing non-union teachers and staff. Public space was reconfigured as a free market dominated by private capital (Ayers & Klonsky, 2006, p. 454). But it is becoming clear that charter schools are incapable of producing better test results than public schools (Miner, 2005). Their students perform poorly on standardized tests, perhaps because their teachers are not held to the same professional standards as those in public schools, or perhaps because they are serving students who suffer the same disadvantages as their peers in public schools. Given this dubious achievement, it is unclear why the mayor of Chicago, the educational philanthropists, or anyone else still considers them preferable to public education. Social justice has been sacrificed to the goal of efficiency, but that goal has not been achieved.

No Child Left Behind

The neoliberal reformers who have worked so hard to dismantle public education have also inspired the most intrusive educational law in the history of our country, *No Child Left Behind*. With its passage, the federal government took on the business of micromanaging every public school that receives federal funds. The law dictates how states should measure school success, specifies punitive interventions for schools that fail, diverts tax dollars to private institutions, mandates exhaustive and internally inconsistent lists of qualifications for teachers, and even tells schools how to teach reading and which textbooks teachers should use if they want to continue receiving federal funding (Wallis & Steptoe, 2007).

All this is monitored through a mandated testing regimen requiring teachers to reconfigure nearly every teaching or planning moment into a form of test preparation. In fact, many teachers spend as much time in test-driven activities (benchmarking, posting standards on bulletin boards, aligning standards with assessments, attending workshops on "teaching to the test," tracking student progress on charts, filling in computerized reports, and teaching test-taking skills), as in teaching itself. Meanwhile, schools are spending hundreds of millions of dollars each year on testing programs that would be better spent on improving instruction. The result is a massive distortion of the entire system, and a punishing regimen for all involved. "The biggest problem with NCLB is that it mistakes measuring schools for fixing them. States have been forced to lower their standards and some schools improve performance by encouraging low-performing students to leave" (Darling-Hammond, cited in Meier & Wood, 2004). Worse, when public schools "fail," as they inevitably will do under NCLB's unobtainable goal of annual improvement for each of 37 subgroups, some of their work is turned over to private tutoring companies (Bracey, 2007). The law mandates that by 2014 all children at every school will be, as in Lake Wobegon, above average (proficient), a logical impossibility.

The law's sanctions are not designed to help schools resolve their specific problems, but rather to punish them, make them fail, and ultimately deliver them over to the free market. In many cases, even though the schools are actually improving each year, they fail to meet the inflexible standards prescribed by NCLB, if one of their 37 target groups has not reached its rigid annual goal in reading or math. One child can make all the difference (Meier & Wood, 2004).

Morale is one casualty of this testing regimen; debasement of the curriculum is another. Teachers teach to the test based on hundreds of discrete standards in each discipline, feeding snippets of knowledge to their students, ready for regurgitation on multiple-choice tests. Broad, scattered coverage replaces comprehension. There is no time to find out if students have mastered a skill before moving on to the next one. Pacing charts determine all. The NCLB focus on proficiency in reading and math for elementary students distorts and narrows the curriculum, privileging basic literacy and math skills over content knowledge, the arts, and critical thinking. Hands-on projects are eliminated in favor of pencil-and-paper test preparation. Even the kindergartens have become test-prep centers. The stakes are just too high to leave them as they were intended: "children's gardens." Paints, easels, and Froebel blocks have vanished, replaced by an academic treadmill. Creativity has been pushed out of the curriculum, along with play and recreational activities, fundamental human rights as defined by the United Nations International Convention on the Rights of the Child (1989).

And finally, school success or failure are largely measured by a single round of multiple-choice tests, even though most researchers and brain theorists have demonstrated that a variety of assessments over time is a more accurate way to measure learning (Shepard, 1996; Gardner, 1983). NCLB accountability is thus inherently skewed and unfair. Many state superintendents around the country have declared that its Adequate Yearly Progress (AYP) system is inflexible, arbitrary, and punitive. For example, some schools in California have made substantial progress by most measures, but because they did not meet their rigid AYP targets they were required to redirect some of their funds to private tutors (often unqualified), or for busing students to another school. Moreover, "proficiency" is a flexible criterion, varying from state to state depending on the difficulty of state standards. As California State Superintendent Jack O'Connell points out:

> State standards were so low in Mississippi that in 2005, 89% of 4th graders were rated proficient in reading under NCLB, and yet they were at the bottom in reading on the more rigorous National Assessment of Educational Progress (NAEP), with only 18% of students at grade level. Although Mississippi was tied for the best score in the country on NCLB, on NAEP (a uniform measure of student knowledge), the state dropped to 50th place. If you make the goal posts wide enough, everybody scores. (cited in Wallis & Steptoe, 2007, p. 5)

Under this regimen students are reduced to the sum of their test scores, heading for slots in a future labor market; teachers are reduced to technicians and supervisors on the educational assembly line. This is bad in itself, but it is also indicative of a broader systemic malaise. Economists had until recently assumed that a large blue-collar workforce with limited skills was no longer needed. But in the new digital age, performance by teachers and students can now be monitored down to the smallest detail. Technologies known as "enterprise systems," or ES, which use computers to standardize and monitor the entire range of tasks being done by a company's or school's workforce, are designed to reduce complex activities, such as teaching, to a series of steps and outcomes that can be monitored by a computer, thus allowing school districts to hold teachers accountable for assembly-line delivery of testable factoids. Particularly in many urban school districts, standards have been turned into mind-numbing piecework, delivered on a conveyor belt monitored by pacing charts.

The spread of ES in education has resulted in a declining emphasis on creativity, individualized instruction, and teacher professionalism. New mandates are all too easily put in place and monitored, keeping teachers wrong-footed as the goal posts are continually moved. These changes are eroding the value of accumulated teaching experience and wisdom, and are concentrating power among school and district administrators, the new floor managers of the electronic industrial revolution. Never before have teachers been required to work as assembly-line workers on an ever-accelerating production line. Taylorism[1] and Fordism[2] are reappearing in an electronic guise, with NCLB and its new industry of assessors holding the stopwatch (S. Head, 2007).

The End of Neoliberal Standardization: Positive Standards as Vision and Goals for Democratic Education

However, change is in the air. The neoliberal project is faltering, and the ideal of democratic education is regaining its strength. Throughout U.S. history, conservative and liberal trends have alternated, each running its course, then giving rise to its opposite. The excesses of the 1890s were checked during the Progressive era; and the McCarthy era was reversed during the 1960s (Kliebard, 1986; Tyack & Cuban, 1995). There are signs now that the neoliberal tide has begun to recede. It has become increasingly difficult for conservatives to ignore the social and environmental costs of their market-driven policies such as urban decay, the healthcare crisis, and the widening chasm between haves and have-nots. In fact, judging by such financial disasters as the Enron scandal, the recent subprime mortgage and banking meltdown, upwardly spiraling national debt, due in large part to an illegal, fraudulent, and privatized war, it has become more and more obvious that the free market is incapable of regulating its own excesses. The failure of neoliberalism's market-based prescriptions means that the government will need to return to state-based solutions not only in healthcare, schools, and the environment, but also to resolve global problems which private capital has failed to remedy: for instance, we must cap carbon emissions, a regulatory task that only governments together can accomplish. Local and global, micro and macro, are inextricably linked, and cannot be left to the caprices of the market.

The failure of the neoliberal reform project creates the opportunity to return to an educational system based on democratic and social justice principles. Led by the Forum on Educational Accountability, more than 100 national groups signed a statement in 2007 calling for fundamental changes to NCLB, in particular changing the law's focus on standardized testing, its over-identification of schools in "need of improvement," and its reliance on punitive sanctions. Each of these groups is also spearheading its own initiative, and providing evidence that NCLB is actually undermining the concept of educational reform. Together they were able to block the reauthorization of NCLB during the Bush administration, clearing the way for a more holistic and progressive education in which social justice, peace, and environmental education can claim their rightful place in the curriculum (Miner, 2007).

At this crucial juncture, schools need to prepare students to address the national and global issues that confront us, and we must devise a strategy to enable educators to respond effectively to these challenges. But in this new era of globalization (defined as the transnational flow and networking of people, communications, labor, products, capital, ideas, culture, and power), it is not enough to go back to Dewey's formula for democratic education, as defined in the Progressive era, or to the Great Society formulae of the 1960s: we must think our way beyond the current crisis, not only repairing the damage wrought by a generation of corporate-inspired educational "reforms," but also looking forward and embracing opportunities that globalbization presents. We now have the chance to make social justice principles a central element in the curriculum, teaching them not only from a local and national perspective, but more importantly, in a global, humane, and ecological context (Aronowitz & Gautney, 2003; Nussbaum, 1998, 2002, 2003, 2006; Schaeffer, 2005; Slattery & Rapp, 2003; Spring, 1997, 1998).

The time has come therefore to lay out a set of positive educational standards for social justice, peace, and environmental education. We can no longer follow a nation-centered curriculum in this new global age. Criteria for social justice, peace and environmental standards must now be subsumed under internationally agreed-upon normative standards. By invoking international treaties and documents to develop their social justice, peace, and environmental education standards, the authors in this book are recasting and re-invigorating the democratic principles on which our educational system has traditionally been based.

Standards for Democratic Education in a Global Context

Schools of Education, teacher educators, teachers, and P-12 students should investigate and deliberate the following:

1. ***The purpose of public education in a democracy;***
2. ***Relationships between the global political economy and issues of social justice, peace, and the environment;***
3. ***Whether globalization reduces or increases inequalities between rich and poor within and between nations;***
4. ***How societal changes (political, economic, religious, and demographic) affect schools, curricula, and teacher practice;***
5. ***How thinking globally and locally rather than nationally can advance the causes of social justice, peace, and environmental education;***

6. ***How a cosmopolitan curricular framework can provide for a flexible citizenship that includes loyalty to the nation-state, but also to the human community, the bioshpere, and the shared challenges that confront us all;***
7. ***Relationships between the global political economy and the way schools are run and what is taught in them;***
8. ***How U.S. public schools have historically served as primary venues for racial, ethnic, religious, and gender inequality* and *equality;***
9. ***How P-12 students benefit from an age-appropriate and humanistic education;***
10. ***The implications of the use of computer systems to control and monitor teaching and learning.***

Notes

1. Taylorism comes from Frederick Winslow Taylor's famous 1911 book, *The Principles of Scientific Management*, which applies science to the management of workers in the industrial age. Scientific management converted skilled crafts into a series of simplified operations that could be performed by unskilled workers following a rigid timetable, thus making industrial output more efficient.
2. Similarly, Fordism, the concept of mass production pioneered by Henry Ford, refers to his assembly line system of mass production based on standardization: standardized parts, standardized machinery, standardized manufacturing processes, and a standardized final product. Parts were interchangeable so that they could be replaced and repaired at minimum cost and effort.

References

America 2000: Excellence in Education Act. H.R. 2460, 102nd Congress, October 24, 1991.

Anyon, J. (1980, Fall). Social class and the hidden curriculum of work. *Journal of Education, 162*(1), 67–92.

Aronowitz, S., & Gautney, H. (2003*). Implicating empire: Globalization and resistance in the 21st century world order.* New York: Basic Books.

Ayers, W., & Klonsky, M. (2006). Chicago's Renaissance 2010: The small schools movement meets the ownership society. *Phi Delta Kappan*. February. Retrieved 8, 2007, from http://www.epx.sagepub.com

Bennett, W. (1984). *To reclaim a legacy. A report on the humanities in higher education.* Washington, DC: National Endowment for the Humanities.

Berliner, D. C., & Biddle, B. J. (1995). *The manufactured crisis: Myths, frauds and the attack on America's public schools.* New York: Longman.

Bracey, G. W. (2007, October). The first time 'everything changed': The 17th Bracey report on the condition of public education. *Phi Delta Kappan, 89*(2), 119–136.

Brown et al. v. Board of Education of Topeka, et al., 347 U.S. 483 (1954).

Cheney, L. V. (1987). *American memory: A report on the humanities in the nation's public schools.* Washington, DC: National Endowment for the Humanities.

Christensen, C. A., & Dorn, S. (1997). Competing notions of social justice and contradictions in special education reform. *The Journal of Special Education, 31*(2), 181-198.

Crawford v. Board of Education of the City of Los Angeles, 17 Cal. 3d 280 (1976).

Cremin, L. A. (Ed.). (1957). *Republic and the school: Horace Mann on the education of free men.* New York: Teachers College Press.

Davis, M. (1990). *City of quartz: Excavating the future in Los Angeles.* New York: Vintage Books.

Dewey, J. (1916). *Democracy and education: An introduction to the philosophy of education.* New York: Macmillan.

Doyle, D. (1982). Way out west in Dixie: The Los Angeles desegregation of schools. *Integrated Education, 20*(1-2), 2–6.

Du Bois, W.E.B. (1903/1999). *The souls of black folk.* New York: Norton.

Elmore, R., & McLaughlin, M. (1982). *Reform and retrenchment: The politics of California school finance reform.* Cambridge, UK: Ballinger.

Finn, C., & Ravitch, D. (1984). *Against mediocrity: The humanities in America's high schools.* New York: Holmes & Meier.

Finn, Jr., C. E., & Ravitch, D. (1987). *What do our 17-year-olds know? A report on the first national assessment of history and literature.* New York: HarperCollins.

Farhi, P. (2007, January 21). Five myths about U.S. kids outclassed by the rest of the world. *Washington Post,* p. BO2. Retrieved from http://www.washingtonpost.com/wp-dyn/content/article/2007/01/19/AR2007011901360.html

Fischel, W. (1989). Did Serrano cause Proposition 13? *The National Tax Journal, 1*(10), 465–474.

Friedman, M. (2002). *Capitalism and freedom* (40th anniversary ed.). Chicago: University of Chicago Press. (Original published 1962)

Gardner, H. (1983). *Frames of mind: The theory of multiple intelligences.* New York: Basic Books.

Goals 2000: Educate America Act (P.L. 103-227), March 31, 1994.

Hayek, F. A. (1978). *The constitution of liberty.* Chicago: University of Chicago Press.

Hayes, W. (2006). *Horace Mann's vision of the public schools. Is it still relevant?* Lanham, MD: Rowman & Littlefield.

Head, S. (2007, August 16). They're micromanaging your every move. *New York Review of Books, 54*(13). Retrieved December 22, 2008, from http://www.nybooks.com/artiles/20499

Head, T. (2007). Tom Head's civil liberties blog. Retrieved January 15, 2008, from http://www.civiliberty.com

Hillocks, G. Jr. (2002). *The testing trap: How state writing assessments control learning.* New York: Teachers College Press.

Jefferson, T. (1781–1784). *Notes on the State of Virginia.* Electronic Text Center, University of Electronic Text Center, University of Virginia Library. Retrieved January 9, 2008, from http://www.masshist.org/thomasjeffersonpapers/virginia/#summ

Keay D. (1987, October 31). Aids, education and the year 2000! *Women's Own.*

Kliebard, H. M. (1986). *The struggle for the American curriculum 1893-1958.* Boston: Routledge & Kegan Paul.

Kozol, J. (1991). *Savage inequalities: Children in America's schools.* New York: Harper Collins.

Lekachman, R. (1978, September). Proposition 13 and the new conservatism. *Change, 10*(8), 22-27.

Lo, C. (1990). *Small property versus big government: Social origins of the property tax revolt.* Berkeley: University of California Press.

Meier, D., & G. Wood (Eds.). (2004). *Many children left behind.* Boston: Beacon Press.

Miner, B. (2005, Summer). Who's behind the money? *Rethinking schools online.* Retrieved April 22, 2007, from http://www.rethinkingschools.org/archive/19_04/who194.shtml

Miner, B. (2007, Spring). Can No Child Be Left Behind? *Rethinking schools online.*

Retrieved April 22, 2007, from http://www.rethinkingschools.org/archive/21_03/nclb213.shtml

National Commission on Excellence in Education. (1983). *A nation at risk: The imperative for educational reform.* Washington, DC: US Department of Education.

No Child Left Behind Act (Jan. 8, 2002). PL 107–110.

Nussbaum, F. (Ed.). (2003). *The global eighteenth century.* Baltimore: Johns Hopkins University Press.

Nussbaum, M. C. (1998). *Cultivating humanity: A classical defense of reform in liberal education.* Boston: Harvard University Press.

Nussbaum, M. C. (2002). *For the love of country?* Boston: Beacon Press.

Nussbaum, M. C. (2006). *Frontiers of justice: disability, nationality, and species membership.* London: Belknap.

Parents Involved in Community Schools v. Seattle School District No. 1 et al., VII, 426 F. 3d, at. 1192 (2007).

Poynor, L., & P. M. Wolfe. (2004). *Marketing fear in America's public schools: The real war on literacy.* Mahwah, NJ: Erlbaum.

Regents of the University of California v. Bakke. 76-811, 438 U.S. 265 (1978).

Ricardo, D. (2004). *The principles of political economy and taxation.* London: Dover. (Original published 1817)

Saltman, K. J. (2000). *Collateral damage: Corporatizing public schools—a threat to democracy.* Lanham, MD: Rowman & Littlefield.

Saltman, K. J., & Gabbard, D. (2003). *Education as enforcement: The militarization and corporatization of schools.* New York: Routledge/Falmer.

Scatamburlo, V. L. (1998). *Soldiers of misfortune: The new right's culture war and the politics of political correctness.* New York: Peter Lang.

Schaeffer, R. K. (2005). *Understanding globalization: The social consequences of political, economic, & environmental change (3rd ed.).* Lanham, MD: Rowman & Littlefield.

Serrano v. Priest, 18 Cal.3d 728 (1976) (Serrano II).

Shepard, L. A. (1996). The role of assessment in a learning culture. *Educational Researcher, 29*(7), 4–14.

Slattery, P., & Rapp, D. (2003). *Ethics and the foundations of education: Teaching convictions in a postmodern world.* Boston: Pearson Education.

Smith, A. (1776/2003). *The wealth of nations.* New York: Bantom Books. (Original published 1776)

Smith, D. (1998). *Tax crusaders and the politics of direct democracy.* New York: Routledge.

Spring, J. (1997). *Political agendas for education: From the Christian coalition to the green party.* Mahwah, NJ: Erlbaum.

Spring, J. (1998). *Education and the rise of the global economy.* Mahwah, NJ: Erlbaum.

Symcox, L. (2002). *The hidden agenda behind Proposition 13: A suburban middle class revolt.* Unpublished manuscript.

Tabb, W. K. (2001). *The amoral elephant: globalization & the struggle for social justice in the twenty-first century.* New York: Monthly Review Press.

Tyack, D., & L. Cuban. (1995). *Tinkering toward utopia: A century of public school reform.* Cambridge, MA: Harvard University Press.

United Nations. (1989). *Convention on International Rights of the Child.* Retrieved February 25, 2008, from http://www.unicef.org/crc/

University of California Regents V. Bakke, 438 U.S. 265 (1978) 438 U.S. 265

Wallis, C., & Steptoe, S. (2007, May 24). How to fix No Child Left Behind. *Time.Com.* Retrieved July 7, 2007, from http://www.nctq.org/nctq/research/1180459263221.pdf, p. 5.

Willis, P. (1981). *Learning to labour.* Hampshire, UK: Gower.

5 Reclaiming Standards for a Progressive Agenda

Human Rights Education Standards for Teachers and Teacher Education[1]

Todd Jennings

Human rights are standards, standards that outline the conditions necessary for people to live in full dignity. Contemporary efforts to define specific human rights include United Nations instruments such as The Universal Declaration of Human Rights (1948), The International Convention on the Elimination of All Forms of Racial Discrimination (1963), The International Covenant on Economic, Social and Cultural Rights (1966), The Convention of the Rights of the Child (1989), The Convention on the Elimination of All Forms of Discrimination Against Women (1981), and The Declaration on the Rights of Indigenous Peoples (1994). Although there is spirited debate over the cultural universality of the work of the United Nations and the specific rights outlined within many U.N. instruments (Donnelly, 2002; Ignatieff, 2003; Mutua, 2002a, 2002b), these instruments nonetheless provide useful examples of potentially universal human rights.

Human actions to promote and protect human rights are improbable if ignorance regarding human rights is as common as research indicates and human rights education (HRE) continues to be ignored in public education (Human Rights USA, 1997). For example, as recently as 2000, only 20 of the 50 states within the United States explicitly included human rights content within public education curriculum (Banks, 2001). Little wonder, then, that many people condone human rights violations through their passive endorsement of the policies and practices of governments and multinational corporations. In an effort to address these concerns, this article proposes a set of standards for classroom teachers in the area of human rights education and suggests an agenda for teacher education. The hopeful outcome of these HRE standards is that students will frame and critique their own actions from a human rights perspective. Another outcome is that students will critique the actions of the organizations in which they participate or who ostensibly represent their interests as citizens, consumers, or stockholders. While it is important that individuals see that human rights violations are committed, or deterred, by the actions of individuals and groups it is equally important that they understand the potential roles of social structures in allowing human rights violations to go unnoticed and unchallenged.

Standards designed to shape educational outcomes are familiar. In the case of classroom teachers, standards often define required competencies for professional practice. Similarly, professional competency standards provide guidance when developing teacher education programs. If constructed properly, a set of human rights education standards could promote human rights education by shaping teacher preparation programs. However, standardization efforts are often approached suspiciously as potential threats to the professional autonomy of educators and the self-determination of local communities regarding education. Therefore, any efforts to establish standards, particularly human rights education standards, must respect the rights of teacher educators, teachers, and ultimately, students. In the end, a set of human rights education standards could promote human rights education and provide a framework to critique any contemporary standardization movement that might undermine the rights of children, teachers, or the communities in which they teach and learn.

Defining Human Rights Education

"Human rights are both abstract and practical. They hold up the inspiring vision of a free, just, and peaceful world and set minimum standards for how both individuals and institutions should treat people" (Human Rights Resource Center, 2000). However, empowering visions must first be learned. Human rights education is the deliberate practice of preparing individuals, groups, and communities with the content, attitudes, and skills that encourage the recognition, promotion, and protection of human rights (Amnesty International, 2005; Lister, 1991), and usually encompasses cognitive, affective, and behavioral elements (Martin, 1997; Tibbetts, 1997). Human rights education routinely includes teaching the various types of human rights (civil, political, economic, social, cultural), the legal basis of human rights (e.g., human rights instruments), historic and contemporary human rights violations, historic and contemporary human rights advocacy efforts, how human rights principles and concepts can be implemented in classrooms and beyond, and how one can design opportunities for students to engage in actions that promote and protect human rights (Council of Europe Committee of Ministers, 1985/1991; Flowers & Shiman, 1997; Meintjes, 1997; Shafer, 1987; Starkey, 1991). Human rights education should also entail the formation of social consciousness whereby students not only examine individual actions and collective actions that promote human rights but work to interrogate any social structures (policies, values, and collective practices) whereby human rights violations might occur under a veil of anonymity.

Human rights education aligns with other justice-oriented educational philosophies and practices such as critical pedagogy (Kanpol, 1994; Smith, 1976; Shor, 1993; Shor & Friere, 1987; Friere, 1970, 1985) and many forms of multicultural education (Sleeter, 1996). Human rights education strengthens these efforts by providing explicit attention to the larger international human rights movement as well as providing content that defines social justice specifically from a human rights perspective (see Baltodano this volume). Likewise, the dialogic nature of critical pedagogy and critical multiculturalism facilitate various skills or attributes related to human rights education such as critical social consciousness, affirmation of diversity, and student empowerment. Critical pedagogy and multiculturalism also offer opportunities for educational communities to wrestle with the tensions between affirming diverse cultures and assertions of the universal nature of human rights.

What Might Human Rights Education Standards for Teachers Include?

"Human rights should be a fundamental organizing principle for professional practice, so that all prospective teachers come to see themselves as human rights educators and advocates" (Flowers & Shiman, 1997, p. 162). This requires that, as professionals, teachers intellectually understand human rights issues, serve as models of human rights advocacy, urge students to act in accordance with human rights principles, facilitate classroom environments that reflect human rights principles, and create experiences for students to act in accordance with the promotion of human rights (Flowers & Shiman, 1997; Osler & Starkey, 1996). Human rights education cannot be accomplished simply by adding human rights content to already overburdened curricula. It must go further toward reform by shaping the curriculum content of schools and teacher education, shaping classroom methodologies for instruction and management, and encouraging teacher-student and student-student interactions not only *about* human rights but that also *embody* human rights (United Nations Education, Scientific and Cultural Organization, n.d.). Contemporary human rights educators recognize the importance of sound cognitive knowledge of human rights principles and concepts as well as affective or dispositional characteristics that incite action (e.g., empathy, perspective taking, a sense of efficacy to affect change, etc.). Cognitively, such content includes an understanding of the concept of human rights and familiarity with contemporary expressions of human rights such as the various instruments of the United Nations. In many contexts, the 1948 Universal Declaration of Human Rights (UDHR) can form the basic content of human rights education (Lister, 1984). The UDHR can be used to explore the political, social, economic, and cultural lives of students across many grade levels and potentially across multiple social contexts (Reardon, 1995; Sebaly, 1987). While U.N. instruments may require some adaptation based upon student developmental characteristics (particularly for young students), the instruments nonetheless represent attempts to define human rights within an international community. They can provide foundations for exploring curriculum content and creating school environments. As mentioned above, they can provide points of departure for students and teachers to debate the universality and nature of particular rights, assess their own actions relative to particular rights, and examine the socio-historical contexts in which they live (Wronka, 1994).

Beyond the UDHR, other international instruments can be useful for teachers as well. For example, The Convention on the Rights of the Child is particularly appropriate for those working with children and in many cases may hold the greatest interest for children themselves. Educators concerned specifically with girls' and women's human rights might use The Convention on the Elimination of All Forms of Discrimination Against Women, while those concerned with indigenous communities and populations can include The Declaration on the Rights of Indigenous People. Similarly, educators teaching natural science or ecology might use instruments related to human rights and the environment such as The Draft Declaration of Human Rights and the Environment (1994). The study of armed conflict historically and contemporarily should include the Geneva Conventions and their protocols. In short, for the teacher committed to the notion of human rights education and infusing pedagogy with a human rights perspective, there are a multitude of human rights instruments and curriculum available to explore virtually any issue salient in local/state school curriculum and/or student's lives and communities (Tibbetts, 1997; Human Rights Resource Center, 2006).

The Necessity of a Comprehensive Approach

Some educators may assert that they already provide human rights education by promoting various prosocial dispositions and skills such as empathy and conflict management (thus avoiding the political nature of human rights per se). However, such apolitical efforts are not human rights education because, while they may promote "good" people, they do not promote a critical awareness that results from exploring human rights theory, the human rights movement, the possibility of universalized rights for all, the accountability of all people and institutions for respecting those rights, and the ways that human rights are tied to larger social structures and government/corporate policies (Tibbetts, 2002). For example, empathy and conflict management skills, although wonderful human capacities consistent with human rights education, do not represent human rights education if the standards for human dignity and conduct (the principles and concepts as codified by instruments) are missing and if the means to critically evaluate how human rights apply to any given situation are absent. Likewise, knowledge of the principles outlined in various human rights instruments, while crucial and foundational, is not necessarily sufficient to bring about the compulsion to take action, the belief that one can affect change, or the dispositions leading to felt responsibilities for the rights of oneself and others. In short, neither an exclusively instrument-based nor a character-based approach is sufficient to fully embody human rights education.

Human rights education in many ways places a premium upon the knowledge and actions of individuals who have responsibilities to protect and promote human rights. In turn, individuals can either singularly or collectively work to combat the two forms of human rights abuses that commonly occur. These include violations committed by individuals as well as violations resulting from government or corporate policies worldwide (to which individuals are always linked). This later category is perhaps the most pervasive and insidious because these violations are shrouded behind impersonal policies justified in the name of economic growth, fighting terrorism, or protecting national security. Consequently, human rights violations are often committed through the systemic actions of collective institutions such as governments and multinational corporations. However, governments and multinational corporations have neither personality nor conscience. Although these organizations, policies, or structures may not have individual identities they do represent the interests of individual citizens, consumers, and benefactors. Therefore, the accountability for the actions of these organizations rests with the conscience of their individual citizens, stakeholders, and constituents. Human rights education recognizes that people have rights and responsibilities not only for their actions as individuals but also for the actions carried out in their political and economic interests as citizens and stakeholders. This is the level where human rights education engages in social change—the will of individuals or individuals in collective action to meld and shape the policies and practices of government and corporate bodies. Understanding the systemic nature of human rights abuses and protections is perhaps the greatest challenge facing human rights education and many teachers. It is a challenge for many teachers and students to develop the consciousness that enables them to see violations as systemic and endorsed actively and passively by those within the political or economic system.

Most scholars and activists working to define human rights education agree that students' experiences in classrooms and schools must be saturated by a comprehensive curriculum and school culture that teach human rights through experience (Tibbetts, 2002). Building upon the knowledge base found in the instruments' contents and relying additionally upon the substantial amount of current curriculum material on human rights education, teachers and students must use human rights principles to shape, if not reform, learning environments. Toward this end, a measurable set of standards could provide the justification and guidance needed to link the conceptual framework of human rights education, the wide variety of disparate curriculum materials currently available, school policies, school values, school norms, and teacher actions. The basic structure and content of the proposed standards to follow are loosely informed by standards established by two accreditation bodies in the United States (one at a state level and the other at the national level): The California Standards for the Teaching Profession (California Commission on Teacher Credentialing, 1997) and the standards established for teacher preparation by The National Council for Accreditation in Teacher Education (NCATE; 2006). It is likely that readers from other regions of the world also have accreditation bodies who promote standards similar in content and structure.

Human Rights Education Standards for Classroom Teachers

Preamble

Throughout history, people have struggled to outline the conditions necessary for human beings to live justly with one another in peace and full dignity. Teaching and education are the primary means by which human rights are secured for current and future generations. Human rights are most secure when embedded in the thoughts and actions of individuals and then embodied by local, national, and international political and corporate communities who represent the interests of individuals and groups. Thus, at its core, human rights education promotes an awareness of human rights and offer explicit opportunities to explore how human rights and their associated responsibilities apply to private and public life. To this end, the following standards for human rights education are proposed for classroom teachers at all levels and with all populations of students.

Standard One: Engages and Supports All Students' Learning About Human Rights

- Relates students' developmental characteristics and needs to human rights themes, principles and concepts such as rights, justice, dignity, and the universal value of all human beings
- Connects students' prior knowledge, life experiences, and personal interests to human rights principles and concepts in both human history and students' contemporary lives
- Uses a variety of instructional strategies and resources to promote learning about human rights, particularly forms of instruction that encourage student participation and opportunities to voice opinion, think critically, and assume multiple perspectives
- Works with students to connect their specific ethnic, familial, racial, gender, sexual, and other identity characteristics to human right principles and concepts, in both history and students' contemporary lives

Standard Two: Creates and Maintains Effective Environments that Embody the Principles and Concepts of Human Rights

- Creates, with students, an explicit and articulated set of classroom and school values that embody and can explicitly be shown to embody human rights principles and specific human rights such as those outlined in The Universal Declaration of Human Rights (UDHR; 1948), The Convention on the Rights of the Child (CRC; 1989), and/or other human rights instruments that may reflect local cultures and contexts
- Plans and implements, with students, classroom and school procedures, disciplinary plans, classroom organizational and management structures that can explicitly be shown to embody human rights concepts and thus support students' learning about human rights concepts and principles through lived experience

Standard Three: Understands and Organizes Subject Matter to Promote Student Learning About Human Rights

- Demonstrates a knowledge of basic human rights concepts and specifics as articulated in instruments such as the UDHR or other instruments. This understanding includes an awareness of the full range of human rights: Civil, political, cultural, economic, and social
- Describes the place of human rights relative to one's own philosophy of education and is able to directly link elements of one's educational philosophy

to human rights principles and concepts as articulated in instruments such as the UDHR or other instruments
- Interrelates human rights concepts and information within and across subject matter areas and/or within the subject area of one's teaching
- Uses instructional strategies that are consistent with human rights concepts and principles in respecting the dignity and rights of students, their families, and their communities
- Uses adaptive materials, resources, and technologies to make human rights concepts and principles accessible to all students

Standard Four: Plans Instruction and Designs Learning Experiences for the Human Rights Education of All Students

- Plans, designs, and sequences human rights education activities and materials that draw upon and value students' backgrounds, interests, and developmental characteristics
- Establishes and articulates specific human rights education goals for students in light of curriculum endorsed by the school's governing body
- Encourages, in an developmentally appropriate manner, student thought and discussion regarding how the articles of various human rights instruments might be interpreted
- Encourages students, in a developmentally appropriate manner, to use their understanding of human rights principles, concepts, and instruments to examine and critically analyze their own experiences and behaviors in the school, home, local community, region, the international community, and the environment
- Work with students to use their understanding of human rights principles, concepts, and instruments to examine and critically analyze the actions of both private and public institutions and organizations (including organizations that represent the political or economic interests of the students themselves domestically and globally)
- Encourages students to use their understanding of human rights principles, concepts, and instruments to interpret and seek understanding of the experiences of people in other social groups, geographic regions, and times in history
- Develops instructional activities that allow students to take positive action relative to their own human rights and their responsibilities to protect and promote the rights of others

Standard Five: Uses Assessment Strategies That Embody Human Rights Concepts and Principles

- Establishes and communicates learning goals specifically related to human rights concepts, principles, and instruments
- Uses assessment strategies that embody, promote, and protect the human rights of students

Standard Six: Develops as a Professional Human Rights Educator

- Reflects on the effectiveness of one's human rights education efforts
- Establishes professional goals and pursues opportunities to develop as a human rights educator
- Works with local and international communities to promote human rights
- Works with families and communities to improve their understanding of human rights
- Works with professional colleagues to promote the practice of human rights education
- Works to ensure that the human rights of educators are protected and promoted

Implications for Teacher Preparation

Among many human rights educators, the promotion of human rights and human rights education is tied to a larger agenda of promoting social justice. Admittedly, social justice efforts within teacher preparation are not without controversy. To illustrate, in 2006 the U.S. based National Council for Accreditation of Teacher Education (NCATE) retracted its use of the term *social justice* as an example of potential dispositional characteristics expected of new teachers (Wasley, 2006). Later, in an apparent compromise between conservative and progressive groups, the organization inserted a separate statement into the standards that clarified its stance on social justice (NCATE, 2008). In this statement, social justice goals were narrowly defined as a commitment to address the educational achievement gap in the United States by providing all children with "well prepared" teachers who understood the impact of discrimination (NCATE, 2008). The removal of the term "social justice" from the description of dispositions and the subsequent narrowing clarification of NCATE's definition of social justice clearly worked to distance NCATE from any number of more radical or progressive definitions of social justice and social justice movements that might challenge current political and economic structures and institutions.

The NCATE example offers clear evidence that professional oversight organizations can, at times, waiver or fall short in offering progressive direction when political pressure is brought to bear upon the values they endorse, particularly when those values have implications for the redistribution of political and economic power. The NCATE decision to clarify its commitment to social justice reinforces the notion that HRE efforts will remain, at least for now, largely decentralized to teacher preparation programs and K-12 classrooms. While it would be ideal if preparation programs and classroom teachers found decisive support for HRE at higher levels, this is never guaranteed. Consequently, most HRE efforts emerge out of the dispositions, values, interests and commitments of classroom teachers themselves. Therefore, the role of teacher preparation programs in promoting HRE is important because of the role programs have in shaping novice teachers' professional commitments.

Human rights education begins with teacher preparation faculty becoming familiar enough with human rights concepts and instruments to locate intersections between human rights education and their own teaching and program design. For example, human rights concepts and instruments can be used to explore the psychological, philosophical, social, and cultural foundations of education. Examinations of economic, social, and cultural human rights can be especially useful in these courses as pre-service teachers examine the purposes of education in light of human rights and the extent to which schools are promoting human rights. For many pre-service teachers, these efforts may stimulate interest in foundation courses as they explore teacher decision-making, schools, and schooling practices in light of contemporary human rights issues and concerns (Jennings, 1995). This is particularly true if such efforts explicitly relate human rights issues to pre-service teachers' own lives, communities, the lives of their future students, contemporary events, and their visions for the future. Such explorations can demonstrate to pre-service teachers the importance of "foundations" to teacher decision-making, schooling practices, and the influence of schooling upon future generations.

Second, it is important that teacher educators act strategically to promote human rights education in situations where it might be otherwise ignored. Returning back to accreditation standards, teacher educators can, within their own programs, offer human rights based *interpretations* of existing professional, federal, and state standards. Additionally, programs can add their own human rights education standards to existing accreditation standards. For example, NCATE standards direct individual teacher education programs (units) to develop their own dispositional outcomes for pre-service teachers. As stated in the glossary of the NCATE standards, "the two professional dispositions that NCATE expects institutions to assess are fairness and the belief that all students can learn. Based on their mission and conceptual framework, professional education units can identify, define, and operationalize additional professional dispositions" (NCATE, 2008). This same sentiment was articulated in a press release offered during the height of the social justice controversy when NCATE stated that "consistent with their mission, *colleges of education may determine* additional professional dispositions they want their candidates to develop" (NCATE, 2006). Thus, despite NCATE's narrow definition of social justice, a commitment to fairness remains and there is still a provision, if not an implied directive, for teacher education programs to establishing *their own* outcomes for teachers—outcomes that can include human rights education.

Continuing further, other NCATE standards provide additional places where strategically minded teacher educators can promote human rights education. For example, the NCATE unit standard for "*Professional And Pedagogical Knowledge And Skills For Teacher Candidates*" states that teacher candidates should be able to "consider school, family, and community contexts in connecting concepts to students' prior experience and applying the ideas to real-world issues" (NCATE, 2008). A human rights perspective provides a framework from which both teachers and their students can assess the "real world issues" they face. Many of the HRE standards proposed in this chapter focus upon students' using human rights concepts as an interpretive framework for understanding their lives, families, communities, organizations, and government. For teachers and teacher educators, a human rights perspective can be used to interpret many accreditation standards not originally written with human rights or human rights education in mind.

Within teacher preparation programs, methods instructors can demonstrate how to search state or district curriculum standards for places where human rights related themes already exist but may not be identified as such. They can then use those content standards to introduce pre-service teachers to human rights concepts. Next, they can use human rights instruments to offer various interpretations and ways of teaching state sanctioned curriculum content. For example, repeatedly in K-12 history-social science education in the United States, students are expected to learn about topics such as slavery, child labor, the women's movement, immigration, significant people in history, indigenous people, geography, and the history of trade movements and unions. Methods faculty can demonstrate how to teach each of these topics from a human rights perspective. For example, *slavery* is not just taught as a "bad thing" or a fact in history (which is as far as many teachers go) but as bad from a *human rights perspective and as a means to teach the broader concept of human rights.* Likewise, the role of unions in U.S. history can be elevated above just facts about history to a means of introducing learners to the larger concept of economic and cultural human rights. Similarly, English and language arts, which routinely include themes such as gender, poverty, slavery, justice, fairness, can be taught in ways that also teach human rights concepts.. The same is true for the visual and performing arts. In mathematics, methods faculty can demonstrate how to use human rights data when teaching specific calculation skills to K-12 students. These can include hunger rates/ratios, poverty rates/ratios, child labor rates, immigration and settlement data, or any numeric data used to describe various human rights related conditions both historically or contemporarily. Thus, math methods faculty can show how to teach human rights via computations skills and using numeric data (from simply to complex). In kinesthesiology, there are of number examples of human rights issues related to sports and sports history that can be integrated into physical education programs. These can reflect human rights in sports history or relate to the rights of all students of all physical abilities to full participation in sports as a cultural and social practice. In earth sciences and life sciences students can explore environmental pollution and ecological systems from a human rights perspective, examining the links between human rights and environmental degradation and preservation. In short, methods faculty can demonstrate for preservice teachers that there are HRE opportunities in each and every content area. This is particularly feasible given the exponentially increasing amount of human rights education curriculum currently being generated that assists in linking academic content areas to the exploration of human rights related topics (Human Rights Resource Center, 2006; Tibbetts, 1997). Rather than seeing human rights education as an "add on," it is important that new teachers see that opportunities for human rights education already exist within official curriculum and need only be uncovered and highlighted.

Teacher education programs can integrate human rights content into assignments and their expected student outcomes for courses and student teaching/practica. A pre-service teacher's basic knowledge of human rights and the ability to articulate how one's pedagogy is informed by a knowledge of human rights is certainly measurable by a variety of means and in multiple contexts during teacher preparation. Furthermore, it is reasonable to assume that the level of clarity and explicitness of that articulation reflects a commitment on the part of the pre-service teacher. The extent of a pre-service teacher's commitment can be evidenced through lesson plans, thematic units, discipline strategies and other competencies that include strong links to human rights awareness as required by the teacher education program. These manifestations could be good indicators that a pre-service teacher's commitment to federal, state, or district standards, as well as HRE, has moved beyond sentiment into deeper understandings expressed in course assignments and then tangible practice during teaching practica.

Among new teachers who so often feel time constraints to cover required material and to comply with district or state requirements for content coverage, it is important to demonstrate in pre-service programs that the integration of human rights education is not so much about adding new material to the day as it is reinterpreting what currently exists and approaching current content from a human rights perspective (Jennings & Eichinger, 1999). With a human rights framework, mandated curricula are (re)interpreted to teach human rights and supplementary materials are chosen to enhance, rather than sacrifice, the basic skills so greatly emphasized in today's teaching culture and schools. Similarly, motivation, classroom management and discipline planning—perennial concerns of many new teachers—can be reinterpreted as opportunities to teach human rights and encourage pupil dispositions consistent with respect for human rights. Discipline and classroom management take on new and engaging dimensions as pre-service teachers explore these topics in light of human rights principles and instruments. For example, how do particular motivational strategies, discipline strategies, and classroom management procedures (indeed the entire created school environment) either teach respect for human rights or create in youth dispositions ignorant of, or antithetical to, such concerns as a result of youths' lived experience in schools?

In addition to approaching teacher preparation from a human rights perspective for the sake of pre-service teachers' dispositions, teaching excellence, and creating humane school environments, such a perspective could also enable novice teachers to approach the profession itself with a new sophistication. For example, teacher preparation programs that teach human rights concepts are likely to help new teachers understand educational environments and schools in new ways. New teachers might better understand and even defend themselves against the often demoralizing socialization of novice teachers if they have a strong framework from which to forge a professional identity. They are able to evaluate and question routine practices in schools that may be antithetical to the protection and promotion of human rights and in the process discover their own voices as educators. In short, a human rights perspective can provide teachers a framework to interpret and understand the humanizing and sometimes dehumanizing nature of schooling and to advocate for themselves, their students, and their students' communities.

In conclusion, teacher preparation from a human rights perspective may be less about new content and more about exploring new interpretations of what many teacher educators already do, going further through examining the possibilities for teacher education to explicitly promote students' understanding of human rights and the critical capacities to interpret the world and their actions in light of those human rights. In the end, using a human rights framework to frame teacher education and teacher competencies (and mandated standards) may result in a deeper understanding of instruction and instructional purposes while strengthening, rather than sacrificing, teachers' and schools' mandates to prepare children academically. Further, a human rights perspective could enhance many teacher educators' and classroom teachers' sense of purpose as they help future generations become daily advocates for human rights as a natural expression of their educational experiences.

Note

1. Portions of this chapter have been previously published in the article "Human Rights Education Standards for Teachers and Teacher Education," *Teaching Education, 17*(4), 287–298.

References

Amnesty International. (2005, January). *A human rights education strategy for Amnesty International.* International Human Rights Education Forum. Morocco. Unpublished manuscript.

Banks, D. (2001). *What is the state of human rights education in K-12 schools in the United States in 2000?: A preliminary look at the national survey of human rights education.* Paper presented at the American Educational Research Association, Seattle, April 2001. ERIC document: ED 454 134.

California Commission of Teacher Credentialing. (1997, January). *California standards for the teaching profession.* Sacramento, CA: California Department of Education.

Council of Europe Committee of Ministers. (1985/1991). Recommendation No. R (85) 7. Reprinted in H. Starkey (Ed), *The challenge of human rights education* (pp. 256–259). London: Cassell Educational Limited.

Donnelly, J. (2002). *Universal human rights in theory and practice* (2nd ed.). Ithaca, NY: Cornell University Press.

Flowers, N., & Shiman, D. (1997). Teacher education and the human rights vision. In G. Andreopoulos & R. P. Claude (Eds.), *Human rights for the twenty-first century* (pp. 161–193). Philadelphia: University of Pennsylvania Press.

Friere, P. (1970). *Pedagogy of the oppressed.* New York: Continuum.

Friere, P. (1985). *The politics of education.* New York: Bergin and Garvey.

Human Rights Resource Center. (2000). *The human rights education handbook: Effective practices for learning, action, and change.* Human Rights Resource Center (part 1). University of Minnesota. Retrieved May 31, 2005, from http://www.hrea.org

Human Rights Resource Center. (2006). Material Resources. Retrieved February 21, 2006, from http://www1.umn.edu/humanrts/edumat/

Human Rights U.S.A. (1997). *Report card on human rights in the USA: Key findings from a nationwide study.* Retrieved April 25, 2005, from http://wwwserver.law.wits.ac.za/humanrts/160.94.193.60/repcard.htm

Ignatieff, M. (2003). *Human rights as politics and idolatry.* Princeton, NJ: Princeton University Press.

Jennings, T. (1995). Developmental psychology and the preparation of teachers who affirm diversity: Strategies for the promotion of critical social consciousness in teacher preparation programs. *Journal of teacher education, 46*(4), 243–250.

Jennings, T. E., & Eichinger, J. (1999). Science education and human rights: Explorations into critical social consciousness and post-modern science instruction. *International journal of educational reform, 8,* 37–44.

Kanpol, B. (1994). *Critical pedagogy.* Westport, CT: Bergin and Garvey.

Lister, I. (1984). *Teaching and learning about human rights.* Strausberg: Council of Europe.

Lister, I. (1991). The challenge of human rights for education. In H. Starkey (Ed.), *The challenge of human rights education* (pp. 245–254). London: Cassell Educational Limited.

Martin, J. P. (1997). Epilogue: The next step, quality control. In G. Andreopoulos & R. P. Claude (Eds.), *Human rights education for the twenty-first century* (pp. 599–609). Philadelphia: University of Pennsylvania Press.

Meintjes, G. (1997). Human rights education as empowerment. In G. Andreopoulos & R. P. Claude (Eds.), *Human rights for the twenty-first century* (pp. 64–79). Philadelphia: University of Pennsylvania Press.

Mutua, M. (2002a). *The Complexity of Universalism in Human Rights.* Paper presented at 10th Annual Conference on "The Individual vs. the State" Central European University. Budapest. June 14–16, 2002.

Mutua, M. (2002b). *Human rights: A political and cultural critique.* Philadelphia: University of Pennsylvania Press.

National Council for Accreditation in Teacher Education (NCATE). (2006). *NCATE News: A statement from NCATE on professional dispositions.* Retrieved December 5, 2008, from http://www.ncate.org/public/0616_MessageAWise.asp?ch=150

National Council for Accreditation in Teacher Education (NCATE). (2008). *Professional Standards for the Accreditation of teacher preparation institutions.* Retrieved December 5, 2008, from http://www.ncate.org/documents/standards/NCATE%20Standards%20 2008.pdf

Osler, A., & Starkey, H. (1996). *Teacher education and human rights.* London: David Fulton Publishers.

Reardon, B. (1995). *Educating for human dignity: Learning about rights and responsibilities.* Philadelphia: University of Pennsylvania Press.

Sebaly, K. (1987). Education about human rights: Teacher preparation. In N. Tarrow (Ed.), *Human rights and education* (pp. 207–222). Oxford, UK: Pergamon Press.

Shafer, S. (1987). Human rights education in schools. In N. Tarrow (Ed.). *Human rights and education* (pp. 191–206). Oxford, UK: Pergamon Press.

Shor, I. (1993). Education is politics: Paulo Friere's critical pedagogy. In P. McLaren & P. Leonard (Eds.), *Paulo Friere: A critical encounter* (pp. 25–35). New York: Routledge.

Shor, I., & Friere, P. (1987). *A pedagogy for liberation.* South Hadley, MA: Bergin and Garvey.

Sleeter, C. (1996). *Multicultural education as social activism.* Albany: State University of New York Press.

Smith, W. (1976). *The meaning of conscientizcao: The goal of Paulo Freire's critical pedagogy.* Amherst: Center for International Education: University of Massachusetts.

Starkey, H. (1991). The Council of Europe recommendations on the teaching and learning of human rights in schools. In H. Starkey (Ed.), *The challenge of human rights education* (pp. 20–38). London: Cassell Educational Limited.

Tibbetts, F. (1997). *The annotated primer for selecting democratic and human rights education teaching materials.* Budapest: Open Society Institute. Retrieved February 28, 2005, from http://www.hrea.org/pubs/Primer/introduction.html

Tibbetts, F. (2002). *Emerging models for human rights education.* Issues of democracy: An electronic journal of the U.S. Department of State. Volume 7(1), March 2002. Retrieved February 28, 2005, from http://usinfo.state.gov/journals/itdhr/0302/ijde/ijde0302.htm

United Nations Education, Scientific and Cultural Organization. (n.d.). *What is human rights education?* Retrieved February 18, 2006, from http://portal.unesco.org/education/en/ev.php-URL_ID=1920&URL_DO=DO_TOPIC&URL_SECTION=201.html

Wasley, P. (2006, June 16). Accreditor of education schools drops controversial 'social justice' language. *The Chronicle of Higher Education* (section: The Faculty), *52*(41), A13.

Wronka, J. (1994). Human rights and social policy in the United States: An educational agenda for the 21st century. *The Journal of Moral Education*, *23*, 261–272.

6 Environmental Education

From International Resolve to Local Experience and Inquiry

David A. Greenwood, Bob O. Manteaw, and Gregory A. Smith

A Warrant for Environmental Education

Environmental and ecological educators go by many names, and some educators committed to teaching about, in, and for the environment prefer not to be labeled at all. Part of the reason for this diverse positioning is that environmental education is inherently interdisciplinary and inherently political. Indeed, as David Orr suggested in his seminal book, *Ecological Literacy* (1992), "all education is environmental education" (p. 90). That is, all of what is taught and learned (or not taught and learned), as well as the pedagogies employed (or not employed), has an impact on the way people relate to their total environments—their selves, other humans, and other-than-humans.

But the claim, "all education is environmental education," frustrates some environmental educators, just as it confuses those educators who never consider their work primarily "environmental." If "all education is environmental education," what constitutes environmental literacy, or essential knowledge of and experience with the environment? What is the relationship between environmental education and education for social justice? What, after all, is education for? This chapter will offer a response to such questions first by mapping the development of the international discourse on the environment with special attention to recommendations for environmental education. Since the 1970s, many international conferences and summits have been convened to examine the growing importance of environmental issues in communities and regions, and in nations across the globe. Many of these meetings have concluded that only through ecological and environmental education will citizens be able to serve the well-being of local communities and the global community.

The international discourse of environmental education that we outline in this chapter is only one place to look for theoretical and practical frameworks for environmental education. A rich theory, research, and practice tradition in the United States and other countries also informs our discussion. The *Journal of Environmental Education*, the *Environmental Education Research* journal, the *Canadian Journal of Environmental Education,* and the more recently founded online journal, the *Ecojustice Review,* are scholarly journals in which one can trace the breadth and depth of environmental education. A brief (and incomplete) list of key authors whose work has helped to create a culturally-grounded discourse of environmental education would include Chet Bowers, David Orr, Edmund O'Sullivan, Bob Jickling, Stephen Sterling, John Fien, Lucie Suave, and John Huckle. We invite readers outside the field to explore these and other authors to appreciate how "environmental education" has long been intertwined with cultural theory and diverse cultural experiences, and has long been associated with issues such as racism, poverty, technology, development, globalization, and moral responsibility.

We focus here on global environmental politics in order to create a warrant for environmental education that reaches beyond academic texts, education policies, and professional organizations. We wish to demonstrate that outside of formal education discourse and practice, there exists a related and diverse global movement for environmental consciousness and care, a movement with a storied history and with significant implications for educators everywhere. A current and momentous manifestation of this wider movement is the United Nations Decade of Education for Sustainable Development, 2005–2014. Unfortunately, this wider movement has existed largely outside of everyday conversations about schooling, and even outside of most conversations that are critical of schooling. Our intent is to show the relevance of this international, multicultural, and multilingual movement to educators committed to rethinking educational purposes and the meaning of educational success. In addition, we wish to connect the lofty goals of environmentally aware political and educational activists with concrete actions that teachers, students, and community members can take at the local, district, and school building level.

We believe that learning about the environment requires both a global awareness and knowledge of the home range—the neighborhood, the community, and the local ecosystems and bioregions in which people live their everyday lives. Therefore, after presenting a context of international resolve and recommendations for the environment, we will present a series of questions, borrowed from diverse sources, aimed at stimulating reflection about how to integrate environmental education in local schools and communities. These questions reflect the kinds of experiences that can lead to the environmental knowledge that so many people on the planet believe to be essential to all of our survival.

An International Sense of Urgency

Unfortunately, environmental and ecological education still connotes to many educators a narrow focus on natural science and/or advocacy for the natural environment. No doubt this perception has contributed to the marginalization of environmental education within the wider educational community, and has limited the development of coalitions between those centrally concerned with the "natural" environment, and those centrally concerned with "cultural" issues such as peace, social justice, civil rights, and anti-racism. However, a look at the history of the international discourse on environment, development, and environmental education reveals that environmental education has been at the vanguard of synthesizing perspectives toward "cultural" and "natural" environments.

Many environmental and ecological educators resist the artificial separation between "nature" and "culture" and embrace environmental education precisely because it provides a language, a theoretical framework, and a rich (and contested) political history for understanding the relationships between social experience and ecological reality. Throughout the development of its theory, practice, and strategic planning in the last three decades of the twentieth century up to the present, environmental and ecological education, as a global educational movement, has become increasingly concerned with the connections between social justice, peace, strong democracy, and ecological sustainability. While some of the early statements of the vision of environmental education focused mainly on mitigating pollution and conserving natural resources, since the 1970s, many environmental educators have come to recognize that environmental and ecological issues are intimately connected with issues of poverty, power, privilege, exploitation, and with a culture of war and violence. Further, it has become increasingly obvious that the looming byproducts of industrialism, the technological revolution, and hyper-consumerism threaten people's livelihood everywhere. Though the immediate consequences of, for example, toxic waste are often shouldered by poor people and people of color (see, e.g., Kuletz, 1998), the impact of global warming, mass extinction, dwindling water resources, genetic contamination, famine, deforestation, depleted fisheries, as well as renewed interest in the "energy crisis"—these environmental/cultural issues threaten everyone's well-being on local and global levels. Non-human communities as well as human communities are at risk. In the wider field of education, it is only the discourse of environmental education that has begun to address these problems that we all face together.

The Role of the United Nations, 1972–1992

The Stockholm conference of 1972, officially named the United Nations Conference on the Human Environment, was organized by the United Nations and attended by 119 countries and 400 non-governmental organizations (NGOs). Many observers have identified this conference as the first event that put the environment on the international political agenda. Its slogan, *Only One Earth*, stressed the finiteness of the planet and the need for conscious and informed human management of the environment. Identifying the role of education in meeting this need, conference proceedings stated that

> The organizations of the United Nations system, especially the United Nations Educational, Scientific, and Cultural Organization, and the other international agencies concerned, should, after consultation and agreement, take the necessary steps to establish an international program in environmental education, interdisciplinary in its approach, in school and out of school, encompassing all levels of education and directed toward the general public, in particular the ordinary citizen living in rural and urban areas, youth and adult alike, with a view to educating him as to the simple steps he might take, within his means, to manage and control his environment.

> (United Nations Conference on the Human Environment, 1972, recommendation 96, sect. 1)

Clearly, the language of this proclamation is problematic in its anthropocentrism, androcentrism, and in its emphasis on management and control. However, the conference did succeed in placing environmental education on the international agenda. It also led to the creation of the United Nations Environment Program (UNEP), which later partnered with UNESCO to establish the UNESCO-UNEP International Environmental Education Program (1975–1995).

The first two major environmental education events convened by this United Nations program were the 1975 International Environmental Education Workshop in Belgrade and the 1977 Intergovernmental Conference on Environmental Education in Tbilisi. These conferences resulted in the respective reports, the Belgrade Charter: A Global Framework for Environmental Education (UNESCO-UNEP, 1976) and the Tbilisi Declaration (UNESCO-UNEP, 1978). The Belgrade Charter stated:

> The goal of environmental education is to develop a world population that is aware of, and concerned about, the environment and its associated problems, and which has the knowledge, skills, attitudes, motivations, and commitment to work individually and collectively toward solutions of current problems and the prevention of new ones. (*Connect*, UNESCO-UNEP, 1976, p. 1).

The Tbilisi Declaration expanded on the Belgrade Charter and described three broad goals for environmental education:

- To foster clear awareness of, and concern about, economic, social, political, and ecological interdependence in urban and rural areas;
- To provide every person with opportunities to acquire the knowledge, values, attitudes, commitment, and skills needed to protect and improve the environment;
- To create new patterns of behavior of individuals, groups, and society as a whole towards the environment. (UNESCO-UNEP, 1978, p. 3)

In the 1970s, the Belgrade Charter and the Tbilisi Declaration expressed an international sense of urgency and resolve to respond educationally to increasingly apparent and interrelated environmental problems as they were experienced in countries throughout the world.

The 1980s and 1990s marked a shift in the United Nations discourse that would gradually focus attention more on the concept of sustainability and sustainable development. The 1987 World Commission on Environment and Development, also known as the Brundtland Commission, published a report titled *Our Common Future* (also known as the Brundtland Report). This report introduced the concept of sustainable development to a global audience and defined it as development that "meets the needs of the present without compromising the ability of future generations to meet their own needs" (World Commission on Environment and Development, 1987, p. 8). Although *Our Common Future* did not focus much attention on the educational implications of sustainable development, it functioned to change the global conversation from one about environmental knowledge and environmental issues to a broader conversation about the problems and possibilities of sustainability. Such a change in emphasis, we remark below, has had both positive and negative consequences for promoting the work of environmental education.

Perhaps the most famous international political event dedicated to the environment was the 1992 United Nations Conference on Environment and Development, popularly called the Earth Summit, held in Rio de Janeiro, Brazil. Its report, *Agenda 21*, clearly stated the interrelationship of social and environment issues as it described the contemporary global context:

> Humanity stands at a defining moment in history. We are confronted with a perpetuation of disparities between and within nations, a worsening of poverty, hunger, ill health and illiteracy, and the continuing deterioration of the ecosystems on which we depend for our well-being. However, integration of environment and development concerns and greater attention to them will lead to the fulfillment of basic needs, improved living standards for all, better protected and managed ecosystems and a safer, more prosperous future. (United Nations Conference on Environment and Development, 1992, Preamble)

Like *Our Common Future*, *Agenda 21* embraced sustainable development and promoted the widespread implementation of environmental education programs across the globe in order to achieve this goal. Two chapters of *Agenda 21* deal specifically with education: chapter 25, Children and Youth in Sustainable Development, and chapter 36, Promoting Education, Public Awareness and Training. Chapter 36 of this momentous historical document states:

> Education is critical for promoting sustainable development and improving the capacity of people to address environment and development issues.... To be effective, environment and development education should deal with the dynamics of both the physical/biological and socio-economic environment and ... should be integrated in all disciplines. (UNCED, 1992, 36, sec. 1)

Agenda 21 does not say so explicitly, but it suggests nothing short of a total rethinking and transforming of the way education, especially in "developed" countries like the United States, is currently conceived and practiced. The same could be said of all the documents introduced above. To incorporate environment and development concerns into basic educational practice would first require an analysis of how every element of education impacts environment and development.

This huge undertaking has clearly not taken place in the United States, where all of the events and publications mentioned above remain largely unknown to all but specialists in environmental education. The 20 years (1972–1992) of international attention toward environmental education did, however, provide a beacon, a sense of hope, and a legitimating discourse to those educators who have sought to integrate environmental awareness into the education of children and youth (see, e.g., North American Association of Environmental Education, NAAEE, 1999). For those educators interested in connecting equity and social justice education with environmental concerns, the first two decades of global environmental politics, and their corresponding calls for environmental and sustainability education, can provide some key focusing themes. In summary, the conferences from Stockholm to Rio acknowledged that:

- Problems of poverty, health, and environmental degradation exist both in rich and poor countries, and there is the need to adopt holistic learning approaches that emphasize the interrelationship between the environment and socioeconomic issues of poverty and underdevelopment.
- The world, from a macro-perspective, is a "global village"; local problems easily become global problems just in the same way as global problems become local problems.
- There is the need for a shift in values in all nations; respect for life, quality of personal life, social justice, aesthetics, the natural environment, and ethical considerations are at the core of environment and development issues and they must be emphasized in all communities.
- Education is an important tool to address basic learning needs relevant for informed and ethical action with respect to the environment; it is therefore imperative that educational systems are "re-oriented" to help people develop the desired attitudes, skills, and values that are essential for such actions.
- While it is important to improve the quality of human life on the planet, it is equally important for individuals and communities to be mindful of the fact that there is a limit to the carrying capacity of the earth's supporting ecosystems.

Contesting the Ruling Discourse

From the beginning of its usage, sustainable development has been a problematic term. The underlying assumption of many of those who advocate for sustainable development, including many supporters of *Agenda 21*, is that meeting needs and improving living standards now and in the future depends on sustaining economic growth as currently practiced in developed countries like the United States. Sustainable development and sustainability are terms currently used by corporate and government leaders to describe those very economic policies, such at those enforced by the World Trade Organization, that disrupt ecological and cultural systems. Even the landmark environmental publication, *Our Common Future*, calls for "a new era of economic growth … that sustains and expands the environmental resource base" (p. 1). Many advocates for sustainability would recognize the irony in this rhetoric: is it possible, for example, to sustain *and* expand our resource base in a finite world with definable ecological limits? At issue here is the meaning of such terms as development and sustainability and the assumptions about environment, growth, and progress that underlie their usage. The terms tend to mean very different things for those who hold power than for those who do not.

International environmental politics, including those events from Stockholm to Rio, have been contested terrain. While the Rio Earth Summit, for example, was the largest gathering of heads of state in history, it was also a hotbed of political activism outside of the state-sanctioned spectacle. Some 2,400 representatives of NGOs and 8,000 journalists attended the official events, and 17,000 people attended a parallel NGO forum. The theme of much of this political activism, which resulted in 46 separate non-governmental treaties, was resistance to an intergovernmental process that failed to name some of the deeper causes of social injustice and environmental decay. One of these treaties, The People's Earth Declaration: A Proactive Agenda for the Future, proclaimed that that the Earth Summit and the corresponding launch of *Agenda 21* (the Agenda for the 21st Century), was a scripted government sham engaged in the fine tuning of an economic system that serves the short-term interests of the few at the expense of the many. The NGO forum repeatedly recognized that leadership for more fundamental change had fallen by default to the organizations and movements of civil society. Resistance to and critique of the shortcomings of intergovernmental conferences such as the Earth Summit, and reports such as *Our Common Future*, has been a constant theme in the three decade history of international environmental politics. This is succinctly evidenced in the title of The Ecologist's 1993 book, *Whose Common Future?*, which was a response the essentialisms (i.e., universal assumptions), and omissions of both *Our Common Future* and the Earth Summit.

Within this milieu of resistance, critique, and non-governmental political activism, other treaties and proclamations from diverse people and places have emerged. In 1991, the First National People of Color Environmental Leadership Summit published *Principles of Environmental Justice in the U.S.* In 1992, the World Conference of Indigenous Peoples on Territory, Environment, and Development resulted in the Kari-Oca Declaration of Indigenous People's Earth Charter. Many other such summits and documents that describe the relationship between culture and environment have sprung from groups whose needs, interests, and experiences have not been well represented in the higher-profile United Nations gatherings and proclamations.

Perhaps the most widely known non-governmental project aimed at describing the appropriate relationship between diverse people and their environments is the Earth Charter Initiative. The Preamble of the Earth Charter, now available in over 40 languages, sets the context for global praxis (i.e., theory and action):

> The dominant patterns of production and consumption are causing environmental devastation, the depletion of resources, and a massive extinction of species. Communities are being undermined. The benefits of development are not shared equitably and the gap between rich and poor is widening.

> Injustice, poverty, ignorance, and violent conflict are widespread and the cause of great suffering. An unprecedented rise in human population has overburdened ecological and social systems. The foundations of global security are threatened. These trends are perilous—but not inevitable. (Earth Charter, 2001, Preamble)

(Most of the remaining document is an outline of 16 principles and subprinciples, which are appended at the end of this chapter.)

Unlike some of the products of intergovernmental environmental politics such as *Agenda 21* or *Our Common Future*, or the Tbilisi Declaration, The Earth Charter is clear and unequivocal that many social and ecological problems stem from dominant patterns of development, production, and consumption. Its explicit critique of economic inequities within and between nations, its long term vision of health and prosperity for all human and non-human communities, and its commitment to demilitarizing national security systems to a non-provocative defense posture, are clearly at odds with the explicit political and educational aims of wealthy and powerful nations such as the United States. Despite the apparent incommensurability between the values of the Earth Charter and the apparent values of powerful nation states, the Earth Charter Initiative continues to seek official acknowledgment at the level of the United Nations. In 2002, with the support of leaders in many nations, organizers sought recognition of the Earth Charter at the World Summit on Sustainable Development, held in Johannesburg, South Africa. However, due to some last-minute, non-public objections from certain governments, reference to the Earth Charter was deleted from the final version of the Declaration of Johannesburg. Apparently, some powerful governments found the language of the Earth Charter too threatening.

Though the Earth Charter remains unacknowledged by certain powerful governments committed to unsustainable patterns of development, including the pattern of aggressive militarization, it has been endorsed by many national governments, as well as states and municipalities in many countries, including the United States. That the Earth Charter serves as a catalyst for social action and reflection among diverse communities is seen in the growing number of endorsements coming from diverse peoples and places. To date, the charter has been endorsed by thousands of organizations and millions of individuals. Community development and education are two sectors of society in which the charter is being used to stimulate dialogue, reflection, and action for social change. The Earth Charter Initiative offers support for educational planning at all levels. The charter itself is a valuable resource to incorporate into courses dealing with themes such as ethics, environment, social justice, democracy, sustainable development, globalization, and peace. At the community level, the Earth Charter provides a framework for assisting local communities to reflect and take action on the interrelated themes of ecological care, social justice, and peace. The Earth Charter Initiative encourages local communities, schools, and community-based organizations to discuss, debate, ratify, and use the charter as deemed appropriate for governance and agenda setting. We believe it is an important tool for connecting local experience to global awareness.

Toward a Framework for Transforming School Experience

At this writing, schooling in the United States and elsewhere is very similar to schooling before any of the conferences and publications mentioned above. Although the environmental movement both globally and nationally has clearly influenced the cultural context of schooling, the purpose of schooling, and the structures and methodologies employed, have not shifted to respond to the international sense of urgency about culturally-rooted environmental problems. The discourse of environmental education or education for sustainable development stands in stark contrast to current federal and state education policies. For example, the U.S. Department of Education, and our own states' offices of public instruction, have been utterly silent about the United Nations Decade of Education for Sustainable Development (2005–2014). But the problem is much deeper than this predictable silence. Many observers have commented that the ideological, structural, pedagogical, and curricular practices of schooling work against the goals of environmental education. A brief list of these pillars of schooling would include: school purposes that are geared for uncritical participation in the growth economy; school structures that are isolated from communities and that cut learning up into small chunks of time; standards-based and teacher-centered pedagogies that frustrate the process of inquiry; curricular fragmentation that works against holistic or systems thinking; and the assumption that school success or student achievement should be measured by content-area test scores or other indicators such as the rate of university attendance. Simply put, the aims of environmental education and the aims of general education are often in conflict (Gruenewald, 2004; Gruenewald & Manteaw, 2007; Stevenson, 1987). This is not only true in federal and state education policy, but also true in most academic discourse in education, whether conservative, progressive, or radical, which remains mostly silent about the relationships between environment, culture, and education.

It is also true, however, that the aims of environmental education can be shown to be commensurate with some of the aims of dominant and conventional education. In their commitment to legitimize environmental education within the institutional practices of conventional education, many environmental education professionals and organizations have emphasized how environmental education meets and furthers some of the goals of conventional education. In one of its key publications, the NAAEE (1999), for example, maintains that its "guidelines for excellence" support environmental education by "Demonstrating how environmental education can be used to meet standards set by the traditional disciplines" (p. 1). This paradox—the fit and the lack of fit between environmental education and the standard school curriculum—complicates the already problematic mission to articulate educational standards, guidelines, or queries for environmental education.

Because of the hegemony of a standards-based school curriculum that already fails to provide students with adequate experience to explore and understand the complex relationship between environment and culture, we are extremely cautious about naming additional standards for environmental education. Further, the appropriate focus of environmental care, concern, and study is something that is contested around the world by diverse coalitions of people who have diverse culturally-rooted environmental experiences. We wish to avoid making universal claims about what counts as appropriate environmental education for people and places with which we are unfamiliar. Still, we share with the other contributors to this volume a desire to strategize for educational change in an educational culture that seems to be moving in the wrong direction. The following recommendations and queries are offered in this spirit.

Key Entry Points: The Decade of Education for Sustainable Development and the Earth Charter

Most educators in the United States are simply unaware that the United Nations declared the years 2005–2014 the Decade of Education for Sustainable Development. We believe that an examination of the Decade should be a starting point for educators at all levels who are considering integrating the environment into their teaching. To ignore the Decade is to ignore over 30 years of international environmental politics (described above). To consider the Decade is to appreciate the intimate connection between culture and environment and to appreciate both the local and global challenges involved in the goal of sustainability.

The UN declaration of a Decade of Education for Sustainable Development shows that cultural and environmental problems as experienced in local, national, or regional levels eventually converge to become global challenges which need to be addressed through conscious and concerted efforts. The Decade was an outcome of the World Summit on Sustainable Development (WSSD), which convened in 2002 to review the results of the Rio Earth Summit, and to adopt concrete measures as well as to identify quantifiable targets for better implementation of *Agenda 21*. The WSSD also renewed attention on the complex and contested meanings of sustainability. First, the Political Declaration of the conference noted that, sustainable development is built on three "independent and mutually reinforcing pillars—economic development, social development and environmental protection—which must be established at local, national and regional and global levels" (Johannesburg Declaration on Sustainable Development, 2002, paragraph 5, WSSD, 2002, p. 5).

The conference also provided a venue to expand and concretize the meanings of sustainable development and focused on such key action themes as overcoming poverty, gender equality, health promotion, climate change, biodiversity, rural development, cultural diversity, peace and human security, and sustainable urbanization (see the Decade's Web site at http://portal.unesco.org/education/en/ev.php-URL_ID=27552&URL_DO=DO_TOPIC&URL_SECTION=201.html). This more focused vision of sustainable development recognized the complexity and interrelationship of critical issues such as education, poverty, wasteful consumption, population, gender issues, conflict, and human rights.

A good example of this interrelationship can be found in the cultural practices of a small and poor rural community in Ghana, Africa. Subsistence farming and fishing have been the main sources of livelihood for this community for years. This makes the natural environment a central focus in the people's lives, as everything they do to survive is either directly, or indirectly, dependent on the environment. As the pressure on the environment increases, resulting in reduction in output, the people adapt more *creative* ways to survive. Creativity, however, is expressed in unconventional or *unsustainable* methods of farming and fishing: dynamite fishing, slashing and burning, and sand winning—a process of fetching and selling coastal sand for construction purposes. These are just a few examples that worsen the people's situations in ways that are not immediately obvious or comprehensible to them. Dynamite fishing does not only deplete intergenerational fish stock, it also destroys the coral reef. Slashing and burning does not only destroy the ecosystem but also creates environmental health hazards especially for women and children. Sand winning, which has become a very lucrative venture in recent times, results in land erosion that threatens the people's habitats. Additionally, sand winning leaves in its trail shallow holes along the coast; these holes collect stagnant water, which in turn serves as the breeding grounds for mosquitoes. This is just one simple way of exploring the complex intersection of environment and cultural issues, and in a situation like this, education must be holistic and must focus on showing how different factors combine to create a common problem. Solutions to these problems depend on this kind of understanding.

To make this complex web of issues associated with sustainable development meaningful to people will require practical and sustained publicity and education efforts at different levels—local, national, regional and global. This is the goal of the UN Decade: to provide momentum for a conscious and concerted educational endeavor. The Decade is currently underway, and even though it is yet to be given the needed attention especially in the United States, some countries around the world (e.g., Australia, Canada, Japan, England, and Zimbabwe) have already taken the necessary policy steps to reorient their educational systems for sustainable development. Even though the Decade is global in its outlook, it insists on local ownership and approaches which are relevant to local particularities. The centrality of the environment within ESD provides a unique opportunity not only to validate environmental education, but also to expand its implications and application through more creative and interdisciplinary ways.

To examine the Decade critically also means uncovering the contested meanings around sustainability and the related themes of environment, progress, growth, and development. We believe that the Earth Charter, which is promoted by the Decade initiative, provides an effective means for starting critical conversations about the diverse cultural meanings of environment and its relationship to the local and global goal of sustainability. In the long process of drafting the Earth Charter, great care was taken to express a complex set of issues in direct language, and in many languages (the Earth Charter is available in over 40 languages at www.earthcharter.org). One of its strengths as a catalyst for social and educational action is that readers, or listeners, can access and begin reflecting on this complex set of issues relatively quickly. The charter is not meant to be a universal set of rules for all to follow, but rather, a statement of principles to catalyze dialogue, reflection, and action, in all sectors of diverse societies, locally, regionally, and globally (see Corcoran, Vilela, & Roerink, 2005).

Queries for Culturally-Conscious Environmental Education

As mentioned in our introduction, we have focused on providing an international, multicultural, and multilingual warrant for environmental education in order to both expand its taken-for-granted meanings and to show other educators interested in social justice issues that environment must be taken as seriously as culture when considering the problems and possibilities of education. The question remains of how to integrate environmental consciousness into educational practice. The study of such movements as the Decade of Education for Sustainable Development and the Earth Charter Initiative can offer educators and students a powerful context for questioning the relationship between environment, culture, and education. The following section offers a list of thought-provoking queries for making culturally-conscious environmental education happen at the school and community level. Though the phrase "culturally-conscious environmental" is a cumbersome modifier, we want to emphasize that environmental education is most effective and relevant when it purposefully seeks to make connections between culture and environment. The queries below also emphasize the relationship between students, schools, and their local communities through the themes of 1) a sense of place and care, 2) conceptual knowledge about the environment, 3) the school environment, 4) practical skills, 5) citizen involvement and activism, and 6) moral/ethical perspectives.

Many of the queries will probably overlap with guidelines in other chapters in this book that focus more explicitly on social justice. Like the principles of the Earth Charter, these queries are offered as conversation starters. Readers, especially teachers, are encouraged to critique, revise, amend, and respond to them in ways that best meet the needs of people and the diverse places they inhabit. The queries are at times purposefully generalized and open-ended in order to start people thinking and talking about shared and different meanings. For example, we pose the question, "Does the school help students develop practical skills required to live well in their places?" Rather than define what "living well" means, we hope that teachers, students, and community members will struggle with the meaning of "living well" together, with an appreciation of other people and the ecosystems that surround them.

Because these queries often focus on the immediate environment of the school, neighborhood, and region, readers are invited to keep in mind other regional, national, and global contexts, and their relationship to the more locally-focused queries. Some of these global contexts, and the diverse places and peoples within them, can be invoked by the Earth Charter, which is appended at the end of the chapter. Making connections between local/global, cultural/environmental contexts is a challenge that we hope educators will undertake in this the Decade of Education for Sustainable Development.

Queries for Culturally-Conscious Environmental Education

Development of Sense of Place and Care

Students:

Do students develop a personal affinity with the natural world and the human community in which they live?

Do students become knowledgeable about and committed to the health and welfare of their own communities and regions?

Do students become knowledgeable about other people and other places, and do they have an opportunity to compare familiar places with unfamiliar, regionally, nationally, and globally?

School:

Does the school develop in students a personal affinity with the earth through practical experiences out-of-doors and through the practice of an ethic of care?

Does the school ground learning in a sense of place, i.e., connection and care for local environment, community, and habitat?

Community:

Does the community help to create safe places for exploration of the natural world, as well as the built environment, especially for girls and women?

Do members of the community accept and embrace an educational process that includes classroom and community-based learning experiences?

Do members of the community provide opportunities for students to participate in internships and service learning opportunities in their workplaces and agencies?

Do members of the community who are knowledgeable about local and translocal phenomena share their expertise with students?

Conceptual Knowledge

Students:

Do students have sufficient knowledge to permit them to make ecologically sound decisions with respect to environmental and cultural issues?

Do students possess the understanding and skills necessary to live less consumer-dependent lives?

Do students understand the way that language processes reproduce shared patterns that are the source of meaning and understanding of relationships and moral norms?

Do students understand the cultural and historical antecedents to local and global environmental problems?

School:

Does the school impart the knowledge and understanding of how natural systems work, as well as a knowledge and understanding of how natural systems interface with social systems? Is this understanding sufficient to permit students to make ecologically sound decisions with respect to environmental issues?

Does the school approach learning in an interdisciplinary manner, exploring interactions across the boundaries of conventional knowledge and experience?

Does the school help students differentiate between cultural traditions that support social and environmental justice and those that erode it?

Does the school examine with students the impact of technology on society and the environment?

Community:

Do professionals who work in the areas of environmental management and protection participate in the shaping and evaluation of curriculum and the teaching of courses that focus on environmental topics?

School Environment (Physical/Social)

Students:

Do students display an openness to and willingness to work with people unlike themselves in terms of nationality, language, race, ethnicity, gender, sexual orientation, intellectual abilities?

School:

Does the school carefully monitor the selection and quality of cafeteria food? Are restricted (i.e., vegetarian) or organic diets available? What are the school policies about serving milk and meat products from hormone-injected animals or other genetically-modified foods? How often and under what criteria is the water tested in the school? Do students have access to pure water?

Does the school actively seek to protect the student environment from chemical ingredients of unknown or potentially harmful effects (e.g., in cleaning solutions, herbicides, pesticides, or airborne contaminants)?

Does the school induct students into an experience of community that counters the press toward individualism?

Does the school encourage students to share their perspectives and participate in the shaping of their education and school governance?

Does the school seek to build or renovate buildings that are energy efficient, constructed with environmentally friendly materials, minimize waste water, and make use of renewable energy systems?

Does the school provide students with the opportunity to grow, process, and cook healthy foods and explore the consequences of their food choices?

Community:

Do community members monitor food and environmental quality in public schools and insist that the school board and educators do all they can to create environmentally healthy settings for learning?

Do community members insist that all building construction and renovation projects seek to achieve a LEED rating of at least silver?

Practical Skills

Students:

Do students acquire practical skills needed to regenerate human and natural environments (e.g., growing food, building simple shelters, using solar energy, restoring damaged ecosystems)?

School:

Does the school help students develop practical skills required to live well in their places?

Community:

Does the community provide opportunities for students to contribute their labor to projects that enhance the welfare of economically marginalized people and/or contribute to ecological clean-ups or restoration activities?

Does the community publicly acknowledge the contributions of children and youth to such projects?

Citizen Involvement/Activism

Students:

Do students and graduates of the school demonstrate a willingness to work, individually and collectively, toward achieving and/or maintaining a dynamic equilibrium between quality of life and quality of the environment?

Do students participate in the monitoring of air, water, and food quality and share their findings with appropriate agencies?

Do students possess the analytical, social, and political skills necessary to address problems successfully?

Do students participate in the restoration of environmentally damaged sites in their community or other activities aimed at enhancing the ecological health of their community?

Do students participate in activities aimed at identifying and correcting instances of environmental injustice in their community and region? Are they encouraged to network with other people dealing with similar issues in other places?

School:

Does the school seek to enhance students' locus of control and encourage the assumption of personal responsibility?

Does the school and its employees participate in activities aimed at solving environmental problems and resolving issues in the broader community and region?

Does the school feature an approach to teaching that is participatory and experiential rather than didactic?

Community:

Do community members welcome the participation of children and youth in public decision-making forums?

Do community agencies (both governmental and non-profit) welcome the help of students in their work?

Do city and county governments adopt resolutions that encourage public agencies to draw upon students as researchers and participants in the planning processes?

School/Community Relations

School/Community:

Do the school and community interact for mutual benefit? Is there broad representation of community organizations in the life of the school, especially those dealing with environmental and social justice?

How well is the school networked to other community services, including community development organizations and other non profits? How does the school facilitate connecting students and families to community and governmental resources?

Outside the school, are there projects in the community that connect the generations, such as student research that is shared with community boards or committees?

Moral/Ethical Perspectives

Students:

Do students develop a clear understanding that humanity is an inseparable part of a system consisting of human beings, culture, animals, and the biophysical environment, and that humans have the ability to alter the interrelationships of this system?

Do students express genuine concern about the welfare of the social and natural environments of which they are a part?

Are students able "…to distinguish between health and disease, development and growth, sufficient and efficient, optimum and maximum, and 'should do' from 'can do'?" (Orr, 1994, pp. 14–15)

School:

Does the school provide opportunities for students to explore the moral and ethical implications of human decisions and actions?

Community:

Are community members willing to allow educators and students to grapple with fundamental moral and ethical issues that inhere in our interconnectedness to one another and the planet, even though these discussions may be outside the context of a single religious tradition?

Conclusion

These locally-focused queries, along with global contexts represented by the Decade of Education for Sustainable Development and the Earth Charter, are a starting point. The challenges ahead are daunting and demand thoughtful action now. The cultural/environmental crisis is as complex as it is real. It is difficult to comprehend and act on the nature of the problems facing the entire world and facing many communities. There is no shortage of research, theory, and practice in the literature about the nature of the problem, or even how to develop culturally-conscious environmental education or education for sustainable development. The problem is that schooling at all levels has been constructed and is currently conducted for different purposes (Callahan, 1962; Spring, 1998). In their relentless push to prepare youth for uncritical participation in the consumer/growth economy, schools have mainly functioned to support increasingly unsustainable relationships between people, cultures, and humans and the earth. What is needed is more people in more places asking the kinds of questions that might be inspired by the Decade, the Earth Charter, and the queries presented above. The queries may be an especially appropriate starting place because they involve learners of all ages in local inquiry, reflection, and action.

The Earth Charter

In the complete text of the Earth Charter, each of the 16 principles is supported by several sub principles that help clarify how the main principle might be translated into action (see www.earthcharter.org).

I. Respect and Care for the Community of Life

1 Respect Earth and life in all its diversity.
2. Care for the community of life with understanding, compassion, and love.
3. Build democratic societies that are just, participatory, sustainable, and peaceful.
4. Secure Earth's bounty and beauty for present and future generations.

II. Ecological Integrity

5. Protect and restore the integrity of Earth's ecological systems, with special concern for biological diversity and the natural processes that sustain life.
6. Prevent harm as the best method of environmental protection and, when knowledge is limited, apply a precautionary approach.
7. Adopt patterns of production, consumption, and reproduction that safeguard Earth's regenerative capacities, human rights, and community well-being.
8. Advance the study of ecological sustainability and promote the open exchange and wide application of the knowledge acquired.

III. Social and Economic Justice

9. Eradicate poverty as an ethical, social, and environmental imperative.
10. Ensure that economic activities and institutions at all levels promote human development in an equitable and sustainable manner.

11. Affirm gender equality and equity as prerequisites to sustainable development and ensure universal access to education, health care, and economic opportunity.
12. Uphold the right of all, without discrimination, to a natural and social environment supportive of human dignity, bodily health, and spiritual well-being, with special attention to the rights of indigenous peoples and minorities.

IV. Democracy, Nonviolence, and Peace

13. Strengthen democratic institutions at all levels, and provide transparency and accountability in governance, inclusive participation in decision making, and access to justice.
14. Integrate into formal education and life-long learning the knowledge, values, and skills needed for a sustainable way of life.
15. Treat all living beings with respect and consideration.
16. Promote a culture of tolerance, nonviolence, and peace.

References

Agenda 21 United Nations Conference on Environment and Development. (1992). *Agenda 21*. Albany: New York State University Press.

Callahan, R. (1962). *Education and the cult of efficiency.* Chicago: University of Chicago Press.

Connect. UNESCO-UNEP. (1976). *Environmental Education Newsletter, 1*(1) 1–9.

Corcoran, P. B., Vilela, M., & Roerink, A. (2005). *The Earth Charter in action.* Amsterdam: Kit Publishers.

The Earth Charter. (2001). *The earth charter.* Earth Charter International Secretariat. Retrieved August 9, 2006, from http://www.eartcharter.org

The Ecologist. (1993). *Whose common future? Reclaiming the commons.* London: Earthscan.

Gruenewald, D. (2004). A Foucauldian analysis of environmental education: Toward the socio-ecological challenge of the Earth Charter. *Curriculum Inquiry,* 34(1), 63–99.

Gruenewald, D., & Manteaw, B. (2007). Oil and water still: How no child left behind limits and distorts environmental education in U.S. schools. *Environmental Education Research, 13*(2), 171–188.

Kuletz, V. (1998). *The tainted desert: Environmental and social ruin in the American West.* New York: Routledge.

North American Association of Environmental Education (NAAEE). (1999). *Excellence in EE—Guidelines for learning.* Rock Springs, GA: NAAEE.

Orr, D. (1992). *Ecological literacy.* Albany: State University of New York Press.

Orr, D. (1994). *Earth in mind.* Washington, DC: Island Press.

Spring, J. (1998). *Education and the rise of the global economy.* Mahwah, NJ: Erlbaum.

Stevenson, R. B. (1987). Schooling and environmental education: Contradictions in purpose and practice. In I. M. Robottom (Ed.), *Environmental education: Practice and possibility* (pp. 69–82). Victoria, Australia: Deakin University Press.

United Nations Environment Programme (UNESCO-UNEP). (1978). Final Report Intergovernmental Conference on Environmental Education. Organized by UNESCO in

Cooperation with UNEP, Tbilisi, USSR, October 4–26, 1977. Paris: UNESCO ED/MD/49.

United Nations Environment Programme (UNESCO-UNEP). (1976). The Belgrade Charter, *Connexion, 1*, 1–3.

United Nations. (2002, September). The Johannesburg Declaration on Sustainable Development, World Summit on Sustainable Development, Johannesburg, 26 August–4 September.

United Nations Conference on Environment and Development. (1992). Agenda 21: The United Nations programme of action from Rio. New York: United Nations Department of Public Information.

United Nations Conference on the Human Environment. (1972). Declaration of the United Nations Conference on the Human Environment. Stockholm: UNEP.

World Commission on Environment and Development. (1987). *Our common future.* Oxford: Oxford University Press.

7 Education for Peace and Nonviolence

Julie Andrzejewski

> A culture of peace will be achieved when citizens of the world understand global problems, have the skills to resolve conflicts and struggle for justice non-violently, live by international standards of human rights and equity, appreciate cultural diversity, and respect the Earth and each other. Such learning can only be achieved with systematic education for peace. (Hague Appeal for Peace)

Even as violence and war permeate our everyday lives, media, and world, peace is rarely a topic in schools. In desperate circumstances, people often respond to violence with violence. Yet, over millennia, many people, individually and collectively, have dedicated their lives to creating peace, often under great duress. This chapter draws upon their collective wisdom and advocacy to explore integrated approaches to peace that are personal, communal, and global. Such non-violent principles and actions can be engaged and practiced through peace education.

Peace Is Integral to Social Justice and Earth Preservation

Peace education is fundamental to justice and ecological well-being. The following examples will illustrate some of the connections. Two questions exemplify the impact of war on the environment: Will a large percentage of the earth's finite resources continue to be wasted on war and domination or can they be redirected to preserve life on earth? Can we reclaim land, water, and air polluted with radioactive or chemical weapons, landmines, or the residue of weapons production and warfare?

Peace education is inextricably linked with human rights and justice for indigenous peoples and peoples of color since White supremacy, ethnocentrism, and religious hegemony have provided the justification for wars of conquest, imperialism, and genocide. Peace is a gender issue as hyper-masculinity, cultivated through violent entertainment, entices young men to demonstrate their manhood through violence, war, torture, misogyny, and sexual assault (Robb, 2002). Because children suffer so grievously in wars, the United Nations has dedicated an International Decade for a Culture of Peace and Nonviolence for the Children of the World from 2001 to 2010.

Education for peace would help prevent harm to many other groups as well. While war and violence are responsible for creating many disabilities, veterans and traumatized civilians are abandoned during and after every war. Though sexual minorities are denied their rights as citizens, they are "allowed" to serve in the United States military but forbidden to reveal personal relationships considered normal and appropriate for heterosexuals. At the same time, they are often denied legal protection from violence and discrimination. Peace and nonviolence are crucial to animals whose habitats and species are destroyed, who are used for cruel military and laboratory testing, or who experience perpetual torture and imprisonment in factory farms, laboratories, zoos, circuses, and aquariums.

In all these areas, education for peace with justice and earth preservation raises important life questions: What kind of societies and world do we desire? What kind of people do we want to be? How can we experience a meaningful, compassionate, generous, and peaceful life? How can we practice personal, communal, and global peace?

To seek answers to these questions, this chapter presents four aspects of peace education:

1. Some Root Causes of War, Violence, and Hatred
2. Principles and Practices for Peace and Justice
3. International Documents for Peace, Compassion, Love, and Justice
4. Educational Practices of Peace for Students, Educators, Schools, and Curriculum

Some Root Causes of War, Violence, and Hatred

Many factors encourage aggression and hatred to dominate peoples' attitudes, political and economic institutions, national and international actions. While the roots of war have been investigated for centuries (Barash, 2000), the root causes presented here are synthesized from two international efforts for peace: the eight characteristics of a culture of war identified by the UN Programme of Action on a Culture of Peace (Culture of Peace Network, 2004) and the Hague Agenda for Peace and Justice (HAPJ) for the 21st Century (2000).

Intertwined in these root causes of war and violence are two key forces: 1) the role of governments and corporations in consolidating economic wealth and power; 2) the actions of individuals in creating or perpetuating violence. Rarely discussed or investigated in schools, the negative consequences of these forces lay the foundations for mobilizing individuals and institutions for peace and nonviolence.

Root Cause #1: Greed and Imperialism (HAJP #4)

To increase their wealth, individuals, groups, nations, and corporations have traveled the globe for thousands of years expropriating land and natural resources that did not belong to them, and exploiting the labor of people and animals.

This process of coercive wealth accumulation may be called imperialism, empire, colonialism, neo-colonialism, or "globalization." When those exploited by such processes try to resist, violence or the threat of violence is often applied to continue the extraction of wealth.

Root Cause #2: Coercive Power of the State (UN Characteristics of War #3)

Corporations do not invade or wage war on other peoples or nations directly. They make large campaign donations and hire lobbyists to influence government policies and actions. Elected and appointed government officials often work for corporations before or after their government service, creating conflicts of interest in their decision-making. Because of these connections, it is not uncommon for governments with substantial military budgets, weapons systems, and spying capabilities to intervene violently in other countries on behalf of business interests (Grossman, 2001). Economies or governments of other sovereign nations may be undermined or overthrown, and then leaders assassinated.

Without constant monitoring by citizens and watchdog organizations, even governments identifying themselves as democratic can be corrupted. States may use military power or intelligence operations to intervene in other countries, overtly or covertly. They may subject their own citizens to conscription, generate public relations campaigns to justify these policies, or indoctrinate citizens through education.

Root Cause #3: Arms Industry and Military (UN Characteristics of War #5)

War profiteering itself creates a formidable support system for global aggression. Enormous public resources are spent on weapons, weapons research, military bases, military infrastructure, and provisions for armed services personnel. The United States military expenditures, for example, far surpass all other countries combined (Marte & Wheeler, 2007). Military contracts, including companies employing private soldiers, are figured on a cost-plus basis, resulting in the highest profit margins of any industry. Even so, no-bid contracts, fraud, and overcharges are rampant (Zepezauer, 2004), and companies are reissued contracts even if convicted. Arms are sold to almost any country with the money to buy them or given to selected governments through foreign aid programs (Shanker, 2007). Contractors partner with military personnel on projects which operate with little or no oversight or consequences for violations of law or human rights (Scahill, 2007).

Root Cause #4: Economics Racism and Inequality of Global Resources (HAPJ #2 and #4)

Imperialism results in the concentration of wealth among a few individuals, countries, and corporations. More than half the wealth of the world is now owned by only 2% of its people, and 90% of the wealth is concentrated in North America, Europe, and a few Asian countries (Davies, Sandstrom, Shorrocks, & Wolff,

2006). Using the ideology of White supremacy (Mills, 2007), countries benefiting from centuries of imperialism now consume a disproportionate amount of the world's resources. Stone (1996) calls this process *economic racism*, "the initial theft of the land, property, resources, and/our labour belonging to another racial or ethnic group by violence as extreme as that required to accomplish the theft, e.g., unprovoked aggression, invasion, full-scale war, massacre, and/or kidnapping" (p. 286).

Hoarding resources creates structural violence—harm and death to millions of people each year through lack of livelihood, nutrition, sanitation, health care, and housing. Institutionalized advantages and disadvantages based on color, culture, class, and gender are normalized globally and to varying degrees within most countries.

Root Cause #5: Propaganda and Censorship (UN Characteristics of War #4)

Very few of the root causes for war and violence could continue without censorship and propaganda. Public relations are purposeful campaigns designed to convince an audience of something that is not necessarily true, or to sell a product or policy that will be profitable to sponsors and often detrimental to the audience (Robb, 2002). Censorship supports propaganda by suppressing information and evidence that might motivate people to come to different conclusions. Propaganda and censorship are not restricted to dictators and totalitarian regimes as many people have been led to believe, but exist in every country to varying degrees.

Many people in the West, taught that they have access to a "free" press, are often surprised to discover that the media from which they receive most of their information consists of large corporations whose primary objective is to maximize profits. Further, these media corporations, with clients and financial interests in imperialism and war, influence how information is packaged and disseminated, including educational texts. Public relations campaigns have been instrumental in selling wars to the U.S. public (Grossman, 2001, 2007; Alper, 2007). Censorship of information that would challenge violence and war is documented every year through Project Censored (Phillips & Roth, 2008, see www.projectcensored.org).

Although the media are a major source of censorship and propaganda, educational institutions, wittingly or unwittingly, participate in these activities as well. If this were not true, why are topics like peace, justice, and environmental issues that have life and death consequences not central to the curriculum of all educational institutions?

Root Cause #6: Overconsumption and Exploitation of Global Resources (HAPJ #3)

Enormous environmental damage has been created by industrialization, imperialism, and technological processes of extracting natural resources from the earth with no regard for the long-term consequences to people, animals, or the earth. These activities have resulted in: 1) the sixth mass extinction of species, 2) pervasive degradation, poisoning, and restructuring of the natural environment (e.g., dams, mountain removals, genetic engineering, exotic species), 3) the disruption of major climate controls (e.g., the ocean conveyor belt), and 4) potential collapse of life support systems (e.g., deforestation, freshwater scarcity). As people and animals are affected by these consequences, conflict and violence will increase.

In capitalist societies and everywhere global media corporations prevail, people are socialized to seek personal happiness through the accumulation of material possessions, most of which they do not need. This overconsumption fuels the unsustainable and inequitable uses of global resources that, in turn, maintains the extraction of wealth and environmental destruction around the world through force.

Root Cause #7: Ideologies of Superiority and Self-Centeredness (UN Characteristics of War #2, HAPJ #5)

Racism, ethnocentrism, nationalism, xenophobia, patriarchy, patriotism, religious, and other belief systems that create and reify hierarchies of nations, cultures, peoples, and animals, provide rationalizations for violence and wars. Such ideologies indoctrinate dominant groups into a sense of superiority, entitlement, and righteousness while influencing subjugated groups to internalize beliefs of their own inferiority. Education intentionally or unintentionally transmits many of these ideologies by the information, viewpoints, and skills that are taught or omitted.

Individualism, for instance, establishes a worldview of self in competition with others instead of considering the well-being and interdependence of all. Under this belief, it is possible to develop or instill apathy, aversion, distrust, distain or hatred toward other people, animals, and even plants or forests (viewed as being "in the way" of a desired outcome) rather than a sense of interconnectedness, care, and compassion. Ignorance, stereotypes, and mis/disinformation about other people or beings is a recipe for violence, whether in the form of discrimination, bullying, hate crimes, or military orders to kill others viewed as the "enemy."

Root Cause #8: Patriarchy and Male Domination (UN Characteristics of War #8, HAPJ#6)

Boys and men in many cultures are socialized to believe they are superior to women and that females are to be despised, degraded, and dominated. This patriarchy is maintained by violence against women pervasive in popular culture, and by culturally tolerated psychological abuse, battery, sexual assault, and femicide. It is supported by normalized gender discrimination that inhibits or prevents women from gaining equal education, employment, and political decision-making authority. Boys and men usually are not aware that they are also victims of gender roles and violence.

Women are seriously disadvantaged on almost every indicator of well-being around the world. Heyzer, Director of the United Nations Development Fund for

Women (UNIFEM), summarized the problem, "It is not acceptable…for women to work two-thirds of the world's working hours, but earn only one-tenth of the world's income and own less than one-tenth[1] of the world's property" (Seager, 2003, p. 102). Violence and the threat of violence are required to maintain such inequitable systems.

Root Cause #9: Selling of Violent Culture, Militarism, and War (HAPJ #9)

Violence is pervasive in every form of media from cartoons, entertainment, music, and sports to video games and news. Boys and men are especially targeted by producers and advertisers to consume these products by connecting "manhood" with exaggerated physical strength, weapons, anger, and violence. Both genders become desensitized to violence, accept violent culture as normal, learn to feel, express, and act on negative emotions, and to solve problems with violence. The military colludes with the entertainment industry for purposes of recruiting young people and training soldiers to kill. Wars and government military interventions are marketed as patriotic adventures where heroic thrill-seekers can take righteous revenge against "evil-doers" (Picker & Sun, 2003).

The Tower of Violence: Interrelationships of Individual and Systemic Violence

These root causes are linked in many ways. Education could provide students with skills to critique media, investigate ideologies of greed and overconsumption, and reconsider the use of global resources. It could help them examine their role in perpetuating hatred, violence, and war. Understanding how individual actions contribute to systemic violence helps students reflect on what kind of decisions they want to make. The Tower of Violence (Figure 7.1) illustrates how negative and judgmental personal thoughts, speech, and actions lay a foundation for institutional discrimination, blatant and extreme cruelty, or global aggression. By reflecting on their own experiences and imagining themselves in the place of the "other," students can begin to see how certain actions may establish an environment where it seems socially acceptable or even desirable to participate in more overt violence.

The lower levels shown in this tower are purposely used by militaries to encourage hatred for the "enemy," camaraderie within units, and to prepare recruits to actually kill other human beings. It is not by accident that militaries use racist and sexist drills to vilify the "enemy." Lt. Colonel David Grossman has exposed the military's use of violent video games as a successful strategy to get soldiers to shoot at other humans (Grossman & DeGaetano, 1999).

There Is No Way to Peace. Peace Is the Way.[2] (A. J. Muste)

As many have pointed out, peace is more than an absence of war and violence, which has been identified as *negative peace* (Barash, 2000). An absence of overt violence can be imposed through coercion, domination, and subjugation. This is

Tower of Violence

Violence feeds upon itself. An environment where individual acts of judgment and harm are encouraged or viewed as normal causes acts of violence (intentional or unintentional) to escalate and intensify until a culture or society emerges that is dangerous for many.

LIFE THREATENING ACTS

- Imperialism/War/Genocide/Extermination/Extinction
- Assassination/murder/lynching/death squads
- Domestic violence/Hate crimes
- Arson/Bombings/Use of hazardous weapons
- Kidnapping/Torture/Rendition/Land mines
- Poverty/Hoarding Resources/Imposing Sanctions
- Environmental/Habitat destruction or contamination
- Systemic Torture/Killing of animals for food, research, education, entertainment, sport, clothing, products

ACTS OF VIOLENCE

- Theft of Land, Labor, & Resources from humans/animals
- Assault (physical, sexual, emotional)
- Beatings/Brutality/Vandalism
- Exposure to toxins, carcinogens, hazardous products
- Imprisonment/Animal agriculture
- Slavery/Sexual slavery/Wage slavery
- Denying food, water, safety, medicine, escape
- Systemic cruelty/exploitation of animals for agriculture, labor, testing, sports, entertainment, education, and products

HUMAN/ANIMAL RIGHTS VIOLATIONS

- Denial of civil rights and due process
- Harassment. abuse, or profiling (based on any characteristic)
- Verbal, non-verbal, or physical threats or vandalism
- Blatant or subtle discrimination (legal or illegal)
- Discriminatory/exclusionary laws, policies & practices (jobs, housing, etc.)
- Any individual/institutional actions that violate other beings or the earth

INDIVIDUAL ACTS OF JUDGMENT & HARM

- Any actions, words, or thoughts that harm people/beings without physical contact
- Avoidance * Name-calling * Verbal insults
- Antagonism or hostility * Rumors & Stereotypes * Negative gestures
- Ridicule, "teasing" * One-up interactions * Paternalism
- Jokes, comments, sarcasm, derision, negative communications
- Bonding/collusion within dominant group (based on "race," gender, class, disability, age, nationality, religion, sexual orientation, physical appearance, ethnicity, species, etc.)

ACTS OF INNER OR INDIRECT HARM

- Aversion, judgment, disgust, anger, hatred, any harmful thoughts toward others
- Denial of judgment, discrimination, or harm of any kind
- Silence or tacit support during acts of harm, discrimination, violence, wars, etc.
- Consuming products, ideas, policies, media that promote or emerge from violence

Figure 7.1 Tower of Violence. Adapted and developed from Outfront Minnesota, Minneapolis, MN by Julie Andrzejewski. *Anti Defamiation League has a similar Pyramid of Violence.

not true peace. *Positive peace* must include justice, harmony, and well-being for all. Positive peace would entail: 1) goals and policies for peace with justice, 2) collective actions based on theories of peace and non-violence, and 3) principles for peace from ancient wisdom and spiritual traditions.

Goals for Peace with Justice

Like the UN Culture of Peace and the Hague Appeal for Peace, other documents identify goals and policies that foster peace, such as: the *Global Environment Outlook 4* (UN Environmental Program, 2007), the *Millennium Development Goals* (UN General Assembly, 2000), *The Earth Charte*r (2001), *The Charter for a World without Violence* (Nobel Peace Laureates, 2006), and other UN conventions supporting rights for children, women, racial equality, disability rights, and indigenous peoples. While there is great agreement among these documents, students could compare them and develop their own lists. *The Better World Handbook* presents a particularly accessible version (Jones, Haenfler, & Johnson, 2001).

Seven Foundations for a Better World

1. **Economic Fairness** ... would strive to meet every person's basic needs so that no one would lack food, shelter, clothing, or meaningful work. Everyone would benefit from economic prosperity.
2. **Comprehensive Peace** ... would shift creative energies to cooperation rather than competing, resolving conflict rather than escalating it, seeking justice rather than revenge, and creating peace rather than preparing for war.
3. **Ecological Sustainability** ... would create a new vision of progress that depends upon our ability to live in harmony and balance with the natural world.
4. **Deep Democracy** ... would empower citizens to participate in shaping their futures every day, (not just on election day), provide broad access to quality information, and democratize powerful institutions.
5. **Social Justice** ... everyone would receive respect and equal access to jobs, education, health care regardless of race, gender, ethnicity, sexual orientation, age, physical or mental abilities, economic background.
6. **Culture of Simplicity** ... would encourage each person to find meaning and fulfillment by pursuing their true passions, fostering loving relationships, and living authentic, reflective lives rather than by seeking status and material possessions.
7. **Revitalized Community** ... creating a healthy, loving environment for people to celebrate shared values while embracing individual differences, provide support for each person's physical, emotional, and spiritual needs. (Jones, Haenfler, & Johnson, 2007, pp. 13–55; www.betterworldhandbook.com/festival/seven.html)

Collective Actions for Peace and Non-Violence

For centuries, peace advocates have organized anti-war and peace efforts in groups small and large. Just as they have drawn inspiration from one another, education about these thinkers, organizers, and movements may motivate students towards new thoughts and courageous actions. Students could benefit from knowing Kant's view of perpetual peace, Goldman's challenge to patriotism, Einstein's support for world government, Hnat Hahn's engaged Buddhism, Mandela's dismantling of apartheid, King's opposition to racism, poverty, and war, Chavez' organizing of farm workers, Maathai's empowerment of women, Gandhi's triumph over colonialism, Aung San Suu Kyi's struggle with the junta in Myanmar, or Menchu's survival of death squads.

In contrast to common misconceptions, nonviolent movements require great courage and have been successful against violent repression and empires (Sharp, 2005, pp. 21–22). Nonviolent movements have been based on three key precepts.

1. Non-resistance (Jesus, Tolstoy)
   Tolstoy influenced peace advocates like Gandhi through interpreting the thoughts and actions of Jesus on non-resistance (Tolstoy, 1894). In non-resistance love and compassion for the oppressors is generated and no actions for self-protection or reprisal against injustice and violence are taken.
2. Satyagraha (Gandhi)
   Satyagraha (truth-force or soul-force) combined truth and nonviolence (ahimsa) to inspire the successful Indian movement for independence from British colonialism (Iyer, 1990). Nonviolent resistance is another name for the methods Gandhi and his followers developed to resist oppression and domination. The main concept is to endure suffering and create nonviolent means to convince the opponent to stop the oppression (Gandhi, 1961). Key practices include: fearlessness, courage, non-possession, and equality (e.g. challenging the caste system in India). Resistance comprises methods like civil disobedience, boycotts, and *swadeshi*—self-sufficiency through producing indigenous goods.
3. Non-violent Struggle (Sharp)
   Sharp's 198 methods of nonviolent action build upon non-violent resistance. They are divided into six categories: 1) nonviolent protest and persuasion; 2) social noncooperation; 3) economic noncooperation: boycotts; 4) economic noncooperation: strikes; 5) political noncooperation; and 6) nonviolent intervention (1973, 2005). Civil disobedience (Thoreau, 1849), military non-cooperation (Tolstoy, 1843), and conscientious objection are among them.

Principles of Peace from Ancient Wisdom and Spiritual Traditions

Ancient wisdom survives today in many spiritual traditions such as indigenous spiritualities, Baha'i, Buddhism, Christianity, Confucianism, Hinduism, Islam,

Jainism, Judaism, Sikhhism, Shintoism, Sufism, Taoism, and Zoroastrianism. While each tradition has different prophets, holy texts or places, cultural and physical environments, they share many common principles pertaining to love, kindness, compassion, generosity, non-violence, and peace at the core of their belief systems (Moses, 2002).

Given the prevalence of these shared beliefs, it is striking how few people, cultures, and social organizations seem willing or able to put these principles into practice. At times, they have been dismissed as too simplistic, too idealistic, too difficult to practice, not activist enough, or lacking the power to address structural violence, wars, and systemic oppression. Yet, ordinary people worldwide have accomplished major changes by practicing these principles. Every continent and era has had people, famous and unknown, who have advocated for and lived their own lives in accordance with principles of peace and nonviolence.

There is disagreement among, and sometimes within, certain intellectual or spiritual traditions about *pacifism*, that violence and war are never justified under any circumstance, and the concept of a "just war," often meaning the use of violence in self-defense. Self-defense, however, can be and has been manipulated to justify wars of aggression. If one critically studies who profits from war, it is difficult to locate a war where imperialism, empire, and profits are not motivating factors. However, this chapter does not take a stand on whether violence is ever justified. The purpose here is to present information and practices to increase peace education. In this respect, some questions educators might consider are presented here and again after each principle:

- What principles of ancient wisdom, intellectual thought, and international agreements can guide people interested in practicing peace, non-violence and justice today?
- Why are these principles so difficult to practice? How could education make them easier?
- Why are they applied to individual behaviors but not to the policies and practices of larger entities like governments, militaries, corporations, or even religious institutions? Who benefits and loses when they are not?
- How might these principles be studied and practiced in schools without favoring any specific spiritual or intellectual tradition?
- Through what opportunities could students practice individual, community, and global principles of peace?

Principle #1: Do not Kill or Harm Others (as Individuals or Under the Auspices of Any Institution)

Not only is this principle universal among religions, it is codified into the legal systems of most countries. Ahimsa, a core principle in Hinduism, Buddhism, Sikhism, and Jainism, goes beyond legal proscriptions, however, to mean do no harm in thought, word, or deed. In some traditions, this primarily refers to humans, in others, like Jainism, the principle applies to all living beings. If this principle were introduced throughout education, and schools began to integrate this practice into policies and activities, the impact on participants, communities, and beyond could be substantial.

There are many contradictions related to these principles. For instance, while it is considered illegal for individuals or groups to kill or harm another person, states and nations reserve the right to kill or harm people for crimes (capital punishment) or in wars. In these cases, there is little to no accountability for harm to innocents, civilians, other beings, or the environment, not to mention combatants. For example, in many countries it may be unacceptable or illegal to harm certain types of animals, but considered normal for humans to kill or harm other animals on the slightest whim.

Questions: What implications might knowledge and practice of the principle "do no harm" have for families? For workplace harmony? For deciding whether to join a military? For deciding what career to pursue? For considering the social responsibility of every citizen? For evaluating the policies of governments and corporations?

Principle #2: Generosity of Material Goods, Effort, and Decision-Making

"Take what you need and leave the rest," expresses the Native American proposition that contradicts the underlying motivation of capitalism—to accumulate as much as possible (LaDuke, 1996). All the major spiritual traditions espouse the importance of sharing, giving, and generosity, yet under capitalism, people are continually bombarded with messages encouraging materialism, self centeredness, consumption, competition, and attachment to one's own selfish desires—in a word, greed. While attempts to encourage sharing occur in elementary schools, some religious institutions, or philanthropic organizations, the knowledge and practice of generosity is not pursued as students mature.

Questions: What might educators teach about cultures that practice simplicity, sharing, and cooperation, including the sharing of power and decision-making to counter individual and corporate greed at the global level? How might generosity be fostered and taught in consumer cultures?

Principle #3: Extend Love to Everyone, Including Those Who Have Harmed You

This principle is sometimes expressed as "love your neighbor," based on the idea that all people are our neighbors. In Buddhism, the concept of love means "wishing happiness for others," which is practiced to antidote aversion, fear, anger, and hatred. Negative emotions towards others often serve as, or are manipulated into, motivation for harm and violence. Further, it is often overlooked that negative emotions create suffering for the people experiencing them. Still, replacing these emotions with love requires a great deal of contemplation, patience, courage, and practice in societies where judgment and hatred towards others are encouraged in blatant and subtle ways. If people were not taught to categorize and hate one another based on race, gender, class, religion, nationality, and other characteristics, it might be more difficult to persuade people that another group is a threat or an enemy.

In every major religion, there is an admonition to love those who have harmed you, who oppress you, or who are perceived as "enemies." An important question to contemplate is why all the spiritual traditions would say something that seems to counter many cultural and media messages. With very few models of these principles, and the prevalence of violent images and "heroes," there is little opportunity or leadership to support the practice of this difficult principle.

Questions: How might such a principle be studied in schools? Is there a place for learning to respond to hostility with love and compassion rather than anger and revenge? What would happen if these principles were practiced by even a few individuals, communities, and nations? How might foreign policy be different if nations promoted skills in diplomacy, negotiation, and non-violence?

Principle #4: You Will Experience the Consequences of Your Own Actions

"You reap what you sow" is a powerful dictum drawn from many traditions that most people understand at a superficial level but rarely consider in their daily lives. The Buddhist concept of *karma,* popularized in the saying, "what goes around, comes around," is also known to people of many countries and cultures. Yet, except for exercises in elementary school, integrating the wisdom of this principle into daily life is not given serious consideration in most educational settings. This principle is vividly exemplified by veterans who never recover from the atrocities they committed, even if they were the result of orders. Suicide, homicide, post-traumatic stress syndrome, mental health problems, assaults and battering, chemical dependency, and homelessness among veterans are epidemic (Winterfilm, 1972; Iraq Veterans Against the War, 2008).

As the Tower of Violence illustrates, people participate in many activities, consciously or unconsciously, which harm others through thought, speech, or action. While these behaviors may seem harmless or justified to the person initiating them, such actions often have unintended consequences that the person may not desire. For instance, people who defend their right to judge others may be unaware that they themselves may be viewed as discriminatory, judgmental, or mean. In a global example, leaders promulgating torture and war may suffer loss of respect and authority, political or economic consequences, or eventually criminal charges. While it may seem that many people responsible for harming others do not experience negative consequences, it is not easy to measure the experiences of another over a lifetime.

Questions: How could people learn to generate love and compassion in the face of irritation, frustration, envy, hatred, or oppression? How might positive, compassionate, and peaceful thoughts, words, and deeds generate similar feelings in others or even reduce our own suffering?

The Tower of Peace and Well-Being

The Tower of Peace and Well-Being (Figure 7.2) provides a model for people to see how their personal actions can effect positive change at many levels. In order

Tower of Peace and Well-Being

ACTIONS FOR SAVING LIVES AND GLOBAL PEACE

- Work on the root causes of violence/war instead of band-aid solutions.
- Work for peaceful and creative solutions to imperialism: help restore land, resources to humans, animals, and living systems.
- Support global economic policies that value all life over profits and greed.
- Refuse to kill, torture or harm any person or being as an individual or by order of the military or state. Become a conscientious objector.
- Make a living doing work for a better world: Refuse any job that supports the root causes of war, violence, or harm of any kind.
- Join organizations to stop wars, killing, torture, and harm conducted in your name with your money.
- Take immediate steps to save the planet and repair the environment.
- Practice living every day in ways that save human and animal lives.
- Work to eliminate non-imperative imprisonment, the death penalty and other violent punishments.

GLOBAL/NATIONAL POLICIES FOR PEACE AND JUSTICE

- Help institutions use resources for people, animals, and the earth—not weapons and dangerous products.
- Support all UN Conventions on human rights, environment, animal well-being.
- Support international law and the International Criminal Court.
- Hold governments, corporations, institutions, and the people within them responsible for repairing their impact on people, animals, & the earth.
- Work peacefully to (re)instate civil rights, due process, and democracy.
- Support peace alternatives to military recruitment, propaganda, manipulation.
- Work for government & corporate accountability to & for people, not profits.
- Help reform laws and the "justice" system for rehabilitation/restoration.
- Join organizations working for a better world on all issues.
- Work for fairness of food, water, homes, safety, and health for all beings.

ACTIONS FOR INSTITUTIONAL JUSTICE & NON-VIOLENCE

- Evaluate candidates for public office on their record and actions, not what they say.
- Enforce rules and accountability for peace, nonviolence, equality, fairness, and safety.
- Work within organizations to eliminate divisions, conflict, discrimination, and hatred.
- Live simply. Use fewer resources. Stop overconsumption. Share with others daily.
- Buy and support fair trade, non-slave, cruelty-free products.
- Access independent non-profit activist media in print, web, radio, music, film.

ACTS OF PERSONAL/INTERPERSONAL PEACE AND RESPECT

- Each day, with pure motivation, do the most good and the least harm in all you do.
- In your thoughts, words, and actions, be compassionate, kind, and caring to everyone, including those you perceive as enemies.
- Practice/encourage generosity rather than greed, attachment, and self importance.
- Counter stereotypical or harmful comments, jokes, and actions with kind and humble education.
- Reach out to any individual, group, species, or being to counter aversion, fear, and hatred.
- Eat organic, local, plant-based food for health, indigenous peoples, other species, and the earth.
- Help stop animal agriculture and genetic engineering.

ACTS OF INNER COMPASSION AND PEACE

- Acknowledge our own role in violence and practice daily to change our thoughts, words, and actions.
- Cultivate motivations of generosity and love. Seek a meaningful beneficial life purpose.
- Relinquish attachment to self, to our own desires, projects, and personal aggrandizement.
- Realize that resentment, aversion, irritation, disgust, judgment, anger, and hatred harm ourselves.
- Refuse to consume/support violent media, ideas, music, or visions of any kind.
- Be continually mindful of eliminating negativity & increasing compassion and kindness for all beings.

Figure 7.2 Tower of Peace and Wellbeing. Julie Andrzejewski created The Tower of Peace and Well-being modeled on Outfront Minnesota's Tower of Violence.

to counteract the Tower of Violence that human beings have constructed and reinforce everyday, we can create a vision of how principles of peace might be integrated into our own lives, individually and collectively. Like the Tower of Violence, the Tower of Peace and Well-Being illustrates the interconnections between our inner thoughts and motivations, our speech, and our actions. It helps portray connections between our personal actions, and policies at the national and global levels.

Instead of feeling cynical and hopeless about the state of the world, we can see in the Tower of Peace and Well-Being that our own decisions and actions have an impact much larger than ourselves. Tolstoy's main solution to war was the conviction that war could not be waged if soldiers refused to serve and obey (1899). Yet, in the United States, military recruiters have greater access to young people than ever before. Despite the exposé of false promises, lies, and other manipulative recruiting techniques, these practices continue (Weill-Greenberg, 2006). Young people have the right to be well informed before making a decision of such import about their lives. Schools have a responsibility to their students, families, and communities to provide an education that equips students with critiques of war, militaries, weapons, and hegemony; to provide alternative visions of how peace can best be achieved.

International Documents and Organizations: Foundations for Peace Education

There are many important international and laws pertaining to war. As part of global understanding, students should become familiar with these agreements, the circumstances that motivated them, and the constituencies involved in their creation. For instance, while many people have heard of the Geneva Conventions, they often have only a vague idea what they are and how they pertain to prisoners, soldiers, and civilians. In particular, U.S. soldiers have reported that they were not taught the rules of the Geneva Conventions, making them vulnerable to committing war crimes (Winterfilm, 1972).

The focus here will be on international and a few national documents, models, and initiatives for non-violence and peace, which are even less well known. These documents can be teaching tools in themselves and can provide a foundation for positive guidelines for peace education.

The Hague Agenda for Peace and Justice for the 21st Century

Hundreds of organizations participated in the Hague Appeal for Peace that has emerged as one of the most comprehensive guides for citizen action yet developed. It is predicated upon the assumption that "in a great many cases, the world's governments have manifestly failed to fulfill their responsibility to prevent conflict, protect civilians, end war, eradicate colonialism, guarantee human rights and create the conditions of permanent peace" (HAPJ Preamble, 2000, p. 2). Thus, the plan proposes that the responsibility and capability for peace can be achieved through the dedication and work of "citizen advocates, progressive governments and international organizations" (p. 2). The strength of the Hague Agenda is the assumption that peace must be built upon the intersections of human rights, social justice, and environmental activism. The solutions to all these issues are indivisible.

A Global Campaign for Peace Education is one of the main actions of the Hague Agenda and is the first action (of fifty) to be taken under four Strand Agendas:

1. Root Causes of War/Culture of Peace
2. International Humanitarian and Human Rights Law and Institutions
3. Prevention, Resolution and Transformation of Violent Conflict
4. Disarmament and Human Security

The Hague Agenda calls for education for peace, human rights, and democracy to be compulsory for all grade levels, at the local and national levels, and infused into teacher education. "In order to combat the culture of violence that pervades our society, *the coming generation deserves a radically different education*—one that does not glorify war but educates for peace and nonviolence and international cooperation. The Hague Appeal for Peace seeks to launch a world-wide campaign to empower people at all levels with the peacemaking skills of mediation, conflict transformation, consensus-building and non-violent social change" (italics added by author, 2000, p. 8).

Manifesto 2000 and Other United Nations Conventions

The United Nations Manifesto 2000 (UN General Assembly, 1999), signed by over 75 million people and written by a coalition of Nobel Peace Prize Laureates, has six principles: *Respect all life. Reject violence. Share with others. Listen to understand. Preserve the planet. Rediscover solidarity.* Other conventions enumerate the rights of peoples of color, women, indigenous people, people with disabilities, and children have been ratified by many nations. In contrast to its stated principles, the United States has yet to ratify any of these.

Global Peace Index (2007)

The first study to quantify negative and positive peace was released in 2007 (Economist Intelligence Unit, 2007). One hundred twenty-one countries were compared on three categories: 1) domestic and international conflict, 2) societal safety and security, and 3) militarization. Problems to be resolved with the index are a failure to include: 1) violence against women and children, (Eisler, 2007) 2) nuclear and radioactive weapons, 3) aspects of structural violence, and 4) implementation of international agreements to ban weapons, torture, or address serious environmental problems. With improvements, the Global Peace Index could encourage or apply pressure to nations to take issues of peace and non-violence more seriously.

Manifesto Against Conscription and the Military System (1930)

This Manifesto, signed by 35 global dignitaries and peace advocates such as Martin Buber, Albert Einstein, M. K. Gandhi, Jane Addams, John Dewey, Bertrand Russell, and Upton Sinclair, describes military training as, "education for war…the schooling of body and spirit in the art of killing" (Manifesto, 1930). Numerous campaigns work to safeguard young people from coercive and unethical military recruitment practices. *10 Excellent Reasons Not to Join the Military* (Weill-Greenberg, 2006) and *Army of None* (Alison & Solnit, 2007) provide compelling evidence against military service.

Japan's Peace Constitution: Renunciation of War

Established in 1946 after experiencing the atomic bombs dropped on Hiroshima and Nagasaki by the United States in World War II, many people are unaware that Japan's Peace Constitution specifically prohibits war.

> Aspiring sincerely to an international peace based on justice and order, the Japanese people forever renounce war as a sovereign right of the nation and the threat or use of force as means of settling international disputes. 2) In order to accomplish the aim of the preceding paragraph, land, sea, and air forces, as well as other war potential, will never be maintained. The right of belligerency of the state will not be recognized. (Pax Christi Queensland, 2007)

While Japan is currently under pressure to change this statement, Hiroshima's mayor strongly reaffirmed it in his 2007 Hiroshima Peace Declaration (*Mainichi Daily News*, 2007).

The Right Livelihood Awards (Initiated 1980) and The Graduation Pledge (Initiated 1984)

Known as the alternative Nobel Prize, The Right Livelihood Award "is widely recognized as the world's premier award for personal courage and social transformation … (I)n striving to meet the human challenges of today's world, the most inspiring and remarkable work often defies any standard classification. For example, people who start out with an environmental goal frequently find themselves drawn into issues of health, human rights and/or social justice. Their work becomes a holistic response to community needs, so that sectoral categories lose their meaning" (2007).

Bringing the ancient concept of "right livelihood" to the attention of graduating students in the United States, *the Graduation Pledge* has been implemented at over 100 U.S. universities including Harvard and MIT. It states, "I ________ pledge to explore and take into account the social and environmental consequences of any job I consider and will try to improve these aspects of any organizations for which I work" (Graduation Pledge Alliance, 2007).

United States Department of Peace Legislation

Introduced in 2003 into the U.S. House of Representatives, this legislation outlines the need, the international and domestic benefits, the responsibilities, and the budget for a Department of Peace. Posing a powerful contrast, it calls for an amount equal to 2% of the U.S. military budget to be dedicated to the promotion of peace and non-violence. A U.S. Peace Academy comparable to the U.S. Military Academy would be established. To date, this proposal has not received serious consideration (The Peace Alliance, 2007).

The wide array of spiritual, philosophical, and activist thought, initiatives, models, and practices for peace and nonviolence created over thousands of years provide an impressive foundation for envisioning and implementing peace and justice education.

Educational Practices for Peace and Justice

Rationale: Since peace and nonviolence are values expressed by most nations, held by most spiritual traditions, and often found in the missions of educational institutions, students of all ages should have the opportunity to study, reflect upon, and practice aspects of personal, community, national, and global peace in their educational experience. To counter propaganda about patriotism, combat, war, empire, militaries, and related issues of ethnocentrism, White and male supremacy, etc., educational institutions have an obligation to provide students with accurate and critical information upon which to make momentous, everyday life, and global citizenship decisions. Peace and justice education should exist as a focus of study as well as infused throughout the entire educational experience. It is hoped that the following standards, modeled after the Alaska Native Knowledge Network Cultural Standards, informed by spiritual and intellectual traditions and international plans for peace, will stimulate creative practices for those striving to educate for and through peace.

What Education Will Assist Students in Working for Nonviolence and Peace in Their Own Lives and in the World?

I. Students can create a safe home and school environment, community, a peaceful nation, and non-violent world (by):

A. Investigating, comparing, and critically analyzing information sources to counteract censorship and propaganda and to identify the root causes of violence and war.

B. Evaluating which aspects of culture, socialization, and media support violence and conflict, or support peace, compassion, and harmony.

C. Learning varied traditions of ancient wisdom and intellectual thought on nonviolence and peace, topics of social justice and environmental preservation integral to them.

D. Developing skills in personal mind training, decision-making, and nonviolent actions to increase calmness and compassion for those creating harm as well as those that are suffering.

E. Practicing life skills of generosity, sharing, cooperation, selfless motivation, patience, and compassion with an overall focus on doing no harm.
F. Contemplating the Towers of Violence and Peace to consider how personal decisions and actions influence and are influenced by larger policies and actions of war or peace.
G. Practicing the art of engaging with others across differences with respect, empathy, equity, peace, and advocacy in all settings.
H. Investigating critical information about military recruitment, military training, military interventions, the consequences of combat for civilians and soldiers, treatment of veterans, conscientious objection, and the rights of students, parents, schools, and communities before making decisions about military service (Peace Alliance, 2007).
I. Seeking out and engaging with non-governmental, non-profit citizen action organizations implementing innovative actions for peace and non-violence.

What Should Educators Know, Model, and Teach about Peace and Nonviolence?

II. Educators can model and inspire peace and nonviolence in their classrooms and schools (by):

A. Participating in a process of personal re-education to critique socialization and indoctrination supporting jingoism, nationalism, colonialism, imperialism, militarism, ethnocentrism, patriarchy, and other beliefs promoting hierarchies of status and privilege.
B. Integrating principles of peace and nonviolence into aspects of the school environment to foster personal and global peace and well-being.
C. Learning, practicing, and modeling mindfulness, compassion, love, kindness, patience, and generosity towards all students and colleagues, especially in conflictual or tense situations.
D. Integrating ancient wisdom, intellectual thought, and practices of peace and nonviolence appropriately into particular grade levels, subject matter, or communities involved.
E. Experimenting with creative methods to support student learning of peace and nonviolence and to address controversial issues that may arise in this context.
F. Engaging other educators, administrators, parents, community members, non-profit organizations, and faith communities interested in sharing ideas and plans for nonviolence and peace education.

How Might Educational Institutions Foster New Paradigms and Life Skills for Peace with Justice, Integrating Them into Everyday Policies and Practices?

III. Schools can place a high priority on educating for peace and nonviolence at the personal, family, community, national, and global levels (by):

A. Creating a mission that reflects education for democracy, social justice, peace, nonviolence, environmental integrity, and interspecies responsibility, implementing a regular evaluation process to assess how the school is meeting this mission.
B. Establishing a socially just and respectful environment to create safety rather than relying upon external controls, surveillance, and punishment.
C. Hiring a diverse faculty, staff, and security personnel with credentials and commitment to fostering peace and nonviolence so every student sees role models in the school leadership able to work across differences to address conflict successfully and model a peace agenda.
D. Hiring administrators and security personnel who have demonstrated success with the creation of a positive nonviolent environment, who operate with vigorous fairness and due process for dispute resolution, and who set the standard for respectful treatment of faculty, staff, and students.
E. Providing faculty and staff development for advanced knowledge, skills, and practice in the principles of peace, nonviolence, justice, and non-judgmental compassion.
F. Establishing a reward structure that recognizes contributions toward meeting this mission.

What Might Be Included in a Peace, Nonviolence and Justice Curriculum?

IV. **Ancient and global knowledge and age appropriate curricula can provide students with alternative perspectives and skills to critique and counteract the culture of violence and to advocate for peace and nonviolence towards all peoples, all species, and the environment.**

A curriculum meets this standard by:

A. Teaching critical analysis and investigation of media, censorship and propaganda.
B. Offering multiple opportunities to study philosophies, spiritual traditions, histories, and practices of peace, pacifism, non-violent resistance, non-violent action, and social justice.
C. Developing skills and habits of compassion, kindness, equity, peace, and advocacy for other peoples, other species, and the environment.
D. Studying international documents on war/peace, the environment, and social justice.
E. Studying social movements working for specific components of peace and non-violence, such as these adapted from the HAPJ:
    1. Establish universal international procedures for war crimes and human rights laws.
    2. Protection and reparations for victims and environmental damage created by war.
    3. Campaigns to stop the use of child soldiers.

4. Protection for advocates, humanitarians, peace workers, and whistle blowers.
5. Establish a universal system for habeas corpus.
6. Shift weapons production/sales and military budgets to positive human and environmental needs.
7. Work for disarmament and non-proliferation of all types of weapons: nuclear, depleted uranium, weapons in space, landmines, biological and chemical weapons, etc.
8. Hold nations and corporations accountable for damage to life and the environment, by:
   a. Developing skills in democratic citizenship including methods of evaluating candidates, exercising voting rights, monitoring campaigns and elections, investigating government decision-making and accountability.
   b. Developing knowledge and skills for global citizenship, demonstrating connections between everyday individual actions, collective organizing, and global well-being.

Conclusion

This chapter has sought to provide a practical and compact overview of some roots of violence and war, some key traditions and principles for peace and justice, and to present a guide to a few inspiring international documents that could be used as a foundation for peace education. The Tower of Violence and the Tower of Peace and Well-Being illustrate how these issues permeate all aspects of our lives and influence actions as individuals, as institutions, and as nations. Initial guidelines may help educators develop their own plans and actions.

Note

1. It is estimated that women may own less than 2% of the land (MacDonald & Nierenberg, 2003).
2. This quote is attributed to A. J. Muste (1885–1967), a pacifist, war resister, and social justice activist. This quote was retrieved from www.ajmuste.org on December 14, 2008.

References

Assembly of Alaska Native Educators (1998). *Alaska standards for culturally-responsive schools.* Fairbanks: Alaska Native Knowledge Network (www.ankn.uaf.edu)

Alison, A., & Solnit, D. (Eds.). (2007). *Army of none: Strategies to counter military recruitment, end war, and build a better world.* New York: Seven Stories Press.

Alper, L. (Producer and Director), & J. Earp (Co-director). (2007). *War made easy: How presidents and pundits keep spinning us to death.* [Documentary Film]. Northampton, MA: Media Education Foundation.

Barash, D. P. (2000). *Approaches to peace: A reader in peace studies.* New York: Oxford University Press.

Culture of Peace Network. (2004). *Values, attitudes and behaviors: Culture of war to culture of peace.* Retrieved October 12, 2007, from http://cpnn-world.org/learn/values.html

Davies, J. S., Sandstrom, A., Shorrocks, & Wolff, E. (2006, December 5). *World distribution of household wealth.* New York: World Institute for Development Economics Research of the United Nations University. Retrieved December 8, 2007, from www.wider.unu.edu/.../2006-2007-1/wider-wdhw-launch-5-12-2006/ wider-wdhw-powerpoint-presentation.pdf

Earth Charter. (2001). *The earth charter.* Earth Charter International Secretariat. Retrieved December 27, 2007, from http://www.earthcharter.org

Economist Intelligence Unit. (2007). *Global peace index.* Retrieved February 2, 2008, from http://www.visionofhumanity.com/artman/uploads/1/EIU_Report.pdf

Eisler, R. (2007, July 26). Dark underbelly of the world's most "peaceful" countries: Some nations that rank well in the global peace index are notorious for violence against women and children. *The Christian Science Monitor.* Retrieved August 2, 2007, from www.csmonitor.com/2007/0726/p09s01-coop.htm

Gandhi, M. (1961). *Non-violent resistance (satyagraha).* New York: Schocken Books.

Graduation Pledge Alliance. (2007). *The graduation pledge.* Retrieved December 30, 2007, from http://www.graduationpledge.org

Grossman, D., & DeGaetano, G. (1999). *Stop teaching our kids to kill: A call to action against tv, movie, and video game violence.* New York: Crown.

Grossman, Z. (2001, September 20). *A century of U.S. military interventions.* Retrieved July 10, 2007, from http://www.zmag.org/CrisesCurEvts/interventions.htm

Grossman, Z. (2007). *History of U.S. military interventions since 1890.* Retrieved July 10, 2007, from http:www.academic.evergreen.edu/g/grossmaz/interventions.html

Hague Agenda for Peace and Justice in the 21st Century-conference edition. (2000). Retrieved November 26, 2007, from http://www.haguepeace.org/resources/HagueAgendaPeace+Justice4The21stCentury.pdf

Iraq Veterans Against the War. (2008). *Winter soldier: Iraq and Afghanistan.* Retrieved on December 17, 2008 from http://ivaw.org/wintersoldier/testimony

Iyer, R. (1990). *The essential writings of Mahatma Gandhi.* London: Oxford University Press.

Jones, E., Haenfler, R.,& Johnson, B. (2007). *The better world handbook.* Gabriola Island, BC: New Society Publishers.

LaDuke, W. (1996, February 14). *Native American land struggles, environmentalism, and indigenous women.* Video of presentation at St. Cloud State University, St. Cloud, Minnesota.

MacDonald, M., & Nierenberg, D. (2003). Linking population, women, and biodiversity. In *State of the world 2003: A Worldwatch Institute report on progress toward a sustainable society* (pp. 38–61). New York: W.W. Norton.

Mainichi Daily News. (2007, August 6). Hiroshima peace declaration 2007: Aim for a nuclear weapon-free world. Retrieved August 10, 2007, from http://www.commondreams.org

Manifesto Against Conscription and the Military System. (1930). Retrieved December 29, 2007, from http://www.themanifesto.info/manifesto.htm

Marte, A., & W. Wheeler. (2007, November/December). The U.S. military: By the numbers. *The Defense Monitor, XXXVI*(6), 7.

Mills, C. W. (2007). Global white supremacy. In P. S. Rothenberg (Ed.), *White privilege: Essential readings on the other side of racism* (3rd ed. pp. 97–104). New York: Worth.

Moses, J. (2002). *Oneness: Great principles shared by all religions.* New York: Ballantine Books.

Nobel Peace Laureates. (2006, November 19). *Charter for a world without violence.* (First draft). Retrieved December 27, 2007, from http://www.nobelforpeace-summits.org/ENG/PDF/2006/CHARTER.pdf

Pax Christi Queensland. (2007, April 10). *Protect article 9 of Japan's peace constitution.* Retrieved December 30, 2007, from http://paxchristi-qld.blogspot.com/2007/04/protect-article-9-of-japans-peace.html

The Peace Alliance. (2007). U.S. department of peace legislation. Retrieved December 30, 2007, from http://www.thepeacealliance.org/content/view/84/111/

Picker, M., & Sun, C. (Producers). (2003). *Beyond good and evil: Children, media and violent times.* [Documentary Film]. Northampton, MA: Media Education Foundation.

Phillips, P., & Roth, A. (2008). *Censored 2009: The top 25 censored stories of 2007–2008.* New York: Seven Stories Press.

Right Livelihood Award. (2007). *The right livelihood awards.* Retrieved December 30, 2007 from http://www.righlivelihood.org

Robb, M. (Producer and Director). (2002). *Toxic sludge is good for you.* [Documentary Film]. Northampton, MA: Media Education Foundation.

Scahill, J. (2007). Blackwater: Hired guns, above the law. *The Nation.* Retrieved September 22, 2007, from http://www.commondreams.org/archive/2007/09/22/4016/print/

Seager, J. (2003). *The Penguin atlas of women in the world.* Brighton, UK: Penguin Books.

Shanker, T. (2007, October 1). US is top arms seller to developing world. *New York Times.* Retrieved November 18, 2007, from http://www.commondreams.org/archive/2007/10/01/4228/print/

Sharp, G. (1973). 198 methods of nonviolent action. *The politics of nonviolent action, Vol. 2: The methods of nonviolent action.* Boston: Porter Sargent.

Sharp, G., (2005). *Waging nonviolent struggle.* Boston: Extending Horizons Books.

Stone, M. (1996). 3000 years of racism. In J. R. Andrzejewski (Ed.), *Oppression and social justice: Critical frameworks* (5th ed., pp. 288–293). Needham Heights, MA: Simon and Schuster.

Thoreau, H. D. (1849). *Civil disobedience.* Retrieved on December 14, 2008, from http://eserver.org/thoreau/civil1.html

Tolstoy, L. (1894). The kingdom of god is within you. Constance Black Garnett (Trans.). Retrieved December 29, 2007, from http://www.online-literature.com/tolstoy/kingdom-of-god/

Tolstoy, L. (1899). How shall we escape? *The complete works of Lyof N. Tolstoi.* New York: Thomas Y. Crowell.

United Nations General Assembly. (1999). *United Nations manifesto 2000.* Retrieved November 15, 2007, from http://www3.unesco.org/manifesto2000/default.asp

United Nations Environmental Programme. (2007, October 25). *Global environmental outlook #4.* Retrieved December 27, 2007, from http://www.unep.org/geo/

United Nations General Assembly. (2000, September 18). *United Nations millennium declaration.* Retrieved December 27, 2007, from http://www.un.org/millennium/declaration/ares552e.pdf

Weill-Greenberg, E. (2006). *10 excellent reasons not to join the military.* New York: The New Press.

Winterfilm Collective in association with Vietnam Veterans Against the War, Directors and Producers. (1972). *Winter soldier.* Aronow, F. et al. USA.

Zepezauer, M. (2004). *Take the rich off welfare.* Boston: South End Press.

8 Social Responsibility and Teaching Young Children

An Education for Living in Ethical and Caring Ways

Beth Blue Swadener and Leigh M. O'Brien

> In the end we will conserve only what we love.
> We will love what we understand.
> We will understand only what we are taught. (Baba Dioum, Senegalese environmentalist, 1968)

Introduction

The impacts of global capitalism and neoliberal policies on domestic infrastructures have been extensively analyzed in terms of economic policies and practices in cross-national contexts (Bloch & Swadener, 2007; Kushnick & Jennings, 1999; Stiglitz, 2002; Wolfe & Vandell, 2002), but the existential impact on children and youth in terms of their daily lives has not been adequately articulated—or translated into policy and practice. As economic and political oppression threaten the development of children and their rights to a healthy childhood and access to education, the issue of children's rights becomes fundamental for any transformative educational or social welfare discourse (e.g., Amnesty International, 1998; Polakow, 2000; Soto & Swadener, 2005).

When attempting to understand and advocate for children's rights in a context of social and global justice, material and social circumstances must be understood in the context of concrete daily realities, across various environments. If children are to be treated with dignity and respect, there are certain universal norms of human capability that, Nussbaum (2000) argues, should form the basis for a set of constitutional principles that citizens have a right to demand from their governments so that children, too, are seen "as agents, each with a life to live, deserving of both respect and resources" (p. 25). This chapter is grounded in respect for the rights of all children and draws from our work with a number of professional and child advocacy organizations, as well as our related scholarship.

In 1999, a Critical Perspectives on Early Childhood Education (CPECE) special interest group (SIG) was founded within the American Educational Research Association (AERA). Attention to children's rights has been one of many broad themes of the critical/reconceptualist movement, with emphasis on respect for children and sensitivity to children's social and cultural contexts.[1] The theoretical interpretations and forms of research employed in reconceptualizing the field of early childhood education have emerged from individuals and groups focused on issues of social justice, equity, oppression and power, and diversity and opportunity. Reconceptualizing the field has included a focus on challenging "grand narratives" that serve to control and limit human beings, and recognizing and embracing diversity in ways of living and being in the world while acknowledging the sociopolitical and historical embeddedness in which all human life resides. Reconceptualist scholars and practitioners see a compelling need for this work in the context of public policy practices in the United States as well as around the world.

The focus on public policy comes from an acknowledgement that, to state the obvious, children are physically smaller and weaker than adults as well as too young to vote and to contribute much economically, and hence are typically voiceless. Because of this relative powerlessness and vulnerability, while many individuals and governments claim they care about children, children often bear the brunt of suffering in the world. Further, in many countries, including the United States, children's rights are weakly defined or ignored. For these reasons, most early childhood educators believe that adults must protect the rights of children in family, educational, and societal contexts.

This chapter has evolved over several years, with the input of a number of early childhood[2] scholars, advocates, educators, graduate students, parents of young children, and members of both the CPECE and Global Child Advocacy Special Interest Groups of AERA. Our work has also intersected with an initiative to identify core values for children and childhood in the United States, initiated by Tom Drummond at Northern Seattle Community College and involving a growing coalition of early childhood educators, teacher educators, and researchers. While members of the CPECE SIG, in particular, would resist prescriptive formulas or "master scripts"—even for social justice, environmental responsibility, and peace—we have put forward some general guiding principles or recommendations for work with and for young children. These principles focus on children's rights, transcend geopolitical location, and cross a number of theoretical, cultural, and ideological borders.

We feel strongly that our present world requires a commitment to interdependence for a more just society and for the sustainability of our physical and social environments. Living in harmony with each other and the natural world have to become our collective priorities. Children and adults must become more aware of what is happening around them and share the responsibility for effecting change. As Ebbeck asserts, "it is our responsibility as educators to foster in children … the capacity to think critically and to reflect on their actions and the actions of others, so that they will, themselves, grow in understanding of their world and all that is in it, and be poised to make a contribution" (2006, p. 356). We have taken up this work because we want to see more early educators join social movements that emphasize humane and ecological values rather than commercial/capitalist and military ones. We believe our work as educators will not be diluted but rather strengthened by our participation in wider struggles for social and ecological justice.

In this chapter we first describe the state of children and childhood around the world. We then briefly review earlier statements and discuss how themes within the early childhood reconceptualist community (and other groups in the field) relate to the themes of this project. Next we identify and describe a number of relevant children's rights as well as key organizations and documents that frame and inform our work. Following this, we discuss grounding theories and research, which then leads to a statement of guiding principles and recommendations based on the pressing children's issues identified. In the final section of this chapter we pose questions relating to students, schools, and communities for early educators to consider.

The State of the World's Children

While we continue to make some progress, the state of the world's children remains precarious. The UNICEF Press Centre (2007) tells us that, although young children's survival and development is the first right of the child, more than 10 million children under the age of 5 die each year. Two-thirds of neonatal and young child deaths—over 6 million deaths each year—are preventable. Many of these deaths are due to inadequate nutrition/clean water and medical care. For example, in 2004, 5.6 million children under 5 died because of undernutrition, and more than 20 million children are born with low birth weight each year. In wealthier countries and among middle- and upper-class children worldwide, childhood obesity is becoming a major issue, and advertising of high-sugar, low-nutritional foods and beverages targeting children has been the subject of increasing medical and public concern. This has also translated into some recent local regulations and legislation in the United States, related to school lunches, availability of soda and "junk food" vending machines, and school-based advertising of such products.

While more than 1.2 billion people gained access to improved drinking water sources and sanitation facilities between 1990 and 2004, more than 125 million children under age 5 live in households without access to an improved water source, and more than 280 million children under age 5 lived in households without access to improved sanitation facilities. Unsafe drinking water, inadequate availability of water for hygiene, and lack of access to sanitation together contribute to about 88% of deaths from diarrheal diseases; more than 5,000 children die every day as a result of diarrhea.

In terms of immunizations, the good news is that immunization coverage of infants for the six major vaccine-preventable diseases has risen from less than 5% to more than 80% in 2004. It is estimated that the vaccinations done in 2003 alone will prevent more than 2 million deaths from vaccine-preventable diseases and an additional 600,000 deaths from Hepatitis B. Despite these achievements, in 2003 an estimated 27 million children below the age of one remained in need of immunization, and in 2004, an estimated 1.4 million children under age 5 died from the six major vaccine-preventable diseases, with an additional 1.1 million deaths from pneumonia and rotavirus. Further, in 2006 an estimated 2.3 million children under age 5 were living with HIV and every day almost 1,500 children worldwide become infected with HIV, the vast majority of them newborns infected through mother-to-child transmission. In addition to infection rates, millions of children, particularly in sub-Saharan Africa, have been orphaned by AIDS, which has also meant that they are less likely to attend school or receive adequate nutrition and health care—not to mention social and emotional support.

An estimated 300 million children worldwide are subjected to violence, exploitation, and abuse including the worst forms of child labor in communities, schools, and institutions; during armed conflict; and to harmful practices such as female genital mutilation/cutting and child marriage. It is estimated that 5.7 million children are trapped into forced or bonded labor, and some 1.2 million children are trafficked worldwide each year. In developing countries, 36% of women are married before age 18, and more than 250,000 children are currently serving as child soldiers. Further, there are an estimated 133 million children who are orphans worldwide, 40%–50% of the people involved in forced commercial sexual exploitation are children, and it is estimated that more than 130 million women and girls alive today have been subjected to female genital mutilation/cutting.

While education is also a basic human right, according to 2002 estimates, approximately 115 million children are out of school. Globally, more than 53% of the children out of primary school are girls, a sobering statistic as educating girls is the key to insuring the next generation receives an education. To achieve universal primary education by 2015, enrollment must increase globally by an average of 1.3% per year over the next 8 years (UNICEF Press Centre, 2007).

A recent report produced by the Organization for Economic Co-operation and Development, *Starting Strong II: Early Childhood Education and Care*, presents the results of research on public expenditures on early care and education by industrialized nations. When comparing public expenditures on early care and education services for children birth to age 6 as a percentage of a nation's Gross Domestic Product (GDP), the report reveals that the United States and Canada both rank in the lower tier. In the top tier are Denmark, Sweden, Norway, Finland, and France, countries that expend at least 1% of their GDP on early care and education. In the lowest tier, countries expending less than .5% of their GDP on early care and education are the United States, Canada, Netherlands, Germany, Italy, and Australia. Could this be one of the reasons why children's experiences and rights in North America are so proscribed?

Add to all this the mass extinction of many species, both plant and animal; the looming and unprecedented changes taking place worldwide due to global warming; genetically engineered plants being introduced with little fanfare and virtually no precautions; the continued rampant production and use of toxic and carcinogenic chemicals and radioactive waste; the lack of concern about population growth as we are rapidly destroying the air, water, and land; and the use of finite global resources to produce and use weapons, and it is clear that much on earth is amiss. These and many more indicators point to a bleak future for current and future generations of children. What actions must be taken immediately to address these compelling issues? How can educators play a vital role?

Children's Rights in Global Context

Because children are both the present and the future of every nation—and, in many cases, the fastest growing age group—they have needs, rights, and intrinsic worth that must be recognized and supported. We believe children's basic rights include but are not limited to the following, all of which, except the last, are taken from the U.N. Convention on the Rights of the Child (CRC, 1989).

The Rights of the Child

- the right to life
- the right (from birth) to a name, the right to acquire a nationality, and, as far as possible, the right to know and be cared for by his or her parents
- to the child who is capable of forming his or her own views, the right to express those views freely in all matters affecting the child
- the right to freedom of thought, conscience, and religion
- the rights to freedom of association and to freedom of peaceful assembly
- the right to the protection of the law against arbitrary or unlawful interference with his or her privacy, family, home, or correspondence, and to unlawful attacks on his or her honor and reputation
- the right to access to information and material from a diversity of national and international sources
- the right to, as needed, special protection and assistance provided by the State
- the right to a full and decent life for all children, including those with disabilities
- the right to the enjoyment of the highest attainable standard of health and to facilities for the treatment of illness and rehabilitation of health
- the right of a child who has been placed by the competent authorities for the purposes of care, protection, or treatment of his or her physical or mental health, to a periodic review of the treatment provided to the child and all other circumstances relevant to his or her placement
- the right to benefit from social security, including social insurance
- the right to a standard of living adequate for the child's physical, mental, spiritual, moral, and social development
- the right to education, with a view to achieving this right progressively and on the basis of equal opportunity
- the right to enjoy his or her own culture, to profess and practice his or her own religion, and to use his or her own language
- the right to rest and leisure, to engage in play and recreational activities appropriate to the age of the child, and to participate freely in cultural life and the arts
- the right to be protected from economic exploitation and from performing any work that is likely to be hazardous or to interfere with the child's education, or to be harmful to the child's health or physical, mental, spiritual, moral, or social development

- the right of every child alleged as, accused of, or recognized as having infringed the penal law to be treated in a manner consistent with the promotion of the child's sense of dignity and worth, and which takes into account the child's age and the desirability of promoting the child's reintegration and the child's assuming a constructive role in society
- the right to clean air and water, and to a non-toxic environment (U.N. Decade of Education for Sustainable Development, 1989)

It is clear that many of these rights are abrogated by the current state of children and childhood worldwide; hence there is much important work for educators, advocates, policymakers, and state and national leaders ahead. In addition to the CRC, which we strongly urge the United States to fully adopt[3] and enact, our work is informed by a wide array of national and international documents, visions, and agreements that address children's rights, a number of which are specifically focused on the early childhood years. Since, for a number of reasons,[4] the United States has been remiss in attending to children's rights at home and on the international stage, many of the documents and movements/organizations we call on to frame our work[5] have been created outside the country.

Recommendations for Early Childhood Guiding Principles

Despite the clear and present need for a stronger focus on children's rights in early childhood, the task of recommending guiding principles grounded in social justice and eco-justice for young children has been a challenging one, particularly in the context of the Critical Perspectives on Early Childhood SIG. An earlier attempt to provide principles to guide our work was made at the 11th Reconceptualizing Early Childhood Research, Policy and Practice Conference, held in Tempe, Arizona, in January, 2003. A statement was drafted and endorsed by the over 120 participants from 14 countries and was then modified and submitted by the Global Child Advocacy SIG for the project addressed by this book. In the following section, we consolidate these rights and principles into a set of 12 recommendations.

Early Childhood Guiding Principles

Recommendation 1:
In all actions relating to children, the child's best interests must be a primary consideration. Above all, we shall not harm children. We shall not participate in practices that are emotionally damaging, physically harmful, disrespectful, degrading, dangerous, exploitative, or intimidating to children.

Examples of ways to apply this recommendation include:

A. Children learning about the rights of all human beings (and other species) and applying those rights to themselves and other children and youth;
B. Curricula for students that are built around the CRC and are used for integrated social studies and language arts units that could have historical,

geographic, and/or local foci, for example, studying child labor through various perspectives;

C. Increasing awareness of children to realize when one is being exploited or abused and learning various ways to prevent and resist harm in different situations;
D. Collaborating with community-based groups and child advocacy groups focused on preventing and addressing child abuse and promoting child welfare.

Recommendation 2:

Adults must ensure that children are encouraged to express their views freely. Such views and perspectives shall be taken into consideration on matters which concern them (e.g., in public decision-making) in accordance with their age and maturity. All programs and initiatives serving children[6] should respect children as young human beings (Cannella, 1997) with rights, voice, and agency. Such programs are strongly encouraged to include young people by involving them in policies and institutions that directly affect their social and educational lives (Hallett & Prout, 2003).[7]

Examples of ways to apply this recommendation include:

A. Encouraging respect for *all* children's opinions in both the classroom and wider society;
B. At the classroom level, using frequent group discussions and consensus decision-making, or other means of arriving at rules and responsibilities that involve children;
C. At the level of civil society, directly involving children and youth in the process of setting policies and monitoring services that affect them; there are abundant examples of ways in which local municipalities and service agencies (c.f., Hallett & Prout, 2003) through national governments remaking their constitutions (e.g., c.f., Cheney, 2007, for the case of Uganda) have directly involved children and youth in the process.

Recommendation 3:

Since every child is entitled to a good and happy childhood, adults must promote the well-being of children and of families with children, increase respect for childhood, and seek to make it more visible.

Examples of ways to apply this recommendation include:

A. Promoting child-centered and "emergent" curriculum that do not impose adult-determined content, but take into account the interests of young children;
B. Focusing on children's rights and empowerment. For instance, in the early childhood programs of Reggio Emilia, Italy, they refer to children with disabilities as children with "special rights," and their image of the child includes descriptors such as strong, rich in potential, and beautiful (Edwards, Gandini, & Forman, 1998). Similarly, the North American

Reggio Emilia Alliance (NAREA) envisions a world where all children are honored and respected for their potentials, capabilities, and humanity (see http://www.reggioalliance.org/);

C. Viewing children as active learners who draw on direct physical and social experience as well as culturally transmitted knowledge to construct their own understandings of the world around them (see, e.g., Bredekamp & Copple, 1997);
D. Promoting policies and practices that support children's healthy development, love of learning, and joy in living (see, e.g., the Alliance for Childhood at http://www.allianceforchildhood.net). This alliance acts for the sake of the children themselves and for a more just, democratic, and ecologically responsible future.

Recommendation 4:
Although the concept of sustainable development has been critiqued (see, for example, Gruenewald, Manteaw, & Smith, this volume), we believe the creativity, ideals, and courage of the youth of the world should be mobilized to forge a global partnership in order to achieve a sustainable future for all.[8]

Examples of ways to apply this recommendation include:

A. Building curricula around themes of earth-keeping, eco-justice, or human-rights-focused topics of study;
B. Saying "no" to those elements of our lives and ways that are unsustainable, and teaching children to do the same;
C. Teaching children to do no harm—to any part of the natural world;
D. Focusing on educating the whole child and whole, interdependent learning;
E. Connecting the world's children with the natural world; age-, individually, and culturally appropriate nature education should be a sustaining and enriching part of the daily lives of children (see, e.g., the World Forum Foundation/the Nature Action Collaboration for Children).[9]

Recommendation 5:
Basic education should be provided to all children, youth, and adults.

As noted, the world faces daunting problems and these problems constrain efforts to meet basic learning needs, while the lack of basic education among a significant proportion of the population prevents societies from addressing such problems with strength and purpose. The right to education, then, is clearly linked with social justice, peace, and environmental preservation.

Examples of ways to apply this recommendation include:

A. Supporting UNESCO's Education for All (EFA; 1990) initiative. In particular, girls and female youth have still not obtained educational parity in participation in many countries. A number of issues prevent their full participation in education ranging from cultural beliefs about early marriage or religious restrictions to lack of sanitary products and even underwear, keeping some girls out of school every month for up to one week;

B. Working for full access to quality early care and education for all children in order to reduce social and educational exclusions in terms of class, language, ability, and citizenship, recognizing that these exclusions lead to high drop-out rates in some communities.

Recommendation 6:

Although this recommendation overlaps with the preceding one, we think it is important to emphasize that educators must envision school and life successes for *all* children, through linguistically, culturally, and ecologically responsive early childhood learning environments. Further, governments and community leaders must promote the education of girls and women worldwide as a potent antidote to global poverty.

Examples of ways to apply this recommendation include:

A. Educators create safe, caring, respectful, and productive learning environments that consider and build on the diverse needs of the children and the communities where they are working;

B. Educators see young children as "of promise" (Swadener & Lubeck, 1995), and work with their governments to insure that all young children are well cared for and educated.

Recommendation 7:

We must fight ageism as it impacts young children and interacts with other forms of social exclusion and oppression. This recommendation requires that we view young children as full human beings.

Examples of ways to apply this recommendation include:

A. Students' rights to know and to act on that knowledge are clearly identified. For instance, in South Australia "*equity is a key curriculum consideration. Learners come to recognize the nature and causes of inequality, and understand that these are socially constructed and can therefore be changed through people's actions*" (http://www.sacsa.sa.edu.au/index_fsrc.asp?t=ECCP);

B. Early educators foreground the principles of holistic development, empowerment, family and community, and relationships;

C. Curriculum strands include well-being, belonging, contribution, communication, and exploration;

D. Early learning and development is seen as occurring within a sociocultural context, and emphasizes the learning partnership between teachers, parents, and families;

E. Teachers weave a holistic curriculum in response to children's learning and development in the early childhood setting and the wider context of the child's world (see http://www.teachnz.govt.nz/curriculum.html).

Recommendation 8:
All governments must protect children and their families from homelessness, hunger, and destitution, and, consonant with Article 24 of the Convention on the Rights of the Child, provide health care to all children, regardless of ability to pay.

This recommendation, as well as Recommendations 9 and 10, which are likewise focused on governmental actions, demand that early educators commit to a life of advocacy for young children and families. As the saying goes, children can't vote—but adults can. We can also write letters, join action-oriented groups, call our representatives, picket, protest, be a part of resistance movements, and so forth. We can also work to find more ways for children's voices to be heard and to support youth-led movements. Given the state of the world's children, we can do no less.

Recommendation 9:
The U.S. government and its allies must pursue, by peaceful and diplomatic means, a resolution of all conflicts across the globe, so that children are not victims of warfare and its corollaries or forcibly conscribed.

Recommendation 10:
The governments of affluent democracies must regulate living and labor conditions in their own countries to alleviate and prevent poverty and economic exploitation of children, and use the forces of globalization to raise living and labor conditions in poor and less affluent countries and to actively work against the exploitation of women and children for global profits.

Recommendation 11:
Adults must ensure that children have the right to such protection and care as is necessary for their well-being. Governments must implement and monitor protections worldwide that protect the young from the brutality of sexual slavery and the global trafficking in children across borders.

Examples of ways to apply this recommendation include:

A. Recognizing that every society has policies and practices that cause harm to children, and these (economic, social, cultural, and political) practices must be critically examined to determine what is harmful to children and work to prevent and stop these practices. Some examples include: (1) child labor, slavery, or trafficking; (2) malnutrition and hunger; (3) lack of clean air and water; (4) lack of adequate health care; (5) sexual abuse and assault; (6) unnecessary surgeries of any kind; and (7) homelessness;
B. Commit to political involvement as outlined in the preceding Recommendations.

Recommendation 12:
All of society is called upon to join a global movement to build a world fit for children.

Examples of ways to apply this recommendation include:

A. Make attention to belonging, well-being, reciprocity, participation, joy, wholeness, and trust central to early childhood practice addressing peace, social justice, and environmental education;
B. Embracing an anti-racism/anti-oppression approach; making equity the key principle in decision making; and caring for and protecting the environment;
C. Integrating conflict resolution, social and emotional learning, and appreciation for diversity into developmentally appropriate practice and curriculum;
D. Asking, is our city (or town) child-friendly?[10] A child-friendly city actively works to fulfill the right of every young citizen to influence decisions about the city; express their opinions on the city they want; participate in family, community, and social life; receive basic services such as health care and education; drink safe water and have access to proper sanitation; be protected from exploitation, violence, and abuse; walk safely in the streets; meet friends and play; have green spaces for plants and animals; live in an unpolluted environment; participate in cultural and social events; and be an equal citizen with access to every service (see http://www.childfriendlycities.org).

Closing Thoughts

Our fundamental beliefs regarding children and childhood include the following: (1) Childhood is a critical phase of life and must be protected to be fully experienced. It should not be hurried; and (2) each child deserves respect as an individual. Each needs help in developing his or her own unique capacities and in finding ways to weave them into a healthy social fabric. Drawing on the slow-food movement premises, Maurice Holt suggests educators concerned with equipping our children with the ability and inclination to act responsibly in a complex world consider Slow Schools. A Slow School suggests an institution where even the youngest students have time to discuss, argue, and reflect upon knowledge and ideas. In such a school, the professional judgment of teachers would be esteemed, students' differing interests and talents would be recognized, and the community would be involved in providing a rich variety of learning experiences. The concept of "Slow" derives its power as a metaphor from its moral force. It is about what is good to do which entails making judgments about conduct, virtue, and balance. Might such an approach help us address the multifaceted moral and political dilemmas we face?

More broadly, early childhood educators might ask, does our teacher education and professional development support the principles articulated here? How can we find work to do—for ourselves and our children—that bears some dignity and earthly discipline: good stories, large fields of thought, "big ideas" that need children to re-think them? Does the curriculum encourage all children to see themselves as social and environmental problem solvers capable of making the world a better place? Is there broad representation of community organizations in the life of the school/center (e.g., environmental and social justice organizations)? Does the curriculum have real-life links? (See, for example, the Edible Schoolyard at www.edibleschoolyard.org.) Is the learning environment protected from chemical ingredients of unknown or potentially harmful effects (e.g., cleaning solutions, herbicides, and pesticides)?

We might also ask, how can we develop and sustain an approach to early childhood education that foregrounds eco-pedagogy and is grounded in eco-justice principles? Are we teaching basic ecological knowledge, one of the key components of ecological literacy?[11] Do our early care and education programs help to bring nature back into the forefront of children's lives (Louv, 2005)? Are we educating students on environmental issues and preparing them to be the stewards of their natural resources? Do we support an integrated, experiential core curriculum with ecologically oriented learning experiences (e.g., the maintenance of a community garden; recycling, reduction, and composting of waste; and a basic understanding of the principles of sustainability)? In sum, how can we ensure that social justice, peace, and environmental education are integrated into and integral to our practices? Might this be a starting place for early educators?

We end our chapter with concerns as well as hope, both of which can be found in the 2007 UNICEF report subtitled, "an overview of child well-being in rich countries." The bad news is that the U.S. and the U.K. tie for last place of the 20 richest nations in overall child well-being. The good news is the measures used—which include material well-being, health and safety, educational well-being, family and peer relationships, behaviors and risks, and subjective well-being—provide clear goals and can help us assess our progress on children's rights. To be sure, addressing young children's well-being is a complex process and an ongoing challenge for all of us.

We believe that taking these rights and recommendations seriously requires that early care and education be oriented toward and supportive of peaceful coexistence, social justice, and care for the environment. We also believe that by attending with care and solicitude to children's unalienable rights to social justice, peace, and a healthy environment, we can teach them to understand, love, and conserve the world. It is our hope that we have in some small way contributed to that process.

Notes

1. We support social justice principles for children and youth that reflect local/national definitions of childhood.
2. In the United States, the term "early childhood" usually refers to children birth to age eight (see, e.g., Bredekamp & Copple, 1997). This age group is our chapter focus.
3. The United States is among a small group of non-signers that includes Iran, Iraq, Libya, Ethiopia, and South Africa. As of 2007, 193 countries have ratified the Convention, demonstrating their commitment to universal child welfare. Despite the fact that the United States was a crucial participant in the decade-long drafting

process, the U.S. and Somalia remain the only two nations affiliated with the U.N. who have not ratified this agreement.

4. Perhaps the main reason is because capitalism comprises a complex tissue of values and beliefs, ultimately producing "...a ruthless totalizing [and increasingly globalized] process that shapes our lives in every conceivable aspect, subjecting all social life to the abstract requirements of the market" (McLaren, cited in Brosio, 2000, p. 401).
5. The European Union Charter of Fundamental Rights (2000), Children's Rights, Article 24; The Mannerheim League for Child Welfare; Reggio Children; The United Nations Special Session on Children, A World Fit for Children (Oct. 11, 2002); U.N. Conference on the Environment & Development (1992), Principle 21; The World Declaration of Education for All (UNESCO, 1990); the Universal Declaration of Human Rights (1948); National Association for the Education of Young Children (NAEYC); Association for Childhood Education International (ACEI); The Early Childhood Equity Initiative; Educators for Social Responsibility; The Vision for Children and Childhood Project; International Covenant on Civil and Political Rights (ICCPR); Canada's National Agenda for Children.
6. These include but are not limited to child care and early education settings, health care programs, child protective services, advocacy projects, and community programs.
7. Quoting from that book (Prout, 2003, p. 22): "... for greater public or political representation of children, [we] have to overcome widespread ideas about children's supposed incapacity to contribute usefully to public debate. In turn, for children's voice to be really heard, even when the institutional arrangements create a notional space for it, requires change in the way that children are seen."
8. The United Nations has decreed 2005–2014 as the Decade for Education for Sustainable Development. In the announcing this campaign, the U.N. declared:
   "There can be few more pressing and critical goals for the future of humankind than to ensure steady improvement in the quality of life for this and future generations, in a way that respects our common heritage—the planet we live on. As people we seek positive change for ourselves, our children, and grandchildren; we must do it in ways that respect the right of all to do so. To do this we must learn constantly—about ourselves, our potential, our limitations, our relationships, our society, our environment, our world. Education for sustainable development is a life-wide and lifelong endeavor which challenges individuals, institutions, and societies to view tomorrow as a day that belongs to all of us, or it will not belong to anyone." (Coad, n.d.)
9. See http://www.worldforumfoundation.org. Their mission is to reconnect children with the natural world by making developmentally appropriate nature education a sustaining and enriching part of the daily lives of the world's children, with a primary focus on age birth to 8 years.
10. This is a question suggested by UNICEF's Child-Friendly Cities initiative.
11. See http://www.ecoliteracy.org/education/sustainability.html.

References

Amnesty International. (1998, November). *Betraying the young: Children in the U.S. justice system.* Washington, DC: Author.

Bloch, M. N., & Swadener, B.B. (2007). "Education for all"—Social inclusions and exclusions: Introduction and critical reflections. *International Journal of Educational Policy, Research & Practice: Reconceptualizing Childhood Studies, 8*(1), 2–11.

Bredekamp, S., & Copple, C. (Eds.). (1997). *Developmentally appropriate practice in early childhood programs serving children from birth through age 8* (Expanded ed.). Washington, DC: National Association for the Education of Young Children.

Brosio, R. A. (2000). *Philosophical scaffolding for the construction of critical democratic education.* New York: Peter Lang.

Cannella, G. S. (1997). *Deconstructing early childhood education: Social justice and revolution.* New York: Peter Lang.

Coad, S. (n.d.). Values and sustainability: Educating for a sustainable future, p. 12. Retrieved December 10, 2008, from http://www.decs.sa.gov.au/valueseducation/files/links/Values_and_Sustainable_Fut.pdf

Cheney, K.E. (2007). *Pillars of the nation: Child citizens and Ugandan national development.* Chicago: The University of Chicago Press.

Dioum, B. (1968). Speech to the General Assembly of the International Union for Conservation of Nature, New Delhi, India. Retrieved December 12, 2008 from http://everything2.com/index.pl?node_id=1482909

Ebbeck, M. (2006). The challenges of global citizenship: Some issues for policy and practice in early childhood. *Childhood Education, 82*(6), 353–357.

Edwards, C., Gandini, L., & Forman, G. (1998). *The hundred languages of children: The Reggio Emilia approach—advance reflections* (2nd ed.). Westport, CT: Ablex.

Hallett, C., & Prout, A. (Eds.). (2003). *Hearing the voices of children: Social policy for a new century.* London: RoutledgeFalmer.

Holt, M. (n.d.). The nature and purpose of education. Retrieved July 2008, from http://www.ecoliteracy.org/publications/rsl/maurice-holt.html

Kushnick, L., & Jennings, J. (Eds.). (1999). *A new introduction to poverty: The role of race, power, and politics.* New York: New York University Press.

Louv, R. (2005). *Last child in the woods: Saving our children from nature-deficit disorder.* New York: Algonquin Books.

Miller, R. (1992). *What are schools for? Holistic education in American culture* (2nd Rev. ed.). Brandon, VT: Holistic Education Press.

Nussbaum, M. (2000). *Women and human development: The capabilities approach.* Cambridge, UK: Cambridge University Press.

Polakow, V. (2000). *The public assault on America's children: Poverty, violence, and juvenile injustice.* New York: Teachers College Press.

Prout, A. (2003). Participation, policy and the changing conditions of childhood. In C. C. Hallett & A. Hallet (Eds.), *Hearing the voices of children: Social policy for a new century* (pp. 11–25). London: Routledge/Falmer.

Soto, L. D., & Swadener, B.B. (2005). *Power and voice in research with children.* New York: Peter Lang.

Starting Strong II: Early Childhood Education and Care. (2006). Washington, DC: Organization for Economic Cooperation and Development, OECD Publishing.

Stiglitz, J. (2002, Winter). Globalism's discontents. *The American Prospect*, A16–A21.

Swadener, B. B., & Lubeck, S. (1995). *Children and families "At Promise": Deconstructing the discourse of risk.* Albany: State University of New York Press.

U.N. Decade of Education for Sustainable Development, 2005–2014. (1989, November 20). Article 40; Convention on the Rights of the Child. Retrieved February 2008 from http://www.unhchr.ch/html/menu3/b/k2crc.htm

UNESCO. (1990). The World Declaration of Education for All. Retrieved April 4, 2007, from http://portal.unesco.org/education/en/ev.php-URL_ID=9213&URL_DO=DO_TOPIC&URL_SECTION=201.html

UNICEF. (2007). Child poverty in perspective: An overview of child well-being in rich countries. Retrieved April 4, 2007. from http://www.unicef-icdc.org/publications/pdf/rc7_eng.pdf

UNICEF. (2007). UNICEF Press Centre: Facts on children. Retrieved May 8, 2007. from http://www.unicef.org/media/media_fastfacts.html

Wolfe, B., & Vandell, D. B. (2002, Summer). Welfare reform depends on good child care. *The American Prospect*, A19–21.

9 Interspecies Education for Humans, Animals, and the Earth

Julie Andrzejewski, Helena Pedersen, and Freeman Wicklund

> The animals of the world exist for their own reasons. They were not made for humans any more than black people were made for whites or women for men. (Alice Walker, cited in Spiegel, 1996, p. 14)

The Need for Interspecies Education

Through various cultural, religious, and philosophical traditions, most educational institutions teach the position that human beings are the highest, most advanced species on earth. Depending upon the particular tradition, the earth and other species are commonly viewed as existing for human use, control, domination, or "stewardship." Even though people are aware that humans are biologically animals too, non-human animals are viewed as "other" in the most profound sense. This chapter will examine the consequences of this anthropocentric (human centered) education on the well-being of humans and animals for justice, peace, and ecological survival.

By any definition, it can be argued that non-human animals are subjected to *oppression*. Under Young's five faces of oppression (1990) non-human animals are *exploited* as their bodies are used for labor, food, clothing, research, education, entertainment, and more "products" than one can imagine, making it almost impossible to avoid their consumption on a daily basis. *Marginalization* takes on new meaning as non-human animals have little to no space on earth to exist where their lives are free of the negative effects of human activities and they are regularly and systemically "subjected to severe material deprivation and even extermination" (p. 53). We have learned to identify our species as "the norm" and the mental, emotional, and physical attributes of all other species are measured, categorized, and devalued in relation to that norm (Young calls this *cultural imperialism*). Under extreme domination of the earth by humans and our technologies, other animals are *powerless* to change their conditions and cannot avoid the many forms of *violence* perpetrated against them. While animal protection and rights groups struggle to bring the suffering of animals to public attention, the oppression of other animals has yet to be considered a legitimate area of social justice, peace, or environmental education. This chapter seeks to aid readers who care about all of these issues to understand the importance of integrating interspecies education into their schools and classrooms.

In contrast to a human centered approach, interspecies education is founded in the holistic process of learning that all forms of life on earth are interconnected and interdependent with one another (Selby, 1995). This implies an educational approach emphasizing that compassion and a sense of justice extends to all humankind, to individual animals, and to all species and ecosystems. Under this definition, students should be able to study, compare, and investigate the interrelationships of species with one another, especially the effects of various human policies and practices on other species. Further, they should have an opportunity to explore what actions can alleviate, prevent, or repair harm to other species.

The knowledge base for critical interspecies education is presented as follows:

1. How is the well-being of humans interdependent with the well-being of other animals? In other words, why is it in human self-interest to learn about and act to protect animals?
2. What is speciesism and why should interspecies education be given the same study and critical examination as other issues of global significance?
3. How is the treatment of other animals and species interrelated with social justice, peace, and ecological survival?

A set of principles, based on these questions, will assist in the integration of interspecies education into schools and curricula for students, teachers, administrators, school personnel, and teacher educators.

Knowledge Base Question #1: How Is the Well-being of Humans Interdependent with the Well-being of Other Animals?

While it may appear beneficial to human beings to use animals for food, clothing, research, education, entertainment, and sport, the negative consequences of these activities for humans are actually quite severe and are rapidly becoming even more deadly. Many belief systems, including aspects of Western science, have evolved to justify human maltreatment, neglect, slaughter, or extermination of other animals, but the consequences to humans, animals, and the ecosystem continue to accrue nonetheless.

Conversely, the benefits (to humans) of biodiversity, intact forests, free flowing rivers, plant-based diets, and respect for the lives of other animals with their own intelligences, talents, and methods of communication are only beginning to be recognized by industrial societies. Long known by many indigenous cultures (LaDuke, 2005) and spiritual traditions like Jainism, Hinduism, and Buddhism (Randour, 2000; Phelps, 2004), models exist for people who seek to live in harmony with, rather than domination over, other beings (Stepaniak, 2000). In the West, consciousness of finite natural resources (e.g. water shortages, peak oil, etc.) has finally raised questions about what is meant by sustainability. Does it mean sustaining a lifestyle of exploitation of other beings or sustaining the earth and its life forms? The right to investigate these issues from new perspectives may hold the key to human well-being.

Because the everyday lives of human beings are permeated with the habitual and unconscious use of animal products, we may find ourselves hesitant to delve into studies that may challenge us to re-evaluate some of the beliefs or behaviors we have been taught. However, key example may illuminate the benefits of including human/animal relations as a core component of education. Let us explore the question: *What are the costs and benefits of eating animals and animal products?* For the most part, schools only teach the *benefits*. While educators want to provide sound nutritional information to students, many of the materials used in elementary and middle schools for decades have been provided "free" from the meat and dairy industries—indoctrinating children into the "necessity" of eating meat, eggs, and dairy at every meal, ostensibly to get adequate protein. To reinforce their marketing message from an "independent" source, these industries have been influential in determining government dietary guidelines. Even as evidence began to accumulate about harmful aspects of their products and the benefits of eating grains, fruits, and vegetables, these industries were successful in assuring that meat, eggs, and dairy were still prominently featured in the government recommended food pyramid.

So, what are the *costs* to humans of eating meat, eggs, and dairy products? The following well-documented consequences of eating animals and animal products are rarely included in the school curriculum at any level, even in universities:

- Meat, eggs, and dairy products are a prominent contributing factor in cardiovascular and heart disease, cancers, diabetes, and other deadly and debilitating diseases (Jacobson, 2006; Nierenberg, 2005; Robbins, 2001).
- While 840 million people suffer from chronic hunger, approximately 70% of the world's grains are fed to animals to produce meat and dairy products (Global Hunger Alliance, 2002).
- Modern animal agriculture (factory farming) uses a large amount of the world's fresh water resources, pumps water from aquifers at unsustainable rates, and pollutes other water systems with manure (Barlow & Clarke, 2002).
- Animal agriculture is a key factor in the desertification of large areas of arable land.
- Beef production is a major factor in the forcible removal of indigenous peoples from their ancestral lands as forests are razed or land is shifted from growing food crops for local people to feeding cows who will be exported and eaten (Rifkin, 1992; Robbins, 2001).
- Cutting down forests for grazing is the leading cause of species becoming extinct or threatened in tropical rainforests and the United States (Robbins, 2001; Motavalli, 2008).
- The 1 billion cows in the world (amounting to nearly double the weight of human beings in the world) have a significant impact on soil, land, and grasses that replace natural forest and prairie vegetation (Robbins, 2001, p. 291).
- Animals raised for food contribute to global warming directly producing about "25% of the anthropogenic methane emissions (those based in human activity)" (Robbins, 2001, p. 267). Further, a heavily meat- and fish-

based diet "generates about 1.5 metric tons of carbon dioxide more per person per year than a plant-based diet yielding the same amount of calories" (Nierenberg, 2006, p. 7; Eshel & Martin, 2006).

- Overuse of antibiotics in factory farming renders them ineffective against human diseases.
- When countries become more affluent, their populations emulate a Western lifestyle by increasing consumption of meat and dairy products and the problems listed above (Delgado, 2003; Motavalli, 2008).

Other areas of human/animal relations have consequences just as serious to humans, to the environment, and to the animals themselves. How is scientific research on animals actually dangerous for humans (Greek & Greek, 2002)? Can different ethical standards about research on human beings versus other animals be justified? What is the relationship between violence against animals and violence against humans? How is factory farming implicated in the development of the Avian flu, mad cow disease, AIDS, and other diseases (Greger, 2006)? What harm is there in zoos or aquariums (Pedersen, 2007)? Aren't they helping to conserve endangered species? What is the empty forest syndrome and how are neocolonialism and resulting human impoverishment driving it? Why has the deer population exploded and isn't hunting the best way to contain it? What happens to animals used for fur? Why are honeybees dying? Our lives intersect with the lives of other animals in important ways yet many, if not most, of these interactions are not included in education or we are purposefully misinformed in order to maintain certain markets.

National and international documents developed over many years by nonprofit and advocacy organizations have much to offer educators and schools interested in addressing some of the crucial issues of human animal relations. The Animals' Platform (2009) presents position papers and legislative platforms on animal issues for education and action. It introduces six animal protection areas: 1) companion animals, 2) animals in agriculture, 3) animals in research, testing, and education, 4) wildlife, 5) captive wildlife, and 6) humane education.

The Humane Society of the United States Statement of Principles and Beliefs (2006) and the Living Planet Report (Loh, 2008) can stimulate exciting classroom investigations on animals. The U.S. Endangered Species Act (1973) and the Convention on International Trade in Endangered Species of Wild Fauna and Flora (1979) present powerful evidence for major changes in human thoughts, words, and actions. While most of these documents focus on the damage to, and abuse of animals, they also raise important ethical issues and explore the intersections between human attitudes, the treatment of animals, and issues of justice, human well-being, and ecological integrity.

By studying non-industry-based information, students, educators, and administrators can re-examine the biases we have been taught, investigate and determine the veracity of information about animals for ourselves, and consider whether human behaviors in relation to other animals are congruent with the values we espouse.

Knowledge Base Question #2: What Is Speciesism and Why Should Interspecies Education Be Given the Same Study as Other Issues of Global Justice and Ecological Preservation?

The cruelties inflicted on animals are deserving of attention in their own right. One theory that can aid discussions is the concept of speciesism. Speciesism is the name given to the presumption of human superiority over other animals and their subjection to oppression based on this belief. Policies and beliefs based on speciesism are pervasive, institutionalized, and publicly accepted. While the corporate media are finally covering controversies on animal treatment, thus legitimizing their importance, education about the life and death experiences of other animals is rarely available.

Except for animal rights activists and smaller informed segments of the public, the exploitation and treatment of animals are seldom included anong issues of social justice, peace, or ecological survival. Social justice, peace, or environmental advocates may still eat meat and dairy products based on the myth that these are necessary to get adequate protein. We may still wear leather belts, shoes, coats, gloves, or even fur because we are not aware of the extreme suffering experienced by the animals who are imprisoned, tortured, and killed for these products. Our education has not included the knowledge base upon which to make informed decisions on these issues.

While educational institutions may claim to be objective and neutral, values, morality, and ethics are integral to the overt and hidden curricula in every institution. It is not unusual for the hidden curriculum to contradict the stated values of the school. For instance, schools that pledge "justice and liberty for all" may be stratified or segregated by race, class, gender, or disability. Or, students may be targeted or abused based on sexual orientation with no consequences. Similarly, animals are often presented as the sympathetic protagonists of children's books, or the focus of environmental concerns. At the same time, live or dead animals may be subjected to experiments or dissection in laboratories, eaten in cafeterias, or worn as clothing with no discussion whatsoever, or these activities may even be vociferously defended if questions are raised about them.

To expand upon our example in the previous section, what are the consequences *to animals* of the human habit of eating meat and dairy products? First, contrary to what most people are led to believe, animals raised to be eaten are not covered by the Animal Welfare Act in the United States.[1] Instead, there are no laws to protect animals from being:

- systematically confined in unnatural spaces and subjected to living in their own waste.
- physically altered without anesthetic (castration, debeaking, branding, etc.).
- forced to eat unnatural unhealthy food including the waste products of slaughterhouses even if they are naturally vegetarians.
- genetically engineered, forced to take antibiotics and hormones to stimulate excessive growth, egg or milk production, or body parts "harvested" for use in humans.

- artificially/forcibly inseminated, forced to remain pregnant for large portions of their lives,
- given little or no medical treatment for harm created by these unsavory conditions.
- transported in crowded stressful conditions resulting in emotional anguish, injury, or death.
- subjected to slaughterhouse speed-up practices where as many as 30% are "disassembled" while conscious (Robbins, 2001, p. 212).
- beaten, electrocuted, or tortured if they do not cooperate with the abusive processes above.

While many of these conditions exist for animals in many parts of the world, factory farming increases the scope and intensity of these cruel practices. Further, as people in industrialized nations become aware of the contamination and extreme cruelty produced by agribusinesses, factory farming is moved to countries that have even fewer laws to protect animals, workers, and communities from their dangerous and abusive consequences.

Given these conditions, what responsibilities do teachers, schools, and teacher educators have to raise such important issues? Since the philosopher Peter Singer wrote his groundbreaking book, *Animal Liberation,* over 30 years ago, issues of animal rights have gained credibility and visibility. In spite of its vilification, the animal rights movement has brought issues to public attention through shocking undercover video footage and investigative reports. Even corporate owned media now view animal issues as legitimate topics for news coverage, columns, and editorials. So, where and how do these issues belong in education? The Declaration of the Rights of Animals (1990), a statement signed by 56 organizations, might initiate the process of critical interspecies education by introducing discussions about the treatment of animals, the concept of speciesism, presumptions or questions about human superiority, and what is a "right."

Declaration of the Rights of Animals

Whereas it is Self-Evident:

That we share the Earth with other creatures great and small;
That many of these animals experience pleasure and pain;
That these animals deserve our just treatment; and
That these animals are unable to speak for themselves;
We Do Therefore Declare that These Animals
Have the RIGHT to live free from human exploitation, whether in the
name of science or sport, exhibition or service, food or fashion;
Have the RIGHT to live in harmony with their nature
rather than according to human desires; and
Have the RIGHT to live on a healthy planet.

Students could investigate these statements, locate and critically evaluate "evidence" for or against these assertions, consider the impact of human/animal relations on humans and the animals themselves, and debate issues of ethics and morality.

Knowledge Base #3: How Is the Treatment of Other Animals and Species Interrelated with Social Justice, Peace, and Ecological Survival?

How does speciesism compare to and intersect with other social justice issues like racism, sexism, classism, and heterosexism where humans experience unequal power relations? How does speciesism intersect with global issues of militarism and peace? The next sections explore a few of these issues that might provide entryways for schools and teachers to include the study of speciesism or human/animal relations as a topic of great significance at all levels of education.

Intersection of Social Justice and Animal Issues

While recognizing that each form of oppression has its own unique circumstances, interspecies education might start with exploring historical interrelations between exploitation of animals and oppression of women, people of color, and other marginalized groups in society. From the perspective of critical sociological theory and using system-based models of oppression (e.g., Noel, 1968), Nibert (2002) presents a history of oppressive human-animal relations in which he argues that racism, sexism, and speciesism arise from economic systems based on greed and profit maximization where human labor and animal bodies are exploited for the creation of wealth for the elite few. These ideas may form one of many possible theoretical backgrounds for critical interspecies education that tie together human rights, environmental, and peace education. They also provide motivations for practical cooperation between different social movements that work for a compassionate, just, and sustainable society.

Speciesism and Sexism

Human-animal relations may be explored as a feminist issue, focusing on the common features between the subordination of women and animals. Ecofeminism states that the ideology that legitimates oppression based on race, class, or gender is basically the same ideology that sanctions the oppression of nature and non-human animals (Gaard, 1993; Warren, 2000). Examples abound.

The common use of nonhuman animal-pejoratives that frequently target women demonstrates the connection between sexist and speciesist language. These often refer to domesticated animals, like the chicken, cow, and dog, who are bred for service to humans (Dunayer, 1999). In a patriarchal social order the role of women and animals are similar: to be the possessed object. Meat and slaughter are used as metaphors for the oppression of women (e.g., "feeling like a piece of meat") and in animal agriculture, female animals are often doubly exploited by first having their femaleness, their reproductive system, manipulated in order to produce milk or eggs for human consumption. When their reproductive efficiency ends, they are butchered for their flesh (Adams, 2002).

Science and hunting also reveal intersections of species and gender. Links between sexism and trophy hunting may include sexualization of animals, women, and weapons in hunting magazines (Kalof, Fitzgerald, & Baralt, 2004), and scientific animal experimentation often encourages "masculine" emotional detachment and desensitization in the struggle for scientific "objectivity," whereas emotional responses toward "lab animals" and identification with them are often seen as "feminine" and as an obstacle to objectivity. Further the knowledge produced in laboratories is often "gendered" (Birke, 1994) as many animal experiments on intelligence, aggression, competition, and dominance are designed to establish essential differences between men and women (Gruen, 1993).

Speciesism and Racism

Links between speciesism and racism can be addressed from several perspectives. Diverse areas such as animal agriculture, the slave trade, hunting, zoos, and scientific experiments show how people of color and animals have historically been subjected to similar strategies of control and violence. Racist propaganda has compared people of color with negative stereotypes of animals, and people of color have been considered belonging to a subhuman species, lacking both reason and rights. Slaves have been treated like production units that can be bought and sold, and runaway slaves have been hunted much like animals are hunted today. Slaveholders thought that people of color quickly overcame separations, thus justifying splitting up families for the slave trade. Many arguments that have been used to justify slavery are used today to justify abusive treatment of animals (Spiegel, 1996).

Throughout history, victimization of animals has served as a model and inspiration for victimization of devalued humans in a number of ways. For instance, the practical arrangements of mass killing and the arguments used to justify it demonstrate parallels between the Nazi extermination of Jewish people during World War II and the industrialized slaughter of animals. The dehumanization of Jews by making them appear "like animals" facilitated the atrocities committed toward them (Patterson, 2002).

Edgar Kupfer-Koberwitz, a Holocaust survivor, saw the parallels between killing animals and humans. He was a vegetarian, pacifist, and conscientious objector whom the Nazis condemned for being a "strong autonomously thinking personality." The Gestapo imprisoned him in Dachau from 1940 to 1945. During his imprisonment he wrote the "Dachau Diaries" which included a section on why he didn't eat animals. "I eat no animals because I don't want to live on the suffering and death of other creatures. I have suffered so much myself that I can feel other creatures' suffering by virtue of my own" (cited in Patterson, 2002, p. 219).

The zoo is another arena for researching speciesism-racism links. Western zoos have a history of exhibiting exotic animals captured during imperialist endeavors in distant continents, and the animal exhibits sometimes took place alongside displays of native peoples (Rothfels, 2002). These people were thereby brought "closer to nature" in a way that legitimated their status as deviating from the identity of white, Western humans (Anderson, 1998). The exotic animal trade established in the late 19th century that sustained both zoos and circuses as well as the pet trade and laboratories, relied on colonial commerce in Africa and Asia (Hanson, 2002). In these ways, the zoo's purpose of education and stimulation of scientific curiosity actually built on colonial domination of both cultures and natures.

In scientific experiments both animals and involuntary, marginalized humans have been used for the purpose of the "common good". Two well-known examples are the medical experimentation on Jews and Slavic people in Nazi Germany and the medical experimentation on Black men in Alabama from the 1930s to the 1970s known as the Tuskegee Syphilis Study (Spiegel, 1996). Like zoos, developments in Western science have gone hand in hand with imperialist efforts, often based on ignoring the accumulated knowledge of people outside the institutions of science, such as indigenous peoples, or on appropriating and renaming their knowledge (Birke, 1995). Commercially driven biotechnology, for instance, can be seen as an invasion of other species, cultures and societies that deepens the exclusion of other knowledge systems (Shiva, 1995).

Speciesism and Classism

Meat production and consumption has been perceived both as a symbol of social progress and as a tool for capital accumulation and has functioned in the interests of elite classes over the ages (Nibert, 2002). As a tool for capital accumulation, modern "livestock" production has developed out of exploitation of militarily acquired and colonially organized land (frequently involving slave labor) for purposes of economic expansion in the 16th to the 19th centuries. Overstocking and overgrazing quickly degraded the pastures, leading the industry to continuously look for opportunities to appropriate new grazing lands (e.g., virgin rainforests; Franklin, 1999). When Third World countries are forced to set apart land for the production of raw materials for the Western animal agriculture industry, food imports become necessary to feed their own population, whose dependence on the West increases (Noske, 1997).

In Western society, meat consumption also has historical origins as a class marker. Fiddes (1991) notes that in medieval Europe meat was consumed in greater than average quantities by those who sought political and economic power. To the elite, meat consumption was a way to manifest privilege and social status and mark their differentiation from common people. Consumption of desirable "choice" cuts of animal flesh was a symbol of social class hierarchy (Nibert, 2002). In analogy with meat consumption, wearing clothes made of animal pelts has also been associated with class, imperialist, and patriarchal oppression, and has been used as a visual marker of social difference. For instance, in medieval England prostitutes were by legislation forbidden to wear fur to differentiate them from "respectable women," while the pelts of finer, rare, and smaller animals were reserved for the aristocracy (Emberley, 1996, 1997).

Both humans and animals easily become vehicles for profit maximization in a social order governed by the rules of capitalism and the world market that mostly benefit the already wealthy. In modern animal agribusiness industries, animals' bodies are frequently modified to optimize their productivity and to suit the production system. By artificial inseminations, genetic manipulation, mutilation, and other measures, animals can be "improved" to meet the profit demands of the food industry. Using the situation of human laborers in the early stages of industrialization as an analogy, the production process in modern animal agribusiness is planned so that all "unnecessary" elements are eliminated. Animals are streamlined to become "specialized" in a certain "skill" (such as producing meat, dairy or eggs), and are then distanced from the products of their own work. This situation applies not only to animals in agribusiness, but often in the pharmaceutical and fur producing industries as well (Noske, 1997). Resistance to cruelty to animals may be understood as resistance against corporate power and the class nature of the system that upholds abusive practices toward both humans and animals (Wilde, 2000).

Vegetarianism, Animal Rights, and Lesbian, Gay, Bisexual, Transgender (LGBT) Issues

Theoretical parallels exist between vegetarian and animal issues and LGBT issues. *Heteronormativity* refers to the practices and institutions "that legitimize and privilege heterosexuality and heterosexual relationships as fundamental and 'natural' within society" (Cohen, 2005, p. 24). Similarly, *meat normativity* refers to the practices and institutions that legitimize and privilege the consumption of meat as fundamental and "natural" within society (Gålmark, 2005). Both of these practices are rooted in and help maintain a patriarchal control of individuals and society by enforcing heterosexuality and the continued exploitation of animals.

Whereas heteronormativity demonizes LGBT people as sexual deviants, and pedophiles, meat normativity demonizes animals as automatons who lack reason and exist for human use. By degrading LGBT people and other animals, individuals and society create simplistic justifications for ignoring the needs and preferences of gay people, animals, and their allies.

The deep prejudices against LGBT people and animals embolden many people to enforce conformity to the heterosexual and meat-eating "norms." Sixteen-year old Zach came out to his parents who sent him to a "reparative therapy" camp run by Love In Action. John Smid, one of the Love in Action leaders, told him: "I would rather you commit suicide than have you leave Love In Action wanting to return to the gay lifestyle. In a physical death you could still have a spiritual resurrection; whereas, returning to homosexuality you are yielding yourself to a spiritual death from which there is no recovery" (Therese, 2005). As heteronormativity encourages people to impose heterosexual norms on others, similarly, meat normativity instigates the enforcement of meat-eating norms. John Robbins tells of a young boy who developed a strong friendship with a pig who protected him from some threatening dogs. In spite of this relationship, his hog-farming father gave him an ultimatum, "You either slaughter that animal or you're no longer my son" (2001, pp. 153–163). Although extreme, these examples illustrate how entitled some people feel to enforce both heterosexual and meat-eating norms. Most acts of norm-enforcement are far more subtle. Still, it can be argued, that these subtle acts, because of their unrelenting and omnipresent nature, may be equally traumatic because of their ability to isolate, alienate, and shame the recipient.

On a personal level, some victims of LGBT hate feel a strong empathy with animals, who they see as facing similar discrimination. Openly gay Dan Matthews, Vice President of People for the Ethical Treatment of Animals, wrote in *The Advocate* how school bullies called him "fag," punched him in the stomach, and laughed at his pain. He then wrote of a fishing trip where, after catching a flounder, his dad's fishing buddies merrily called the fish a "booby prize," stomped on it, and ripped the hook out of his lips while laughing. Matthews concluded, "In that instant I felt like I'd become one of the terrorizing bullies I dreaded so much in school.... I never ate fish again, and I soon stopped eating anything else with eyes" (Matthews, 2003, p. 10).

Former director of the American Civil Liberties Union, William Kunstler, concurs: "I cannot help thinking that our exploitation of animals has a direct link to our exploitation of perennial human victims: African-Americans, poor whites, Latinos, women, lesbians and gays, social activists, and Asians, to name a few disempowered groups.... If we feel that we may exploit nonhumans simply because we are more powerful, and we judge that we will benefit from that exploitation, then discrimination against other disadvantaged groups becomes that much easier" (McCarthy, 2006).

Interspecies Education and Peace Studies

There are many intersections between anti-war issues and animal protection. Animals have been used to fight wars, to test weapons, and to foster domineering attitudes. Animals are also directly or indirectly killed and injured during warfare. What follows are some specifics to better illustrate these intersections.

Dolphins, whales, orcas, seals, pigeons, rats, and other animals are forcibly "drafted" to fight or aid human wars. During World War II, the American military trained dogs for suicide missions by starving them and only feeding them under tanks. These dogs were then fitted with explosives and sent into combat zones. The hungry dogs searched for food underneath the panzers of the Third Reich where the bombs exploded (Selby, 1995, p. 23).

Chemical, biological, and nuclear weapons designed to kill people are developed and tested using animals. Napalm, Agent Orange, 245T, chlorine, and mustard, riot, and nerve gasses were all tested in animals. Groups of animals are repeatedly infected with biological agents such as ebola, anthrax, biotoxins, and malaria (Stop Animal Exploitation Now, n.d; In Defense of Animals, n.d.). This research is ostensibly to help the U.S. counter military threats, but the results simultaneously provide a better understanding of how to use these weapons offensively.

Just as wars leave a trail of dead, injured, and displaced humans, they similarly leave a trail of dead, injured, and displaced animals. Hundreds of thousands of animals were killed during the first Gulf War including marine birds, threatened sea turtles, and marine mammals who died from the release of crude oil into the Persian Gulf; migrating birds who died from inhaling the toxic smoke from burning oil fields; and horses, camels, cows, and sheep who were killed by munitions fire (Loretz, 1991).

Many great thinkers believe the exploitation of animals provides the necessary mindset for war, domination, and the expropriation of others' resources. Historical peace advocates including Mohandas Gandhi, "Peace Pilgrim" Mildred Norman, and Anna Kingsford have argued that the human exploitation of animals perpetuates war. Early feminist and World War I opponent Agnes Ryan wrote, "Wars will never cease while men still kill other animals for food, since to turn any living creature into a roast, a steak, a chop, or any other form of 'meat' takes the same kind of violence, the same kind of bloodshed and the same kind of mental processes required to change a living man into a dead soldier" (quoted in Adams, 2002, p. 126). Thus, they argue, the same logic that allows one to harm innocent animals can equally be used to justify war against an "enemy" who is first vilified as on par with animals (i.e., less than human). This explains why Tolstoy wrote, "As long as there are slaughterhouses, there will be battlefields" (quoted in De Leo, 2000).

Peace educators understand the role of power, domination and aggression in perpetuating war. These same concepts define much of humanity's relationship to other animals and raise a thorny question: How can anti-war advocates expect those in power to live by a nonviolent ethic when they indirectly inflict violence on other beings for taste or convenience despite readily available non-violent alternatives? Such questions have led many justice-seeking people to adopt a vegan lifestyle as an expression of their "commitment to peace and freedom for everyone" (Jones, 2005).

Teaching the connections between peace studies and human-animal studies will help students develop critical thinking, consider all the ramifications of war, have a broader view of potential solutions, and be empowered to live nonviolent values in their daily life. These multidisciplinary teachings are suited for civics, history, current events, or peace studies courses.

A Practical Vision: Interspecies Education Principles

The three knowledge bases presented above provide a foundation for proposing the following principles or standards to be considered in the development of critical interspecies education for students, teachers, schools, curriculum, and teacher education.

What Should Students Know About the Interdependence of Life on Earth and About Other Animals?

Species respectful students critically investigate the relationship of human animals to other animals[2] (individually and collectively), the consequences of human policies and practices on the lives of other species, and the positive changes students can make for the long-term well-being of all life and the planet.

Students who strive to live in accordance with these principles:

A. Study, understand, and respect the complexities, intricacies, and global histories of the interdependence of all life on earth: animals (human and non-human) and plants.
B. Explore and appreciate the lives, abilities, intelligences, uniqueness, personalities, emotions, the inherent and independent value of animals and their roles within natural ecosystems.
C. Investigate, compare, and critically examine various philosophies and cultural perspectives about animals, especially indigenous and spiritual traditions which value animals.
D. Learn the concept of speciesism and explore the consequences of it on humans, on animals, and on the environment.
E. Critically examine underlying assumptions and justifications for control, use, and economic exploitation of animals for food, clothing, research, education, entertainment, and sport.
F. Explore the connection between the abuse of animals and violence against humans so humans will recognize the importance of stopping animal abuse.
G. Practice skills, develop everyday habits, and create school and community norms for ethical behavior, compassion, respect, non-violence, and justice for all species and individual members of these species.

What Should Educators Know, Model, and Teach About Animals and Other Living Beings?

Interspecies educators model and teach knowledge and skills for respect, compassion, peace, advocacy, and sharing resources across species differences.

Educators who strive to teach in accordance with these principles:

A. Conduct an in-depth personal re-education of research, evidence, and beliefs about the human treatment of animals and the interdependence of life on earth including scientific, spiritual, ethical, and philosophical traditions that have been excluded, censored, denigrated, or dismissed.
B. Actively integrate previously excluded perspectives on animals, speciesism, and the practices of respect, compassion, equanimity, peace, and advocacy into the curriculum.
C. Practice and model these characteristics toward animals on a daily basis within the school setting and curriculum.
D. Teach the connection between the respectful or abusive treatment of animals and how this relates to respect or violence against humans (interpersonal, community, global).
E. Provide leadership and mentoring for students to alleviate animal suffering and abuse at the individual, classroom, institutional, and policy levels.

How Might Schools, and Higher Education Institutions, Foster New Paradigms Toward Other Animals and the Earth?

Species respectful educational institutions emphasize the importance of fostering a new ethic of respect, compassion, equanimity, peace, and advocacy for other animals, species, and the natural world. Institutions striving to operate in accordance with these principles:

A. Integrate the importance of respect, compassion, justice, peace, nonviolence toward animals, the interdependence of life, environmental integrity, and personal responsibility into the institutional mission.
B. Develop a regular evaluation process to assess how the institution is meeting this mission.
C. Examine school policies and practices with regard to other animals/species and strive to eliminate those that are exploitative, violent, and harmful, such as:
    1. The curriculum is examined and evaluated for bias and misinformation with regard to animals and other species (see Curriculum Principles below).
    2. Alternatives to the use of live and dead animals for educational purposes are pursued with regard to such activities as dissection, vivisection, classroom "pets" or exhibitions, entertainment, research, fund-raisers, etc.
    3. Vegan options are available at every meal with accompanying information about the benefits of a plant-based diet to human health, the environment, social justice, and animals.
D. Hire faculty and staff who bring expertise about and advocacy for animals based on various cultural traditions to provide previously excluded perspectives.
E. Provide regular faculty/staff development to advance knowledge and skills of respect, compassion, peace, and advocacy for animals, species, and the natural world.
F. Hire administrators who have demonstrated interest, support, and success implementing an institutional mission that includes interspecies education.

What Might be Included in an Interspecies Education Curriculum?

The curriculum for an animal friendly school draws upon diverse knowledge systems and age appropriate materials to demonstrate the rights of all peoples, all animals (individual and collective), respect for integrity of the environment, and the interdependence within the natural world. Such a curriculum would:

A. Foster the study of the intersecting issues between humans, animals and other species as appropriate in each discipline, such as:
    1. Studying the root causes of species extinction, habitat destruction, and animal exploitation and suffering.

2. Studying the intersections between social justice for humans (the "isms"), and the treatment of other animals and species.
3. Studying the connection between animal cruelty and violence against humans (interpersonal and global).
4. Studying the impact of factory farming and the consumption of animal products on global hunger, the environment, human health, the land and lives of indigenous peoples, and animal cruelty and abuse.
5. Studying the impact of animal research on human health and animal cruelty.
6. Studying the impact of animals used for entertainment on human health, animal cruelty, and animals in their natural habitats.
7. Studying the use of animals for "sport" and the impact on the natural environment, human health, and animals in their natural habitats.
8. Studying industries using animals and animal products for profit and their impact on animal cruelty, the environment, and violence against humans (e.g., fur, leather, dissection, vivisection, exotic animal breeding/sales, "pet" breeding/sales, poaching).
9. Studying appropriate and respectful guardianship practices for non-human family members.

B. Provide opportunities to study various cultural, spiritual, and philosophical traditions, and policies and practices pertaining to speciesism, peace, non-violence, respect for individual animals and other species, and principles of eco-justice.

C. Teach skills in the critical analysis of media, evaluation of information, peaceful conflict resolution, problem solving, democratic action, and the development of ethical and socially responsible everyday behaviors in relation to animals and other species.

D. Provide specific opportunities to practice new skills and develop new habits for respect, empathy, equanimity, peace, and advocacy for all peoples, other animals (individually and collectively), and the environment.

E. Develop knowledge and skills for active local/global social change for animal and species supportive policies, and global well-being.

What Might Interspecies Teacher Education Look Like?

Teachers can only teach what they know themselves. Therefore, teacher education programs should foster interspecies education by providing teacher candidates with knowledge and skills about respect, compassion, justice, peace, and non-violence toward other animals and species as well as environmental integrity. Teacher education programs striving to educate in accordance with these principles provide teacher candidates with:

A. Instruction on animal attributes, the interrelationship of other species to the web of life, the consequences of seemingly harmless human endeavors on this delicate balance, and actions that can be taken to restore balance.

B. Instruction on the philosophies, cultural, spiritual, and ethical traditions, and practices of peace, nonviolence in relation to animals, people, and the earth.

C. Skills in critical analysis of the roles and representations of animals in media, schools, and other parts of society.
D. Skills in integrating appropriate content into their own teaching and disciplines.
E. Instruction on the abuse and exploitation of animals in educational institutions, and appropriate alternatives to such educational practices.
F. Opportunities to practice new habits of respect, compassion, nonviolence, and justice toward other animals and species in order to model and teach new behaviors to students.
G. Instructional and assessment strategies to create curricula and learning environments for students to learn knowledge and skills regarding other species and the environment.

Conclusion

We propose this initial set of interspecies education standards or principles in order to stimulate thinking and discussion within higher education, preK-12 schools, communities, and the academic community in general. We would hope to see critical interspecies education becoming a core component of the curriculum and environment in schools and post-secondary education at every age level. We do not expect these to be adopted in their entirety but we hope that individual students, teachers, schools, communities, and educational organizations may adapt them to their own educational environments, share critiques and suggestions for change with us and with their colleagues, and work collaboratively to change the knowledge, attitudes, and behaviors of human beings towards our fellow earth inhabitants—animals.

Notes

1. In some other countries the laws may cover them but are not enforced. Still other countries may have no protections for animals considered "livestock."
2. The term "other animals" is used to denote animals other than human animals (Nibert, 2002).

References

Adams, C. J. (2002). *The sexual politics of meat. A feminist-vegetarian critical theory.* Cambridge, UK: Polity Press.

Anderson, K. (1998). Animals, science, and spectacle in the city. In J. Wolch & J. Emel (Eds.), *Animal geographies. Place, politics, and identity in the nature-culture borderlands* (pp. 27–50). London: Verso.

Animal and Society Institute. (2009). The animal's platform. Retrieved January 26, 2009, from http://www.animalsandsociety.org/resources/index.php?pid=40&tpid=8

Barlow, M., & Clarke, T. (2002). *Blue gold: The fight to stop the corporate theft of the world's water.* New York: The New Press.

Birke, L. (1994). *Feminism, animals and science: The naming of the shrew.* Buckingham, UK: Open University Press.

Birke, L. (1995). On keeping a respectful distance. In L. Birke & R. Hubbard (Eds.), *Reinventing biology: Respect for life and the creation of knowledge* (pp. 75–88). Bloomington: Indiana University.

Cohen, C. J. (2005). Punks, bulldaggers, and welfare queens: The radical potential of queer politics? In E. P. Johnson & M. G. Henderson (Eds.), *Black queer studies* (p. 24). Durham, NC: Duke University Press.

Convention on International Trade in Endangered Species of Wild Fauna and Flora. (1979). Retrieved December 12, 2008, from http://www.cites.org

Declaration of the Rights of Animals. (1990, June 10). Retrieved August 2, 2006, from http://animalsvoice.com/PAGES/write/editorial/essays/anirites/declare_rights.html

De Leo, S. (2000). *Vegetarian nutrition is the diet of the 21st century.* Retrieved January 12, 2007, from http://www.europeanvegetarian.org/evu/english/news/news001/nutrition.html

Delgado, C. L. (2003, November). Rising consumption of meat and milk in developing countries has created a new food revolution. *The Journal of Nutrition. 133*, 3907S–3920S.

Dunayer, J. (1999). Sexist words, speciesist roots. In C. J. Adams & J. Donovan (Eds.), *Animals and women: Feminist theoretical explorations* (pp. 11–31). Durham, NC: Duke University Press.

Emberley, J. V. (1996, Spring). The libidinal politics of fur. *University of Toronto Quarterly 65*(2), 437–443.

Emberley, J. V. (1997). *The cultural politics of fur.* Ithaca, NY: Cornell University Press.

Eshel, G., & Martin, P. (2006, April). Diet, energy, and global warming. *Earth Interactions, 10*, 1–17.

Fiddes, N. (1991). *Meat: A natural symbol.* New York: Routledge.

Franklin, A. (1999). *Animals and modern cultures. A sociology of human-animal relations in modernity.* London: Sage.

Gaard, G. (1993). Living interconnections with animals and nature. In G. Gaard (Ed.), *Ecofeminism: Women, animals, nature* (pp. 1–12). Philadelphia: Temple University Press.

Gålmark, L. (2005). *Skönheter och odjur. En feministisk kritik av djur-människa-relationen* [Beauties and beasts. A feminist critique of the animal-human relation; in Swedish]. Göteborg och Stockholm: Makadam förlag.

Global Hunger Alliance. (2002). Retrieved September 21, 2006, from http://www.globalhunger.net

Greek, C. R., & Greek, J. S. (2002). *Specious science: How genetics and evolution reveal why medical research on animals harms humans.* New York: Continuum.

Greger, M. (2006). *Bird flu: A virus of our own hatching.* New York: Lantern Books.

Gruen, L. (1993). Dismantling oppression: An analysis of the connection between women and animals. In G. Gaard (Ed.), *Ecofeminism: Women, animals, nature* (pp. 60–90). Philadelphia: Temple University Press.

Hanson, E. (2002). *Animal attractions: Nature on display in American zoos.* Princeton, NJ: Princeton University Press.

Humane Society of the United States. (2006). *Statement of principles and beliefs.* Retrieved October 10, 2006, from http://www.hsus.org/about_us/policy_statements/principles_and_beliefs.html?print=t

In Defense of Animals. (n.d.). *Military Research Facts.* Retrieved October 24, 2006, from http://www.idausa.org/facts/military.html

Jacobson, M. (2006). *Six arguments for a greener diet*. Washington, DC: Center for Science in the Public Interest.

Jones, P. (2005, June). Of brides and bridges: Linking feminist, queer, and animal liberation movements. *Satya*. Retrieved December 18, 2006, from http://www.satyamag.com/jun05/jones_bridges.html

Kalof, L., Fitzgerald, A., & Baralt, L. (2004). Animals, women, and weapons: Blurred sexual boundaries in the discourse of sport hunting. *Society & Animals*, *12*(3), 237–251.

LaDuke, W. (2005). *Recovering the sacred: The power of naming and claiming*. Cambridge, MA: Southend Press.

Loh, J. (2008, April). *2010 and beyond: Rising to the biodiversity challenge*. Gland, Switzerland: World Wildlife Fund. Retrieved June 3, 2008, from http://www.wwf.org.uk/filelibrary/pdf/2010_and_beyond.pdf

Loretz, John. (1991). *The animal victims of the Gulf War*. Retrieved October 24, 2006, from http://fn2.freenet.edmonton.ab.ca/~puppydog/gulfwar.htm

Matthews, D. (2003, October 9). Fruits and vegetables. *Advocate*, 10.

McCarthy, C. (2006, October 6). Seeking justice for animals more daunting than croc wrestling. *National Catholic Reporter*. Retrieved December 14, 2008, from http://findarticles.com/p/articles/mi_m1141/is_43_42/ai_n17093196

Motavalli, J. (2008, July/August). The meat of the matter. *E magazine*.

Nibert, D. (2002). *Animal rights/human rights. Entanglements of oppression and liberation*. Lanham, MD: Rowman & Littlefield.

Nierenberg, D. (2005, September). *Happier meals: Rethinking the global meat industry*. Washington, DC: Worldwatch Institute.

Nierenberg, D. (2006, July/August). Eat vegetables, save energy. *Worldwatch*, *19*(4), 7.

Noel, D. (1968). Theory of ethnic stratification. *Social Problems*, *16*, 157–172.

Noske, B. (1997). *Beyond boundaries. Humans and animals*. Montréal: Black Rose Books.

Patterson, C. (2002). *Eternal Treblinka. Our treatment of animals and the holocaust*. New York: Lantern Books.

Pedersen, H. (2007). *The school and the animal other: An ethnography of human-animal relations in education*. Göteborg Studies in Educational Sciences 254. Göteborg, Sweden: Acta Universitatis Gothoburgensis.

Phelps, N. (2004). *The great compassion: Buddhism and animal rights*. New York: Lantern Books.

Randour, M. L. (2000). *Animal grace: Entering a spiritual relationship with our fellow creatures*. Novato, CA: New World Library.

Rifkin, J. (1992). *Beyond beef*. New York: Dutton/Penguin Books.

Robbins, J. (2001). *The food revolution*. Berkeley, CA: Conari Press.

Rothfels, N. (2002). *Savages and beasts: The birth of the modern zoo*. Baltimore: The John Hopkins University Press.

Selby, D. (1995). *Earthkind. A teachers' handbook on humane education*. Stoke-on-Trent, UK: Trentham Books.

Shiva, V. (1995). Democratizing biology: Reinventing biology from a feminist, ecological, and third world perspective. In L. Birke & R. Hubbard (Eds.), *Reinventing biology: Respect for life and the creation of knowledge* (pp. 50–71). Bloomington: Indiana University Press.

Singer, P. (1975). *Animal liberation*. New York: Random House.

Spiegel, M. (1996). *The dreaded comparison: Human and animal slavery*. New York: Mirror Books.

Stepaniak, J. (2000). *Being vegan: Living with conscience, conviction, and compassion.* Los Angeles: Lowell House.

Stop Animal Exploitation Now. (n.d.). *Military experiments: The war on animals.* Retrieved October 24, 2006, from http://www.all-creatures.org/saen/articles-military.html

Therese, M. (2005). Meet Zach—16 years old, gay and trapped. *News Hounds.* Retrieved October 24, 2006, from http://www.newshounds.us/2005/06/23/meet_zach_16_years_old_gay_and_trapped.php

U.S. Endangered Species Act. (1973). Washington DC: Department of the Interior. Retrieved December 14, 2008, from http://www.fws.gov/endangered/pdfs/ESAall.pdf

Warren, K. J. (2000). *Ecofeminist philosophy: A western perspective on what it is and why it matters.* Lanham, MD: Rowman & Littlefield.

Wilde, L, (2000, Autumn). The creatures, too, must become free: Marx and the animal/human distinction. *Capital & Class, 72.* Retrieved December 9, 2008, from http://marxmyths.org/lawrence-wilde/article.htm

Young, I. M. (1990). *Justice and the politics of difference.* Princeton, NJ: Princeton University Press.

Part III

Community Struggles for Global Justice, Peace, and Environmental Education

Introduction

One of the challenges of this section was how to illustrate the connections between identity, community, social justice, peace, and environmental education without falling into the essentializing trap that has dominated most educational discourses on diversity. The challenge was more complex as the initial conversation on social justice guidelines emerged out of multiple meetings with the diverse special interest groups (SIGs) of the American Educational Research Association (AERA) that were already doing scholarly and activist work on social justice. Because many of these SIGs had emerged as part of the movement to diversify education, and during a time in which issues of identity and representation were central to unmask privilege and oppression, the ideas for community-based chapters evolved almost naturally. However, it was clear to all the authors in this section that these chapters were not going to provide recipes on how to educate children of color, girls and boys, students with disabilities, or gay students. The cooption of the multicultural movement has resulted in innumerable lesson plans, textbooks, and curricula that have assigned each cultural group static and fixed characteristics that represent culturally diverse students in a degrading and stereotypical manner. The chapters in this section have made a conscious decision to confront these essentializing discourses and have put forward a more fluid and complex framework to understand the social construction of the Other.

This section addresses issues of identity within a perspective that identifies the larger hegemonic forces that have coalesced in the creation of categories of "deficient" people. The kinds of Otherness presented in this section—disability, sexual orientation, ethnicity, race, and gender have been socially constructed by an unbridled capitalist system to justify the plunder of natural resources, land, and labor. This supremacist ideology has been masked under the myth of normalcy, universality, and neutrality to keep power, privilege, and resources in a few hands, and assigning the Other an identity of deviance to justify their exploitation and marginalization. The chapters in this section speak about these experiences. They inquire about who benefits from the creation of Otherness and whose interests are privileged when people are labeled disabled, gay, Latina, Asian, African American, or female. This section presents a different framework to understand identity and diversity particularly within the context of schooling. The struggle for social justice will be initiated when as a society we take responsibility for perpetuating these myths of Otherness and when we begin connecting these social constructions to decisions, habits, and policies that confer privilege.

In the first chapter of this section, Yvette Lapayese provides an in-depth analysis of the racialization of labor and unmasks the connections between the debilitating schooling conditions of Latina/o students and their tracking into the bottom positions of the service industry. Lapayese (citing Robinson) identifies Latina/os as one of the most flexible, transnationally-mobile, labor force at the service of global capitalism. The creation of a domesticated, cheap labor force takes place through racial and economic segregation, linguistic genocide and a deficient education that prepares Latina/os to get only low-paid, menial jobs. Lapayese argues that the hegemonic oppression of Latinos is not only reduced to their schooling conditions, but their lives have been tainted by environmental policies that have additionally debilitated their quality of life. Environmental racism in the form of toxic waste in low income communities of color and depletion of their natural resources is just one of the many ways that White capitalism imposes its rule over the lives, land and labor of Latino/a people. Lapayese proposes some "starting points" to articulate a liberatory education for Latina/os and others. She advocates for a representation of Latina/os that breaks away from hegemonic stereotypes to focus on the subjugated epistemologies and counter-narratives of people of color. This possibility of rewriting history, she argues, will awaken multiple consciousness and make explicit that Latina/os are not a single essentializing category but as everyone else, they navigate through cultural boundaries and are shaped and conditioned by their dialectical positioning with the center and others in the margin. Lapayese proposes a counterdiscourse against master narratives of capitalism, patriarchy, white supremacy, ableism, and normative heterosexuality.

In chapter 11, Glenn Omatsu unveils how the myth of Asians as the model minority has been created by hegemonic forces to further dehumanize and degrade other racial minorities and to invite them to follow the example of the best assimilated Others. Omatsu argues, that Asians were considered social pariahs for centuries until capitalist forces realized that they could use their labor for the economy and as an example of successful assimilation. Omatsu describes how the model minority myth has harmed the Asian community by masking the rampant poverty in some of their communities and by imposing unrealistic expectations on their youth. The social construction of Asians as a racial category is an ideological invention grounded in colonialism, and as such, Omatsu proposes an alternative framework for exploring the Asian American experience. He suggests looking at the past as histories that liberate and using these narratives to create anti-colonial, community-based frameworks to teach about social justice. An anti-colonial framework, he argues, would help educators and students understand that the lives of African Americans, Latina/os, indigenous peoples, and other minorities are connected to the transnational forces that have benefited from their oppression. The anti-colonial education that Omatsu proposes implies not simply a re-conceptualization of the curricula but an awakening of critical consciousness to eradicate colonial thinking, teaching, and learning.

In their chapter 12, Nola Butler Byrd and Menan Jangu describe the root causes of the African Diaspora (colonization, slavery, neo-colonization, and globalization) and their parallel effects on Africans in Africa and around the world. They also explore the tools used to dominate African economies and resources and devastating impacts of these processes. For instance, they argue that Western education has been used as a hegemonic instrument to control, exploit, and dehumanize people of African descent through cultural, racial, and linguist supremacy. Thus, they propose an educational framework grounded on indigenous knowledge and African-conscious social and environmental justice activism to move away from the pathologization of Africans and African Americans as troubled, conflictual, and inferior groups. They propose African-Centered educational principles to address human rights, environmental preservation, partnerships between continental Africans, Africans in the Diaspora, and other groups, affirmation of indigenous knowledge, the reduction of overconsumption, and interdependence between humans and other species, among others. They further delineate specific principles drawn from the ontology, axiology, cosmology, epistemology, and praxis of the African worldview that promote personal and environmental health, peace, and well-being for all.

In chapter 13, Renée Martin contextualizes gender oppression within the larger ideological framework of global capitalism that has dramatically benefited from patriarchal and stereotypical gender roles. While each form of oppression has distinct characteristics, she notes that the tools and infrastructure erected to support one form of oppression inevitably affect and support other forms. Thus, the empowerment of girls and women (educationally, economically, politically, etc.) is widely viewed by global organizations as a key to solving many serious world problems. Martin proposes standards for gender education that are based on international human rights organizations and feminist movements across the world. She further argues that to eradicate patriarchy, boys and men have to be educated to value and practice gender justice.

In chapter 14, Robin Smith, Deborah Gallagher, Valerie Owen, and Thomas Skrtic propose using disability studies to move away from the clinical model that has justified the exclusion, experimentation, segregation, tracking, sorting, violence, death, and dehumanization of people with disabilities through history. The authors rightfully argue that disability should be addressed as a cultural signifier in the same way that race, gender, sexual orientation, age, and religion are examined. They propose an interdisciplinary examination of disability anchored on the humanities that exposes how the deficient views of people with disabilities have supported the glorification of meritocracy, competition, and social Darwinism. They argue that an emancipatory education for people with disabilities should include a discussion of how the media, literature, and history have constructed images of disabled people as economically unproductive, invisible and in need of being fixed, rather than unique individuals with different strengths and limitations. They point out how women have historically been considered disabled as part of this clinical model to justify patriarchal domination. The authors formulate a comprehensive educational framework in which disability is seen as another cultural signifier.

In the final chapter of this section, Darla Linville, Christopher Walsh, and David Lee Carlson propose a Queered curriculum to challenge the hegemonic heterosexual normativity that has dominated most educational discourses in the Western world. A sexual justice curriculum seeks to revert the dichotomized vision of the world that divide people between female and male. The authors refer to the "international rights for same-gender sexuality and non-binary gender" as concerted global efforts to stop violence, discrimination, and oppression against people who do not fall into the rigid, binary categories of women and men. They address one of the most overlooked educational problems affecting schools: the bullying and degrading of students who do not fit the "universal" gender roles and stereotypes created by the dominant society. They propose the integration of queer studies into the examination of heterosexuality because it provides a fluid framework to understand homophobia and gender oppression. They argue for the necessity to "queer the curriculum" as a key to interrupt homophobia. The "interruption of that heteronormativity" would be achieved by uncovering how history has hidden the sexual identities of famous people, the experiences of people with different gender roles and sexual orientations, and the cultures that have normally embraced different expressions of sexuality.

10 (Re)Imagining New Narratives of Racial, Labor, and Environmental Power for Latina/o Students

Yvette V. Lapayese

Barriga llena, corazon contento (When the stomach is full, the heart is full). My mother often refers to this underground slogan used during the Cuban revolution which pointed to the simple correlation between ideology and social materiality. In this chapter, I bring the relationship between a full stomach and a full heart to the fore—to critically envision social justice education for Latina/o students is to re-imagine our material conditions.

The racial category of Latina/o[1] is associated with sociopolitical, economic, and environmental practices that relegate Latinas/os to the least desirable schooling, working, and living experiences. The identification and intersections of these avenues of oppression ultimately set the stage for starting points to dismantle White, androcentric, and global capitalist oppressions. To radically liberate our sense of being, living, and thinking, these starting points may include resurrecting other ways of knowing; awakening multiple consciousness; and regenerating cultural and natural spaces.

Naming the Intolerable Is Itself the Hope

This section highlights the intolerable living and schooling conditions that diminish Latina/o well-being. Pressing the critique is a form of hope in that, as Prakash and Esteva (1998) have so aptly stated, "Naming the horror impels people to do something about it" (p. 13). For Latinas/os in the United States, variables such as national origin, resident status, political history, racial identification, language, and transnationalism are essential parts in the axis of inequality worldwide, where racialized class relations dominate. The way in which class relations of exploitation intersect with racial/ethnic oppression and discrimination illustrates the realities of Latina/o working, schooling, and living ecologies.

Global capitalism, defined as an economy that connects capitalistic actors from all over the world via production and consumption markets, intensifies a new geography of centrality that sustains the peripheral status of Latinas/os. In post-industrial economies such as the United States', global capitalism requires a highly stratified labor force. This labor force includes the necessity for a dramatic increase in service jobs, which are highly segmented by wages, education, and benefits (Castells, 1996; Sassen, 2002). The ability of this flexible workforce to perform multi-task, part-time, and temporary jobs with few to no benefits is essential in the new globalized economy (Ray & Mickelson, 1993; Sassen, 1998).

These intensified global race/class relations impact and complicate the standing of Latina/o workers vis-à-vis groups in power. From the viewpoint of dominant groups, Latinas/os are the perfect workforce in a global capitalist system. As William Robinson (2007) noted, "They are a transnationally-mobile resource, deployed when and where capitalists need them throughout North America, and utterly dehumanized in the process" (p. 1).

But while the global capitalist system rests upon the exploitation of Latina/o labor, White privileged strata in the United States fear that a rising tide of Latina/o immigrants will lead to a loss of cultural and political control. Latinas/os are now the largest minority group, 44.3 million, comprising 14.8% of the total population (U.S. Census Bureau, 2006). This dynamic evolves into a racialized hostility towards Latinas/os, resulting in a rising tide of xenophobia and nativism, both of which escalate racism in our institutions, especially, for the purpose of this chapter, in both our cultural and natural spaces (Bacon, 2006).

Backlash in Our Cultural Spaces of Work and School

The interplay of global capital and education is particularly salient for Latina/o students. The marginalization fueled by global capitalism in the labor market runs parallel to the marginalization of Latina/o students in the U.S. public schools. Policies such as California propositions 187, 227, and 209 have directly attacked the Latina/o community's right to public services, a bilingual education, and access to higher education. Although one can argue that there exists an intimate relationship between the economy and schools for all racial groups, the way in which it plays out for the Latina/o student includes its own unique group of idiosyncrasies: hyper-isolation, linguistic genocide, and tracking into low-skilled jobs.

Hyper-Isolation

The most significant obstacle to Latina/o achievement in schools is the de facto segregation that many Latina/os face when they step onto their school campuses. According to Orfield & Lee (2006), Latina/o students are the most segregated group of students, on average attending schools that are 55% Latina/o and attending schools with the lowest proportion of White students. Because of this segregation, most Latina/o students are educated at public high schools that are very different than the public schools educating White, African American, or Native American students. Nearly 37% of Latinas/os are educated at public schools with a student/teacher ratio of 22:1, in comparison to 14% of African American students and 13% of White students (Fry, 2005). Finally, 45% of Latina/os are concentrated in high poverty and low-achieving schools, resulting in the highest drop-out rate of any ethno-racial group (Rumberger & Thomas, 2000).

The possibility of Latina/o students going on to attend college is reduced, as

Latina/o students are concentrated in schools poorly prepared to graduate students, much less, send them on to receive university-level education. The situation is compounded by the fact that most Latina/o students live in California, Texas, and Florida, three densely populated states with high-stakes high school graduation tests and no affirmative action programs for college admissions. Even given important victories such as *Méndez v. Westminster* and *Brown v. Board of Education* (Jennings, 2004), as well as *Williams v. California,* the efforts to provide desegregated education for Latina/o students have failed. Latina/o students (and other students of color) often attend schools that are only 1% less segregated than they were after *Brown* in 1954 (Kozol, 2005).

Linguistic Genocide

Schools are committing linguistic genocide daily (Darder, 2006). They do it by forcibly moving Latina/o children from one language group to the dominant language group through linguistic and cultural forced assimilation in schools. By the third generation, only 10% of Latina/o students speak Spanish well, and almost all prefer English (Portes & Rumbaut, 2001).

The current authority of English monolingualism in federal and state policies insists that students give up their first language, despite the evidence that demonstrates monolingualism is not natural, necessary, or beneficial (Wiley, 2002). On the contrary, bilingualism is an asset to the student and actually contributes to increased cognitive flexibility and adaptability. When children are thrown into an English-only situation where they are expected to learn unfamiliar content in an unfamiliar language, their chances of achieving academic success are slim (Zentella, 1997; Macedo, Dendrinos, & Gounari, 2003).

By severely reducing academic achievement, linguistic genocide also serves to reproduce unequal access to power and material resources. In an increasingly global society, Latina/o children are losing a skill that could give them an edge in the job market. By hamstringing immigrants with a linguistically irrelevant English-only education, the system's privileging of English language fluency intersects with capital's needs for an assimilated and manageable workforce. In the United States, the English language becomes a gatekeeper to education, employment, business opportunities, and popular culture (Phillipson, 2000). According to the Latino Labor Report (2005), the vast majority of new jobs for Latina/o workers are in relatively low-skill occupations calling for little other than a high school education. In the expanding service and construction sectors with occupations such as janitors, gardeners, tailors, plasterers, and stucco masons, low-skilled immigrants are disproportionately represented. In contrast, White workers secured large increases in employment in higher-skill occupations requiring at least some college education. The Korn/Ferry International Executive Recruiter Index (2005) shows that 88% of executive recruiters say the ability to speak more than one language is critical to international business success. Seventy-nine percent of North American recruiters cited Spanish as the additional language most in demand by employers. The educational reality that Latina/o students are denied bilingual education resonates with Tollefson's (2002) claim that policies limiting the use of languages other than English must be viewed as an effort to restrict minority access to economic resources.

Violations of linguistic rights, especially in education, lead to a reduction of linguistic and cultural diversity on our planet. The language (and cultural) rights of Latina/o children are not being protected. Formal education in the United States is controlled by the English-only movement which does not aspire to make children high level multilinguals, truly multicultural, or even appreciative of linguistic and cultural diversity. Education systems reflect monolingual reductionism where monolingualism is seen as normal, inevitable, desirable, and sufficient.

Tracking Into Low-skilled Jobs

The many facets of tracking—ethnic/racial, linguistic, economic—each contribute to the lowered educational achievement and accomplishment of Latina/o students. Carlson (1996) explains that "Globalization has participated in the construction of a new post-industrial working class … of clerical, data processing, janitorial, and service industry jobs. The new entry-level jobs increasingly require more in the way of basic reading (word and sentence decoding), comprehension and direction-following skills" (pp. 282–283). Global capitalism facilitates the "basic skills" restructuring of urban schools around standardized testing and a skill-based curriculum that responds to the changing nature of work. The Latina/o youth population comprise a large section of the potential new labor force and are, from the standpoint of capital, increasingly dispensable and have no work at all in the white collar economy (Castells, 1996).

Tying teaching and learning ever more tightly to jobs has particularly negative consequences for poor Latina/o students. Latina/o students are tracked into different curricular programs based on race and gender. In general, Latina/o students are underrepresented in gifted and college-prep tracks and overrepresented in remedial and vocational tracks (Oakes, 2003). For instance, vocational school enrollments demonstrate that Latinas are steered into gender-specific jobs with minimal career or income advancement (Romo & Falbo, 1996). Latina high school students are frequently enrolled in cosmetology or home-economics classes, or tracked into non-college preparatory general education programs (Kozol, 2005). The same happens for Latino males. Both males and females, in turn, internalize these expectations; in a sample of Mexican-Americans in rural areas, the number one career choice of 9th grade Latinas was cosmetology, and for males, automobile mechanic (Ginorio & Huston, 2001). Few vocational programs encourage Latina/os to enter nontraditional fields or offer them reasons to remain in school (Romo & Falbo, 1996).

Indeed, schools and the economy work hand-in-hand to marginalize Latina/o youth and prepare them for a life of insignificance in the eyes of dominant society. By warehousing Latina/o students in substandard schools, with little or no hope of achieving even moderate academic success (let alone an academic future), schools perpetuate the cycle of academic and economic poverty.

Backlash in Our Natural Space

Latina/o students suffer the whole gamut of global capitalist contradiction. As discussed previously, this is expressed through limited access to a socially just, culturally meaningful, and academically strong education. Although it is vital we understand how race, gender, and class discrimination are built in the very structure of schooling, we cannot divorce issues of social justice in education from issues of eco-racism. In effect, to fully understand the experiences and struggles of Latina/o students, it is important we turn our attention to how the racial ecology of Latina/o community flows from a language of global capitalism that disguises the racism that is so deeply inscribed in U.S. society.

Because of Latinas/os' perceived "primitive" cultures, people placed within the lower levels of the socioeconomic hierarchy are generally perceived as closer to nature. This form of racialization simply functions to diminish their rights as human being by giving ethnic minorities an "animalistic" quality (Park & Pellow, 2004). In addition, this ideology presents People of Color as beings in need of constant discipline and order, lest they return to their "wild" ways (Santa Ana, 2002). This racist logic justifies the concentration of People of Color in jobs and residential areas that are particularly dangerous or "dirty."

In order to see the Latina/o situation clearly through the lens of environmental racism, we must fully acknowledge that throughout U.S. history, the exploitation of natural resources has gone hand-in-hand with the exploitation of People of Color. This racialization was present in the ideology of Manifest Destiny, the concept that justified the "conquering" of nature and indigenous peoples as the country expanded westward— "The underlying motivation prompting the genocide of Native Americans, the lust for their territories and the resources within them, is typically hidden behind rhetoric extolling the settlement of 'vacant' lands. To admit otherwise risks revealing that the past motive for genocide exists as much today, and in some ways, more so" (Churchill, 1993, p. 7).

Environmental racism complicates the role of natural resource exploitation as a form of racial oppression. Western societies' extensive and continued dependence upon natural resources are crucial to maintaining white supremacy and environmental injustices (Krieg, 1998; Pulido, Sidawi, & Vos, 1996; Bullard, 1993). Moreover, environmental racism relegates Latina/os and indigenous peoples to the most inferior land on the continent. The landmark study, Toxic Wastes and Race in the United States (Commission for Racial Justice, United Church of Christ, 1987) described the extent of environmental racism. In this study, race was the most significant variable associated with the location of hazardous waste sites. Furthermore, the greatest number of commercial hazardous waste facilities were located in communities with the highest composition of racial and ethnic minorities.

For Latina/o communities the effects of environmental racism are real and tragic. Over 300,000 Latina/o farm workers and their families, including a large percentage of women of childbearing age, are seriously affected by pesticide-related illnesses. For example, an industrial toxic waste site located in the predominantly Latino community of Tucson, Arizona, has caused a high rate of cancer, birth defects, genetic mutations, and other illnesses among Latinas/os, as the site has tainted the community with 20 times the acceptable levels of trichloroethylene, a chemical solvent that damages the nervous system and may cause liver damage, lung damage, and in extreme cases may result in death (Mohai & Bryant, 1992).

Environmental racism crosses borders as well. Approximately 2,000 *maquiladoras* (factories located on the Mexican side that import raw materials to turn them into exported manufactured goods) allow U.S. companies to exploit Mexican labor and land. Corporate headquarters remain north of *la linea* (the line, or border that separates the United States from Mexico), while the *maquiladoras* are mushrooming south of the border. Corporations reap record profits, while poor and working communities on both sides of *la linea* are consigned to low-wage jobs and environmental health hazards. The U.S.-Mexico border is a microcosm of North-South relations in a global economy where corporations call the shots, and poor nations sell off labor rights and the environment to the highest bidder. There is no "right to know" law in Mexico, so both workers and communities are denied information about the toxins to which they are exposed. Companies pollute freely, degrading the border environment. Toxic waste, which should by law be returned to the United States or other countries of origin, is often stored on site, posing a health risk to both workers and surrounding communities. Border communities report a deterioration of public health ranging from respiratory problems to skin irritations and neurological disorders believed to be caused by industrial pollution.

Latinas/os in the United States have been racialized as inferior in the context of white capitalist rule over land and labor (Almaguer, 1994). Their exploitation continues to be justified as both natural and logical, just as the manipulation of the ecosystem is also sanctioned. Yet from the viewpoint of the dominant group, neither people of color nor the environment are being exploited; they are simply being "developed" (Park & Pellow, 2004).

Speaking from Cracked Spaces

> Learning is a space where paradise can be created ... In that field of possibility we have the opportunity to labor for freedom, to demand of ourselves and our comrades, an openness of mind and heart that allows us to face reality even as we collectively imagine a way to move beyond boundaries, to transgress. This is education as the practice of freedom. (hooks, 2000, p. 207)

The schooling of Latina/o students in U.S. public classrooms assaults their sense of being, living, and thinking. Monolingual language use, racist curricula, watered-down content, multicultural curricula based on essentialized notions of Latina/o, not only defines schooling for Latina/o students, but ultimately denies them the opportunity to engage in critical inquiry and praxis in an academic setting.

In the field of education, there are several efforts to research and intellectualize alternative educational pathways for Latina/o students and their communities (Gonzalez, Moll, & Amanti, 2005; Nieto, 2002). For instance, educational frameworks aimed at Latina/o students are often based on the cultural differences concept, and assume that academic achievement of Latina/o students will improve if schools and teachers make an attempt to ensure that classroom instruction is conducted in a manner responsive to the student's home culture. This type of research is known in the literature in a number of different ways: as culturally compatible (Gallimore & Goldenberg, 2001), culturally congruent (Au & Kawakami, 1994), culturally responsive (Gay, 2002), and culturally relevant pedagogy (Ladson-Billings, 1990). These studies recognize the centrality of social and cultural factors in school learning, and the urgent need for schools to develop culturally responsive content and processes to ensure equity and excellence for all students.

Other studies highlight the specific schooling conditions that provide an optimal learning space for Latina/o students, such as a supportive school-wide climate, use of native language and culture in instruction, a balanced curriculum that includes both basic and higher-order thinking curricula, explicit skill instruction, opportunities for student-directed instruction, and home and parent involvement (August & Hakuta, 1997; Stanton-Salazar, 2001; Stanton-Salazar & Dornbusch, 1995).

For language minority students, studies point to constructive schooling conditions that benefit Spanish-speaking students. These include high expectations; staff development designed to help teachers and staff to serve bilingual students effectively; variety of specifically designed courses and programs; and school counseling program giving special attention to the needs of language minority student (Lucas, Henze, & Donato, 1990).

The great upsurge of interest among researchers and educators in developing educational strategies designed to bolster academic achievement for Latina/o students remains at the micro-level. This is not to dismiss the importance of micro-level research and its constructive impact on the day-to-day schooling experiences of Latina/o students. But there is a danger that educational research focused on Latina/o students reduces the solution of the "achievement gap" to merely finding the "right" teaching methods, strategies or prepackaged curriculum purported to work with Latina/o students who have not historically benefited from regular streamlined instruction. This one-size-fits-all mentality runs the great risk of stereotyping subordinated students and engenders instructional recipes that quickly reduce the complexity of educating Latina/o students to a "technical method" issue (Bartolome, 1994).

In the following section, I highlight starting points to push education for Latina/o students from culturally centered discourse to critical inquiry and praxis. What I put forth recognizes a holistic and fluid framework that takes into account both micro- and macro-level dimensions. Socially just education for Latina/o students must move beyond the classroom walls to reconfigure a space where the self and other, local and global, converge.

Radical liberation of Our Sense of Being, Living, and Thinking

> An act of violence is any situation in which some men prevent others from the process of inquiry…any attempt to prevent human freedom is an 'act of violence.' Any system which deliberately tries to discourage critical consciousness is guilty of oppressive violence. Any school which does not foster students' capacity for critical inquiry is guilty of violent oppression. (Freire, 1970, p. 74)

Forty years after the East Los Angeles student "blow-outs" of 1968, where an estimated 10,000 Chicana/o students walked out of classes to protest the unequal conditions of their education, I highlight three conceptual starting points—representation, intersectionality, and praxis—to imagine a liberatory education for Latina/o students. This reconfigured space opens up possibilities for Latina/o students to hear alternative voices; to critically understand the complicated and intersectional layers of oppression; and to act upon this knowledge. Far from "cultural education" where the focus is tightly wrapped around ethnicity and language, education based on representation, intersectionality, and praxis is designed to radically undermine and transform androcentric, White, and capitalist systems of oppression.

To avoid homogenized standards on how to educate Latinas/os, I took the approach of identifying sophisticated theories existent in Latina/o communities that may point us in different directions. These starting points are not a recipe for education that can be exported anywhere without local contextualization. As Giroux (1992) stated, "Pedagogy is less about providing a universalized set of prescriptions than it is about rewriting the relationship between theory and practice as a form of cultural politics" (p. 3). In effect, I write these starting points cautiously, cognizant of our salvational urges as educators to empower and conscientize.

Representation—Educacion to Insurrect Other Ways of Knowing

> She remained faceless and voiceless, but a light shone through her veil of silence. And though she was unable to spread her limbs and though for her now the sun has sunk under the earth and there is no moon. She continues to tend the flame. The spirit of the fire spurs her to fight for her own skin, a piece of the ground to stand on, a home ground from which to view the world. (Anzaldua, 2003, p. 25)

The representation of Latina/o youth as a homogenized category, one characterized by controlling images of academic failure, pregnancy, machismo (to name a few) serves to define what and how to teach Latina/o students, and similarly, what labor and ecology they will participate in. For instance, Latinas tend to be represented as sexualized objects, as victims of particularly repressive traditions, and/or as backward impediments to development and progress. These narratives impact educational policy and practices, like when we see the high percentage of Latina students enrolled in "domestic" tracks at the high school level.

Representation of the Other, in this case Latina/o youth, must be brought to light in our classrooms. Different ways of knowing can emerge from different spaces, what Fanon in *The Wretched of the Earth* and Bhabha in *The Location of Culture*, refer to as subjugated knowledge. This subjugated knowledge resides in a space/sensation/state of betweenness and transition where interlocking systems of oppression lie deep. These *third* spaces become a possible place of emergence for different voices and ways of knowing.

Educacion that originates from colored epistemologies decenters Eurocentric ways of seeing and understanding issues in education, particularly issues impacting historically marginalized students. "The experiential knowledge of Women and Men of Color is legitimate, appropriate, and critical to understanding, analyzing, practicing, and teaching about ... racial subordination (Solorzano, 1998, p. 7). Subjugated epistemologies offer unique ways of knowing and understanding the world based on the various raced experiences of People of Color. By organizing our curricula around the subjugated knowledge of People of Color, we recognize there is more than one way to look at the world and thus, open up possibilities for understanding the schooling experiences of Afro-Latinos, for example, in new and different ways.

These margin perspectives can take the form of counterstories. Counterstories are narratives that challenge the dominant version of reality and lead to the development and acceptance of epistemologies that recognize that People of Color make sense of the world in ways that differ from the dominant white view (Delgado, 1998; Lynn, Yosso, Solorzano, & Parker, 2002). For example, Pulido's work, *Environmental and Economic Justice,* reveals that the environmental struggles of Chicana/o communities do not fit the mold of mainstream environmentalism, as they combine economic, identity, and quality-of-life issues. Examination of the forces that create and shape these grassroots movements clearly demonstrates that environmentalism needs to be sensitive to local issues, economically empowering, and respectful of ethnic and cultural diversity.

Including counterstories in the *educacion* of Latina/o youth can connect students to outside literature that may speak to their experiences and interests. Students could explore the works of Chicana narratives that demand environmental justice in novels such as Ana Castillo's *So Far From God* and Helena Maria Viramontes's *Under the Feet of Jesus,* in testimonials as exemplified by Maria Elena Lucas's *Forged Under the Sun/Forjado Bajo el Sol*, in theory by Cherrie Moraga and Castillo, in drama by Lucas and Moraga, in performance art such as Belinda Acosta's piece "Objects in Mirror Are Closer Than They Appear."

The starting point of representation captures Other knowledge—radically different ways of seeing, speaking and representing. This opens up a space for students to critically understand how they are represented in history, in the economy, in schools, and in other social discourse. Latina/o students would be called on to think, write, and speak against the grain; to be attentive to elite appropriations of their voices and struggles, and to reflect how consciousness may be reconstituted to effect a more socially just world order.

Intersectionality—Educacion to Awaken Multiple Consciousness

Intersectionality goes beyond racialized and cultural consciousness, which often fails to consider the more complex issues of class, culture, national origin, gender, and even sexuality. Intersectionality is an analytical framework that allows us to see linkages among group experiences and highlights how oppression based on race, class, nation, sexuality and gender (as well as oppression based on age and physical ability) interacts to produce institutionalized inequity. As Anderson and Hill-Collins (1992) point out, "Race, gender, and class are interlocking categories of experience that affect all aspects of human life … and are indeed the basis for many social problems" (p. xii). Race, class, and gender are not independent variables that can be tacked onto each other or separated at will. Instead, they are concrete social relations that are enmeshed in each other (Price & Lugones, 2003).

Similarly, rather than simply identifying stories, experiences, and knowledges excluded from the mainstream, the lens of intersectionality also highlights systems of power, which provides tools to "think about changing the system, not just documenting the effects of that system on different people" (Anderson & Hill-Collins, 1992, p. 6).

Educacion for Latina/o students suggests a nonsynchronous strategy that focuses on race as well as class, gender, and the environment to move beyond the essentialism, reductionism, and dogmatism that plague current theories of diversity in education. Latina/o children's identities are constituted by a complex mosaic of cultural fragments. The educational aim of locating and understanding these cultural fragments develops multiple consciousness.

Ultimately, the starting point of multiple consciousness allows Latina/o students to conceive of the self as a subject in process. As a result, there is more room to grow, to travel both in and between worlds because "we are not fixed in particular constructions of ourselves" (Lugones, 2003, p. 400). Latina/o students may be encouraged to live on those borders in order to understand that notions of self, community, and culture are grounded in processes of struggle and resistance rather than coherence and consensus. With its principles of mobility, partiality, nonessentialism—the intersectional nature of consciousness can undermine master narratives of racism, patriarchy, and capitalism that feed off of singularity, homogeneity, and totality, and move students to access multiple social points of view (Sandoval, 2000). As a result, students may recognize alliances with others committed to egalitarian social relations. By stepping outside their own frames of reference, students may relate to "others" in new ways, nurture mutual respect, and establish conditions for a more just social world order. As Iris Young aptly argues,

> The dissolution of cultural imperialism … requires a cultural revolution which also entails a revolution in subjectivity. Rather than seeking a wholeness of self, we who are the subjects of this plural and complex society should affirm the otherness within ourselves, acknowledging that as subjects we are heterogeneous and multiple in our affiliations and desires. (1990, p. 125)

Praxis—Educacion to Regenerate Cultural and Natural Spaces

Praxis is the "reflection and action upon the world in order to transform it" (Freire, 1970, p. 36). Under the construct of praxis, Latina/o students would map inequalities and injustices; trace those inequalities and injustices to their sources; and seek, propose, and act upon remedies to those injustices.

Developing praxis globally involves "shifting the unit of analysis from the local, regional, and national culture to relations and processes across cultures" (Alexander & Mohanty, 1997, p. vxii). This alludes to the possibilities of building transnational links with other movements around the world, i.e. social movements of poor, indigenous, and working people in Latin America and elsewhere (Robinson, 2006). For instance, Latina/o students could access and engage with grassroots environmental justice groups like People Organized in Defense of the Earth and her Resources (PODER), Southwest Organizing Project (SWOP), and Mothers of East Los Angeles (MELA), which have promoted environmental justice on radio programs, field trips, and video, in manifestos, community flyers, poster art, graphic art, and other forms of public art.

The international human rights paradigm may also be considered an indispensable element in a liberatory education for Latina/o students. International human rights organizations and documents provide alternative paradigms that move us closer to creating a socially just society. The International Convention on the Elimination of all Forms of Racial Discrimination and the climactic event of United Nations' Durban Conference in 2001 against World Racism, Discrimination, and Xenophobia brought international recognition to the plight of People of Color from around the globe vis-á-vis White Europeans and other colonizers. Subsequent documents like the Declaration on the Rights for Indigenous Peoples highlight issues such as linguistic rights, self-determination, which could conceptually apply to various Latina/o experiences in the United States. However, while the U.S. government has a poor record in participating in these reforms, and even voted against the latter document, these instruments have been ratified by most nations of the world and can provide an impetus for resistance to U.S. racist ideologies.

Under the framework of human rights, linguistic human rights may be one of the most relevant avenues of action for Latina/o students. The U.N. Declaration on the Rights of Persons Belonging to National or Ethnic, Religious and Linguistic Minorities (1992), provides an alternative articulation of the protection of minority languages. Specifically, Article 4.3 contends that States should take appropriate measures so that, whenever possible, persons belonging to minorities have adequate opportunities to learn their mother tongue or to have instruction in their mother tongue. Access to this knowledge base insurrects new modes of action to preserve the languages of Latina/o communities.

In the following paragraphs, I begin to materialize how the constructs of representation, intersectionality, and praxis interrogate alternative interpretations of education for Latina/o students. These starting points are informed by a wide variety of theoretical and conceptual pieces, in particular, the theoretical works of Paolo Freire, Gloria Anzaldua, Chela Sandoval, bell hooks, and Cesar Chavez, the First National People of Color's Environmental Justice Summit Principles, and the UN Declaration on the Rights for Indigenous Peoples.

It should also be noted that these starting points are informed by but not limited to the racial category of Latina/o students, and may make more sense when not couched in a "raced" chapter, such as this one. It is imperative that all students, particularly students of the dominant group (White, heterosexual, upper class, male, able-bodied, etc.), participate in these educational processes.

Ultimately, I write these starting points as a middle-class mother of two Latino sons, a mother who would like to step outside the limitations of existing educational canons so that I can imagine a socially just *educacion* for Diego and Carlo. This is a work in progress, a work that is highly context-specific and historically particular, and ultimately limited by the fact that my sons will probably construct entirely different *starting points* that will lead their mother-scholar to ask entirely different questions.

Starting Points for Representation, Intersectionality, and Praxis

Representation—Educacion to Insurrect Other Ways of Knowing

1. Students unveil the origins of dominant ideologies (White, heterosexual, able-bodied, to name a few)
2. Students imagine alternative representations of cultural norms
3. Students write nonexistent histories and cultures and rewrite suppressed ones
4. Students destabilize representation of "other as victim" and "other as threat"
5. Students explore counter-narratives, such as the writings of Third World feminists
6. Students are attentive to elite appropriations of their voices and struggles and take positive action to reclaim them
7. Latina/o students counter the linguistic genocide of their mother tongues
8. Latina/o students redefine the limits of social tolerance and the acceptance of cultural diversity

Intersectionality—Educacion to Awaken Multiple Consciousness

1. Students dismantle binary categories and ideologies and engage in alternative paradigms, such as *la conciencia de la mestiza* (towards a new consciousness, Anzaldúa, 2003) and Black feminist thought
2. Students recognize alliance with others committed to egalitarian social relations
3. Students enact a politics of identity that is nonessentialist and differentiated to encompass the ironies and contradiction of the capitalist world system
4. Students recognize and integrate multiple ways of knowing and multiple ways of presenting that knowing so that their learning experiences are connected to the global context

5. Students reimagine themselves as incomplete, as works-in-progress, as multiple and contradictory subjects
6. Students step outside their own frame of reference so that they can relate to "others," nurture mutual respect, and establish the conditions for cultural democracy
7. Students build bridges between the diverse elements of the Latina/o community while at the same time engage the broader society
8. Students academically engage in multiple social points of view

Praxis—Educacion to Regenerate Cultural and Natural Spaces

1. Students engage in "political clarity" (Bartolome, 1994) to creatively examine unjust power structures and to engage in differential modes of action to conceive alternative remedies
2. Students replace culture of domination with values of love, mutuality, honesty, respect, non-violence, and interdependence (hooks, 2000)
3. Students configure and (re)configure identities to engage other in transforming society
4. Students take part in multiethnic and multinational communities
5. Students identify conditions that limit possibilities for human becoming to devise alternative economic arrangements that redistribute social goods
6. Students responsibly use land and renewable resources in the interest of a sustainable planet for all species
7. Students oppose exploitation of lands, peoples and lands, and all other life forms
8. Students create a communal place of learning that can be sustained by a collective process of inquiry and engagement

Note

1. The Institute of Puerto Rican and Latino Studies defines the supra-ethnic label of Latina/o to include people who have recently arrived and those whose heritage of living in what is now the continental U.S. stems over 500 years. National origin, socioeconomic conditions, generational status, geographical location, residence status (including citizenship), political histories, racial identification, languages other than Spanish, dialects, religious and spiritual affiliations, histories of discrimination/oppression, circular migration, and level of transnationalism among other variables add to this population's complexity and diversity. I acknowledge that any study of Latina/o experience in the United States is hampered by the limited amount of empirically based research on Latina/os, a legacy that essentializes Latina/oismo.

References

Alexander, J., & Mohanty, C. (1997). Introduction: Genealogies, legacies, movements. In M. J. Alexander & C. T. Mohanty (Eds.), *Feminist geneaologies, colonial legacies, democratic futures* (xxiii–xxiv). New York: Routledge.

Almaguer, T. (1994). *Racial fault lines: The historical origins of white supremacy in California.* Berkeley: University of California Press.

Andersen, M, & Hill-Collins, P. (1992). Preface. In M. Andersen (Ed.), *Race, class and gender: An anthology* (pp. x–xii). Belmont, CA: Wadsworth.

Anzaldúa, G. E. (2003). La conciencia de la mestiza: Towards a new consciousness. In C. R. McCann & S-K. Kim (Eds.), *Feminist theory reader: Local and global perspectives* (pp. 179–187). Routledge: New York.

August, D., & Hakuta, K. (Eds.). (1997). *Improving schooling for language-minority children: A research agenda.* Washington, DC: National Academy Press

Au, K., & Kawakami, A. (1994). Cultural congruence in instruction. In E. Hollins, J. King, & W. Hayman (Eds.), *Teaching diverse populations: Formulating knowledge base* (pp. 5–23). Albany: State university of New York Press.

Bacon, D. (2006). *Communities without borders: Images and voices from the world of migration.* Ithaca, NY: Cornell University Press.

Bartolome, L. I. (1994). Beyond the method fetish: Toward a humanizing pedagogy. *Harvard Educational Review, 64*(2), 173–194.

Bhabha, Homi K. (Ed.). (1990). *Nation and narration.* New York: Routledge.

Bullard, R .D. (Ed.). (1993). *Confronting environmental racism: Voices from the grassroots.* Boston: South End Press.

Carlson, D. (1996). Education as a political issue: What's missing in the public conversation about education? In J. L. Kincheloe & S. R. Steinberg (Eds.), *Thirteen questions: Reframing education's conversation* (2nd ed., pp. 281–291). New York: Peter Lang.

Castells, M. (1996). *The rise of the network society.* Cambridge, MA: Harvard University Press.

Churchill, W. (1993). *Struggle for the land: Indigenous resistance to genocide, ecocide and expropriation in contemporary North America.* Monroe, ME: Common Courage Press.

Commission for Racial Justice. United Church of Christ. (1987). *Toxic wastes and race in the United States: A national report on the racial and socio-economic characteristics of communities with hazardous waste sites.* New York: Public Data Access.

Darder, A. (2006, April 9). *Linguistic genocide: The racialization of language and the empire of capital.* Paper presented at the American Education Research Association conference, Long Beach, CA.

Delgado, R. (1998). Using a Chicana feminist epistemology in educational research. *Harvard Educational Review, 68*(4), 555–582.

Fanon, F. (1965). *The wretched of the earth.* New York: Grove Press.

Fry, R. (2005). *The high schools Hispanics attend: Size and other key characteristics.* Washington, DC: Pew Hispanic Center.

Gallimore, R., & Goldenberg, C. (2001). Analyzing cultural models and settings to connect minority achievement and school improvement research. *Educational Psychologist, 36*(1), 45–56.

Gay, G. (2002). Preparing for culturally responsive teaching. *Journal of Teacher Education, 53*(2), 106–116.

Ginorio, A. B., & Huston, M. (2001). *¡Sí, se puede! Yes, we can! Latinas in schools.* Washington, DC: American Association of University Women.

Giroux, H. (1992). *Border crossings: Cultural workers and the politics of education.* New York: Routledge.

Gonzalez, N., Moll, L., & Amanti, C. (2005). *Funds of knowledge: Theorizing practices in households, communities, and classrooms.* Mahwah, NJ: Erlbaum.

hooks, b. (2000). *Where we stand: Class matters.* New York: Routledge.

Jennings, L. (2004, May). The end of the "Mexican School." *Hispanic Business, 26*, 28.

Freire, P. (1970). *Pedagogy of the oppressed.* New York: Continuum.

Korn/Ferry International Executive Recruiter Index. (2005). Global survey of multi-language capabilities. Retrieved August 23, 2006, from http://www.kornferry.com/PressRelease/3609

Kozol, J. (2005). *The shame of the nation: The restoration of apartheid schooling in America.* New York: Crown.

Krieg, E. (1998). The two faces of toxic waste. *Sociological Forum, 13*(52), 3–20.

Ladson-Billings, G. (1990). Culturally relevant teaching: Effective instruction for black students. *The College Board Review, 7*(15), 20–25.

Latino Labor Report. (2005). Washington, DC: Pew Hispanic Center.

Lucas, T., Henze, R., & Donato, R. (1990). Promoting the success of Latino language-minority students: An exploratory study of six high schools. *Harvard Educational Review, 60*(3), 315–340.

Lugones, M. (2003). *Pilgrimages/peregrinajes: Theorizing coalition against multiple oppressions.* Lanham, MD: Rowman & Littlefield.

Lynn, M., Yosso, T., Solorzano, D., & Parker, L. (2002). Foreword: Guest editor's introduction. *Qualitative Inquiry, 8*(1), 3–6.

Macedo, D., Dendrinos, B. & Gounari, P. (2003). *The hegemony of English.* Boulder, CO: Paradigm.

Mohai, P., & Bryant, B. (1992). Environmental injustice: Weighing race and class as factors in the distribution of environmental hazards. *University of Colorado Law Review, 63*(4), 177–203.

Mohanty, C. (1997). Women workers and capitalist scripts: Ideologies of domination, common interests, and the politics of solidarity. In J. Alexander & C. Mohanty (Eds.), *Feminist genealogies, colonial legacies, democratic futures* (pp. 3–29). New York: Routledge.

Nieto, S. (2002). *Language, culture, and teaching: Critical perspectives for a new century.* Mahwah, NJ: Erlbaum.

Oakes, J. (2003). *Critical conditions for equity and diversity in college access: Informing policy and monitoring results.* Los Angeles: University of California, ACCORD.

Orfield, G., & Lee, C. (2006). *Racial transformation and the changing nature of segregation.* Cambridge, MA: The Civil Rights Project at Harvard University.

Park, L., & Pellow, D. (2004). Racial formation, environmental racism, and the emergence of Silicon Valley. *Ethnicities, 4*(3), 403–424.

Portes, A., & Rumbaut, R. (2001). *Legacies: The story of the immigrant second generation.* Los Angeles: University of California Press.

Price, J. M., & Lugones, M. C. (2003). The inseparability of race, class, and gender. *Journal of U.S. Latino Studies, 1,* 1.

Phillipson, R. (Ed.). (2000). *Rights to language: Equity, power, and education.* Mahwah, NJ: Erlbaum.

Prakash, M. S., & Esteva, G. (1998). *Escaping education: Living as learning within grassroots cultures.* New York: Peter Lang.

Pulido, L. (2000). Rethinking environmental racism. *Annals of the Association of American Geographers, 90*(136), 12–40.

Pulido, L., Sidawi, L., & Vos, R. (1996). An archaeology of environmental racism in Los Angeles. *Urban Geography, 17*(51), 419–439.

Ray, C. A., & Mickelson, R. A. (1993). Restructuring students for restructured work: The economy, school reform, and non-college-bound youths. *Sociology of Education, 66*, 1–20.

Robinson, W. (2006). Aqui estamos y no nos vamos!: Global capitalist and the struggle for immigrant rights. *Race and Class, 48*(2), 33–45.

Robinson, W. (2007, February). Keynote presentation at El Gran Paro Americano Immigrant Rights Conference, Los Angeles.

Romo, H. D., & Falbo, T. (1996). *Latino high school graduation: Defying the odds.* Austin: University of Texas Press.

Rumberger, R. W., & Thomas, S. L. (2000). The distribution of dropout and turnover rates among urban and suburban high schools. *Sociology of Education 73*, 39–67.

Sandoval, C. (1991). US Third World Feminism: The theory and method of oppositional consciousness in the postmodern world. *Genders, 10*, 1–24.

Santa Ana, O. (2002). *Brown tide rising: Metaphors of Latinos in contemporary American public discourse.* Austin: University of Texas Press.

Sassen, S. (1998). *Globalization and its discontents.* New York: The New Press.

Sassen, S. (2002). Global cities and survival circuits. In B. Ehrenreich & A.R. Hochschild (Eds.), *Global woman: Nannies, maids, and sex workers in the new economy* (pp. 149–162). New York: Owl Book.

Smith, L. T. (1999). *Decolonizing methodologies.* London: University of Otago Press.

Solorzano, D. (1998). Critical race theory, racial and gender microaggressions, and the experiences of Chicana and Chicano scholars. *International Journal of Qualitative Studies in Education, 11*, 121–136.

Spivak, G. C. (1987). *In other worlds: Essays in cultural politics.* New York: Routledge.

Stanton-Salazar, R. (2001). *Manufacturing hope & despair: The school and kin support networks of U.S.-Mexican youth.* New York: Teachers College Press.

Stanton-Salazar, R., & Dornbusch, S. (1995). Social capital and the reproduction of inequality: Information networks among Mexican-origin high school students *Sociology of Education, 68*(2), 116–135.

Stromquist, N., & Monkman, K. (2000). *Globalization and education: Integration and contestation across cultures.* Lanham, MD: Rowman & Littlefield.

Tollefson, J. (2002). *Language policies in education: Critical issues.* Mahwah, NJ: Erlbaum.

U.N. Declaration on the Rights of Persons Belonging to National or Ethnic, Religious and Linguistic Minorities. (1993). G.A. res. 47/135, annex, 47 U.N. GAOR Supp. (No. 49) at 210, U.N. Doc. A/47/49

U.S. Census Bureau. (2006). Hispanic origin population. Retrieved August 22, 2006, from http://www.census.gov/Press-Release/www.releases/archives/population/006808/htm

Weis, L., & Fine, M. (1993). *Beyond silenced voices: Class, race, and gender in United States schools.* New York: State University of New York Press.

Wiley, T. G . (2002). Accessing language rights in education: A brief history of the U.S. context. In J. Tollefson (Ed.), *Language policies in education: Critical readings* (pp. 39–64). Mahwah, NJ: Erlbaum.

Zentella, A. (1997). *Growing up bilingual.* Oxford, UK: Blackwell.

11 Liberating Minds, Hearts, and Souls

Forging an Anti-Colonial Framework to Explore the Asian American Experience

Glenn Omatsu

In the first edition of the classic book *Occupied America,* chronicling Chicano struggles for justice, Rudolfo Acuña (1972) distinguished between "histories that oppress" and "histories that liberate." Writing at the birth of ethnic studies, he analyzed previous scholarship on people of color as histories that oppressed. What were needed were new histories that could liberate people.

What are histories that liberate, and how do we create them? For Asian American scholars and community activists, these have been the central questions for more than four decades. Significantly, today these questions carry even more weight due to the growing recognition of the achievements of Asian Americans. According to influential policy experts (Bell, 1985), Asian Americans have transformed from a pariah group that was banned from even entering the United States for many decades into a "model minority" to one that can serve as an example for Blacks and Latinos—and even Whites—in postindustrial America.

This major shift in the status of Asian Americans in the U.S. racial hierarchy has created new challenges, especially for those of us engaged in struggles for justice in communities. Today, we confront new histories that oppress and that now require new histories that liberate. It is no longer enough for scholars and activists to show the ways that Asian Americans suffer oppression. Paradoxically, we must also confront what many in mainstream society regard as the image of our own liberation: the attainment of success. Is this image really a mirage that disappears upon closer scrutiny? Or is it a partially true picture? These are the questions that now dominate Asian American discourse. Increasingly, some activists and scholars recognize the need to reframe the debate by asking new questions: Who created this image, and why has it emerged at this particular time? And, if politically conscious Asian Americans reject this image, what alternative can we propose? What are the new histories of liberation that we advance?

This chapter presents fragments of an alternative framework for exploring the Asian American experience. The framework is anti-colonial, community-based, grassroots, and holistic. More important, it recognizes that the struggle against colonialism is not simply a struggle for rights but requires the repairing of human consciousness. Five hundred years of colonialism have warped not only human behavior but also human souls. Thus, the alternative framework focuses on liberating minds, hearts, and souls. This chapter presents fragments of this framework because it is far from being complete. Yet, the fragments provide enough direction for intrepid educators to explore the Asian American experience, and, more broadly, the experiences of all groups in America.

Asian Americans: A Demographic Overview

Who are Asian Americans? According to the U.S. Census, Asian Americans are a very small population. In 2004, there were 12 million Asian Americans, accounting for 4% of U.S. society (U.S. Census Bureau, 2004). Although Asian Americans can be found in every region of the country, half of the population lives in three states: California, Hawaii, and New York. Asian Americans are a rapidly growing population, doubling in number in each of the past three decades; the population is expected to double again between 2000 and 2010 (Ong, 1993). The growth is driven by immigration. In 2000, 90% of Asian Americans either were foreign-born or had at least one foreign-born parent (U.S. Census Bureau, 2000). The heavily immigrant nature of Asian communities has important consequences. In California, for example, although Asian Americans now account for 12% of residents, their percentage as voters is between 3% (*Los Angeles Times*, 2006) and 6% (*Los Angeles Times*, 2002). This low percentage is not due to political apathy but a reflection of many immigrants still going through the process of becoming citizens.

In terms of economic status, Asian Americans seem not only successful but highly successful. In 2000, their median household income surpassed all other racial groups, including Whites (U.S. Census Bureau, 2000). In fact, the Asian American median household income ($55,552) dwarfed that of White Americans ($44,232). Because these statistics are used by mainstream analysts to prove their assertion of Asians as the model minority, we need to look at them closely and also listen to what Asian Americans themselves say. According to researchers in Asian American studies (Fong, 2008), the statistics are misleading. They point to another measure in the U.S. Census—per capita income—that divides household income by the number of people in that household. In 2000, the per capita income for Asian Americans was $22,352, compared to $25,278 for Whites. Researchers (Ong, 1994; Chen, 2006) explain the lower per capita income of Asian Americans as due to larger households with more working members than other U.S. families.

Researchers (Ong, 1994) have also focused on other data from the U.S. Census that has been ignored by mainstream analysts. The U.S. Census (2000) divides incomes into percentiles, making it possible to identify those who are in poverty and those who are relatively well-off. For the U.S. population, the distribution tends toward a bell curve with most families clustered around the median. In contrast, the Asian American distribution is bipolar with larger numbers of poor and well-off households than other racial groups. In 2000, 24% of Asian households had incomes below $25,000, while 37% were above $75,000. No other racial population has such an extreme bipolar profile. Thus, researchers (Ong, 1994) conclude that there are actually two Asian communities—one privileged and the other poor. The emergence of these two communities is a new phenomenon, forming only in the last three decades, and is shaped by U.S. immigration policy that has favored newcomers who are well-educated. Mainstream analysts working from the model minority stereotype focus on the privileged sector. Largely ignored, except for researchers in Asian American studies, is the sector in poverty.

Asian American activists (Aguilar-San Juan, 1994) have further critiqued the model minority stereotype by focusing on three harmful effects. First, the stereotype causes others looking at Asian Americans to ignore problems, such as the aforementioned poverty. Social service providers in Asian communities state that the biggest obstacle blocking them from gaining funds is the assumption by foundations and government offices that Asian Americans have less urgent needs than other racial groups. Even when decision-makers acknowledge problems, they often believe that Asians—in contrast to Blacks and Latinos—will work hard and persevere to overcome these problems without "outside assistance."

Second, the stereotype harms race relations. Some politicians and social scientists call for Blacks and Latinos to follow the example of Asians by working hard, not complaining about racism, and persevering without demanding entitlements. Of course, the designation of one group as a model for others does not promote better intergroup relations. In fact, it can cause severe problems. For Korean immigrants, the 1992 Los Angeles riots—where more than 2,000 Korean small businesses were looted, burned, or destroyed in Latino and Black neighborhoods—are a grim reminder of the destructive impact of this stereotype on race relations.

Finally, social service providers focus on the harmful effects of the stereotype on Asian Americans themselves, especially youth. It is not unusual for racial minorities to begin to internalize a stereotype imposed on them by the dominant group. The stereotype becomes the defining framework, and the only two courses of action are to either conform to it or to oppose it. In other words, one of the most damaging effects of any stereotype is to rob a person of their humanity. Some immigrant parents have begun to internalize the stereotype and expect their child to excel in all work (Abboud & Kim, 2005). When the child does not do well or rebels against the stereotype, the parents exacerbate the problem by stating that something is wrong with the child. Counselors working in Asian communities note an increase in family conflicts. These conflicts are often rooted in clashing expectations between immigrant parents and teens raised in the United States (Lee, 1996).

Researchers (Noh, 2007) have also identified a deadly new trend. Asian American women between the ages of 15 and 24 now have the highest rate of suicide of all racial groups. Teens in immigrant households, especially females, are expected to conform to both the standards of success in American culture and in traditional Asian cultures. Thus, young women are expected to do well in school and pursue professional careers while at the same time becoming "good sisters, wives, and mothers." Combined with the daily stress of living in a racist and sexist society, they face an impossible predicament: "to succeed or die trying" (Eng, 2005). Increasing numbers are dying, victims of the model minority stereotype.

The Historical and Political Construction of Asian Americans

As we interpret statistics about Asian Americans, it is often easy to forget that we are talking about a racial group that is politically and historically constructed (Omi & Winant, 1986). In the real world, there is no biological Asian race. The concept "Asian American" actually represents an aggregate of different ethnic groups that in the U.S. became one racial group. In fact, one of the most intriguing questions in Asian American studies is how Asian communities constantly form and re-form through the interaction between objective factors and subjective actors. Today, the racial category of Asian American encompasses more than thirty ethnic groups, most having distinct languages and cultures. From 1980 to 2000, Asians were lumped together with Pacific Islanders in a classification called Asian Pacific American. However, in the 2000 U.S. Census, Pacific Islanders became a separate race. Today, there are about 45 ethnic groups that comprise the Pacific Islander classification, the largest being Samoan, Tongan, and Hawaiian.

Understanding how racial groups are political and historical constructions presents paradoxes, such as the rapid creation of new races and the redefinition of older categories such as White during the past century. In the United States, it is possible to be born of one racial group, to live one's life as a different group, and to finally die as another group. It is in these paradoxes that we can understand why race is a dynamic and not static concept. It is in these paradoxes that we can see the colonial origins of race and why this concept remains a contested terrain today.

Racial classifications were created by European scientists several hundred years ago to study societies "discovered" by colonial explorers. The first categories were influenced by botany and divided the world into four groups based on skin color. This crude system persists today, even though most scientists quickly moved away from seeing it as significant. For example, scientists today state that racial differences explain little about human differences (American Anthropological Association, 2007). Yet, it is common to hear people talk about racial differences in personality and intelligence—despite scientific evidence to the contrary. Why?

Racial categories emerged at the time of Western colonialism, and popular thinking today continues to carry its imprint. European colonizers did not simply adopt the racial classifications of scientists. They augmented them by identifying dominant and subordinate races to justify conquest and exploitation. Thus, the starting point for understanding racial categories is recognizing how they are grounded in colonialism and how their redefinition is connected to anti-colonial struggles.

The earliest classification used for Asians—the political construction "Oriental"—reflects colonial oppression. In the early 1900s, ethnic groups such as Chinese and Filipinos were regarded as separate races in the United States. However, through the impact of nativist groups demanding exclusion of immigrants, laws lumped them together as Orientals. In this sense, the "Oriental race" in the United States was created through a shared history of oppression by different groups that until then had little in common. In fact, in the early 20th century, various groups fought to be not defined as Oriental so as not to be denied rights. In one U.S. Supreme Court case in 1923 (*United States v. Bhagat Singh*), immigrants from India fought unsuccessfully to gain the right to naturalized U.S. citizenship, arguing that racially they were Caucasian. Court justices agreed partially, stating that Indians were Caucasian but not White and thus were subject to the ban for people from Asia. In contrast, Armenian immigrants fought successfully in 1909 in a U.S. circuit court (*In re Halladjian*) to be defined as not Oriental, beginning the long struggle to become White.

The current racial classification of Asian American emerged from anti-colonial struggles. Among the first to use the term was Yuji Ichioka (2000), a pioneer Japanese American historian and activist in the late 1960s. Ichioka formed one of the first groups in the Asian American Movement, uniting activists from Japanese, Chinese, Filipino, and Korean communities. They named their group the Asian American Political Alliance, and in their founding documents (AAPA, 1968, 1969) defined Asian Americans in terms of three principles: grassroots mobilization against war and racism, solidarity with national liberation struggles throughout the world, and uniting with other people of color to change society. Similar activist formations emerged across the country embracing the same principles (Third World Liberation Front, 1968; Asian Americans for Action, 1969). Not surprisingly, others in the community refused to be identified as Asian American, considering the new term as radical. However, by the late 1970s, the term was embraced officially by government agencies (U.S. Census Bureau, 1988) but redefined as a biological and geographical classification and stripped of its earlier political content.

The creation of the term "Asian American" and its subsequent redefinition symbolize the evolving status of Asian Americans. On the one hand, by the late 1960s, Asian Americans had gained enough power to self-define themselves, shedding the definition imposed by dominant groups. On the other hand, Asian Americans did not have enough power to prevent dominant groups from redefining the new term, stripping it of its political meaning. This tension confronting Asian Americans—the ongoing struggle for self-definition and the countervailing efforts of redefinition by others—provides the context for understanding the shifts in status in the past century.

Asian Americans: From Pariah to Model Minority?

At the beginning of the 20th century, the future was bleak for Asian Americans. In fact, most believed there was no future at all (Ichioka, 1988). The Chinese had been banned from entering the U.S. under the 1882 Chinese Exclusion Act, and similar restrictions were enacted against immigrants from Japan, India, and the Philippines. These restrictions culminated in the 1924 Immigration Act, ending legal entry from the entire Asia Pacific region for the next 40 years. In the early 1900s, Asians toiled in the United States as laborers and had few rights. They could not own land, marry people of other races, nor become naturalized U.S. citizens. Politicians from both the right and the left justified these harsh measures as necessary to protect U.S. society from dangerous aliens. They presented findings from scientists showing that of all races in the world Asians were the least intelligent and, therefore, could irreparably harm Americans if allowed to intermarry. They cited the widely held belief that "Oriental despotism" was incompatible with American values of democracy and individualism. Finally, the beginning of the 20th century marked the first of a series of major U.S. wars in the Asia Pacific region: the Philippine-American War. For the next 80 years, the U.S. fought wars against Japan, Korea, China, and Vietnam. These wars shaped the perceptions of other Americans, who saw Asian Americans as not only coming from foreign lands but from enemy lands.

Today, in the early years of the 21st century, the status of Asian Americans has changed in ways unimagined 100 years ago. Today, the common theme used in both popular media and by mainstream policy analysts is of Asian Americans as the model minority. Earlier in this chapter, we examined the critique of this stereotype by Asian Americans. Now, we need to tackle harder questions: Who created this stereotype, and why has it emerged at this particular period in history?

For the first five decades of the 20th century, no Asian American was ever called a model minority, no matter how hard they worked. The transformation of Asian Americans into a model minority began in the 1960s and flourished in the 1980s. What happened in those two time periods that caused this transformation? It would be easy to attribute the birth of the model minority stereotype to a single factor, such as the passage of the 1965 Immigration Act that ended Asian exclusion and that by the 1980s changed the composition of Asian communities by favoring entry of highly educated immigrants. However, because race is socially constructed, we also need to examine the interplay of larger historical and political forces in these two decades. Both decades were times of intense crisis for the American empire. During the 1960s, mass mobilizations by African Americans demanding civil rights forced changes in the U.S. social order. In this period of upheaval, the designation of one racial group as a model minority served as an attempt by dominant groups to counterpose patient endurance of oppression to militant protest. Nevertheless, significant numbers of racial minorities, including Asian Americans, seized the time, identifying their struggles with the worldwide democratic movements of "shirtless and barefoot people" (King, 1967a). The decade of the 1980s—marked by the Reagan presidency and the birth of neoconservatives—is often described as a period of counterrevolution against the democratic gains of the 1960s. More broadly, it was a time of crisis caused by corporate-driven economic restructuring, resulting in job losses and uncertain futures for millions of Americans. To counter widespread ferment, neoconservatives celebrated Asian immigrant entrepreneurs as the model for reinvigorating urban economies and resurrecting capitalist values of self-reliance and hard work. Yet, no matter how hard these immigrants worked, they could not rescue economies undermined by transnational corporations. By the end of the century, the reality of capitalism for ordinary people was not small business ownership; rather, the reality consisted of low-paying jobs, bankruptcies, and homelessness. However, the neoconservative promotion of Asian immigrants as a model minority partially helped right-wing forces achieve one key objective: that of fracturing alliances among racial minorities by redefining the "language of civil rights" (McGurn, 1991). In the 1990s, multiethnic riots erupted in various cities, with Blacks battling Latinos and both groups targeting Asian immigrant small businesses.

The model minority stereotype is pernicious—not only because it is misleading and harms race relations, but because like other stereotypes imposed by dominant groups it has the effect of obliterating alternative viewpoints and new visions for the future. Because of the promotion of this stereotype in mainstream society, researchers from Asian American studies and activists (Woo, 2000; Fong, 2008) have devoted time and energy to show why it is harmful. This expenditure is necessary, but it has also shifted attention away from the central mission of forging alternative visions for liberation. In this period, how can the experiences of Asian Americans contribute to forging new liberatory visions? To answer this question, we need to revisit how colonialism has shaped the identity of Asian Americans and how Asian Americans have responded.

Colonialism, Anti-Colonialism, and Asian Americans

Asian Americans were created by colonialism and recreated through the struggles against colonialism. Colonialism is a system of political, economic, and ideological domination in which one nation oppresses others. Politically, colonial powers invade other nations, taking away sovereignty and other rights. Economically, colonizers plunder resources from other nations and transform colonized peoples into sources of cheap labor for the benefit of the colonizers. Ideologically, colonizers impose new religions, new philosophies and other systems of thought on the colonized to justify exploitation and domination. Starting in the late 1400s, nations of Europe systematically colonized Africa, Asia, and the Pacific, and the Americas, plundering resources, exploiting people, and transforming how people apprehended the world and themselves.

The first Asians came to the U.S. at the end of the 19th century from nations ravaged by colonialism. In China, for example, Western powers used military might, one-sided treaties, and opium to partition the nation. Amidst turmoil, millions of Chinese left their homeland, settling in nearby nations of Southeast Asia and journeying as contract laborers to the Americas. Western colonialism also changed patterns of conquest in Asia, introducing new levels of brutality. For example, in the late 19th century, rulers of Japan—alarmed by the partition of China—embarked on a strategy of Westernization, using military power to plunder Korea and China. Japan justified its invasions as designed to free Asia from Western colonialism, although its proposed Greater East Asia Co-prosperity Sphere replicated colonial practices of racism by placing Japan at the top of a proposed new Pacific world order.

Through colonialism, Asian American history is intertwined with the histories of African Americans, Latino Americans, and indigenous peoples. For example, the development of the global sugar industry can be traced to the plantation labor of African slaves in the Caribbean and Asian indentured workers in Hawaii. In Hawaii, hundreds of thousands of Asian workers were recruited by sugar plantation owners in the late 19th century due to the labor shortage caused by the rapid decline of the native population; within 100 years of first contact with English colonists, the indigenous population dropped by 90% due to genocide (Stannard, 1989). In California agricultural fields in the late 1800s and early 1900s, Asian immigrants served as the first mass farm labor force, until exclusion laws banned Asian workers, forcing agribusiness to turn to another source of cheap labor from Mexico.

As mentioned previously, the term "Asian American" emerged in the late 1960s to encapsulate three anti-colonial principles: grassroots mobilization against war and racism, solidarity with national liberation struggles, and unity with other people of color in the United States to change society. Where did these principles come from, and how did the reshape Asian American consciousness?

Although solidarity among peoples fighting against colonialism has occurred frequently, the 1955 Bandung Conference attended by 29 newly-independent African and Asian nations is recognized as a milestone in world history as well as for U.S. communities of color (Wright, 1956). The 10-point Declaration on Promotion of World Peace and Cooperation emphasized a third force of non-aligned nations in global politics that stood in opposition to the two superpowers. By the 1960s, national liberation struggles occurring in Latin America, Africa, and the Asia Pacific coalesced around the concept of "Third World liberation." In the late 1960s, this new concept was embraced by Black, Latino, and Asian American activists (Louie & Omatsu, 2001).

The liberation movements of people of color in the United States in the late 1960s are sometimes narrowly interpreted as efforts to reclaim cultural heritage. In reality, these movements redefined political consciousness as activists linked community organizing to worldwide struggles for justice (Omatsu, 1994). For example, Asian American activists began to define themselves as part of the Third World and to connect their struggle with global movements. Groups founded by activists (Asian Community Center, 1970; I Wor Kuen, 1970) emphasized in mission statements a commitment to grassroots organizing, solidarity with national liberation movements, and unity with people of color to change society. They drew from ideas of Black, Puerto Rican, and Chicano organizations, notably the Black Panther Party and its 10-point program (Foner, 1970). The Panthers, in turn, were influenced by national liberation struggles in Africa, Latin America, and Asia, especially the Chinese revolution. These struggles emphasized mobilization of ordinary people as the key for social change. This focus on grassroots organizing was embraced by all Asian American activist groups in the early 1970s (Louie & Omatsu, 2001).

Also, common to the founding missions was a new vision of education. Activists demanded not only access to education but also "relevant education" (AAPA 1969; I Wor Kuen, 1970). Relevant education meant an anti-colonial approach to teaching and learning that provided people the tools for liberation (Louie & Omatsu, 2001). For Asian Americans, the first struggles for relevant education occurred at San Francisco State College and UC Berkeley in the late 1960s when students—with the support of community activists—went on strike to gain Asian American studies. At both campuses, Asian Americans joined Blacks, Latinos, and American Indians to form Third World Liberation Fronts to fight for ethnic studies.

The founding philosophy for Asian American studies centered on an approach to education that was grassroots, community-based, and holistic (Omatsu, 2003). Activists drew from model of Freedom Schools in the Civil Rights Movement (Payne, 1997) as well as early experiments by Asian immigrants with worker centers. Freedom Schools were created by African American parents in the segregated South to provide education to children excluded from White schools. Aside from providing basic instruction, these schools helped children develop leadership skills by taking up neighborhood issues, such as campaigns for voting rights. Similarly, Asian immigrant worker centers emerged in the late nineteenth and early twentieth centuries due to the exclusion of Asians from U.S. labor unions (Lai, 1976). These worker centers provided support for worker struggles, and like Freedom Schools served as mobilizing centers informing immigrants about their rights. One example is the Chinese Workers' Mutual Aid Association (Lim, 1982) in San Francisco Chinatown in the 1930s. This worker center functioned as a community gathering place for learning, organizing, and ultimately, collective empowerment. These concepts became part of the founding mission of Asian American studies and community groups in the early 1970s.

The vision of anti-colonial education that emerged for Asian Americans in the late 1960s has continued to develop through ongoing community mobilizations. Two examples are the birth of the environmental justice movement in the late 1980s and the recent opening of a Freedom School in Philadelphia Chinatown. In the 1980s, Asian Americans and other activists of color redefined environmentalism by emphasizing issues of public health, worker rights, housing, transportation, and community empowerment. These issues had been ignored by mainstream groups led by Whites (People of Color Environmental Groups Directory, 2000). The organizing culminated in the 1991 First National People of Color Environmental Leadership Summit and the drafting of the Principles of Environmental Justice (1991). This document affirmed the "fundamental right to political, economic, cultural, and environmental self-determination of all peoples" and opposed "military occupation, repression, and exploitation of lands, peoples, and cultures and other life forms." Like the activist movements of the late 1960s, the environmental justice movement is a grassroots effort built on an alliance of people of color that emphasizes a broad educational vision. However, unlike earlier movements, this struggle expanded concerns of Asian Americans to embrace environmental issues from an enlarged political consciousness.

Similarly, in the late 1990s, members of Asian Americans United (AAU) in Philadelphia expanded an anti-colonial vision of education by creating a multi-ethnic Freedom School in Chinatown. The Folk Arts-Cultural Treasure Charter School officially opened in 2005. According to its mission statement, the school "realizes an alternative vision of education rooted in community and folk arts as vehicles for learning and social change … the school provides a nurturing, culturally rich learning environment for diverse children and families" (Asian Americans United, 2005). Like other Freedom Schools, the Chinatown school helps young people develop leadership skills by responding to neighborhood problems, such as low-rent housing and protection of immigrant worker rights. Thus, central to the mission of this school is a redefinition of teaching and learning to emphasize grassroots organizing and community-building.

Contending Frameworks for Teaching about Asian Americans

The birth of the environmental justice movement and the creation of the Chinatown school point to the ongoing efforts of Asian Americans to redefine themselves. This ongoing struggle provides the framework for educators grounded in Asian American studies to teach about the Asian American experience. However, because Asian American studies exists on the margins of academia and is usually not included in teacher training programs, what is the more common framework used in schools to teach about Asian Americans? Until the late 1960s, Asian Americans were defined as an immigrant group assimilating into U.S. society and as a racial minority dealing with discrimination. Working from the rubric of assimilation and acculturation theory (Gordon, 1964), social scientists defined Asian Americans in terms of dual identity (i.e., half-Asian and half-American) and marginal man and produced numerous studies from the 1920s to the 1950s describing personality disorders and other maladies in various Asian ethnic groups relating to their difficulties of adapting to American life. The emergence of Asian American studies in the late 1960s brought forward a new, anti-colonial perspective for understanding the Asian American experience. Early researchers in the field (Tong, 1971), writers (Chin, Chan, Wong, & Inada, 1974), and activists (AAPA, 1969; Asian Community Center, 1970) critiqued acculturation-assimilation theory, raising the question of what Asian Americans were assimilating into. They proposed that Asian Americans could best be understood as a unique American identity shaped by struggles against oppression. This concept was similar to the self-definitions of Blacks and other people of color during that period. Historians (Lai, 1976) and activists (Asian Americans for Action, 1969) further criticized assimilation theory for failing to account for the ways that Asian Americans changed U.S. society. For example, Ichioka (1971) overturned the prevailing perspective of historians who had studied Asian immigrants as "Orientals" acted upon by racism and redefined Asian Americans as subjects who actively created their own history.

Today, assimilation-acculturation theory remains the mainstream framework for understanding Asian Americans, although educators using this framework should be aware of its relationship to colonialism. While educators can use alternative frameworks, such as cultural pluralism (Newman, 1973), they should also explore more recent frameworks created by Asian Americans themselves. Today, scholars in Asian American studies (Fong, 2008) argue that Asian American identity is socially constructed not only by conditions within the United States but by transnational forces, thus creating multiple identities rather than an homogenous racial identity. Studies of young Asian Americans (Lee & Zhou, 2004) focus on their multiple identities, and one survey of teens (Asian American Youth, 2006) highlights how they define themselves as "trendsetters influencing American pop culture," such as in technology and gadgetry.

For K-12 educators, two valuable resources for teaching about Asian Americans are the lesson plans of teacher-activists, notably Debbie Wei of Philadelphia and Tony Osumi of Los Angeles. Wei (1998), a founder of Asian Americans United, shows how immigrant children can create their own "action comic strips" to tell their life stories. Osumi, a muralist and community organizer, has mobilized his elementary school children to create their own "peoples' encyclopedia" (Osumi, 2003). For community groups, Osumi has also created a "feast of resistance" (Osumi, 2006)—an interactive activity for teaching Asian American history through food. For college professors, there are two resources: *Teaching Asian America* (Hirabayashi, 1998) focuses on pedagogical challenges facing faculty in Asian American studies, while *Teaching about Asian Pacific Americans* (Chen, 2006) is a volume of lesson plans on issues ranging from the immigrant and refugee experience to the model minority stereotype.

Taken together, these resources reflect how Asian Americans continue to redefine themselves. For educators, these resources show the intriguing ways that the Asian American experience can be introduced into classrooms, beyond the standard assimilation-acculturation framework. For intrepid educators, there is a special challenge: that of experimenting with an anti-colonial approach to teaching and learning to explore the experiences of Asian Americans and other communities. What is an anti-colonial approach to teaching and learning?

Education as a World View and Way of Living

Central to anti-colonial movements is the concept of education. In these movements, education is defined not simply as a curriculum to enable people to gain rights. Education takes on a larger meaning as a worldview and a way of living (Gandhi, 1953; Meyer, 2003). Under colonialism, oppressed peoples are robbed of their culture and taught to adopt the colonizer's worldview (Smith, 1999). Thus, anti-colonial education focuses on changing consciousness, or perhaps more accurately, healing consciousness. Education, thus, is visionary, and seeks to create an approach to teaching and learning that can liberate human consciousness. Hawaiian educator Manulani Aluli Meyer (2003) captures this visionary understanding by emphasizing the difference between colonial and indigenous peoples' epistemologies. By epistemology, Meyer refers to the foundations of human consciousness—our ways of understanding and interacting with the world. Epistemologies deal with questions relating to knowledge: how we know, where we believe knowledge comes from, and what we believe knowledge is used for (Meyer, 2003). For educators, epistemologies are fundamental for defining approaches to teaching and learning. Yet, although they are fundamental for thinking and action, in Western societies we usually do not take the time to examine them. In Western societies, epistemologies are relegated to the subject areas of philosophy and religion and seldom studied in other areas, such as teacher training programs. In contrast, in indigenous peoples' cultures and anti-colonial struggles, the creation of an anti-colonial epistemology stands at the center of educational programs (Smith, 1999; Meyer, 2003).

Indigenous peoples (Sotsisowah, 1978; Smith, 1999; Meyer, 2003) and anti-colonial thinkers (Gandhi, 1953; Freire, 1970) have summarized the colonial approach to education as focusing on the mind while ignoring the heart and separating thinking from doing. Similarly, in classes I teach in Asian American studies, I have found that most students enter with the following assumptions: that learning is dependent on textbooks and lectures, that learning is an individual activity that takes place in the minds of individual learners, that learning can only occur within the four walls of a classroom, and that students learn only from professors and other academic experts. The existence of this colonial mindset in students in Asian American studies—a field founded on anti-colonial struggle—is a constant reminder to me of the powerful influence of colonial epistemology on those growing up in Western societies.

How can educators introduce an anti-colonial approach to learning in a classroom permeated by a colonial mindset? Or more specifically, how can educators subvert the colonial approach while simultaneously promoting an anti-colonial approach? For my courses, I emphasize constructing classes with a culture of experimentation around five principles. These principles are based on critiques of colonial epistemology and by my own involvement in grassroots struggles. I describe these principles as grassroots, community-based, and holistic. They are grassroots because they are rooted in struggles of oppressed peoples striving for justice. They are community-based because they highlight the importance of community-building in education. They are holistic because they recognize factors such as the centrality of human relationships that are not usually acknowledged in classrooms influenced by Western culture.

Anti-Colonial Principles for Teaching and Learning

1. ***Education needs to emphasize not only minds but also hearts and souls, and we have the responsibility to give back knowledge to the communities that nurtured us.***
2. ***Thinking and doing are not separate things but intricately connected, and the relationship between knowing and acting is not linear.***
3. ***Good teaching is more about "drawing ideas out from" our students than it is about "putting ideas into" them.***
4. ***Learning occurs not within the individual person but for a person within a web of relationships.***
5. ***There can be no social change without simultaneously changing ourselves.***

Education needs to emphasize not only minds but also hearts and souls, and we have the responsibility to give back knowledge to the communities that nurtured us. Gandhi (1959) critiqued colonialism as focusing only on the head while ignoring the hand and the heart. True education must be about the head, hand, and heart. And because we learn with the head, hand, and heart, we must also give back in the same way. Thus, in our classes we need to emphasize ways teachers and students can give back to communities. For the past decade, students from my classes have produced for community groups an array of projects, including a trilingual (Spanish-Korean-English) comic book on health and safety rights for immigrant restaurant workers in Los Angeles Koreatown, a trilingual children's coloring book on the campaign for justice by Koreatown immigrant market workers, a carnival on issues facing Asian Americans for high school youth in Chinatown, Asian American superhero anti-colonial comic books for young teens, and a participatory research project on worker struggles that served as the foundation for a documentary video, *Grassroots Rising: Asian Immigrant Workers in Los Angeles* (Winn, 2005).

Thinking and doing are not separate but intricately connected, and the relationship is not linear (Mao, 1967; Freire, 1970; Sotsisowah, 1978). Under colonialism, we intellectually separate thinking from doing and conceptualize knowing as always preceding acting. However, this is really an artificial separation since in life there is a constant interplay. Thus, for our classes, it is best to have students simultaneously think and do and help them develop a non-linear understanding of the process. Among assignments I include in my classes are political tours of communities. Political tours are different from the more commonly found community tours because they focus on the largely hidden dynamics of neighborhoods, such as interethnic relations and labor struggles. I require students to work in teams to organize these tours. I emphasize student leadership of these tours to move them away from reliance on professors for knowledge. In preparations for their tours, students quickly learn that information that they need cannot be found in campus libraries, the Internet, or assigned readings. They need to find other sources of knowledge, such as community groups. Students also learn that important neighborhood struggles for justice are not commemorated by monuments. They are part of the rich oral tradition of communities and can only be discovered by talking to long-time residents. By participating in political tours and interacting with residents, students gain an understanding of community issues different from that of textbooks and lectures. Many define the experience as empowering and providing them a new perspective on the important role they can play in communities.

Good teaching is more about "drawing ideas out from" our students than it is about "putting ideas into" them (Werner & Bower, 1982). We must help students understand that information is not something outside of them but is connected to their experiences. In Western societies it is common for teachers to separate the teaching of history and current events from students' lives (Mills, 1959). A better approach is to help students see the connections. For my classes, the first assignment is an essay having students identify the intersection of their lives with history. Following the insights of C. Wright Mills (1959), I also ask students to explain why the discovery of that intersection is both "terrible and magnificent" and how they can use their new awareness to change their communities. Giving this assignment enables me to also talk about the founding mission of Asian American studies, especially the contributions of historian-activist Yuji Ichioka. Ichioka (1971) adopted Mills' ideas to redefine Asian Americans as active subjects who create history by asserting their rights. His perspective emphasizes the linkage between history and autobiography and the importance of using that awareness to change society. This perspective defines the mission of Asian American studies (Omatsu, 1994).

Learning occurs not within the individual person but for each person within a web of relationships (Vygotsky, 1978; Wink & Putney, 2002). If we want to increase learning outcomes for one student, we need to enhance human relationships. Thus, we need to conceptualize our classrooms as learning communities. Emphasizing healthy group dynamics (i.e., community-building) is a major responsibility of teachers (Werner & Bower, 1982). In my classes to help students complete the community projects, I include activities on leadership development and activist training. Following the model of Freedom Schools (Payne, 1997), I believe that leadership and activist training are an integral part of classes. Unlike the tradition framework of the university where these aspects of student life are defined as "extracurricular activities" outside of academia, the founding mission of Asian American studies placed them at the center of curriculum (Omatsu, 2006). My approach emphasizes shared leadership, a model adapted from indigenous peoples' movements (Sotsisowah, 1978), the organizing experiences of early Asian immigrant labor leaders such as Philip Vera Cruz (Scharlin & Villanueva, 1992), and the women's movement (Kokopeli & Lakey, 1983). In contrast to leadership models in Western societies that focus on attributes of a few special individuals, the model of shared leadership requires people to become aware of leadership qualities in all they work with. Members of the team then work together to use each person's existing skill while also nurturing development of a targeted new skill in each individual. For students in my classes, shared leadership is not simply a classroom activity but an essential part of the process for completing the community project.

There can be no social change without simultaneously changing ourselves (Boggs, 1998). One struggle does not precede the other; both must occur at the same time. Boggs (1998) critiques revolutionary movements of the twentieth century as prioritizing structural change above personal transformation, with leaders oftentimes arguing that large-scale changes in society, such as increases in production and state ownership of the means of production, were pre-conditions for ending racism, sexism, and other forms of human exploitation. Boggs (2004) believes that the liberatory visions needed in the 21st century should draw from the insights of Martin Luther King, Jr. (1967b), especially his call for building movements that are simultaneously "self-transforming and structure-transforming." Boggs highlights King's belief that community-building must be accompanied by "a revolution of values," replacing the current focus in Western society on racism, militarism, and materialism (King, 1967b). In my own classes, I emphasize how students' community projects can be "self-transforming and structure-transforming" by sharing my own first experiences as a community activist in the early 1970s (Omatsu, 2001). As a student activist, I entered San Francisco Japantown with the mission of organizing the community. However, through my interactions with low-income residents and immigrant workers, it was the community that really organized and changed me. This valuable experience was not simply a lesson in humility but a revelation about the connection between social change and personal transformation.

What, then, is an anti-colonial approach to teaching and learning? Based on the experiences of Asian Americans, an anti-colonial approach is one that enables people to discover and develop the potential that exists deep within themselves. An anti-colonial approach provides people with the power to overcome the pernicious impact of stereotypes so that they can define their own lives. An anti-colonial approach heals consciousness ravaged by centuries of colonialism. An anti-colonial approach enables people to move beyond "histories that oppress" (Acuña, 1972) and to create their own "histories that liberate." For Asian Americans and others throughout the world, these are the needed histories that can liberate minds, hearts, and souls.

References

Asian American Political Alliance. (1968). *Asian American political alliance* (UC Berkeley), *1*(1), 2.

Asian American Political Alliance. (1969, October). *AAPA perspectives* (UC Berkeley), *1*(6), 4.

Abboud, S., & Kim, J. (2005). *Top of the class: How Asian parents raise high achievers—and how you can too.* New York: Berkley Books.

Acuña, R. (1972). *Occupied America: The Chicano's struggle toward liberation* (1st ed.). New York: Canfield.

Aguilar-San Juan, K. (Ed.). (1994). *The state of Asian America: Activism and resistance in the 1990s.* Boston: South End Press.

American Anthropological Association. (2007). Are we so different? Retrieved December 20, 2007, from http://raceproject.aaanet.org/home.html

Asian Americans for Action. (1969). *Asian Americans for Action newsletter, 1*(1) (New York City), 1.

Asian Americans United. (2005). Retrieved December 20, 2007, from http://www.aaunited.org/facts.html

Asian American youth: America's new trendsetters. (2006). United Business Media. Retrieved December 20, 2007, from http://sev.prnewswire.com/entertainment/20060726/LAW05826072006-1.html

Asian Community Center. (1970, November). *Rodan, northern California Asian American community news* 1(5).

Bell, D. (1985, July 15–22). The triumph of Asian-Americans: America's greatest success story. *New Republic,* 24–31.

Boggs, G. (1998). *Living for change: An autobiography.* Minneapolis: University of Minnesota Press.

Boggs, G. (2004). The beloved community of Martin Luther King. Retrieved December 20, 2007, from http://www.yesmagazine.com/article.asp?ID=704

Chen, E. (2006). Deconstructing the model minority image: Asian Pacific Americans, race, class, gender, and work. In E. Chen & G. Omatsu (Eds.), *Teaching about Asian Pacific Americans: Effective activities, strategies, and assignments for classrooms and communities* (pp. 41–56). Lanham, MD: Rowman & Littlefield.

Chin, F., Chan, J., Wong, S., & Inada, L. (Eds.). (1974). *Aiiieeeee! An anthology of Asian American writers.* New York: Mentor.

Eng, M. (2005, November 13). Succeed or die trying: Fear of failure and competitive stress haunt Asian American women. *Chicago Tribune.* Retrieved November 15, 2005, from http://www.chicagotribune.com/news/opinion/chi-0511130298ov13,0,2168226.story?coll=chi-newsopinionperspective-hed

Foner, P. (1970). *The Black Panthers speak the manifesto of the party: The first complete documentary record of the Panthers' program*. New York: Lippincott.
Fong, T. (2008). *The contemporary Asian American experience: Beyond the model minority* (3rd ed.). Upper Saddle River, NJ: Pearson Education.
Freire, P. (1970). *Pedagogy of the oppressed* (M. Ramos, Trans.). New York: Seabury Press.
Gandhi, M. (1953). *Towards new education*. In B. Kumarappa (Ed.) (pp. 67–78). Ahmedabad, India: Navajivan.
Gordon, M. (1964). *Assimilation in American life: The role of race, religion, and national origins*. New York: Oxford University Press.
Hirabayashi, L. (1998). *Teaching Asian America: Diversity and the problem of community*. Lanham, MD: Rowman and Littlefield.
I Wor Kuen. (1970, February). 12 point platform and program. *Getting Together, 1*(1).
Ichioka, Y. (1971). A buried past: Early Issei socialists and the Japanese community. *Amerasia Journal, 1*(1), 1–15.
Ichioka, Y. (1988). *The Issei: The world of the first-generation Japanese immigrants*. New York: Free Press.
Ichioka, Y. (2000). A historian by happenstance. *Amerasia Journal, 26*(1), 32–53.
King, M. (1967a, April 2). Beyong Vietnam —A time to break the silence. Speech to Clergy and Laity Concerned, Riverside Church, New York City. Retrieved December 1, 2007, from http://www.americanrhetoric.com/speeches/mlkatimetobreaksilence.htm
King, M. (1967b). *Where do we go from here: Chaos or community?* New York: Harper & Row.
Kokopeli, B., & Lakey, G. (1983). *Leadership for change: Toward a feminist model*. Gabriola Island, Canada: New Society Publishers.
Lai, H. (1976). A historical survey of the Chinese left in America. In E. Gee (Ed.). *Counterpoint: Perspectives on Asian America* (pp. 63–80). Los Angeles: UCLA Asian American Studies Center.
Lee, J., & Zhou, M. (Eds.). (2004). *Asian American youth: Culture, identity and ethnicity*. New York: Routledge.
Lee, S. (1996). *Unraveling the ëmodel minority' stereotype: Listening to Asian American youth*. New York: Teachers College Press.
Lim, H. (1982). The Chinese Workers' Mutual Aid Association. *East Wind*. Retrieved December 1, 2007, from http://www.aamovement.net/history/eastwind/11/lim1.html
Los Angeles Times. (2002, November 7). Times exit poll. Retrieved December 20, 2007, from www.latimes.com/news/custom/timespoll/
Los Angeles Times. (2006, November 9). Times exit poll. Retrieved December 20, 2007, from www.latimes.com/news/custom/timespoll/
Louie, S., & Omatsu, G. (Eds.). (2001). *Asian Americans: The movement and the moment*. Los Angeles: UCLA Asian American Studies Center Press.
Mao, Z. (1967). On practice. In *Selected works of Mao Zedong*. Beijing, China: Foreign Languages Press.
McGurn, W. (1991, June 24). The silent minority. *National Review*, pp. 19–20..
Meyer, M. (2003). Our own liberation: Reflections on Hawaiian epistemology. *Amerasia Journal, 29*(2), 139–164.
Mills, C. (1959). *The sociological imagination*. New York: Oxford University Press.
Newman, W. (1973). *American pluralism: A study of minority groups and social theory*. New York: Harper & Row.
Noh, E. (2007). Asian American women and suicide: Problems of responsibility and healing. *Women & Therapy, 30*(3/4), 87–107.
Omatsu, G. (1994). The four prisons and the movements of liberation: Asian American

activism from the 1960s to the 1990s. In K. Aguilar-San Juan (Ed.), *The state of Asian Pacific America: Activism and resistance in the 1990s* (pp. 19–69). Boston: South End Press.

Omatsu, G. (2001). Listening to the small voice speaking the truth: Grassroots organizing and the legacy of our movement. In S. Louie and G. Omatsu (Eds.), *Asian Americans: The movement and the moment* (pp. 307–316). Los Angeles: UCLA Asian American Studies Center Press.

Omatsu, G. (2003). Freedom schooling: Reconceptualizing Asian American Studies for our communities. *Amerasia Journal, 29*(2), 9–33.

Omatsu, G. (2006). Making student leadership development an integral part of our classrooms. In E. Chen & G. Omatsu (Eds.), *Teaching about Asian Pacific Americans: Effective activities, strategies, and assignments for classrooms and communities* (pp. 183–194). Lanham, MD: Rowman & Littlefield.

Omi, M., & Winant, H. (1986). *Racial formation in the United States: From the 1960s to the 1980s*. New York.

Ong, P. (1993). The growth of the Asian Pacific American population: Twenty million in 2020. In *The state of Asian Pacific America: Policy issues to the year 2020*. Los Angeles: LEAP Asian Pacific American Public Policy Institute and UCLA Asian American Studies Center.

Ong, P. (Ed.). (1994). *The state of Asian Pacific America: Economic diversity, issues & policies*. Los Angeles: LEAP Asian Pacific American Public Policy Institute and UCLA Asian American Studies Center.

Osumi, T. (2003). Teamwork and people power: Liberatory teaching in the elementary classroom. *Amerasia Journal, 29*(2), 92–118.

Osumi, T. (2006). Feast of resistance: Asian American history through food. In E. Chen & G. Omatsu (Eds.), *Teaching about Asian Pacific Americans: Effective activities, strategies, and assignments for classrooms and communities* (pp. 19–26). Lanham, MD: Rowman & Littlefield.

Payne, C. (1997). *I've got the light of freedom: The organizing tradition and the Mississippi freedom struggle*. Berkeley: University of California Press.

People of Color Environmental Groups Directory. (2000). Retrieved December 20, 2007, from http://www.ejrc.cau.edu/poc2000.htm

Principles of Environmental Justice. (1991). Retrieved December 20, 2007, from http://www.ejnet.org/ej/principles.html

Scharlin, C., & Villanueva, L. (1992). *Philip Vera Cruz: A personal history of Filipino immigrants and the farmworkers movement*. Los Angeles: UCLA Asian American Studies Center Press.

Smith, L. T. (1999). *Decolonizing methodologies: Research and indigenous peoples*. London: Zed Books.

Sotsisowah. (1978). Thoughts of peace: The great law. In Akwesasne Notes (Ed.), *Basic call to consciousness* (pp. 9–17). Summertown, TN: Native Voices.

Stannard, D. (1989). *Before the horror: The population of Hawaii on the eve of western contact*. Honolulu: University of Hawaii Press.

Tong, B. (1971). The ghetto of the mind: Notes on the historical psychology of Chinese Americans. *Amerasia Journal, 1*(1), 36–49.

TWLF (Third World Liberation Front). (1968). *Statement of the third world liberation front philosophy and goals*. (San Francisco State College). Mimeograph.

Understanding AAPA. (1969). *Asian American political alliance* (UC Berkeley), *1*(5).

U.S. Census Bureau. (1988). 1980 census of population. Subject reports. Asian and Pacific

Islander American population in the United States. Washington, DC: U.S. Government Printing Office.

U.S. Census Bureau. (2000). *Profile of selected economic characteristics: 2000.* Washington DC: U.S. Government Printing Office.

U.S. Census Bureau. (2004, December). *We the people: Asians in the United States.* Retrieved November 25, 2007, from http://www.census.gov/prod/2004pubs/censr-17.pdf

Vygotsky, L. (1978). *Mind in society: The development of higher psychological processes.* Cambridge, MA: Harvard University Press.

Wei, D. (1998). Students' stories in action comics. In E. Lee, D. Menkart, & M. Okazawa Rey (Eds.), *Beyond heroes and holidays: A practical guide to anti-racist taching and professional development* (pp. 216–227). Washington, DC: Network of Educators on the Americas.

Werner, D., & Bower, B. (1982). *Helping health workers learn: A book of methods, aids, and ideas for instructors at the village level.* Palo Alto, CA: Hesperian Foundation.

Wink, J., & Putney, L. (2002). *A vision of Vygotsky.* Boston: Allyn & Bacon.

Winn, R. (Director). (2005). *Grassroots rising: Asian immigrant workers in Los Angeles* [Video]. Los Angeles: Visual Communications.

Woo, D. (2000). *Glass ceilings and Asian Americans: The new face of workplace barriers.* Walnut Creek, CA: AltaMira.

Wright, R. (1956). *The color curtain.* Cleveland, OH: World Publishing.

12 "A Past Is Not a Heritage"

Reclaiming Indigenous Principles for Global Justice and Education for Peoples of African Descent

Nola Butler Byrd and Menan Jangu

Throughout Africa, the Americas, and many other parts of the world, peoples of African descent continue to suffer the devastating effects of colonization, capitalism, racism, and poverty. As Tandom and Solarin so aptly express:

> All over Africa, poverty has increased rather than decreased. If conflicts stem from poverty and the struggle for scarce resources, then the re-colonization of Africa that is taking place right in front of our eyes is the principal cause of poverty in Africa. There can be no peace in the continent as long as the bulk of its population is poor, and there can be no growth or development as long as the invisible market forces continue to enable foreign owners of capital and technology to plunder Africa's rich resources at a fraction of their value, and as long as the debt overhang continues to enslave Africa to the mercy of its creditors. (Tandom, 2000, p. 181)

> These (African American) communities are the descendants of the Africans that were transported to these countries the long era of the African Holocaust and Dispersal (slavery and colonialism) of the 15th–19th century. What is truly sad and sobering is that their plight is not that much different from that of the majority of their kinfolk in the African content from where they were displaced. And we are talking of 500 years. (Solarin, 2004, p. 67)

This chapter examines these intersecting, sobering realities while speaking to the tools and effects of exploitation, as well as paths to their elimination.

Education is a key to offsetting and eventually eliminating racism and colonialism. With this goal in mind, we draw together critical principles of African and African-centered education, vision-building, and decision-making to create a set of principles to contribute to educational change for social and global justice. The principles we offer to guide such education focus on teaching the interconnections between the problems of people of African descent in the United States and Africa, how violence and environmental issues are intertwined, and how these problems might be addressed by future generations who learn about them. The principles offered encourage efforts by all people to overcome the negative impacts of historical and current racism, environmental devastation and violence, and to become healthy active global citizens. We recognize that attempting social change without also attending to the needs of currently existing individuals is a futile exercise. Healthy whole individuals hold the greatest hope for making positive social change in the future.

Root Causes of the African Diaspora

People of African descent in Africa and in the diaspora bear the disproportionate burden of political, economic and ecological interventions in the form of the slave trade, colonization, neocolonization, and globalization. This chapter briefly explores the root causes of cultural transformation, migration, resource conflicts and wars, poor health conditions, and environmental damage. Films such as *Blood Diamonds*, *Darwin's Nightmare* (eating exotic fish heads), and *Black Gold* (coffee in Ethiopia) document the environmental injustice, and violation of human rights and animals taking place in Africa. People in Africa are now exposed to bio-prospecting, bio-piracy, poverty, exotic species, infectious diseases, and water scarcity. Despite these challenges, some communities in Africa have proven resilient and inspirational by becoming activists for positive change.

Africa is a continent rich in human and natural resources (renewable and non-renewable), cultural diversity, and bio-diversity. At the same time, Africa remains poor in economic terms expressed by the gross domestic product and the human development index. These two scenarios result in contradictory perceptions of Africa. Despite a diverse ecology and resource abundance, the continent is often described as a disease ridden region with staggering poverty.

In brief, the rich resources of Africa attracted Europeans and Arabs who extracted African wealth through waves of exploitation. Using euphemisms such as civilization and modernization, Africans were (and still are) often portrayed as lacking the technological know-how to make use of their economic potential. The disruption of African societies has been devastating, resulting in mass displacement, imprisonment, torture, slavery, death, child labor, environmental destruction, and wars. Millions of Africans were disbursed around the world through kidnapping for the slave trade, fleeing hostile or desperate conditions, or seeking a better life.

Slavery and Migration

The Atlantic slave trade was the forced dispersal of African peoples in the Atlantic world, especially in the Western hemisphere (Alpers, 2001). It devastated the labor base, economic opportunities, social networks, species diversity, the environment, and technological advancement in Africa. This involuntary migration through the trans-Saharan, trans-Atlantic, and Indian Ocean slave trades accounts for most of the Black presence outside of Africa today. Slaves became the major source of labor in the regions where Africans were shipped. The establishment of communities of people of African descent outside the African continent is known as the *African diaspora*. Thus, people of African descent are found in North America, South America, the Caribbean, and Asia. Between 650 and 1900, almost 23 million Africans were shipped around the world as slaves, over 11 million to the new world (Maddison, 2005). According to census figures, people of African descent now represent 12%–13% of the population of the United States.

Though illegal, slavery continues today in Africa, North and South America. Slave holders now control enslaved people without owning them, exploiting their labor without the responsibility of supporting them. There are more enslaved people than ever before requiring new efforts to interrupt diverse forms of human trafficking such as sexual slavery, child labor, and child soldiers.

Vestiges of Slavery: Racism in the United States

Racism is alive and well in most countries outside of Africa. Many people believe that slavery is an historical fact that has no meaning in the modern world. Yet, across all relevant indicators, people of African descent continue to experience severe consequences for their history of oppression in the United States. In the United States, people of African descent:

- have $31,408 medium household income compared to $47,199 median White household income according to the U.S. Census Bureau (YWCA, n.d.);
- are more likely to live in poverty than people of European descent (24% to 8%, respectively) according to US Bureau Census data (Rizvi, 2007);
- experience twice the infant mortality rates as do Whites (Abdullah, 2007);
- are more likely to be illegally prevented from voting than people of European descent (Colb, 2004);
- are approximately 7 times more likely to go to jail or prison than people of European descent (Kaiser Family Foundation, 2006).

In nearly every aspect of life, there are costs associated with being a Person of African descent. For example, in the United States People of African descent suffer modern-day overt and covert oppression by being profiled, suspected, and falsely accused of crimes by store owners, teachers, neighbors, employers, and ultimately the police. "Driving while Black" is an expression used to describe the at-risk position of drivers of African descent who are stopped by the police in highly disproportionate numbers. We could adapt this expression to just about any circumstance encountered in everyday life: "applying while Black," "going to school while Black," "working while Black," or "looking for an apartment while Black." The list is long and shows few signs of getting shorter over time. Because African Americans are less likely to receive a good education and thereby get a good job, they are less likely to afford a lawyer to defend them once they are accused of a crime. It is also the case, that the poorer you are, the more likely it is that you will be suspected of wrong doing—producing double jeopardy for people of African descent when it comes to avoiding encounters with the law.

Thus people of African descent experience serious oppression throughout the diaspora as the exploitation of African countries continues via numerous extraordinary global programs. These programs, such as international trade agreements and international organizations led by multinational corporations, continue the quest for cheap labor and resources via new forms of colonization.

Colonialism and Neocolonialism

The economic influence perpetuated by colonial powers altered social and economic activities in Africa. Africans were forced to work under colonial programs while underpaid and underfed. Time allocated to subsistence farming was reduced, leading to more frequent famine and malnutrition. To justify the exploitation, African colonizers stereotyped people in Africa as backward, and culturally and technologically primitive. The land was assumed not to be fully utilized. Brutality was imposed on the colonized peoples on the assumed superiority of European men and their exclusive status as fully human. Colonial administrators promoted cash crops employing huge amounts of fertilizers and pesticides that had detrimental effects on the environment.

Direct domination of African countries was economically and militarily expensive, thus colonizers embraced neocolonialism. Under this type of colonialism, corporations assured the maximization of their profits by controlling most African resources, economies, labor, markets, and political processes either by supporting corrupt governments or anti-government movements. The eight most powerful industrialized nations that make up the G8,[1] interested in securing African resources, initiated different neocolonial strategies such as offering loans and grants to the African governments through private creditors. Many African countries quickly accumulated large debts to the G8 countries and international agencies such as the World Bank and International Monetary Fund. Currently African countries struggle with unpayable debt recorded at $300 billion in 2004 (Booker & Colgan, 2004). Meanwhile G8 countries control international markets and trade by restricting trade among African countries so they are forced to trade under unfair terms with the industrialized G8 countries.

Globalization

Neocolonialism continues under the general canopy of globalization—a contemporary euphemism for a system that releases corporations from the constraints of national and international laws. Globalization *could* mean an integrated world without territorial boundaries, where countries have equal opportunities to interact, trade, acquire, and share knowledge and technologies. Instead, globalization refers to international policies and practices imposed by industrialized countries that permit multinational corporations to invest in Africa and other former colonies to acquire natural resources at bargain prices, and take advantage of cheap labor, lax or unenforceable safety laws, and little to no environmental protection.

"Free trade" agreements thus shift jobs from industrialized countries leaving millions unemployed, affecting people of the African diaspora disproportionately. In the United States, they experience internal colonialism as profits continue to be extracted from their underpaid labor, from fraudulent or exorbitant loans, from inflated prices in neighborhood stores, theft or property, and unjust imprisonment.

Tools Used to Dominate African Economies and Resources

Continental Africans and Africans in the diaspora have endured different forms of violence that can be traced to the colonial period where initial military interventions and bribes of the chiefs were common. In response, Africans have challenged colonial interventions using different approaches including nonviolent diplomacy, armed resistance, and appeals to national and international governing bodies. The effectiveness of these efforts, however, has been limited by the ability of major powers to continue domination through violence, media, language, loans, laws, and trade mechanisms.

Military Interventions and Police Violence

Systems of domination and resource extraction cannot be imposed or sustained without force or the threat of force. When people of African descent have challenged their oppression, resistance is usually curtailed by military, police, or government repression using direct force, targeted assassination, mass killing, imprisonment, or unjust laws. The most recent example of neocolonial intervention is the United States African Command (AFRICOM), the building of United States military bases in Africa. Ostensibly created to protect African countries from terrorism, the military presence will assure continued resource extraction against any interference, including resistance from those who own or live on the lands affected. In the United States, preferred methods of control are poverty, inequitable education, massive unemployment, imprisonment, police violence, and the death penalty. These methods work together to hamper African-American progress.

Education

Imperialists have used education and science to exploit resources from Africa and people of African descent for centuries. African forms of education (indigenous knowledge passed through oral traditions) are characterized as primitive, backward and associated with witchcraft. To control people, communities in Africa and the diaspora are inundated with propaganda and education purporting the benefits of capitalism. Colonial languages such as English or French widely dominate. Educational institutions in exploited communities and countries extol the virtues of Western knowledge and corporations. Western researchers or people of African descent trained in Western education ignore or disparage native values, knowledge, customs, culture, and identity. Indigenous people are viewed as having undeveloped mental abilities: not fully human, not civilized, not educated. All these strategies justify continued exploitation. Research is used as an entry point to native communities, followed by new waves of exploration, discovery, exploitation, and appropriation. Smith (1999) contends, "Western researchers enter communities armed with good will in their front pockets and patents in their back pockets; they bring medicine into village and extract blood for genetic analysis" (p. 24).

Discriminatory educational practices and disparate treatment of are major forms of social and economic control in countries such as the United States. In particular, African Americans are overrepresented in the *school to prison pipeline*, which includes (NAACP Legal Defense Fund, 2006):

- experiencing inadequate school resources;
- being over-identified as special needs students;
- experiencing more severe disciplinary responses than White peers for the same conduct (34% of school suspensions, 45% of juvenile arrests).

Media

The media plays a significant role in shaping how people view the world. People in different countries rely on Western and corporate owned radio, television, newspapers, and Internet to access information. Media owners and sponsors determine what these publics consume. As in the West, advertisements, programs, and public relations campaigns exert a powerful influence over human thoughts, behaviors, and consumption patterns. Through media, people of African descent within industrialized and re-colonized countries are taught to desire and emulate the unsustainable and environmentally destructive beliefs and life-styles of the West. Further, people of African descent are discredited and targeted through blatant and subtle media portrayals.

Economic Policies

Despite statements asserting dedication to the interests of poor people, international financial and trade institutions (World Bank, International Monetary Fund, World Trade Organization), support the interests of big corporations through international economic policies. Poor countries are seduced or coerced into borrowing money and adopting policies that maximize profits for foreign investors at the expense of the people, the environment, and other species. Structural adjustment programs, engineered by industrialized countries, subject populations to great deprivation through the devaluation of their currency and the subsequent cutting social programs. Exports and imports are manipulated to the advantage of foreign corporations.

Impacts: The Legacy of the Slave Trade, Colonialism, and Globalization

The massive exploitation of resources and people in Africa has left devastating effects that have yet to be fully quantified. The continent is now stricken by poverty, migration, child labor, child solders, ethnic conflicts, wars, diseases, corruption, and environmental damage. Africa remains the poorest region in the world and it is getting poorer. Its share in international trade transactions is said to be less than 3% (Souare, 2004). Meanwhile, countries in the North enjoy large shares of benefits obtained from African resources. The condition has created scarcity among Africans. Likewise, the region now is a battleground for ethnic tensions and wars. The civil wars reported in Sierra Leone, Angola, and Congo are indicative of the unequal access and distribution of resources linked to trade between industrialized countries and developing nations. Under neocolonialism affluent countries exploit resources from Africa and escape the burden of their environmental and human impacts.

Food Scarcity

The agricultural revolution purported to solve the hunger problem has instead produced food scarcity and led to the accumulation of hazardous materials in the food chain. Both food and cash crops are now continuously exported from the same countries where people are experiencing famine. Numerous countries report famine and riots based on skyrocketing food prices. High food prices have devastating effects in poor countries, where food often accounts for more than half a family's spending. It is estimated that over 2.8 million people live on less than $2 per day (World Watch Institute, 2002). Poverty has led to high mortality and morbidity rates. Life expectancy has declined dramatically. In 2002, life expectancy for the 680 million people living in sub-Saharan Africa was only 45.8 years (Preux & Druet-Cabanac, 2005).

Violence, Wars, and Political Instability

Armed conflicts, ethnic crises, and fraudulent elections sparking violence (e.g., cases of Zimbabwe and Kenya) have taken a heavy toll in Africa and are increasing. More than thirty internal wars have been fought in Africa since 1970 (Tandom, 2000). Many armed struggles since World War II have arisen from disputes over territorial boundaries established by colonial powers and competition over resource access and domination (Murphy, 1990; Le Billion, 2001).

The violent scenarios in the Sierra Leone, Sudan, the Niger Delta, and the Democratic Republic of Congo show how resource extraction and exportation have triggered imbalances of power and political instability in the region. Abundant mineral and oil resources in these countries have spawned violence, wars, poverty, migration, and child labor. Sierra Leone has been devastated by a war that has lasted for more than 10 years. Despite incredible wealth from diamonds, Sierra Leone remains one of the world's poorest countries with the highest maternal and infant mortality rates (Zack-Williams, 1999; Ahmad, Lopez, & Inoue, 2000).

Coltan, a key component in electronic devices such as mobile phones and computers, is mainly produced in the Democratic Republic of Congo (DRC). Despite the high prices of Coltan and other Congo minerals, Congo is among the countries significantly devastated by war, poverty, population displacement, and widespread rape. Available estimates suggest that 3.3 million have died in the DRC war in a population of 60 million people (Coghlan et al, 2006). Weak political institutions, inequality, and unequal distribution of resources based on "free market" capitalist principles escalate violence and perpetuate civil wars.

Spread of Disease

In places like Central Africa, forests threatened by logging and road construction are linked to disease outbreaks. For instance, in Central Africa, rates of Ebola hemorrhagic fever increased dramatically as forests disappeared. Mining activities in the DRC are directly related to an increase in prostitution and sexually transmitted diseases. Sexual exploitation and violence are widespread especially among military personal and rebels in war zones. Major displacements of people and deepened inequalities have increased the vulnerability of women and children to sexual assaults and sexually transmitted diseases such as HIV/AIDS. Conflicts, displacement, food insecurity, and poverty have the potential to make populations more vulnerable to HIV transmission. The HIV prevalence rate is estimated to be between 15% and 24% in the general population in the eastern DRC (Spiegel, 2004).

Environmental Degradation and Extinction of Species

A stable physical environment is essential to sustain humans and other living organisms. Climate change, ozone layer depletion, acid rain, exposure to hazardous materials, deforestation, loss of bio-diversity, pollution, and decline of water quality and quantity are the results of massive resource exploitation and haphazard disposal of waste.

The environmental damage caused by the world's richest countries amounts to more than the entire third-world debt of $1.8 trillion (*Guardian,* 2008). In addition to $2.3 trillion worth of environmental damage related to greenhouse gases, dam construction in Africa (floodplain of the Pongolo River in South Africa and Kenya's Tana River) has displaced and endangered millions of people and numerous other species of life (Pottinger, 1996).

The Coltan mining activities that rarely benefit communities in Congo have devastating effects on animals and bio-diversity where miners or loggers in areas such as the Kahuzi Biega National Park consume bush meats. As roads intrude into previously inaccessible forests, all types of animals are hunted for sale and consumption in the bush meat trade, giving rise to the empty forest syndrome and intensifying the endangerment and extinction of species. Hunting and poaching further threatens the ecosystem balance, rainfall cycles, and creates paths for the transfer of diseases from animals to humans.

Loss of Indigenous Knowledge and Culture

African indigenous knowledge, culture, and languages are disappearing as a result of the ongoing colonial and globalization strategies. The sense of interconnection and interdependence among human beings, animals, and their surroundings has been seriously degraded. Preservation schemes initiated and funded by international agencies ignore the role and knowledge of indigenous people and thus, are based on inadequate information about local conditions whereas African communities have sustained their natural environments through indigenous knowledge for millennia. In East Africa, farmers planted drought resistant crops in dry areas such as varieties of millet, sorghum, and legumes. Crops like yams, sweet potatoes, and plantains were grown in wet and fertile areas (Wangari, 1996. p. 190). Soil fertility was maintained through crop rotation, shifting cultivation, and mixed cropping. In contrast, Western monocultures and chemical agriculture have resulted in soil degradation and desertification. Further, Western plans for conservation of wildlife were motivated by attracting more tourists. This process included little involvement from local communities in the protection of the environment. Instead, local communities, like Maasai people in Kenya and Tanzania, were expected to entertain tourists.

The Importance of African-Centered Learning

What do the historical and current sociopolitical conditions of people of African descent mean for educators in industrialized countries? What principles can we employ to assure that change will take place at the macro level of international relations and at the micro level of individual behavior and personal fulfillment? Before we can answer that question we must examine how the colonization, enslavement, exploitation, and diaspora of Africans have impacted on people of African descent within the United States—personally, as individuals. What is the human experience? How can educational institutions be accountable for the welfare of learners of African descent? What is our social responsibility as educators to correct the injustices against people of African descent, and how do we fulfill that responsibility?

People of African descent and culturally responsive allies have invested considerable time and resources into education and literacy resulting in the development of numerous organizations and movements for social justice in the United States, including the National Association for the Advancement of Colored People (NAACP), The National Urban League, and the United Negro College Fund (UNCF). The freedom school movement in urban communities occurred from 1960 into the 1970's, inspired by the civil rights and Black Power Movements leading to the development of survival programs based on the idea of self-determination. Through these programs, the Black Panthers established a network of community service projects designed to improve the life chances of African American people (Jackson, 2001; Abron, 1998; Pollard & Ajirotutu, 2000). Other recent examples include the development of African-centered schools including the Nairobi Day School in East Palo Alto, California, in operation from 1966–1984, that used African and African American history, culture, and language as the basis of its curriculum making use of pedagogical techniques that responded to African American children's learning styles. In 1991 the African American Immersion School model was implemented in Milwaukee (Wisconsin) Public Schools in response to the critical need to provide quality, meaningful, empowering education for African American learners in that city. Today, the numbers of African-centered learning projects and schools, independent schools and charter schools, as well as home schooling, continue to grow in the quest by people of African descent for self-determination and well-being (Jackson, 2001; Pollard & Ajirotutu, 2000).

Consequences of Oppression: Humiliation, Natal Alienation, and Exilic Agony

The long-standing mistreatment and isolation of People of African descent led community psychologist Donald Klein (1991) to describe the resultant individual behavioral characteristics as the Humiliation Dynamic, an interpersonal phenomenon endemic to dominating, warring cultures:

> The Humiliation Dynamic is used to socialize children and engineer conformity among adults. It poisons relationships between individuals and groups and…is a major weapon in the oppression of women, people of color, and other stigmatized groups. The experience of humiliation and the fear of humiliation are implicated in a variety of mental illnesses and engender rage which is manifested in anti-social behavior, murder, and suicide. Moreover, the dynamics of humiliation, both that which is experienced and that which is feared play an important part in perpetuating international tensions and violence. (p. 2)

Humiliation demoralizes people and communities and creates a culture of alienation and pessimism, which often causes people to give up on themselves, others, and life.

Alienation and Its Effects on Identity and Empowerment: A Past Is Not a Heritage

African-centered scholar Marimba Ani (1980, 1994) describes European cultural thought and behavior as key components of the complex tangle of the European culture of domination. From an African-centered perspective, she has inspired many scholars, educators, and activists to reclaim African heritage and move beyond the deficit approach that focuses on slavery as the definitive "past" experience of people of African descent. In support of the African-centered principle of self-definition, she uses the Kiswahili term, *Maafa* (meaning terrible occurrence or disaster) to reclaim the right of people of African descent to tell their story of the incomprehensible human death and destruction beginning with the enslavement and murder of Africans and the destruction of African cultures, first by Arabic forces, then by Europeans, and the continuing oppression and intergenerational effects of this trauma on people of African descent today.

The *Maafa* has led to significant negative consequences for people of African descent, including Patterson's contention that there is a natal alienation from Africa, or at the very least a secular excommunication. He contends that this occurred because enslaved Africans were denied all claims and obligations to their parents and living relations, and by extension all claims and obligations to ancestors and descendants. Skinner (1999) describes this significant alienation and questioning about Africa and identity as an "exilic" agony about Africa that is suffered by many torn from its shores, and a similar alienation and questioning of Africa suffered by some Africans born and colonized there. This was a profound loss, because heritage and ancestralization are critical parts of African culture. Coupled with the social isolation of slavery, enslaved Africans were left devoid of significant social connection and the power of social relations that human cultures need in order to function and thrive. Patterson (1982) provides a sound rationale for indigenous African-centered education, by contending that a "past is not a heritage":

> He had a past, to be sure. But a past is not a heritage. Everything has a history, including sticks and stones. Slaves differed from other human beings in that they were not allowed freely to integrate the experience of their ancestors into their lives, to inform their understanding of social reality with the inherited meanings of their natural forebears, or to anchor the living present in any conscious community of memory. That they reached back for the past, as they reached out for the related living, there can be no doubt, unlike other persons, doing so meant struggling with and penetrating the iron curtain of the master, his community, his laws, his policemen or patrollers, and his heritage. (p. 5)

When Someone Is Sick, Everyone Is...

In *The Miner's Canary: Enlisting Race, Resisting Power, Transforming Democracy,* Guinier and Torres (2002) compared the plight of people of African descent and other peoples of color with "miners' canaries" whose highly sensitive metabolisms detected methane and carbon monoxide gas traces that signaled potential explosions, poisoned air, or both. People of African descent serve as life insurance for Eurocentric capitalist "miners" to test the volatility in the environment of Eurocentric capitalist "mines." Africans and other people of color are the first to suffer the dire consequences of this dysfunctional, toxic system, but not the last.

While Africa, Africans, and other peoples of color throughout the diaspora are experiencing physical deprivation, Eurocentric cultures are experiencing a spiritual or soul hunger that is threatening to consume the world. Indigenous African scholar Somé (1998) cites a shaman from his village,

> We Africans also believe that we need healing at the hands of the white man. This is why our children leave us. You see, it's the same world, the same house. When someone is sick, everyone is. Why should we remain passive while the white man searches the world for the means to save himself? We are together in this struggle. All our souls need rest in a safe home. All people must heal, because we are all sick. (p. 17)

Indigenous African-Centered Education

Three other factors are relevant to the renewed interest in African-centered education in recent years: demographic shifts and political changes due to immigration, the most recent educational reform movement, and renewed attention and scholarship by African American scholars concerning Afrocentrism and African-centered education. These factors play a significant role in the increase in the numbers of educators and parents who are advocating African-centered educational alternatives. This renewed focus has been observed throughout the United States, England, Canada, and other European-dominated societies, and is most evident in urban areas where large groups of people of African descent reside (Pollard & Ajirotuto, 2000).

In using the term *African-centered*, we are not suggesting that these values are necessarily understood or practiced the same way in all African cultures and societies, nor are they unique to Africa; however, there are sufficient commonalities across the cultures of African people to establish common themes (Gyekye, 1996). African-centered education places people of African descent at the center of the educational experience as a subject, rather than an object. From a traditional African worldview, this placement supports an inclusionary, emancipatory, multicultural learning environment incorporating reciprocal relationships and the sharing of power and resources, by giving equal representation to all groups—rather than one group over or below any other.

African-centered education is holistic, transdisciplinary learning, designed to achieve high academic standards, social development, critical and creative thinking, and the development of self-knowledge and individual gifts for the betterment of community and spirit. African-centered refers to the collective community values of indigenous African people exhibited in the ancient Kemetian concept of *Ma'at* (truth, justice, balance, and harmony). These values are also integrated into the principles of the *Nguzo Saba* (unity, self-determination, collective work and responsibility, cooperative economics, purpose, creativity, and faith) (Karenga, 1965). Karenga uses the Kiswahili term, *Kawaida*, to describe the philosophy behind African-centered orientation. *Kawaida* is the ongoing synthesis of the best of African thought and practice in constant exchange with the world. Culture, one of its key principles, is described as the source of people's identity, purpose and direction. *Kawaida* is a continuous dialogue with African culture, in search of the answers to critical concerns of the African and human community.

African-centered education is designed to support the development of health, self-esteem and empowerment by helping people own African ancestry, history and accomplishments, the beauty and intelligence of Africa, African worldview and values, and the value of Africa to the world. It is designed to overcome exilic agony (angst of being cast out from one's homeland), humiliation, hegemony, individualism, consumerism, and other destructive results of colonization. African-centered education is the way of beauty, peace, community, and love.

Educating people from an African-centered perspective emphasizes heritage through the veneration of ancestors, nature and spirit in daily life. This is accomplished by attuning to and balancing with the natural rhythms of nature and spirit through individual and group processes, education, rituals and ceremonies. Developing methods and spaces in which to honor the natural expression of these traditions should be carefully considered as part of African-centered pedagogy. Collaborating with African and African-centered educators, healers, elders, and teachers knowledgeable in sharing traditional knowledge in traditionally appropriate ways in modern environments is part of the developmental process of successful infusion.

Implementing African-Centered Education for Global Justice

History has shown that implementing any type of educational reform is a challenge. However, infusing African-centered learning into existing traditional curricula or developing African-centered learning communities can be especially challenging because of the *Maafa* and the ongoing negative attitudes and behaviors toward Africa and people of African descent. Individuals and communities implementing African-centered learning must have support in order to be successful.

One example of how needs were addressed in the implementation of a successful project is the African America Immersion elementary school in Milwaukee. The founders began with basic aspects of African-centeredness, such as clothing, and basic principles and rituals, while simultaneously preparing learners to deal effectively with the bicultural reality they negotiate in U.S. society. Gradually, over a 5-year period, they integrated deeper levels of African worldview into all aspects of the curriculum and environment. Their project allocated resources, including time for education and training, support staff, and consultants to assist educators in learning African history, pedagogy, and world view; ongoing assistance with the development and implementation of curriculum into the learning environment; and formative and summative assessment (Pollard & Ajirotutu, 2000).

Developing and implementing education of this nature is a process that involves transformative strategies that work with and through individuals and communities where they are, and then uses decolonizing African-centered democratic decision-making and learning strategies to help learning communities scaffold themselves to more liberating spaces.

Basic Needs: Community, Educators, and Learners

Learning Community Needs. Learning community leaders, educators, and learners need principles, values, and missions to guide their work and the development of successful African-centered learning. They need to learn and implement effective home-school-community partnerships that support them in their work. They also need adequate resources so they can develop and implement a healthy, socially just learning environment. In order to be truly liberating, African-centered democratic decision-making processes must be used to establish and maintain socially just learning strategies and environments. Projects also need to develop clear visions, missions, and goals that are constructed from African-centered principles through collaborative processes that engendered ownership by members of the learning community.

Needs for Educators

Attracting, developing and retaining committed African-centered professionals who are dedicated to serving people of African descent is crucial to successful implementation. Key to educator success is support from those in power and from the community for their professional development and personal growth for the benefit of the learning community. They need to learn how to partner effectively with home-school-community partnerships to support learner growth and development. They also need the freedom to develop and implement creative African-centered curriculum in their learning environments, without penalty or microagressions directed toward them. They also need formative and summative assessments of their work that align with African-centered principles for academic excellence, as opposed to oppressive Eurocentric standards focused on testing and other deficit approaches.

Needs for Learners

Learners need to be loved and appreciated as people of African descent by culturally competent educators and other professionals who have high expectations for them, based on international standards, not the Euramerican norm. They need educators, professionals, and allies who are excellent teachers, competent advocates, and role models who support them in developing self-advocacy and inoculating themselves against overt and covert oppression. Learners should study principles and ethics that engender peace, well-being, and social and environmental justice.

International Documents on Human Rights, Bio-diversity, Environmental Justice, and Empowerment of Indigenous Peoples

Many organizational documents advocate human rights, social justice and peace. Yet educators and students are often unaware of their existence. These documents encourage grassroots movements to simultaneously address problems associated with democracy, environmental stability, economic justice, bio-diversity, indigenous knowledge, and peace. They challenge colonial politics that have created miserable conditions for people of African descent everywhere. The documents are divided into four sections.

Equality, Democracy, Commitment to Justice and Human Rights

The following documents advocate partnerships among African countries and other countries in the world to design a shared common vision to eradicate poverty, and create sustainable economies, peace, democracy, good governance, respect for fundamental rights and freedoms, gender equality, and environmental protection.

- African Charter on the Rights and Welfare of the Child, adopted in 1990 and entered into force in 1999 (OAU, 2001)

- Conference of Ministers of Education of African Member States (UNESCO, 1976)
- The African Charter for Human and Peoples' Rights (OAU, 1979)
- The World Conference Against Racism, Racial Discrimination, Xenophobia and Related Intolerance (United Nations, 2001)

Indigenous Knowledge, Culture, and Beliefs

Indigenous values (languages, cultures, traditions, and spiritualities) are largely missing from existing education programs widely dominated by Western paradigms. These documents show how loss of languages is accompanied by loss of knowledge about species, medicine and methods for protecting the environment. They reveal different forms of racism on a global level, highlighting the worth of indigenous spirituality, beliefs, and ceremony, and provisions for improving living standards for indigenous peoples.

- The Coolangatta Statement on Indigenous Peoples' Rights in Education (WIPCE, 1999)
- A Universal Declaration of a Global Ethic (Global Dialogue Institute, 1998)
- Indigenous Environmental Network Declaration; Environmental Racism and Racial Discrimination (IEN, 2001)

Environmental Protection and Equal Access to Natural Resources

These documents show that humankind is only one part of nature. All life depends on the uninterrupted functioning of natural systems to ensure the supply of energy and nutrients. They highlight the symptoms and causes of environmental degradation, teaching people to discern the linkages between conserving biodiversity, alleviating poverty, and peace, and how key groups can take action.

- The Green Belt Movement and Wangari Maathai (2008[2])
- The African Convention on the Conservation of Nature and Natural Resources adopted by the African Heads of State and Government, adopted on September 15, 1968, and entered into force on June 16, 1969 (African Union, 2003)
- The World Charter for Nature (United Nations, 1982)

Protecting Humans and Bio-diversity

These documents present strategies and actions to protect the natural, animal, plant, and human resources to ensure improved and sustainable lives for all.

- The Convention on International Trade in Endangered Species of Wild Fauna and Flora signed on March 3, 1973, and amended on June 22, 1979 (CITES, 1979)

- The 1992 Convention on Biological Diversity (United Nations, 2001)
- Bushmeat Crisis Task Force (2008; engages local communities in preventing the commercial bushmeat trade, promoting alternatives, and protecting individual animals and spaces).

Basic Principles of African-Centered Education

Seven overview principles and 18 specific principles address both macro/global and micro/individual action aspects of African-centered education that can be applied in schools and academic institutions. The overview principles emphasize the need and commitment among educators and students to address problems such as wars, violence, corruption, human rights violations, and environmental devastation.

Seven Overview Principles of African-Centered Education

Education by, for, and about people of African descent would:

Advocate for human rights, environmental preservation, and social justice
African-centered education would emphasize the need to achieve equality in human societies, while recognizing equal protection for other species and the environment. This requires interdisciplinary learning that links social, environmental, and economic sustenance for all.

Value identity, uniqueness, dignity, and interdependence of humans and other species
This principle acknowledges that the earth and all forms of life depend on each other in intricate ways. Understanding interdependence will help students value diversity among people and species. People must relearn respect for other creatures and plants to protect life support systems.

Create partnerships between continental Africans, Africans in the diasporas and other groups
Global cooperation, the partnership of Africans in Africa and in the diaspora, as well as other peoples and nations, is necessary to create and maintain programs in education, environmental management and economic development that are fair, equitable, and effective. Educators, scholars, and the intelligentsia of African descent have the responsibility to critically examine the role of the continent and its peoples in the whole spectrum of global engagement (Solarin, 2004).

Advocate for peace through forgiveness, acceptance of differences, sharing resources, and cherishing common roots
Education should teach skills to prevent violence and assist victims of violence, wars, and ethnic conflicts to negotiate peace. Many people hold grudges because of inequality, discrimination and power relations

that have created racial inequities and economic injustice. Nelson Mandela, former president of South Africa, is a vivid example of the art of forgiveness for the common good for both the victims and perpetuators of apartheid in South Africa.

Affirm indigenous knowledge and contributions

African communities, like other indigenous communities, have survived over millennia using traditional knowledge and practices. Despite the importance of traditional knowledge, most schools and colleges do not incorporate traditional languages, spiritual learning and ethnic sciences. Schools should support language reclamation and indigenous knowledge along with other knowledge bases.

Offer alternatives to human consumption trends

Education must encourage protection of bio-diversity, freshwater resources, air and land by examining the causes and reducing human commercialization and consumption of resources. Alternatives must be studied and practiced.

Extend love to all other humans and other creatures

Learning to love will reduce violence, wars, and threats. Through love and appreciation of each life (humans and animals) peaceful dialogue, decisions, and actions can improve human lives and protect bio-diversity. Reducing military spending, and expanding budgets for social services such as education and health care services should be the priority.

Principles Derived from African-Centered Sources

The following African-centered principles are derived from traditional African and African-centered sources for the purpose of encouraging the development of project-specific visions, missions and goal statements, support for leaders and educators, as well as guidelines for socially just education of people of African descent. These principles reflect an African-centered worldview that provides a lens through which to see the world and a map by which to negotiate life. The ontology, axiology, cosmology, epistemology, and praxis of this worldview reflect its cornerstone values: ancestor veneration, social collectivity, and the spiritual basis of existence (Grills, 2002). These principles promote the development of environmental health, while engendering peace and well-being for all people.

Sources for these principles range from traditional African philosophies including *adinkra* symbols from the West African Akan people and ancient Kemetian philosophies, including *Ma'at*; to African-centered philosophies based on traditional African philosophies such as Maulana Karenga's (1965) *Nguzo Saba* or Seven Principles, Marimba Ani's (1994) critique of European world view from an African-centered perspective, and Cheryl Grills's (2002) philosophies for African-centered psychology.

Concepts of Spirit, Universe, Self–Cornerstones for African-Centered Education

Spirit. In traditional African worldview, spirit refers to the life force, energy, or incorporeal, animating principle that reflects the essence and sustenance of all matter. It is as important as the physical incarnation of the self. Spirit and religion are not necessarily synonymous (Grills, 2002).

Metaphysical interconnectedness. As human beings, we are always in relationship with and influenced by other forces and beings. There is a metaphysical component to each person that requires certain social and natural obligations. Examples include the cycle of life (birth through death) and breathing (inhalation and exhalation) (Dukor, 1993 cited in Grills, 2002).

Love ethic. In an African-centered context, love is defined and employed in the way that hooks (2000) describes in *All About Love: New Visions*, as extending oneself for the nurturing of spirit in oneself or others. Individuals practice skills and develop everyday habits that include care, affection, recognition, respect, commitment, responsibility and trust, as well as honest and ethical communication toward other African Americans and other human beings (Karenga, 1965).

Nature. Nature and the environment consist of all elements contained within the natural world. Nature provides a window to the human spirit and principles for living peacefully in relationship with society and the environment. Natural processes provide lessons on human functioning, the rhythms of life, and natural order (Grills, 2002). *Nyamenti* (By God's grace) is the *adinkra* symbol of faith and trust in God or Great Spirit. The tree-like stalk in this symbol represents the staff of life in many cultures, which symbolizes the Akan belief that nature is the basis of life (Willis, 1998).

Social and Environmental Justice. *Ma'at* (truth, justice, balance, and harmony) regulates physical and moral law, the stars, seasons, and the actions of humans and all life forces. *Ma'at* established and maintains the order of the universe from chaos since the moment of creation. *Ubuntu*, from the Bantu languages, or *Unhu* in the Shona languages of Zimbabwe is a traditional African ethic that focuses on alliances and relationships between people, ancestors and the environment. It constitutes the core of traditional African law, leadership, and governance.

Self-Determination and Responsibility

Africa-centeredness places people of African descent at the center of education and human processes as the subject rather than object and creates an inclusionary process which gives equal involvement and the sharing of power with all groups, rather than domination by one group (Parham, White, & Ajamu, 1999). African-centered education designs and develops learning environments where people individually and collectively own and use their power and resources to make decisions using African-centered principles about the purpose, pedagogy, philosophies, goals, and objectives of the learning environment.

History and Humanity

Historical connection. The *Sankofa* symbol and maxim, "Go back and fetch it," stresses the importance of knowledge based on hindsight, critical reflection, and intelligent, patient investigation and action (Agbo, 1999). Understanding the history of African people, knowledge and values and the role that Africa has played in the world throughout history is crucial to well-being.

Unity in diversity. The Adinkra *Funtimfunafu Denkyem Funafu* symbol and maxim stresses the oneness of humanity in spite of cultural diversity and the inherent difficulties of reconciling individual and group interests in a democratic system (Agbo, 1999). This value stresses the importance of cultural pluralism and the freedom of different cultures to express and live their own world view. African-centered education creates environments where diverse views and beliefs can be shared and new knowledge developed collaboratively.

Community and Self-Awareness

Communal order and self-knowledge. In African world view, individuals come to know themselves through their relationships with others and the environment. Individuals exist because of the community and the community is responsible for its individual members. Being human means belonging to the whole community, so much so that in many African languages, there is no word for "I", because "I" is not conceptualized without a "we" (Grills, 2002).

Individual and community well-being. The health and well-being of individuals and communities are intricably intertwined, and are not something that can be maintained alone or in a vacuum. Healing, ritual, and community—these three elements are vitally linked." (Somé, 1998, p. 22).

Reciprocity and cooperation vs. competition. In African-centered world view, it is important to learn to differentiate individualism from the appreciation of individual uniqueness and gifts that strengthen community. Individuals learn to appreciate and develop their unique talents and gifts as contributions to community, and how to support others in the development of their gifts for the benefit of community. "If you have something unique in you and you want to do it, do it harmoniously in such a way that it will have a positive influence on your community"—Ghanian artist, James Cudjoe (2007). *Kuumba* or creativity from the *Nguzo Saba* stresses the need to always do as much as we can, in the best way that we can in order to leave our community more beautiful and valuable than we inherited it (Karenga, 1965).

Self-knowledge and awareness of others. Community members are encouraged to explore and appreciate themselves and others' lives, abilities, intelligences, uniqueness, personalities, and emotions. Through their interactions with other individuals and the community, learners become aware of aspects of themselves they were not aware of. They also become aware of sociocultural and psychosocial dynamics, their own behaviors, and their effects on others and the community.

Ritual and Healing

Ritual. Rites of passage and other rituals as simple as the act of breathing help individuals develop good contact and relationships with themselves and community. "Ritual is an art, an art that weaves and dances with symbols, and helping to create that art rejuvenates participants. Everyone comes away from a ritual feeling deeply transformed. This restoration is the healing that ritual is meant to provide" (Somé, 1998, p. 23).

Knowledge and Education

Perspective. African-centered pedagogy stresses the need to study and understand the history and contributions of Africa and people of African descent in the context of the web of life. It also respects the complexities, intricacies and histories of the interdependence of diverse ethic groups on the earth and their relationship with nature and spirit from the perspectives of scholars from different cultures and ethnic backgrounds, contrasted with dominant Eurocentric scholarship.

Balance. In order to heal intergenerational trauma from the *Maafa*, and promote well-being, individuals are encouraged to develop emotional management skills that promote psychophysiological coherence, health, and well-being and reduce stress.

Intellectual curiosity. Investigate, compare, and critically examine various philosophies and perspectives about other cultures and ethnicities, especially indigenous African and spiritual traditions which value community, nature, and spiritedness.

Emotional intelligence, stamina, and management. Through self-awareness and self-knowledge in relationships with others and the community, learners are encouraged to become aware of their emotions, the effects of their behaviours on others, and learn to manage their emotions and behaviors for health and well-being. Through these processes, learners develop emotional intelligences, stamina, and resilience when facing challenges.

Informed appraisal. African-centeredness stresses the importance of critically examining Eurocentric and other dominating cultures from other worldviews, especially African. This includes examining the humiliation dynamic, violence, and justifications for control. It also examines issues of power, including the exertion of power-over others, versus power-with others, and the exploitation of other human beings, especially people of African descent. It further stresses the importance of understanding culture as a process that gives people a general design for living and patterns for interpreting their reality (Ani, 1994).

Notes

1. The G8 is composed of Canada, France, Germany, Italy, Japan, Russia, the United Kingdom, and the United States.
2. Wangari Maathai and The Green Belt Movement have created a framework to teach community members to recognize and differentiate between the causes and symptoms of violence, oppression, and environmental degradation and to discern the linkages between them. The Green Belt Movement addresses the role of civil society, especially women, in protecting the environment, developing a democratic culture, pursuing participatory development, and promoting accountable and responsible governance.

References

Abdullah, H. (2007, September 29). Racism may affect infant mortality rates. *McClatchy Newspapers*. Retrieved August 17, 2008, from http://www.mcclatchydc.com/227/story/20099.html

Abron, J. (1998). "Serving the people": The survival programs of the black panther party. In C. E. Jones (Ed.), The black panther party reconsidered. Retrieved November 23, 2007, from http://www.mindfully.org/Reform/BPP-Serving-The-People1998.htm

Agbo, A. H. (1999). *Values of adinkra symbols*. Kumasi, Ghana: Ebony Designs and Publications.

Ahmad, O. B., Lopez, A. D., & Inoue, M. (2000). The decline on child mortality: A reappraisal. *Bulletin of the World Health Organization*, *78*, 1175–1191.

Alpers, E. A. (2001, October 25). *Defining the African diaspora*. Paper presented to the Center for Comparative Social Analysis Workshop at the University of California, Los Angeles.

African Union. (2003). *The African Convention on the Conservation of Nature and Natural Resources*. Retrieved May 7, 2008, from http://www.intfish.net/treaties/africa2003.htm

Ani, M. (1980). *Let the circle be unbroken*. Trenton, NJ: Red Sea Press.

Ani, M. (1994). *Yuguru: An African-centered critique of European cultural thought and behavior*. Trenton, NJ: Africa World Press.

BCTF. (2008). *Bushmeat Crisis Task Force*. Retrieved May 12, 2008, from http://www.bushmeat.org/docs.html

Booker, S., & Colgan, A. (2004). Africa Policy Outlook 2004. *Africa Action*. Retrieved May 27, 2008, from http://www.africaaction.org/resources/docs/2004PolicyOutlook2.pdf

Convention of Biological Diversity (CBD). (1992). *The 1992 convention on biological diversity*. Retrieved May 6, 2008, from http://www.cbd.int/convention/

Convention on International Trade Endangered Species of Wild Fauna and Flora (CITES). (1979).*The convention on international trade in endangered species*. Retrieved on May 6, 2008, from http://www.cites.org/

Coghlan, B., Brennan, R. J., Ngoy, P., Dofara, D., Otto, B., Clements, M., & Stewart, T. (2006). Mortality in the Democratic Republic of Congo: A nationwide survey. *The Lancet, 367,* 44–51.

Colb, S. (2004, October 29). *Racially-based suppression of the African-American vote: The role it may play in the upcoming presidential election.* Retrieved August 17, 2008, from http://writ.news.findlaw.com/colb/20041029.html

Cudjoe, J. (2007, May). *James Cudjoe featured artist. Contemporary art from Ghana and Zimbabwe.* San Diego, CA: Museum of Man.

Global Dialogue Institute. (1998). *A universal declaration of a global ethic.* Retrieved May 2, 2008, from http://astro.temple.edu/~dialogue/Center/declarel.htm

The Green Belt Movement. (2008). *Greenbelt movement and Wangari Maathai.* Retrieved April 2, 2008, from http://www.greenbeltmovement.org/a.php?id=113

Grills, C. (2002). African-centered psychology: Basic principles. In T. Parham (Ed.), *Counseling persons of African descent: Multicultural aspects of counseling and psychotherapy* (pp. 10–21). Thousand Oaks, CA: Sage.

Guinier, L., & Torres, G. (2002). *The miner's canary: Enlisting race, resisting power, transforming democracy.* Cambridge, MA: Harvard University Press.

Gyekye, K. (1996). *African cultural values: An introduction.* Accra, Ghana: Sankofa Publishing.

hooks, b. (2000). *All about love: New visions.* New York: Perennial.

IEN. (2001). Indigenous environmental network declaration; environmental racism and racial discrimination. Retrieved May 4, 2008, from http://www.ienearth.org/ienej_enviro.html

Jackson, C. (2001). *African American education: A reference handbook.* Santa Barbara, CA: ABC-CLIO.

Kaiser Family Foundation. (July 2006). Young african american men in the united states. *Race, ethnicity & health care fact sheet.* Retrieved August 17, 2008, from www.kff.org/minorityhealth/upload/7541.pdf

Karenga, M. (1965). The Nguzo Saba (Seven Principles). Retrieved ,August 20, 2007, from http://www.officialkwanzaawebsite.org/NguzoSaba.shtml

Klein, D. (1991). The humiliation dynamic: an overview. In D. C. Klein, (Ed.), The humiliation dynamic: Viewing the task of prevention from a new perspective Special Issue, *Journal of Primary Prevention* (Part I, special issue), *12*(2).

Le Billion, P. (2001). The political ecology of war: natural resources and armed conflicts. *Political Geography, 20,* 561–581.

Maddison, A. (2005). Growth and interaction in the world economy: the roots of modernity. Washington, DC: The AEI Press. Retrieved from http://www.ggdc.net/maddison/other_books/Growth_and_Interaction_in_the_World_Economy.pdf

Murphy, A. B. (1990). Historical justification for territorial claims. *Annals of the Association of American Geographers, 80*(4), 531–548.

National Association for the Advancement of Colored People (NAACP) Legal Defense Fund. (2006). *Dismantling the school-to-prison pipeline.* New York: NAACP LDF.

Organization of African Unity (OAU). (1979.) *The african charter for human and peoples' rights.* Retrieved May 16, 2008, from http://www.hrcr.org/docs/Banjul/afrhr2.html

OAU. (2001). African charter on the rights and welfare of the child. Retrieved May 7, 2008, from http://www.wunrn.com/reference/pdf/African%20Charter_Rights_Welfare_Child.PDF

Parham, T., White, J., & Ajamu, A. (1999). *The psychology of blacks: An African centered perspective* (3rd ed.). Upper Saddle River, NJ: Prentice Hall.

Patterson, O. (1982). *Slavery and social death: A comparative study.* Cambridge, MA: Harvard University Press.

Preux, P., & Druet-Cabanac, M. (2005). Epidemiology and aetiology of epilepsy in sub-Saharan Africa. *The Lancet, 4*, 21–31.

Pollard, D., & Ajirotutu, C. (Eds.). (2000). *African-centered schooling in theory and practice.* Westport, CT: Bergin & Garvey.

Pottinger, L. (1996). Environmental impacts of large dams: African examples. Retrieved April 24 , 2008, from http://internationalrivers.org/en/africa/environmental-impacts-large-dams-african-examples

Rizvi, H. (2007, September 1). US poverty data raise new questions about cost of war. Retrieved August 17, 2008, from http://us.oneworld.net/node/152804

Skinner, E. (1999). The restoration of African identity for a new millennium. In I. Okpewho, C. Davies, & A. Mazrui (Eds.), *The African diaspora: African origins and new world identities* (p. 24). Bloomington: Indiana University Press.

Smith, L.T. (1999). *Decolonizing methodologies: research and indigenous peoples.* London: Zed Books.

Solarin, I. (2004). Globalization and African identity; The case of communities of African descent in Latin America. *African Renaissance, 1*(2), 62–67.

Somé, M. (1998). *The healing wisdom of Africa: Finding life purpose through nature, ritual and community.* New York: Jeremy P. Tarcher/Putnam.

Souare, I. K. (2004). Can the G-8 and IFIs Help Africa? *African Renaissance, 1*(2), 115–20.

Spiegel, P. B. (2004). HIV/AIDS among conflict-affected and displaced populations: Dispelling myths and taking action. *Disasters, 28*(3), 322–339.

Tandom, Y. (2000). Root causes of peacelessness and approaches to peace in Africa. *Peace & Change, 25*(2), 166–187.

UNESCO. (1976). Conference of ministers of education of African member states organized by UNESCO with the co-operation of OAU and ECA Lagos (Nigeria) January 27–February 4. Retrieved on May 10, 2008, from http://portal.unesco.org/education/en/ev.php-URL_ID=31048&URL_DO=DO_TOPIC&URL_SECTION=201.html

United Nations. (1982). *The world charter for nature.* Retrieved May 6, 2008. from http://www.un-documents.net/a37r7.htm

United Nations. (2001). *The world conference against racism, racial discrimination, xenophobia and related intolerance.* Retrieved May 10, 2008, from http://www.hrcr.org/docs/Banjul/afrhr3.html

Wangari, E. (1996). Intersection of gender, race environment: Colonial and post colonial policies. In J. Andrzejewski (Ed.), *Oppression and social justice: Critical frameworks* (pp. 190–195). Needham Heights, MA: Pearson.

Willis, B. W. (1998). *The adinkra dictionary: A visual primer on the language of adinkra.* Washington, DC: The Pyramid Complex.

World Indigenous Peoples' Conference on Education (1999). The Coolangatta statement on indigenous peoples' rights in education. Retrieved May 2, 2008, from http://www.win-hec.org/docs/pdfs/Coolangata%20Statement%201999.pdf

World Watch Institute. (2002). *State of the world peport: Special world summit edition.* New York: W.W. Norton. Retrieved March 23, 2008, from http://www.worldwatch.org/system/files/ESW201.pdf

YWCA. (n.d.). *Statistics on racial justice.* Retrieved August 17, 2008, from http://www.ywcabham.org/Racial/stats.asp

Zack-Williams, A. B. (1999). Sierra Leone: The political economy of civil war, 1991–98. *Third World Quarterly, 20*(1), 143–162.

Zack-Williams, A. B. (2008, January 21). Rich countries owe poor a huge environmental debt. *Guardian Unlimited.* Retrieved on July 7, 2008, from www.guardian.co.uk/science/2008/jan/21/environmental.debt1/print

13 Achieving Conceptual Equilibrium
Standards for Gender Justice in Education

Renée Jeanne Martin

Introduction: Setting the Stage for Gender Justice

This chapter is predicated upon the mission of the Research on Women and Education Special Interest Group of the American Educational Research Association. It asserts the following goals: (a) to promote research concerning the education of women and girls; (b) to provide a mechanism to facilitate communication among researchers and practitioners who are concerned about women in education at the intersection of race, class, gender, and culture; and (c) to support education. Addressing the topic of gender justice is a vast and inclusive undertaking. Gender, like race and social class, is a positionality that intersects with other social justice concerns. One of the tasks of the gender justice educator is to enable all people to understand why it is in the best interests of society to redress the injustices enacted against women. It is important to clarify that whenever any segment of society is oppressed, by extension, the opportunities and privileges that are withheld from that group are implicated in the privileges and opportunities accorded other groups. As we educate students in all facets of the educational arena, we must strive to overcome the temptation to create oppositional stances and competing oppressions. No form of oppression is better or worse than another. Each has its distinct characteristics and the tools and infrastructure that are erected to support one form of oppression inevitably affect and support other forms.

A chapter such as this cannot remediate all of the problems associated with gender injustice; what it can do is suggest possibilities to scrutinize and cure some of the ills that plague the society and women's lives. As we do so, we can begin to envision a society in which the lives and accomplishments of women are recognized, a society which is ultimately more just, humane and democratic. Toward that end, this chapter sets forth gender equity standards that can serve as an impetus to address sexism and gender oppression in schools. The chapter calls attention to the need to create guidelines or standards that (a) help educators recognize gender oppression and (b) initiate approaches that will lead to its eradication. It is anticipated that the creation of standards that meet the various educational needs of women and girls will facilitate learning for all students and foster inclusive and empowering educational communities as well as promote social change.

Gender equity standards have the potential to:

- Counteract current trends to overlook or eliminate issues of gender justice at all educational levels;
- Promote sound and intentional pedagogical decisions regarding gender fair curriculum;
- Interrogate and analyze issues of gender justice in a variety of social and educational institutions;
- Probe the nature of assumptions about the education and schooling of women and men in a gendered context;
- Develop inquiry skills and abilities to identify contradictions and inconsistencies, question assumptions regarding policies and practices, as well as interrogate normative and ethical behavior relative to issues of gender justice;
- Promote research concerning women and girls in educational environments;
- Create an understanding of the implications of gender injustice for men and the social expectations for them;
- Facilitate a conceptual understanding of the role that men and boys can play in advocating for gender justice;
- Facilitate communication and link scholarly research about women and girls among social theorists, researchers, and classroom educators;
- Comprehend the intersection of positional stances such as race, ethnicity, social class, and gender;
- Develop appreciation for the complex nature of the issues that affect women's lives especially as they pertain to the education of women and girls in a global society;
- Develop schema germane to education with an eye toward sustained, lifelong initiatives to eradicate sexism;
- Create an understanding of the ethical dimensions of gender justice and equity.

Progressive and activist educators at all levels working in formal and informal settings might benefit from the suggestions in this chapter which focuses primarily upon the development of standards for gender justice in education in the United States. In this work, I will refer to the broad category of "educators" which is meant to be inclusive of teachers, administrative personnel, guidance counselors, and all those persons who educate students in U.S. public schools. The suggestions in this chapter are meant to serve as a foundation upon which additional work might be constructed in virtually all educational disciplines and arenas.

If teachers and other school personnel are appropriately educated about social and in particular gender justice, they have the potential to influence people in all walks of life. Kincheloe and McLaren (2007) suggest that the act of teaching "goes beyond providing the conditions for the simple act of knowing and understanding and includes the cultivation of the very power of self-definition and critical agency" (p. 3). And they note that "Pedagogy is the space that provides a moral and political referent for understanding how what we do in the classroom is linked to the wider social, political and economic forces" (2007, p. 3).

Gender Equity as a Global Issue

Given the changing nature of society and technology, it is important for educators to grasp the relevance of the policies and practices that affect women and girls, not only in the United States, but in all parts of the world. The enhancement of global communications facilitates the political and economic aggregation of countries across borders that have previously separated them. Thus our relationships with each other have been intensified globally as have the roles that corporate and governmental entities play in each of our lives.

Key global and national documents have helped identify and legitimate issues to be addressed by gender justice advocates. In particular, increased attention to global gender equity is intertwined with increased concern for the environment, the HIV/AIDS pandemic, drug trafficking, international monetary and financial transactions, the acquisition of nuclear power, and corporate as well as economic and global industrialization. On a global level, the empowerment of girls and women is widely acknowledged as a key to solving such serious world problems. For instance, the United Nations Millennium Development Declaration:

> ...maintains that giving women their fair share is the only way to effectively combat poverty, hunger and disease and to stimulate development that is truly sustainable...(in fact) promoting gender equality and the empowerment of women is an effective strategy to ensure that the other Millennium Development Goals are achieved. (United Nations Department of Economic and Social Affairs, 2005, p. 1)

Women's roles in restoring and establishing peace and non-violence are also being highlighted. As United Nations Deputy Secretary-General Louise Fréchette stated,

> ...while women are often the first victims of armed conflict, they are now becoming recognized as a key to preventing, managing or resolving it. They can be powerful forces for peace, for the reconciliation of their communities, for bringing war-torn societies back to health. (2001)

As global political boundaries dissolve and democratic traditions and customs are more closely scrutinized, it will become increasingly important for citizens of democratic societies to effectuate the goals that they purport to endorse. There is, therefore, a necessity to renegotiate our roles as global citizens and as women and men within a global context (Clark, 1999).

Commenting on the document *Beijing and Beyond*, the United Nations International Development Fund for Women (UNIFEM, 2002) noted, "Although there are positive and practical examples in almost every country of actions taken that have improved women's status, significant challenges remain" (p. 3). For example, of the nearly one billion adults in the world who cannot read, two-thirds are female. For countries in which education is not yet universal, the education of girls typically lags behind that of their male counterparts. The links between being uneducated and impoverished versus educated women who achieve independent economic stability, improved housing and better and more comprehensive health care are clear. Improving girls' education results in a wide range of individual, social, and economic benefits. For example, better-educated women have healthier babies and experience lower rates of infant mortality; they tend to be more actively involved in the governance of their worlds; are more financially stable; more economically independent; and have lower rates of HIV/AIDS.

The advances and impediments to gender justice globally have been well documented. A 2007 report by the International Labour Office (ILO) provides a snapshot of job-related discrimination, "The global picture of the struggle to overcome wage discrimination shows a mixture of major advances and failures" (p. 1). One emergent theme of the report is that there is a "persistence of gender gaps in employment and pay" and a "need for integrated policies addressing sex discrimination in remuneration and occupational segregation by sex while reconciling work and family responsibilities" (2007, p. 1). On the positive side the report notes that the ILO member states share a commitment to stamp out workplace discrimination and that, the commitment is "almost universal." However, the report cautions that the need to combat discrimination is urgent noting "In the face of a world that appears increasingly unequal, insecure, and unsafe," gender discrimination may lead to "political instability, and social upheaval, which upset investment and economic growth" (p. 3).

The *Progress of the World's Women* report (UNIFEM, 2000) found that

> …although women have made great strides in recent years, there is still much to be done to move forward and to prevent falling back. At this critical time in international politics, world leaders must find a way to ensure growth, development and hope for everyone—women and men alike. Public policy for the empowerment of women has to focus on new ways of including women and enabling them to shape the institutions that structure their lives. Empowerment is essentially about the ability to make choices and exercise bargaining power; to have a voice; to have the ability to organize and influence the direction of social change; to create a just social and economic order nationally and internationally. (p. 63)

The goals of the UNIFEM document that set time-bound targets and indicators of accomplishment are ambitious. Thus far, more than 40 countries have produced reports relative to the annual goals, but the extent to which gender justice efforts have been initiated has not been encouraging. The document notes that "Specific policy issues concerning women and girls, such as work-related rights, gender-based violence, reproductive and sexual health and rights, education and social security, access to productive resources including credit and nutrition require sustained attention" (p. 3). These concerns are echoed by the Development Alternatives with Women for a New Era (DAWN), launched in the context of the United Nation's Third World Conference on Women. DAWN "represents third world women's increasing concerns about the impact of debt, food security, environmental degradation, deteriorating social services, militarism, political conservatism, and religious fundamentalism on the lives of poor women" (Bunch, Dutt, & Fried, 1996, p. 224).

While a variety of international organizations and all forms of feminism voice concerns for gender justice, global feminists, in particular, seek to create awareness of how the issue of gender is connected to other social justice issues throughout the world. Banks (2007) notes that global feminism attempts first to convince all nations to honor women's rights to make free choices about matters related to their reproductive and sexual responsibilities. She asserts that without the ability to control their own bodies and the course of their destiny, women cannot feel like full human persons. The second goal is to bring women and men together to create a more just social and economic order at the global as well as national level (p. 51). Knowledge of such initiatives is integral to an understanding of gender justice and must become part of the fabric of schools.

The AIDS pandemic and a rise in the number of sexually transmitted diseases serve as a powerful reminder of how women and men must work together to solve societal problems. Masculine behavior often puts women at risk—reluctance to wear condoms or practice safe birth control, multiple sexual partners, bisexuality—all of which can influence the health of women and none of which can be solved by women alone (Gillespie, 1993, p. 443). A thriving international sex industry affects many poor and uneducated women throughout the world who turn to prostitution as a way to support their families. The international sex industry is supported by male international travelers and often by military personnel. A failure to interrupt such trafficking indicates that some governments either look the other way or tacitly approve of the sex trade. Additionally, poor women are the least likely to have adequate health care and are very likely to become pregnant, which means that there are vast numbers of children being born with sexually transmitted diseases to mothers who are unable to support them or to provide adequate health care.

A United Nations report released late in 2007 indicated that, primarily due to better reporting mechanisms and increased awareness, there has been a leveling off of AIDS in some countries. However, it is noteworthy that the current estimate of between 30.6 and 36.1 million people with HIV/AIDS is not a healthy profile. Sixty eight percent of the global total of AIDS cases are in sub-Saharan Africa and eight countries account for nearly one third of all new HIV infections and deaths globally (World Health Organization, 2006). It is not coincidental that in the countries where the statistics are most grave, women are not well educated, are poor and are politically disenfranchised.

It is apparent that throughout the world female disadvantage permeates nearly all elements of sociocultural, economic, and personal life. Through the gender division of labor (i.e., women assigned to childcare and domestic labor, or to jobs that pay less well than those men are able to attain), male superiority is underscored, and female subordination ensues. Power, wealth, and prestige belong to people who control the distribution of resources in the economic and political public spheres—not in the private sphere of the home, the traditional domain of women (Richardson, Taylor, & Whittier, 2001, p. 563). In nearly all nations, men control access to resources and possess the ability to marshal those resources to accomplish their goals. Linking the conditions under which women work live and learn with civil rights legislation actualizes those conditions. As McKinnon (2006) notes, it is possible to transform the definition of equality, not by making women the same as men, "entitled to violate and silence, or by reifying women's so-called differences, but by insisting that equal citizenship must encompass what women need to be human, including a right not to be silenced or violated" (p. 48).

One of the many challenges is to educate teachers and administrators to value global concerns and comprehend the implications for inclusion of those who have historically been marginalized. Educators must be taught to critically analyze what occurs when any segment of the population is deprived of adequate food, shelter, or health care and is subjected to economic and political exploitation. And, they must investigate the effects of such exploitation which reverberate around the world in order to determine how adequately educating tomorrow's citizens can transform society and create equitable conditions for women.

Imperialism

Those who work for global gender justice face numerous, inextricably linked issues. For example, within the context of macro-economic and global capitalism job security, pay equity, racism, poverty, violence against women, and various other forms of sexism prevail. Economic exploitation, military aggression, gender repression, and violence have been employed by governments to coerce women and men to engage in hegemonic cultural reproduction typified by cultural imperialism. Women's bodies and minds have been colonized by governments in cooperation with multi-national corporations for the sake of economic development and that often results in exploitation.

Imperialists invoke political and economic power to exalt and spread the values and habits of a foreign culture at the expense of a native culture (Bullock & Stallybrass, 2003, p. 3). Imperialism facilitates conditions in which women are under-represented in government, paid inequitable wages, and forced to work in demoralizing and dangerous global industries that exploit their labor and endanger their health. Put simply imperialism is used to enforce the way productive forces operate and to maintain a private sector in which women's labor is marginalized, excluded, subordinated, and under-compensated.

Countries with global corporate interests and the military industrial complex to protect such interests have sought cheap pools of labor in colonized and neo-colonized nations thereby invoking an imperialist paradigm. Women in developing nations constitute just such pools of cheap labor, and according to Banks (2007) "do so to help support their families and/or to avoid having to work in the sex tourism industry which caters to men from developed nations" (p. 52). Historically, women in such countries have not only been economically disenfranchised, but they have lacked the political power to effectuate resolutions to grave social problems. Because multinational corporations, most of whom emanate from the United States, control most of the wealth, production of materials, and labor, as well as world markets, their ability to penetrate neo-colonized nations and affect their growth and development has been profound. As corporate America has permeated the economic and political borders of other nations, it has appropriated the raw materials, natural resources, and human capital of those nations. In so doing, it has undermined the internal development of policies, governments, and institutions that have quite literally traded the exploitation of their lands and people for imperialist development. While a discussion of the magnitude of such exploitation is beyond the scope of this particular chapter, it is noteworthy that such development has been reliant upon the reification of patterns of oppression, namely the racist and sexist exploitation of the inhabitants of so-called Third World women and people of color.

Violence Against Women

Social justice educators need to identify numerous issues in order to redress gender injustice. One of the most daunting is providing safe spaces where women can work, live, and learn. The United Nations has recognized an urgent need to address the violation of basic human rights, violence against women that nullifies their progress. Noting that domination and discrimination against women has been characterized by inequitable power relations, which have often been manifested in violence against women, the United Nations has advocated the elimination of all forms of discrimination against women and most notably the violence that has prevented them from attaining their full human potential. The United Nations defines violence against women as:

Article 1
Any act of gender-based violence that results in, or is likely to result in, physical, sexual, or psychological harm or suffering to women, including threats of such acts, coercion or arbitrary harm or suffering to women including threats of such acts, coercion or arbitrary deprivation of liberty, whether occurring in public or in private life.

Article 2
Violence against women shall be understood to encompass, but not be limited to, the following:

(a) Physical, sexual and psychological violence occurring in the family, including battering, sexual abuse of female children in the household, dowry-related violence, marital rape, female genital mutilation and other traditional practices harmful to women, non-spousal violence and violence related to exploitation;
(b) Physical, sexual and psychological violence occurring within the general community including rape, sexual abuse sexual harassment and intimidation at work, in educational institutions and elsewhere, trafficking in women and forced prostitution;
(c) Physical, sexual and psychological violence perpetrated or condoned by the State, wherever it occurs." (http://www.un.org/documents/ga/res/48/a48r104.htm)

The United Nations Convention on the Elimination of All Forms of discrimination against Women (UNCEDAW) established an international bill of rights for women in which it advocates that "States commit themselves to undertake a series of measures to end discrimination against women in all forms including:

- to incorporate the principle of equality of men and women in their legal system, abolish all discriminatory laws and adopt appropriate ones prohibiting discrimination against women;
- to establish tribunals and other public institutions to ensure the effective protection of women and discrimination against women;
- to ensure elimination of all acts of discrimination against women by persons, organizations or enterprises. (http://www.un.org/womenwatch/daw/cedaw)

Education is a crucial step in stopping the gendered oppression against women. Teachers and students must work toward an understanding of how the information and images that are generated in all social institutions including schools, religious groups, and media, as well as in the products that are manufactured and purchased by Americans influence our perceptions of women. We must teach students that while some of us perceive that Americans benefit from the cheap pools of female and child labor that produce inexpensive food, and material goods, the rights of those women to live healthy, productive lives are negated by their exploitation. Further, it is essential to introduce students to the work of social justice activists such as Wangari Maathai, who underscores links among a range of oppressive issues such as environmental racism, poverty, and gender oppression. Maathai, a recipient of the Nobel Peace Prize, has urged Kenya's farmers (who are women) to prevent soil erosion by planting trees that would, in turn, regenerate natural resources such as lumber and firewood. The wood can be used to create homes and products that benefit the workers and the economy. Asserting that the environment is a barometer of a nation's health she has called on governments to "expand democratic space and build fair and just societies" devoid of the environmental and human exploitation that has characterized much of the for-profit industry in Africa (Sethov, 2004).

Theoretical Framework for Gender Justice

Efforts to generate standards in U.S. educational institutions often overlook fundamental notions of how knowledge is privileged, constructed and disseminated. This chapter is founded upon the development of standards that are guided and influenced by the work of social justice educators and feminist scholars as well as by the work of scholars engaged in critical, liberatory, multicultural education who are proponents of transformative pedagogy (Adams, Bell, & Griffin, 2007; AAUW, 1992, 1995, 1996, 1998; Brody et. al., 2000; Collins, 1990; Darling-Hammond, French, & Garcia-Lopez, 2002; Horgan, 1995; Ladson-Billings, 1995; Maher & Tetreault, 1994; Maher & Ward, 2002; Sleeter, 1996). Authors such as these challenge the validation of Eurocentric and patriarchal ideology and the exclusion of the knowledge and experiences of members of historically marginalized groups. Knowledge of their work is an essential component for the development of gender justice standards. Such scholars posit that knowledge is not neutral but is political and influenced by collective, human interests. Further, they recognize that all knowledge is a reflection of the power and relationships within society and assert that comprehending the nature of knowledge and the ways in which it is socially constructed has the potential to transform and improve society (Banks, 1993, p. 9).

One transformative theoretical disposition, feminist theory, consists of a widely conceived body of work comprised of multiple theoretical perspectives, methodologies, disciplinary interests, philosophies, and goals. Most feminist theory is typified by an analysis of sexism that challenges patriarchy and asserts new visions of social interactions between women and men (hooks, 2000). In addition, feminists share a common interest in understanding and improving the lives and relations between women and men economically, socially, culturally, and personally. Feminists concur that women live in societies that are structured and organized around principles and practices of male supremacy and domination, and that due to those conditions, women have not enjoyed the same power and privileges as men either in the public or private spheres. "Research conducted within a feminist framework is attentive to issues of difference, the questioning of social power, resistance to scientific oppression, and a commitment to political activism and social justice" (Hess-Biber & Leavy, 2004, p. 3).

Whereas much mainstream research has historically focused upon men and was rooted in male dominated social spheres, feminist research has broadened the theoretical framework as well as expanded and focused upon the lives and experiences of women. Opening up a dialogue to critical analysis has led feminists to challenge traditional notions of knowledge building and to develop new and innovative epistemological approaches to research and education. As feminist theorists repositioned women from the periphery to the center of social analysis, they adopted a post-structural examination of gender justice thereby demanding the deconstruction of master narratives (Luke & Gore, 1992). The dismantling of dominant narratives has led to new understandings of the role of feminist, emancipatory pedagogy.

> Feminist pedagogy is the attempt to disrupt the taken-for-granted assumptions about what it means to be a man or a woman, assumptions that maintain exclusive realms of privilege and power for boys and marginalization for girls. Feminist teachers draw upon diverse disciplines and theories to ask critical questions about the way we live our lives as men and women, questions that...demand that we take seriously the politics of identity, compassion, and caring, equality of opportunity and outcome. (Martusewicz & Reynolds, 1994, p. 15)

hooks (1989) underscored an important distinction regarding feminism, noting that it is not an effort to marginalize or oppress men or to reify oppressive structures, rather it is an effort to "talk back" to establish a "dialectical context where there is serious and rigorous critical exchange" (p. 51). She clarified that feminism is

> a movement to end sexism, sexist exploitation, and oppression.... it so clearly states that [the]movement is not about being anti-male. It makes it clear that the problem is sexism. And that clarity helps us remember that all of us, female and male, have been socialized from birth on to accept sexist thought and action. (hooks, 2000, pp. viii–ix)

To effectively integrate feminist theory into education, we must find ways for groups that have historically been alienated from each other, women and men, people of color and Whites, people with disabilities and the able-bodied, etc. to coalesce around issues of social justice. Further, it will be necessary to overcome reductive and divisive notions of what it means to be female or male. To not do so is to polarize women from men and fail to use the power of collective agency to unite for gender justice. Mohanty (1991) cautioned against a binary analysis of sexist exploitation based on a generalized and wrongly constructed notion of gender and its ensuing subordination.

> What [frequently] characterizes women as a group is their gender (sociologically, not necessarily biologically, defined) over and above everything else, indicating a monolithic notion of sexual difference. Because women are thus constituted as a coherent group, sexual difference becomes coterminious with female subordination, and power is automatically defined in binary terms; people who have it (read: men), and people who do not (read: women). Men exploit; women are exploited. Such simplistic formulations are historically reductive; they are also ineffectual in designing strategies to combat oppressions. All they do is reinforce binary divisions between men and women. (p. 83)

All forms of feminism assert that women have the right to live healthy, productive lives, free of violence and oppression, as should their male counterparts. As noted previously, however, feminism and feminist theory are not monolithic, and feminist researchers and scholars will continue to differ about theoretical dispositions, as well as, how to conduct research, and how to enact feminist goals, but they do not differ about the importance of researching the lives of women and girls.

Gender Justice Education in the United States

There is a growing body of research on the educational status of girls and women in the United States. The National Center for Educational Statistics (NCES, 2004) *Trends in Educational Equity of Girls and Women* contains a selection of indicators that illustrate the educational gains as well as the gaps that continue to exist. This statistical report highlights the extent to which women and men "have access to the same educational opportunities, avail themselves equally of the opportunities, perform at similar levels throughout schooling, succeed at similar rates, and reap the same benefits from their educational experiences" (Introduction). According to the NCES data in the 1999–2000 school year, 75% of all teachers were female, underscoring the feminization of the profession that accompanies low wages and low prestige. The proportional representation of women is highest in elementary schools, decreasing as grade levels rise. There are greater numbers of men in secondary administrative positions than there are women, and men experience more opportunities to coach despite the increased participation of girls in sports during the past three decades. Nationally, about 44% of all principals were women, however as the grade level increases, the numbers of women in administration declines. Nationally, women constitute about 55% of principals at the elementary level; 31% of principals at the middle school level; and only 21% of principals at the secondary level. The number of women in superintendencies increased to about 13% in 2000, an increase of 6% since 1992; however, the highest percentage of women in administration occurred during the decade of the 1920's. According to Tallerico (2007), the patterns illustrate

> continuing gender stratification and sexual divisions of labor. More specifically, regularities and differences include: the relative scarcity of males and preponderance of females in teaching; the persistence of men managing and women teaching in schools nationally; the pattern of women administrators being more likely to occupy staff rather than line positions and elementary rather than secondary leadership positions; and the increasing percentages of men in administration as the scope of authority, status, and salaries of particular roles rise (e.g. from elementary to secondary school principalships and, at the central administration levels, from coordinator to assistant superintendent to superintendent). (cited in Banks, 2007, p. 646)

Research over the last 30 years demonstrates that educational institutions in the United States have been marginally successful in meeting the needs of women and girls (AAUW, 1992, 1995, 1996, 1998; Sadker & Sadker, 1995; Sadker, 1999). Gender bias continues to characterize interactions in classrooms, persists in the curriculum, and is reflected in staffing patterns and wages. There has been an increase in the numbers of women with graduate educational degrees, however, research by Cooper and Stevens (2002) revealed that "despite efforts to increase the visibility of women scholars in academe ... women make up only 31 % of full-time faculty in American higher education today, an increase of only 5% in the past 75 years" (p. 6).

Although Title IX generated some improvements for women and girls in the years immediately following its inception, a neo-conservative backlash during the nineteen eighties and nineties against civil rights, in general, and women's rights, in particular, took hold with the major shifts in political power at the state and national levels. Those shifts have resulted in a steady erosion of legal and civil rights gained during the civil rights and the women's movements of the last century. Setbacks have occurred through lack of support and funding for existing legislation and by overt actions to undermine initiatives, such as Title IX and affirmative action.

Teacher education programs still lag behind in addressing gender inequities in deep and meaningful ways. For example, teacher education textbooks are woefully lacking in information about gendered issues. After completing a content analysis of 23 key teacher education texts for their inclusion of gender and education, Zittleman and Sadker (2003) reported, "Despite decades of research documenting gender bias in education … these 23 teacher education texts devote only about 3 percent of their space to gender" (p. 59). Masculine superiority and patriarchy are reinforced in all facets of schooling, the effect of which is a normalizing of patriarchy and masculine supremacy.

Concern among educators has led to some educational reform initiatives by professional education and accreditation organizations. However, many of the reforms are ambiguous and rely upon the caring and goodwill of the individual as opposed to attending to the systemic nature of gender injustice.

Virtually no mechanisms exist to remediate those who fail to comply with existing social justice efforts. Nor are there any consequences for those who promote institutionalized, systemic forms of oppression whether it be sexism, racism, elitism, or homophobia. For educational institutions to alter the existing paradigm of gender injustice, they must institute deliberate measures to combat gender inequity. Invoking gender equity standards, helping faculty to meet them, and remediation of those who do not meet the standards are necessary steps for successful transformation.

Educators will also need to become better informed about how to align their content with issues of gender justice. Prioritizing gender issues, establishing inservices and workshops, and mentoring educators who are unacquainted with gender justice issues are important components of the transformative process. It would also be helpful for educational institutions to revise existing mission statements to be inclusive of issues of social justice, and especially gender equity. Additionally, there is a need to develop thoughtful approaches to staffing patterns; the assignation of traditionally female and male duties; recruitment and retention of women, especially women of color; and the alignment of pay equity scales of female educators with those of their male counterparts. Tangible incentives such as formal recognition of gender equitable pedagogy and curriculum as well as awards and stipends can be infused into the fabric of education institutions at all levels. Enacting such changes sends powerful messages to educators and students that the lives and accomplishments of women and girls are taken seriously. The persistence of sexism and gender inequities in all educational institutions in the United States and internationally compels the synthesis of professional standards that are deliberate, rigorous, and comprehensive.

The Role of Men in Perpetuating Gender Justice

In *Feminism is for Everybody,* bell hooks (2000) articulates the struggle to create critical consciousness in university classrooms. She writes about the imposition of class and corporate power, the backlash against feminism, and numerous difficulties regarding the teaching of social justice issues and feminist values to college students. The issues of which she speaks are central to the struggles that educators face when they introduce alternative analytical lenses for the discussion of social justice issues such as gender equity. hooks (2000, p. 118) notes that "Feminism is for everybody." Convincing boys and men of the efficacy of gender justice issues to their lives and persuading young women, most of whom have no understanding of contemporary feminism, to advocate for gender justice is a challenge.

Human beings derive what it means to feminine or masculine from the socializing agencies in which they participate. Families, schools, governmental agencies, media, religious affiliations, and social groups of all sorts promote standards for what is deemed culturally normative. The basic assumptions of a patriarchal society are that male dominance and aggression are "just the way things are." Strict sex-role stereotypes maintain male dominance and female subordination. Deeply held beliefs about traditional forms of femininity and masculinity have damaging effects on the images and self-worth of women and men, harm their relationships, and impede potential economic, political, and social opportunities and alliances.

It is important for boys and men to understand gender equity and the potential that it has to liberate women and men. A binary construction of gendered oppression frames relations between men and women in oppositional political, social, and economic terms resulting in institutional and social patterns that are structured to maintain and perpetuate gender inequality. When gender oppression is present, the lives of both women and men are negatively affected. For example, when sexist paradigms prevail, normative gender expectations force men to engage in behaviors that often go unquestioned such as military service, violence against women and gay men, and the pursuit of dangerous sports and athletic competition. Not only do many men engage in such activities without question, but they pressure other men to acquiesce to masculine stereotypes. In addition, many men do not feel free to exercise a full range of human qualities such as vulnerability, artistic creativity, a willingness to seek help solving problems or engage in domestic labor and child-rearing behaviors. Traditional beliefs about gendered roles also harm men by excluding them from intimacy and connection in relationships and have a tendency to perpetuate unhappiness and conflicts in family life. Further, when men do venture outside traditional masculine behaviors, they are threatened with negative labels such as those used to perpetuate homophobia. Because that which is feminine is de-valued in the culture and because male homosexuality is often wrongly associated with being feminine, men who engage in non-traditional, i.e., feminine behaviors, are haunted by the specter of homophobia. That fear keeps men from associating with that which has traditionally been regarded as feminine including advocacy for gender issues such as reproductive rights, childcare, domestic labor, and pay equity. Female oppression becomes a way to insure masculine power, and in some cultures, the subjugation of women is presented as a way for men to bond and assert their masculinity.

To create binary opposition to gender equity is to deduct men from an important part of the equation. Because men often occupy positions of power, they can serve as powerful allies in the fight for gender justice. It is in everyone's interest to educate men to the ways in which gender oppression affects the ability to live authentic lives and to achieve our fullest human potential. When women and men are depicted as opposites and their lives as oppositional, and when they are pitted against each other, they are robbed of opportunities to coalesce around important human, social issues.

Proposed Standards for Gender Equity in Education

There is no single entity to which we can look to solve issues of gender justice. What is needed is a comprehensive and sustained effort in all societal and educational institutions. "The structures that perpetuate gender inequality and discrimination pervade economic, social, political, cultural, legal and civic institutions, norms and practices around the world (UNIFEM, 2000, p. 3). Transformation from a world where gender injustice is pervasive to one where gender justice is prevalent will only occur if social institutions such as schools, governments, media, industries, and religious groups initiate change.

A crucial component in redressing gender injustice is creating a comprehensive approach for the remediation of gender inequity in all facets of education. While many reports have focused primarily upon initiatives aimed at empowering girls and women, it is incumbent upon us to educate all students to understand the debilitating and destabilizing effects of gender inequity upon all social constituencies.

The nature of the pedagogical and epistemological alterations must not only be inclusive of quantitative representation, but must take into account the quality of women's lives. Educational standards must ensure that women do not merely achieve numerical parity. Duncan Wilson (2004) recommends, "The human rights protection and promotion of gender equality requires more than numerical equilibrium, it also requires conceptual equilibrium, and a conscientious effort to redress inequality, as it exists" (p. 12). Schools, and in particular colleges of teacher education, must create more balanced representations of the accomplishments of women, as well as an understanding of the issues and injustices that they face.

This section outlines standards to underscore gender equity in education. Gender equitable education must be available, accessible, and adaptable. No standards or attempts to alter pedagogy or curriculum are inherently liberating or just. It is the blending of conscientious social justice constructs with democratic vigilance and a willingness to transform ourselves, as well as our classrooms, that will create a world where the lives and accomplishments of women will be valued and treasured, a world in which men as well as women will advocate for peace and gender justice. Standards cannot prescribe how to accomplish our goals. They can, however, be guideposts along a path of social transformation that suggest and encourage those who educate teachers to explore alternative landscapes and terrain. What is certain is that the world, as it currently exists, has not fulfilled the democratic ideals that are so frequently touted. UNIFEM (2000) has cautioned, "The world can no longer afford to make commitments that cannot or will not be kept. Future stability and progress itself depend upon the decisions we make now-to fulfill commitments and to ensure that the world's most desperately poor people, many of whom are women, have the guarantee of a better future" (p. 64).

Proposed Standards for Gender Justice in Education

I. Educational Accreditation Agencies Should

1. Incorporate standards for gender equity and justice into their mission statements, goals, and accreditation standards;
2. Institute remediation and/or restrictions for institutions that fail to demonstrate gender justice and issues of equity in pedagogy, curriculum, and research;
3. Articulate, clarify, and communicate goals that all prospective administrators and teachers must have in order to be competent regarding issues of gender justice.

II. Educational Institutions at All Levels Should

1. Integrate gender equity standards into their mission statements;
2. Influence accreditation agencies to actively pursue gender equity initiatives that serve as examples of excellence;
3. Create links with external community, health, medical, and social agencies that address gender issues such as teen pregnancy, reproductive rights, peace and environmental issues, as well as those that address violence against women and school violence in order to promote safe and healthy students in healthy educational environments;
4. Work across school districts, schools, and disciplines to collaborate on gender justice initiatives that are reflective of the entire community's female population.
5. Conduct workshops and professional seminars to acquaint administrators and faculty with gender justice issues and links to global peace and environmental issues;
6. Provide opportunities for professional development about global gender justice and international organizations that are working for gender and social justice;
7. Establish resource centers with materials by and about women, their lives, and contributions for students, teachers, community leaders, and parents;
8. Create institutional incentives such as grant money, technology, educational resources, and awards to support the investigation of gender justice issues;
9. Highlight, celebrate and reward teachers, administrators, and staff who model and create gender justice initiatives in their teaching, research, and service;

10. Establish mentors for those faculty and administrators who may be unfamiliar with gender justice issues;
11. Promote a range of curricular and pedagogical strategies such as action research that enable students to engage in discovery, develop research paradigms, share information, and articulate causal factors for understanding and interrogating issues of gender justice;
12. Articulate classroom and pedagogical values that embody human rights values and that are explicitly linked to global initiatives regarding gender justice;
13. Employ pedagogical strategies that reflect and utilize global gender initiatives, resources and technologies;
14. Create gender justice materials, resources, and technologies that are accessible to a range of students with varying learning modalities and physical abilities;
15. Actively infuse, teach, and model democratic, gender fair principles in all disciplines and classrooms;
16. Create opportunities to critique and investigate social institutions such as government and corporate media in order to understand their relationship to the enactment of gender justice issues in schools;
17. Integrate the work of transformative theorists including a range of feminist authors, social justice and critical multicultural scholars as integral components of all disciplines;
18. Help students establish global connections among their own ethnicity, race, and social class identities with those of people in other countries;
19. Articulate, clarify, and communicate goals that all teachers must have in order to be competent regarding issues of gender justice;
20. Establish specific strategies to assess educators' abilities to incorporate gender justice in the curriculum, pedagogy, and learning initiatives that they create;
21. Create learning opportunities in which students actively demonstrate gender justice proficiency.

III. Standards for Educators: Teachers and School Administrators Should Be Able To

1. Articulate a range of theoretical dispositions that aid in the development of gender justice, and support the pedagogical and curricular choices that they will make as educators;
2. Understand global women's rights issues and the relationship of those issues to the disciplines they teach;
3. Demonstrate that they are acquainted with a range of local, national, and international organizations working for the advancement of gender equity;
4. Link gender equity to human and civil rights initiatives in the development of curricula and pedagogy;

5. Demonstrate an understanding of the history of civil and women's rights in the United States;
6. Demonstrate a capacity to disrupt institutional sexism in their written and academic work;
7. Be conversant with work by major scholars in the field of social and gender justice;
8. Display an understanding of the nature of sexism and of its systemic characteristics as well as its inter-connectedness to other social justice issues;
9. Develop holistic approaches to eradicate social and in particular gender injustice in school and society;
10. Collaborate with people from a range of social justice advocacy groups across racial, ethnic, gender and social classes in order to promote and practice equitable gender, racial, ethnic, sexual orientation, and disability policies in schools;
11. Demonstrate gender equity knowledge, concepts, skills, dispositions, and praxis in all disciplines and field experiences;
12. Exhibit a commitment to foster social and gender justice issues through pedagogy and curricular initiatives that are just, fair, comprehensive, and equitable as they interact with prospective educators in field experiences and student teaching;
13. Create original and innovative social justice curricula while infusing new approaches that have the potential to positively affect the lives of the students in order to transform schools and society.

References

Adams, M., Bell, L. A., & Griffin, P. (Eds.). (2007). *Teaching for diversity and social justice: A sourcebook* (2nd ed.). New York: Routledge.

American Association of University Women. (1992). *The AAUW report: How schools shortchange girls.* Washington, DC: The AAUW Educational Foundation.

American Association of University Women. (1995). *Growing smart—what's working for girls in school.* Washington, DC: The AAUW Educational Foundation.

American Association of University Women. (1996). *Girls in the middle—working to succeed in school.* Washington, DC: The AAUW Educational Foundation.

American Association of University Women. (1998). *Gender gaps—where schools still fail our children.* Washington, DC: The AAUW Educational Foundation.

Banks, J. A. (1993). The canon debate, knowledge construction, and multicultural education. *Educational Researcher, 22*(5), 4–14.

Banks, B. (Ed.). (2007). *Gender and education: An encyclopedia.* Westport, CT: Praeger.

Brody, C., Fuller, K., Gosetti, P., Moscato, S., Nagel, N., & Pace, G., et al. (2000). *Gender consciousness and privilege.* London: Falmer Press.

Bullock, A,. & Stallybrass (Eds.). (2003). *The Fontana dictionary of modern thought* (2nd ed.). London: Fontana Books.

Bunch, C., Dutt, M., & Fried, S. (1996, Summer). Beijing 95: A global referendum on the rights of women. *Canadian Women's Studies, 16,* 221–231

Clark, J. D. (1999). *Ethical globalization: The dilemmas and challenges of internationalizing civil society.* Paper presented at the International NGO Conference, Birmingham University, London.

Collins, P. H. (1990). *Black feminist thought: Knowledge, consciousness, and the politics of empowerment*. London: Harper Collins Academic.

Cooper, J., & Stevens, D. (2002). *Tenure in the sacred grove: Issues and strategies for women and minority faculty*. Albany: State University of New York.

Darling-Hammond, L., French, J., & Garcia-Lopez, S. (2002). *Learning to teach for social justice*. New York: Teachers College Press.

Fréchette, L. (2001, August). *Women can be powerful force for peace and reconciliation and must be integrated more effectively in peace processes worldwide, says deputy secretary-general*. Retrieved July 6, 2008, from http://www.un.org/News/Press/docs/2001/dsgsm123.doc.htm

Gillespie, M. A. (1993). HIV: The global crisis. In L. Richardson & V. Taylor (Eds.), *Feminist frontiers III* (pp. 443–446). New York: McGraw-Hill.

Hess-Biber, N., & Leavy, P. (Eds.). (2004). *Approaches to qualitative research: A reader on theory and practice*. New York: Oxford University Press.

hooks, b. (1989). *Talking back: Thinking feminist, thinking black*. Boston: South End Press.

hooks, b. (2000). *Feminism is for everybody—Passionate politics*. Cambridge, MA: South End Press.

Horgan, D. (1995). *Achieving gender equity*. Needham Heights, MA: Allyn & Bacon.

International Labour Office (ILO). (2007)'. *Declaration on fundamental principles and rights at work*. International Labour Conference, 2007.

Kincheloe. J., & McLaren, P. (Eds.). (2007). *Critical pedagogy: Where are we now?* New York: Peter Lang.

Ladson-Billings, G. (1995). Toward a theory of culturally relevant pedagogy. *American Educational Research Journal, 32*(3), 465–491.

Luke, C., & Gore, J. (Eds.). (1992). *Feminisms and critical pedagogy*. New York: Routledge Press.

Maher, F., & Tetreault, M. (1994). *The feminist classroom*. New York: Basic Books.

Maher, F., & Ward, J. (2002). *Gender and teaching*. Mahwah, NJ: Erlbaum.

Martusewicz, R. A., & Reynolds, W. M. (Eds.). (1994). *Inside out—Contemporary critical perspectives in education*. New York: St. Martin's Press.

McKinnon, C. A. (2006). *Are women human?* Cambridge, MA. The Belknap Press of Harvard University Press.

Mohanty, C. T. (1991). Under western eyes: Feminist scholarship and colonial discourses. In C. T. Mohanty, A. Russo, & L. Torres (Eds.), *Third world women and the politics of feminism* (p. 338). Bloomington: Indiana Universtiy Press.

National Center for Educational Statistics (NCES). (2004). Washington, DC: United States Department of Education.

Research on Women and Education (2008). The American Educational Research Association. Washington, DC; http://www.aera.net

Richardson, L., Taylor, V., & Whittier, N. (2001). *Feminist frontiers* (5th ed.). Boston: McGraw-Hill.

Sadker, D. (1999). Gender equity: Still knocking at the classroom door. *Educational Leadership, 56*(7), 22–26.

Sadker, M., & Sadker, D. (1995). *Failing at fairness: How our schools cheat girls*. New York: Touchstone Press.

Sethov, I. (2004). Nobel winner Maathai sounds alarm over planet.

Sleeter, C. E. (1996). *Multicultural education as social activism*. Albany: State University of New York Press.

United Nations Convention on the Elimination of All Forms of Discrimination against Women, (1979). New York: United Nations.

United Nations Department of Economic and Social Affairs. (2005). *Progress towards the millennium development goals, 1990–2005.* Retrieved on July 7, 2008, from http://mdgs.un.org/unsd/mdg/Resources/Attach/Products/Progress2005/goal_3.doc

United Nations Development Fund for Women (UNIFEM). (2000). *Progress of the world's women: 2000.* New York: United Nations.

United Nations General Assembly, Violence Against Women Act. (1993). New York: United Nations.

United Nations International Development Fund for Women (UNIFEM). (2002). *Beijing and beyond.* New York: United Nations.

Wilson, D. (2004). Human rights: Promoting gender equality in and through education. *Prospects, XXXIV*(1), March, 11–27.

World Health Organization. (2006). *Uniting the world against aids.* Press release. New York: WHO.

Zittleman, K., & Sadker, D. (2003). Teacher education textbooks: The unfinished gender revolution. *Educational Leadership, 60*(40), 59–63.

14 Disability Studies in Education
Guidelines and Ethical Practice for Educators

Robin M. Smith, Deborah Gallagher, Valerie Owen, and Thomas M. Skrtic

The Dehumanizing Consequences of the Traditional Special Education Model

In this chapter we explore the growing tension in special education discourse and practice. Traditional special education, steeped in positivist, medical, and behavioral assumptions, relying heavily on the methodologies of prediction and control, has remained astoundingly resistant to the postmodern critiques of social science and educational practices, and of disability studies (Owen, Neville, & Smith, 2001). The alternative perspective of the Disability Studies in Education Special Interest Group (SIG) reveals the deep division between educators who uphold the foundational assumptions of traditional special education and those who espouse different constructions of disability as they are related to the principles of social justice and disability rights in schools.

Special education emerged from the civil rights (and by extension the disability rights) era of the 1960s. It has evolved, however, not as a vehicle of emancipation and social justice but rather as a system of segregation and inequality. Despite its avowed goals to promote the educational equality and dignity of students with disabilities, special education's ideological foundations and frameworks of liberal functionalism, empiricism/positivism, and behaviorism, further explained below, resulted in a coordinated system that has undermined its very purpose. Simply put, this ideological trifecta contains within it a number of erroneous assumptions entirely at odds with the field's fundamental, or at least stated, aspirations.

The central thrust of liberal functionalism is the opportunity for social mobility based on merit (Hurn, 1993). Liberal functionalism then is "liberal" in the sense that, as a conceptual framework, its intent was to foster rationality, equality, and humanitarian ideals. As one of the foundations of special education and despite good intentions, liberal functionalism has not realized these goals. The roots of liberal functionalism can be traced back to the end of the nineteenth century. Schools were to serve as the institutions in which all had equal opportunity to realize their "potential." Faced with an overwhelming diversity of students and pressures to conform them into a unified, standardized whole, teachers took on many roles. One role involved the identification of abnormalities in students that may handicap their learning. These included defects in posture, hearing, eyesight, and health habits. In addition to surveying students for potential defects, the teacher was expected to make some accommodations for students with learning or physical difficulties and was mandated to teach "good health habits." To encourage students and their parents to comply with these "good health habits," educators posed physical deformities, mental derangements, and social segregation as threats for non-compliance with the suggested habits. Individuals who were already considered deviant or deformed were presented as deserving of their oppression and segregation because they failed to comply. Implied was the connection between disability and personal choice. Segregation was justified, therefore, through threats of moral and health contamination or physical degradation. "Conforming" parents were those for whom "good health habits" were possible, and they passed on their privilege to their children (Owen, Neville, & Smith, 2001).

Under the liberal functionalism framework, special education became yet another constituent in the sorting and selecting function of schooling, thus enforcing the social class hierarchy and the racial caste system no less effectively than was previously the case (Sleeter, 1986; Tomlinson, 1982). Liberal functionalism and assumptions of merit continue to impact special education practices. For example, in spite of the Individuals with Disabilities Education Act (IDEA) and mandates for culturally fair testing, students from economically disadvantaged and diverse cultural backgrounds are still overrepresented in classifications such as "mentally retarded" and "emotionally disturbed" (Turnbull, Turnbull, & Wehmeyer, 2007). Children in segregated special education classes experience lower academic expectations. Children labeled "emotionally disturbed" have a higher proportion (two-thirds) of unqualified teachers and academic failure spawns further behavior difficulties. Those who are segregated to learn social behavior skills may also lose out on the academics needed to reintegrate into general education classes (Turnbull et al., 2007). Children with severe intellectual disabilities may be perceived as incapable of meaningful thought and excluded from the curriculum even in inclusive classrooms (Kliewer, 1998; Kliewer & Biklen, 2001).

The medical model of disability attempted to counter these harsh conceptions by defining some disabilities as medical/biological conditions that were not necessarily controlled by choice. The medical model rests on the empiricist/positivist philosophy; meaning it employs strict scientific method and objectivity. The tools (e.g., medical and psychometric testing) used to make the distinctions also provide the technology to distinguish between normal and abnormal. Disability, therefore, is seen as a deficit within the child. Traditional special education has long held a tenacious allegiance to the assumptions of this deficit oriented empiricist/positivist framework (Brantlinger, 2006; Gallagher, 1998, 2004; Heshusius, 1989, 2004a; Iano, 1986, 2004; Skrtic, 1991). Empiricist/positivist research throughout the twentieth century has attempted to increase knowledge of biological or neurological deficits, refine diagnostic procedures and instruments, and improve the effectiveness of prescriptive and therapeutic interventions. These forms of knowledge heralded the potential for disability cures and were used to argue the worthiness of special education services. This framework's claim of neutrality and objectivity, however, has demonstrably worked against the goals of educational and social equality by objectifying and stigmatizing people labeled as having disabilities (Heshusius, 2004a), impoverishing the instructional approaches used to educate them (Gallagher, 2005; Iano, 1986; Poplin, 1988), and institutionalizing educational segregation (Skrtic, 1991). Bogdan and Kugelmass (1984) concluded that teachers are not only trained in premises of disability as an in-person deficit and that disabled/typical are useful distinctions, but also that special education is rationally conceived and coordinated system of services that help children who are labeled disabled. They continue by saying that the positivist assumption is that increased knowledge of psychometrics, disabling conditions and special prescriptive teaching strategies correlate with successful educational opportunities.

Heshusius (2004a) captures quite eloquently the manner in which the empiricist/positivist obsession of measuring and ranking obscures diversity and therefore preempts the honoring of it and even prevents rather than honors diversity:

> A particularly sad dilemma involved is that the perceived obligation to measure, and thus rank, often flies in the face of the rhetoric everywhere in education, also within traditional special education, of "honoring diversity." Diversity and ranking are singularly incompatible. You *cannot* measure and rank diversity; doing so flattens and thus kills it. Diversity is flattened and disappears in the very act of being measured and ranked. When those referred to as "diverse" in ability (by those who probably consider themselves as belonging to the norm, or at least to know the norm) are measured against a desired goal or standard, the goals and standards are always less diverse than diversity itself, and thus reduce diversity to the limited diversity *allowed* by the standards and measurement devices. (pp. 213–214, italics in original)

Nevertheless, the field's dogged commitment to positivism/empiricism has proven difficult, if not impossible, to dislodge. The medical model commitment to ranking, sorting, and diagnosing continues to perpetuate the marginalization of students with disabilities.

Behaviorism, or the philosophy of the science of human behavior (Skinner, 1974) has long informed traditional special educational practices. From this framework, behavior is seen as simply responses to stimuli. If you control the stimuli (or environment), you control the behavior. In fact, applied behavior analysis (systematic application of behavioral principles outside the laboratory or clinic), positive reinforcement, and the use of token economies are cited often as the *gold standard* of effective (or evidence-based) practices in the special education research literature (see, for example, Forness, Kavale, Blum, & Lloyd, 1997; Hallahan, 1998; Lloyd, Forness, & Kavale, 1998; Maag, 2001; Kauffman & Hallahan, 2005). Ostensibly, the goal of behavioral interventions is to improve the life and condition of the person. As with the assumptions of the medical model, these behavioral interventions are believed to be empirically tested and "scientifically" effective, and therefore, humanitarian, benevolent, and benign. For persons with disabilities, however, they have more often been used to punish and control. This is played out in classroom management textbooks and practices that promote point and level systems and other systems of rewards and punishments (Smith, 2006). Students are rewarded for good behavior by points to spend toward trinkets, candy, or preferred activities; they may be restricted in activity from having too few points, a type of class distinction since students who are struggling with some of these issues easily give up when they see they can never catch up. These reward systems are related to behavior and compliance training but actually interfere with the inherent rewards of learning and the practice of social skills and citizenship skills (Smith, 2006; Kohn, 1996).

Devastating critiques of behaviorism and behavioral interventions reveal their speciousness, their plausibility built on false premises, not only on their philosophical merits (Robinson, 1981) but also on their moral and practical viability (Kohn, 1993; Danforth & Smith, 2005). In blunter terms, behavioral interventions are essentially dehumanizing and objectifying as the emphasis is placed on engineering students' behaviors rather than engaging them as human beings. Consequently, the field's deep commitment to behaviorism is decidedly at odds with its claims of egalitarianism.

Moving Toward Disability Studies Perspectives

In a movement away from the empiricist/positivist, deficit oriented, and behavioral driven assumptions of traditional special education, disability studies is an interdisciplinary perspective combining contributions from the arts, social science, education, and the humanities. Scholars in these fields have explored the ways in which disability is socially constructed. Examinations of how people with disabilities are portrayed in our culture include revelations of how disempowering attitudes are embedded in our culture and are invisible to most of us (Linton, 1998; Thompson, 1997; Wendell, 1989). For example, Thompson (1997) explores the marginalization of people with disabilities in literature and identifies patterns that also apply to non-fiction and academic narrative (see Smith, 2000a, 2000b, 2006).

Therefore, the study of disability typically addresses research, policy, or practice that relates to treatment and intervention, categories of disabilities, or discussions of implications within the traditional logical positivist and norm-based frameworks using language that relies on methods of research in the physical sciences. For example, despite the many uses for comparing performance of groups of individuals against norms, the actual educational career and success of an individual with a disability is more dependent on the perceptions and values of the educators than on any inherent characteristics or differences of the person (Smith, 1999, 2000b). In short, the relationship between the presence of a disability and the provision of education or interventions is more than the relationship between learners, tasks, and settings (Smith, 1998). Equally important are the relationships between the individual, the educators, and the culture that defines the tasks and settings within which the individual is required to perform.

The social construction model holds that disability resides in the set of social relationships and outcomes of social practices that tend to disadvantage and marginalize people with impairments (Abberley, 1987; Allan, 1999; Linton, 1998;

Paterson & Hughes, 1999). However, the actual impairment a person experiences is a real and important part of daily life but generally poses considerably less handicap than what the society imposes due to assumptions of deficit and incompetence. For example, students labeled with severe disabilities may in fact be literate but not allowed to read in school (Kliewer & Biklen, 2001). Such restrictions reside within institutional, cultural, and interpersonal social structures.

Cultural definitions can result in assumptions about individuals that are based on lack (the person is broken and unrepairable), deviance (the person is abnormal and therefore threatening), or invisibility (the person is a social non-entity and a medical object to be acted upon). These attitudes unconsciously govern practices such as exclusion and isolation. Thus, the field of disability studies is uniquely situated to disrupt the privileging of social paradigms and practices that prioritize deficit, inherent failure, deviance, or invisibility of all or part of an individual. Disability may be understood best by listening to "disabled people" tell about their lives and the real life experience of living with a disability. For example, the social model of disability has been further developed in light of the relevance of women's experiences which include notions related to the idea thta being female is a disability itself thus rendering females as less competent to make sound life choices. Further, medical model sociology has explored both social structures and social relationships in the context of medicine and disability (Thomas, 1999). Disability studies further challenges us to explore the intricacies of disability identity that include choosing disability and taking pride in it (Michalko, 2002). Disability identity results in a resistance to societal expectations of "overcoming" disability, a prevailing rehabilitation counseling model where individuals are encouraged to adapt (or use adaptations with the goal of the disability not making a difference) in order for the disability to disappear entirely. This attempt at normalization is more about the person fitting into a rigid and predetermined society without consideration of the variety of the human condition, which thus renders the person either invisible or "unfixable," or both. Ferguson (1994) examined the institutionalization of people considered mentally retarded in terms of the outcomes for them that reflect social justice principles of critical pedagogy and disability studies. Toward that end, he stated:

> Failure became transformed into chronicity through the application of the therapeutic perspective. Chronicity is created by the merger of professional judgment with the other dimensions of failure. The prominence of this judgment is currently enshrined in official policy and in law. However, professional judgment ratifies only; it does not originate success or failure. The problem is that professionalism has some very powerful reasons of self protection to endorse the continued presence of a percentage of failure, poverty, custody, and hiddenness that economic, ethical, and aesthetic dimensions seem to demand. (p. 170)

Thus people labeled "retarded" were considered failures as people and since they could not be repaired, were considered to be chronically defective. Professionals became invested in this chronic failure as it provided them with lifelong employment as service providers. This attitude has the strength of a paradigm that precludes or makes it very difficult for people to perceive otherwise. Attempts to change this paradigm have resulted in laws such as IDEA, the Rehabilitation Act of 1973, and the Americans with Disabilities Act of 1990. Policy changes such as person-centered planning, positive behavioral supports (Jackson & Panyan, 2002; Albin, Lucyshyn, Horner, & Flannery, 1996; Artesani & Maller, 1998), and supported employment are in direct contrast with the culture of chronicity, but progress is still inhibited to the extent this culture (paradigm) continues to exist in society. TASH (formerly The Association of Persons with Severe Handicaps) is an organization that has had significant influence in progressive person-centered paradigm policies and practices (www.tash.org).

From Activism to the United Nations: Disability Studies and Ethical Practice

When these incoherencies of conflicting paradigms gained recognition throughout the 1980s and 1990s, deep divisions among academics within special education began to emerge (Gallagher, 2007). A small contingent of scholars began by offering serious critiques of the field, critiques that were not well received by mainstream academics. Heshusius (2004b) provides a detailed overview of the "waves of discontent" flowing into the previously placid world of special education. Yet these efforts to reexamine the field and its organizing frameworks were largely ignored or rebuffed. In the late 1990s, special education's dissenters coalesced and turned toward the field of disability studies as a vehicle for "providing alternative ways to think and talk about disability in educational research" (Gabel, 2005, p. 1). In 1999, they formed the Disability Studies in Education Special Interest Group (SIG) at the American Educational Research Association (AERA).

Disability studies education scholars continue to critique educational practices in the service of social justice. Such critiques range from countering the isolating positivist ideologies of special education embodied in arguments against inclusion (Brantlinger, 1997), and in textbooks (Brantlinger, 2006), to the oppressive nature of degrading behavioral programs (Danforth, 2006). An international perspective is essential to our standards. The DSE Standards take into account the United Nations Convention on the Rights of Persons with Disabilities, which was signed by a record 81 nations on the first day it opened for signatures in March 2007. The Convention, which Yannis Vardakastanis of the International Disability Caucus characterized as "a very drastic paradigm shift in the way the international community looks at disability" (UN News Centre, 2007), asserts that people with disabilities often encounter attitudinal and environmental barriers that prevent their full, equal, and active participation in society. "These barriers impinge particularly on the well-being of persons with intellectual, mental or multiple disabilities. They add to the disadvantage customarily experienced by disabled persons belonging to such populations or social groups as women, children, the elderly and refugees." The proposed convention emphasizes accessible environments.

To enable persons with disabilities to live independently and participate fully in all aspects of life, States Parties shall take appropriate measures to ensure to persons with disabilities access, on an equal basis with others, to the physical environment, to transportation, to information and communications, including information and communications technologies and systems, and to other facilities and services open or provided to the public, both in urban and in rural areas (Article 9).

Five essential characteristics include:

- Accessibility—can you get to where you want to go?
- Accommodation—can you do what you want to do?
- Resource Availability—are your special needs met?
- Social Support—are you accepted by those around you?
- Equality—are you treated equally with others?

The United Nations convention sets the tone for specifics of ethical practice in education.

Disability Studies and Ethical Practice: Evolution of Our Standards

The participation of the DSE SIG members in the project culminating in this book included discussions at the SIG business meeting, the Second City Disability Studies and Education Conference held each year, as well as email conversations. At the 2004 DSE annual business meeting, the SIG members agreed that our standards should be assertively oriented toward social justice and move institutions applying them to take a more active stance. Given that the structures of oppression are interlocking in nature, a disability studies framework can be used to evaluate, even influence, the ethical impact on practice, not only for disabled students, but for all students. While education standards may help target areas of curriculum to be improved in teacher education, they may also be framed in such a way as to perpetuate practice that will impair the abilities of teachers to grow in understanding of their students and to actually limit educational possibilities for students perceived as deviant due to their disabilities or individual learning needs. At the 2007 Second City DSE Conference, SIG members and others interested in the standards suggested further refinement, particularly in terms of possible misunderstandings of jargon.

The standards presented here result from a number of influences in addition to disability studies. The first was the guidelines from the Assembly of Alaskan Native Educators (2000, 2001). An earlier version of our standards used the categories from the Alaskan Guidelines. The second was the idea of ethical impact discussed by Michael Lerner (2000) from outside the educational establishment. The third is the disability rights movement. An international perspective was gained from the United Nations Comprehensive and Integral International Convention on Protection and Promotion of the Rights and Dignity of Persons with Disabilities (2003).

Lerner's idea of requiring an ethical impact statement as a requirement for contract bids (the winning bid would have the highest social responsibility rating) caused the first author to try and apply the concept to standards in order to not only make standards ethical but to raise the bar on what ethical standards evoked. Lerner proposes engaging in emancipatory spirituality or a politics of meaning as the center of a program for social change. He suggests for both private and public sectors

> … a new bottom line so that institutions, economic practices and individual decisions are judged rational not only to the extent that they maximize money and power but also to the extent that they maximize our capacities to be caring about others, ecologically and ethically coherent, and capable of responding to the world not only in narrow and utilitarian ways but with the awe and wonder of the grandeur of creation. (p. 8)

Thus, he is proposing a procedure that values compassion, creativity, ecological sanity, awe and wonder, and not just money and power.

In the case of educational policy and practice, the ethical impact of any proposal or pilot project should be evaluated by a standard of social responsibility as a condition of approval or continuation. In an age when standards are controversial regarding whether they are helpful or harmful, we are part of a movement exploring how standards might further and actively promote social justice and responsibility. An ethical impact standard can help educators think through and foster needed conversations about approaches that best serve our students. Disability studies principles inherently lend themselves to such a frame of reference and provide an activist thrust.

Such a standard or guideline should contradict the national trend in education towards an extrinsic and superficial focus to maintain competitive advantage. This would include changing priorities of standardization and conformity to priorities of social and individual growth, responsibility, and creativity. The "new bottom line" for education calls for restructuring education.

If your goal is to create a human being who is loving, capable of showing deep caring for others, alive to the spiritual and ethical dimensions of being, ecologically sensitive, intellectually alive, self-determining, and creative, there are ways of restructuring education to foster this kind of person (see Lerner, 2002, pp. 233–259). There is no objective test for these things, according to Lerner, but they occur in a context of meaning and relationship. For example, capacities for compassion and awe and wonder might be defined and evaluated "by the relevant communities from which people emerge" (Lerner, 2000, p. 242) or alternative tracks such as ethnic, religious or voluntary communities asked to participate in such evaluations (pp. 242–243).

Teaching "awe and wonder" would begin with a focus on integrating "knowledge about" (in the external left-brained sense) with a deeper right-brained emotional and experiential focus (p. 244). "Knowledge about" would be in a context of meaning, appreciation, responsibility and stewardship for the uniqueness, interconnection, and survival of the world. Disability studies goes beyond evaluating such an ethical impact to creating one. Evaluation or promoting social justice oriented ethical impact would inherently include and promote key ethical concepts such as inclusion, dignity, respect for diversity, liberation, social responsibility, justice, and fellowship.

The Disability Rights Movement has led to the creation of a community of individuals with disabilities who collectively and actively strive to achieve social justice and end discrimination through political action. The recent history of the movement has included political actions ranging from civil rights to a free appropriate public education, employment, access to public transit, appropriate interpreters for the deaf, access for people with visual impairments (Fleischer & Zames, 2001) and elimination of government work disincentives (Longmore, 2004). In recent years activism has taken on ethical issues such as physician assisted suicide (or murder; see www.notdeadyet.org) and the right to live outside institutions or "unincarcerated" (see www.adapt.org). The movement has significant implications for creating ethical impact standards for education. The educational system should have a goal of creating human beings who further social justice by recognizing discrimination, stereotyping, oppression, and marginalization and using political and social actions to counteract them. Lerner's call for "awe and wonder of creation" includes the precious nature and contribution of each human being. In this model, teachers and students identify real problems and create real solutions.

Disability Studies Assumptions and Standards for Educators

The shift to a disability studies perspective can assist in understanding the ethical impact of educational policy and practice. Standards for educators emerging from policy bodies to instructional and support personnel and students would be based on the following principles common to those who support disability studies as a tool for social justice. Each of the following assumptions provides the foundation for suggested standards which can assist educators and policy makers in establishing goals, developing curricula, creating a positive environment, and so forth.

1. Challenge the Social Construction of Disability is socially constructed.

Disability resides in the set of social relationships and outcomes of social practices that tend to disadvantage and marginalize people with impairments, perceived impairments, and physical differences. These relationships are institutional, cultural, and interpersonal social structures. Cultural definitions result in deficit oriented assumptions that govern oppressive practices such as exclusion and isolation. Therefore:

- Educators must assure that students with disabilities or who are perceived to have disabilities are fully participating citizens of the educational community.
- Steps must be taken to contradict exclusive and marginalizing cultural norms so that disability is recognized as another interesting way to be alive. As everyone needs some kind of support, and most supports for people

with disabilities are useful to many people, these should be made available to all; unique supports should be viewed as a norm.

2. *Address Actual Life Challenges Rather than Handicapping Sterotypical Assumptions*

Disability studies prioritizes the complex aspects of peoples' lives over the privileging of paradigms and practices that prioritize deficit(s) over other aspects of their lives. Therefore:

- Labeling should be replaced with useful knowledge about the individual and practices that support learning.
- The use of aversive practices as "treatments" for differences in behavior should be considered ethically and morally untenable and should be replaced with respectful methods such as interpreting behavior as meaningful communication and thus providing/accepting alternative means of communication, changing environments and recognizing differences in behavior as "normal."
- Educators must avoid and prevent the use of coercive versions of approaches such as person-centered planning and positive behavioral supports, which though generally non-coercive when conducted from a strength-based perspective, can become coercive when differences in behavior are viewed as deficits and as abnormal.
- Educators should adopt the *Criterion of The Least Dangerous Assumption* which "holds that without conclusive data educational decisions should be based on assumptions which, if incorrect, will provide the least danger for independent functioning" (Donnellan, 1984, p. 141). This means assuming competence in all students and honoring their contributions so that their education proceeds in age-appropriate ways and according to high expectations as with nondisabled students (see Jorgensen, 2005).

3. *Assume Competence and Honor Contributions*

The actual impairment a person experiences is a real and important part of daily life. This lived experience, which may include considerable challenges, generally poses considerably less restriction than what the society imposes due to assumptions of deficit and incompetence. The deficit assumptions prevail resulting in the naming of people with differences as "incompetent," when in fact disability is part of the normal spectrum of life. Therefore:

- Educators should take steps to avoid such deficit assumptions and aversive "treatments" and actively support strength based assumptions and activities.
- Adversive tactics should be replaced with respectful approaches such as interpreting all behavior as meaningful communication, providing and accepting alternative means of communication, changing and adapting environments to foster participation, and recognizing differences in behavior as natural to humans.

4. *Explore Both Social Structures and Social Relationships*

Disability studies explores both social structures and social relationships (Thomas, 1999). As with other marginalized groups, institutions develop around disabled people to justify and govern their marginalization. At the same time, disabled people form relationships to both cope with and transform their situations. The complexity of the lived experience should not be overlooked in struggles for social justice. Therefore:

- Educators should take steps to understand and communicate the difference between disabling and enabling social structures and relationships.
- A key indicator relates to quality of life. Educators should ask whether he or she would put him/herself or most beloved person in the same situation and, if not, take appropriate steps.

5. *Foster Disability Pride*

Exploring the intricacies of disability identity includes choosing and taking pride in it, in contrast to societal expectations of overcoming, adapting, and making disability irrelevant or invisible. Therefore:

- Educators should take steps to help the students feel pride.
- Educators should provide the supports students need, including the development of self-determination skills, to be fully visible and participating in life.

6. *Listen to People with Disabilities*

Disability is best understood by listening to disabled people tell about their lives. Disability perspectives and experiences have a significant contribution to make to teacher learning. Therefore:

- Educators should be soliciting feedback from their disabled students and colleagues to improve their own connection and effectiveness.
- Educators should learn the perspectives of their students in order to evaluate the ethical impact of their practice.

7. *Empower Self-Determination through Liberation from the Medical Model*

The medical model of sorting, ranking, and diagnosing has led to professional obscuring of disabled students' strength, talents, and insights. Therefore:

- Educators should understand the social model of disability, the way social structures, institutions, and cultural artifacts impact the experience of disability, and contribute to it, as it is still a work in progress.
- Educators should thus actively promote liberation (flourishing, self-determination), collaboration, and acknowledgment of students' competence and lived experience regardless of the physical impact of their disabilities.

8. Integrate Social Disability Justice into the "Hidden Curriculum"

Curriculum is seen as a means to achieve social justice. Curriculum is a process and is more than just an imparting of knowledge. Therefore:

- Educators must be aware of the "hidden curriculum" of processes and their ethical impacts. These processes of control and compliance should be actively eliminated in favor of educative and liberating processes.
- The "hidden curriculum" must include processes that are educative themselves, promote critical thinking about required content, promote advocacy for self and others, and full citizenship. Understandings of the hidden curriculum must also apply to those with severe disabilities who also deserve access to an interesting and academic curriculum and social skills development approaches that are socially and contextually meaningful rather than geared toward compliance training.

9. Integrate Disability Studies into Teacher Education

Achieving these disability studies dispositions, perspectives, and practices in educators requires developing them in teacher educators and the institution of teacher education.

- The culture and curriculum of teacher education should be transformed to prepare educators who exemplify disability studies principles and realize them in practice.
- The institution of teacher education should engage citizens and policymakers in understanding, identifying, and ameliorating disabling social structures and relationships in schools and communities.
- Teacher educators should increase their use of interpretive and participatory forms of research because their conventional positivist orientation and quantitative methods preclude the type of moral inquiry and social engagement inherent in the disabilities studies perspective.

Implications for Practice

Readers who might be familiar with implications for practice may need to rethink carefully how they construct "the other" in their own classroom. The cultural paradigms around normalcy may cause the most culturally relevant teachers to overlook the children with disabilities. For example, in a study of inclusion of deaf-blind students, Giangreco, Dennis, Cloninger, Edelman, and Schattman (1993) found that teachers who were initially skeptical of these students began to see and treat them as real students in their classroom, one even exclaiming, "I've counted Jon!" in terms of making sure he got the handouts and worksheets (assuming competence, full citizenship).

Teachers often seek classroom management strategies to engage their students and find certain students with learning and attention challenges need particular attention. In seeking advice, strategies range from community building and positive behavioral support strategies to bribes and rewards and point level systems. When they carefully evaluate practice, they can ask where the technique under consideration is also used in society. Sometimes "prison" comes up as a stark answer as they realize that, if the bribes do not work, the next option is exile.

A search for educative solutions has yielded strategies such as the following: A student who was particularly distracted and prone to be in motion was sent on an errand. After the walk he returned ready and eager to focus on the work at hand. Later, he learned that he could take walks whenever he needed to "collect himself" as long as he didn't disrupt others. Sometimes he went for a drink. Sometimes a walk around the room was sufficient (lived experience included a need for movement). Another student was clocked at being off-task 25 times during the day. He was surprised to learn this and agreed to a self-monitoring program where he kept track of the time on and off task. After a week, he got the hang of staying focused and worked out a secret reminder with the teacher for when he went astray. He was pleased that his work improved and got done sooner yielding him more "choice time" (self-determination, collaboration). A student who was constantly "in trouble" due to his lack of social skills (greeting, asking for things, turn taking) was engaged by an offer of leadership training. He learned a game that his peers did not know. In the process, he learned the importance of following the instructions, helping people, and turn taking. He taught the game to his classmates transformed his relationship with them. An understanding of what it was like to be this student in this class led to the idea of the game (social structures for acceptance/inclusion, collaboration, educative process, collaboratively developing student competence, and belonging). A non-verbal teenager student with Rett syndrome did no meaningful work and had scant communication with a speech therapist who did not think the student would understand much of anything. The speech therapist's successor, who assumed and expected competence (the least dangerous assumption), supported the student in taking multiple-choice tests and engaged the student in typed conversations about things that were upsetting. Thus, the eyes of the beholders, in this case two professionals in the same role, seemingly transformed this student from "not understanding very much" to a flourishing and communicative student.

These few examples point out that using the ethical guidelines can help teachers evaluate practice and make sure their practices are to the students' benefit.

Conclusion

As policies and guidelines can become rigid and co-opted, we propose this as a base for furthering social justice in education. Our guidelines went through some changes, which included making them less generic. A generic version could yield applications to every topic but disability, mirroring the current state of marginalization of disabled people and their related issues. Our explicitly disability studies perspective invites readers to integrate these into other issues presented in this book. We experience the guidelines of disability studies as core and useful in all arenas of human endeavor. The ethical impact standards can be adapted or used to formulate or inspire policy for various educational roles from policy generation and enforcement to staff, support personal, families, and students in schools. They also inspire more questions about ethical practice. For example, what is the ethical impact of deciding that a nonverbal student is illiterate and incapable of meaningful choices? How do you determine the ethical impact of teaching desired behaviors by bribing presumably incompetent students with meaningless rewards rather than using educative means that result in rewarding experiences and relationships? What do these approaches do to our relationships with students and each other? If we replace "disabled student" with another category (gender, race, ethnicity, etc.) how do the questions change? How do we evaluate ethical impact? The concept of ethical impact evaluation could usefully expand to the whole social fabric.

Contributors in the process: Robin M. Smith, Valerie Owen, Deb Gallagher, Tom Skrtic, Susan Peters, Mara Sapon Shevin, Roger Slee, Linda Symcox, Nancy Rice, and other members of the Disability Studies in Education Special Interest Group.

References

AERA Social and Environmental Justice SIG's. (2003). *Drafts of social and environmental justice standards.* Washington, DC: AERA.

Abberley, P. (1987). The concept of oppression and the development of a social theory of disability. *Disability, Handicap & Society, 2*(1), 519.

Albin, R. W., Lucyshyn, J. M., Horner, R. H., & Flannery, K. B. (1996). Contextual fit for behavioral support plans. In L. K. Koegel, R. L. Koegel, & G. Dunlap (Eds.), *Positive behavioral support: Including people with difficult behavior in the community* (pp. 81–98). Baltimore: Paul H. Brookes.

Allan, J. (1999). *Actively seeking inclusion: Pupils with special needs in mainstream schools.* London: Falmar Press.

Artesani, A. J., & Maller, L. (1998). Positive behavior supports in general education settings: Combining person centered planning and functional analysis. *Intervention in School and Clinic, 34*(1), 33–38.

Assembly of Alaska Native Educators. (2000). *Guidelines for respecting cultural knowledge.* Anchorage: Alaska Native Knowledge Network. Retrieved October 13, 2006, from http://www.ankn.uaf.edu

Assembly of Alaska Native Educators. (2001). *Guidelines for strengthening indigenous languages and guidelines for nurturing culturally sensitive youth.* Anchorage: Alaska Native Knowledge Network.

Bogdan, R., & Kugelmass, J. (1984). Case studies of Main Street: A symbolic interactionist approach to special schooling. In L. Barton & S. Thomlinson (Eds.), *Special education and social interests* (pp. 173–191). New York: Nichols.

Brantlinger, E. (1997). Using ideology: Cases of nonrecognition of the politics of research and practice in special education. *Review of Educational Research, 67*(4), 425–459.

Brantlinger, E. (2006). The big glossies: How textbooks structure (special) education. In E. Brantlinger (Ed.), *Who benefits from special education? Remediating (fixing) other people's children* (pp. 45–76). Mahwah, NJ: Erlbaum.

Danforth, S., & Smith, T. J. (2005). *Engaging troubling students: A constructivist approach.* Thousand Oaks, CA: Corwin Press.

Danforth, S. (2006). Compliance as alienated labor: A critical analysis of public school programs for students considered to have emotional/behavioral disorders. In S. L. Gabel (Ed.), *Disability studies in education: Readings in theory and method* (pp. 85–102). New York: Peter Lang.

Donnellan, A. M. (1984). The criterion of the least dangerous assumption. *Behavioral Disorders, 9*(2), 141–150.

Ferguson, P. M. (1994). *Abandoned to their fate: Social policy and practice towards severely retarded people in America. 1820–1920.* Philadelphia: Temple University Press.

Fleischer, D. Z., & Zames, F. (2001). *The disability rights movement: From charity to confrontation.* Philadelphia: Temple University Press.

Forness, S. R., Kavale, K. A., Blum, I. M., & Lloyd, J. W. (1997). Mega-analysis of meta-analysis: What works in special education and related services. *Teaching Exceptional Children, 29*(6), 4–9.

Gabel, S. (2005). Introduction: Disability studies in education. In S. Gabel (Ed.), *Disability studies in education: Readings in theory and method* (pp. 1–20). New York: Peter Lang.

Gallagher, D. J. (1998). The scientific knowledge base of special education: Do we know what we think we know? *Exceptional Children, 64*(4), 493–502.

Gallagher, D. J. (2004). Entering the conversation: The debates behind the debates in special education. In D. J. Gallagher, L. Heshusius, R. P. Iano, & T. M. Skrtic (Eds.), *Challenging orthodoxy in special education: Dissenting voices* (pp. 3–26). Denver, CO: Love Publishing.

Gallagher, D. J. (2005). Searching for something outside of ourselves: The contradiction between technical rationality and the achievement of inclusive pedagogy. In S. Gabel (Ed.), *Disability studies in education: Readings in theory and method* (pp. 139–154). New York: Peter Lang.

Gallagher, D. J. (2007). Challenging orthodoxy in special education: On longstanding debates and philosophical divides. In L. Florian (Ed.), *The Sage handbook of special education* (pp. 515–527). Thousand Oaks, CA: Sage.

Giangreco, M. F., Dennis, R., Cloninger, C., Edelman, S., & Schattman, R. (1993). "I've counted Jon": Transformational experiences of teachers educating students with disabilities. *Exceptional Children, 59*(4), 359–372.

Hallahan, D. P. (1998). Sound bytes from special education reform rhetoric. *Remedial and Special Education, 19*(2), 67–69.

Heshusius, L. (1989). The Newtonian mechanistic paradigm, special education, and contours of alternatives: An overview. *Journal of Learning Disabilities, 22*, 403–415.

Heshusius, L. (2004a). From creative discontent toward epistemological freedom in special education: Reflections on a 25-year journey. In D. J. Gallagher, L. Heshusius, R. P. Iano, & T. M. Skrtic (Eds.), *Challenging orthodoxy in special education: Dissenting voices* (pp. 169–230). Denver, CO: Love Publishing.

Heshusius, L. (2004b). Special education knowledges: The inevitable struggle with the "self." In D. J. Gallagher, L. Heshusius, R. P. Iano, & T. M. Skrtic (Eds.), *Challenging orthodoxy in special education: Dissenting voices* (pp. 283–309). Denver, CO: Love Publishing.

Hurn, C. J. (1993). *The limits and possibilities of schooling: An introduction to the sociology of schooling.* Needham Heights, MA: Allyn & Bacon.

Iano, R. P. (1986). The study and development of teaching: With implications for the advancement of special education. *Remedial and Special Education, 7*(5), 50–61.

Iano, R. P. (2004). The tale of a reluctant empiricist. In D. J. Gallagher, L. Heshusius, R. P. Iano, & T. M. Skrtic (Eds.), *Challenging orthodoxy in special education: Dissenting voices* (pp. 231–249). Denver, CO: Love Publishing.

Individuals with Disabilities Education Act. 20 U.S.C. (1975).

Jackson, L., & Panyan, M. V. (2002). *Positive behavioral support in the classroom: Principles and practices.* Baltimore: Paul H. Brookes.

Jackson, P. W. (1968) *Life in classrooms*. New York: Holt, Rinehart & Winston.

Jorgensen, C. (2005). The least dangerous assumption: A challenge to create a new paradigm. *Disability Solutions, 6*(3), 1, 5–9, 15. Retrieved April 3, 2007, from http://www.disabilitysolutions.org/pdf/6-3.pdf

Kavale, K. A., Blum, I. M., & Lloyd, J. W. (1997). Mega-analysis of meta-analysis: What works in special education and related services. *Teaching Exceptional Children, 29*(6), 4–9.

Kauffman, J. M., & Hallahan, D. P. (2005). *Special education: What it is and why we need it*. Boston: Pearson.

Kliewer, C. (1998). *Schooling children with Down syndrome: Toward an understanding of possibility*. New York: Teachers College Press.

Kliewer, C., & Biklen, D. (2001). School's not really a place for reading: A research synthesis of the literate lives of students with severe disabilities. *Journal of The Association for People with Severe Handicaps, 26*(1), 1–12.

Kohn, A. (1993). *Punished by rewards: The trouble with gold stars, incentive plans, A's, praise, and other bribes*. Boston: Houghton Mifflin.

Kohn, A. (1996). *Beyond discipline: From compliance to community*. Alexandria, VA: Association for Supervision & Curriculum Development.

Lerner, M. (2000). *Spirit matters*. Charlottesville, VA: Hampton Roads Publishing.

Lerner, M. (2002). Wall street meltdown. *Tikkun, 17*(5), 8–9.

Lloyd, J. W., Forness, S. R., & Kavale, K. A. (1998). Some methods are more effective than others. *Intervention in School and Clinic, 33*(4), 195–200.

Linton, S. (1998). *Claiming disability: Knowledge and identity*. New York: New York University Press.

Longmore, P. K. (2004). Why I burned my book. In *Why I burned my book and other essays on disability* (pp. 230–259). Philadelphia: Temple University Press.

Maag, J. W. (2001). Rewarded by punishment: Reflections on the disuse of positive reinforcement in schools. *Exceptional Children, 67*(2), 173–186.

Michalko, R. (2002). *The difference that disability makes*. Philadelphia: Temple.

Owen, V., Neville, P., & Smith, T. J. (2001, April). *Challenging representations of disability in the professional standards for special education*. Paper presented at the American Education Research Association, Seattle, WA.

Paterson, K., & Hughes, B. (1999). Disability studies and phenomenology: The carnal politics of everyday life. *Disability & Society, 14*(5), 597–610.

Poplin, M. S. (1988). Holistic/constructivist principles of the teaching/learning process: Implications for the field of learning disabilities. *Journal of Learning Disabilities, 21*, 401–416.

Robinson, D. N. (1981). *An intellectual history of psychology*. New York: MacMillan.

Skinner, B., F. (1974) . *About behaviorism*. New York: Vintage.

Skrtic, T. M. (1991). *Behind special education: A critical analysis of professional culture and school organization*. Denver, CO: Love Publishing.

Skrtic, T. M. (1995). *Disability and democracy: Reconstructing (special) education for postmodernity*. New York: Teachers College Press.

Sleeter, C. E. (1986) Learning disabilities: The social construction of a special education category. *Exceptional Children, 53*, 46–54.

Smith, C. R. (1998). *Learning disabilities: The interaction of learner, task, and setting*. Needham Heights, MA: Allyn & Bacon.

Smith, R. M. (1999). Academic engagement of students with significant disabilities and educators' perceptions of competence. *The Professional Educator, 22*(1), 17–31.

Smith, R. M. (2000a). Mystery or typical teen? The social construction of academic engagement and disability. *Disability & Society, 15*(6), 911–924.

Smith, R. M. (2000b). View from the ivory tower: How academics construct disability. In B. B. Swadner & L. Rogers (Eds.), *Semiotics and Disability: Interrogating the categories of difference* (pp. 55–73). Albany: State University of New York Press.

Smith, R. M. (2006). Classroom management texts: a study in the representation and misrepresentation of students with disabilities. *International Journal of Inclusive Education, 10*(1), 91–104.

Thomas, C. (1999). *Female forms: Experiencing and understanding disability.* Philadelphia: Open University Press.

Thompson, R. G. (1997). Feminist theory, the body, and the disabled figure. In L. Davis (Ed.), *The disability studies reader* (pp. 279–292). London: Routledge.

Tomlinson, S. (1982). A sociology of special education. London: Routledge & Kegan Paul.

Turnbull, A. P., Turnbull, H. R., & Wehmeyer, M. J. (2007). *Exceptional lives: Special education in today's schools* (4th ed.). Columbus, OH: Prentice Hall.

United Nations (2003). *Towards a society for all: Long-term strategy to implement the world programme of action concerning disabled persons to the year 2000 and beyond.* New York: United Nations: Division for Social Policy and Development.

United Nations News Centre (2007, June 13). Record number of countries sign UN treaty on disabilities on opening day. Retrieved May 21, 2007, from http://www.un.org/apps/news/story.asp?NewsID=22085&Cr=disab&Cr

Wendell, S. (1989, Summer). Towards a feminist theory of disability. *Hypatia, 4*, 104–124.

15 Queered Standards

Living and Working for Peace and Justice

Darla Linville, Christopher Walsh, and David Lee Carlson

Framing the Issues

When contemplating proposing a sexuality justice curriculum that is applicable in all locales globally, the authors of this chapter become nearly paralyzed. There is no standard understanding of sexuality worldwide, and many Western beliefs about sexuality in Africa, Asia, and the Middle East persist from the era of Western imperialism. An imposed Western standard of sexuality that was disseminated during the era of expansion and Christian proselytizing denies the variety of sexualities and sexual practices that colonists encountered in their travels (Murray & Roscoe, 1998). Similar miscategorization, oversimplification, and moralizing still occurs in 21st century dissemination of economic and social aid by international humanitarian groups (Vasagar & Borger, 2005). Western aid organizations and journalists sometimes bring unwanted attention and conflict to local groups working for sexuality justice in countries outside of the United States and Western Europe, and frequently "get it wrong" when they advocate for outcomes that would isolate those not in traditionally heterosexual relations from their families, religions, and cultures (Roshan & Shemirani, 2006; Ahmed, Shafqat, Shemirani, & Toor, 2006). Various scholars have documented cultures where same-sex sexual practices have existed concurrently with heterosexuality and received acceptance and ritualized, codified significance in the cultures (Murray & Roscoe, 1998; Peplau, 2001). Because so many beliefs and understandings about sexuality exist, it is challenging to think or teach about sexuality in schools.

In countries where persecution of lesbian, gay, bisexual, transgender, and queer (LGBTQ)[1] persons is perceived to be excessive, violent, and sponsored by the state, U.S., British, and international gay advocacy groups have often proposed interventions to protect the human rights of the targeted persons. This impulse is often appreciated by activists working within the country in question, but the methods and the results can be unhelpful (Arondekar, 2005). Outside groups may request that LGBTQ persons in another country "come out," or publicly declare themselves gay as a part of their liberation movement, a strategy that may flout sexuality conventions within the society. Sometimes just being involved with international gay advocacy organizations results in further endangering or exclusion of the group. Also, in some cases, the advocacy work and language of the Western LGBTQ activist group may be picked up by the U.S. or British, or other European government and used as an excuse to attack, either diplomatically or militarily, a country for its human rights abuses. This tactic is seen by the activists in other countries not as a genuine concern for the rights of the LGBTQ persons in that country, but as an excuse for further imperialist incursions into regions where the West has economic interests (Roshan & Shemirani, 2006).

Within the United States and Western European nations, queer issues are often posited as issues of social exclusion and inequality for those who do not participate in heterosexuality. In some other places, however, the very right to exist is threatened for those who have sexual relations outside of the construct of heterosexual marriage. On the other hand, in many places, homosocial behaviors that would incite speculation as to the participants' sexuality and perhaps precipitate violence in the United States or Western European countries, such as two men holding hands, is commonplace and expected. What constitutes the boundaries of sexuality justice will need to be defined rather flexibly, and the definition will need to be contextual, for the purposes of creating curriculum content and educational policy that will speak to the needs of many communities. In the end, it must be remembered that people around the world are losing their lives because of the sexual pleasures that they seek, because of the sexual desires that they feel, and/or because of the person with whom they choose to act. This is where the social justice claim resides.

Our contention will be that love can exist in myriad forms, that it can be expressed in many ways, and that love, intimate relationships, and sexual pleasures are rights that one should have access to in life. Although sexual relations and marriages are often viewed as economic, political, and social arrangements that reinforce systems of power and consolidate wealth, they are equally often imbued with spiritual values in which persons are united to one another through religious ceremonies. Around the world, connections of family and love create the support networks and social settings in which people's needs and desires are met. Focusing education on the importance of human relations and love, on the ability to interact with others in peace without the need for conquest or domination, may help create greater possibilities for all students, and open spaces for non-heterosexual love and sexuality to enter.

International Rights for Same-Gender Sexuality and Non-Binary Gender

Queer youth and adults worldwide have very few sites of refuge. That does not mean that there are very few people who have sex or intimate relations with persons of the same sex or gender. It often means that if this activity is known about it is only tacitly accepted and not spoken about; it remains, at least in the public sphere, a secret. In other countries homosexuality is an "open secret," at least in larger, urban areas. The LGBTQ people may be visible, have social networks and gathering spaces, community and political organizations, and have a certain amount of security in expressing their sexuality, even if legal protections for their rights to a job, housing, education, and for their relationships do not exist. Additionally, there are currently 21 countries[2] in which homosexual marriages or civil unions have acquired legal status (Civil Union, 2007). In these countries, public debate about the rights and place in society of LGBTQ persons has been held. Although Canada, Great Britain, and New Zealand all offer some legal recognition for same-sex relationships, in the United States and Australia the issue has not yet been decided nationally.

Internationally, global human rights groups have recently included sexual orientation, gender identity and gender expression to the list of categories on which people should expect equal treatment from nations and avoid being discriminated against. Of special importance, an ad hoc international group of human rights experts from various organizations and countries convened in Jogjakarta, Indonesia, in November 2006 and created a policy document called the Yogyakarta Principles proposing international standards for human rights for LGBTQ persons (Human Rights Watch, 2007). These standards suggest equality should be enforced in all nations for all persons regardless of sexuality or gender identity or expression, based on human rights principles that many states have already agreed to. The standards proposed by the Yogyakarta Principles on the Application of International Law in Relation to Issues of Sexual Orientation and Gender Identity make explicit that access to human and civil rights should be extended to LGBTQ persons, as it is to non-LGBTQ persons (Yogyakarta Principles, 2007).

The Yogyakarta Principles cover human rights such as protection under the law, the right to cultural, social and economic goods, freedom of movement and expression and the right to redress for wrongs. Specifically on the topic of education, the document calls for "the right to education, without discrimination on the basis of, and taking into account, their sexual orientation and gender identity" (p. 21). Actions recommended to governments include:

a. ensuring equal access to education and equal treatment regardless of sexual orientation or gender identity;
b. ensuring that students are nurtured in their sexuality and gender expression;
c. ensuring that students are educated about human rights, including respect for diverse sexualities and gender identities;
d. ensuring safety for students, staff and teachers of diverse sexualities and gender identities;
e. ensuring that students are not isolated or marginalized in the name of protecting them from bullying;
f. ensuring that disciplinary measures in schools respect human dignity and do not penalize students on the basis of their sexuality or gender identity; and
g. ensuring that adults who have suffered a loss of education due to discrimination have access to adult educational resources without discrimination. (pp. 21–22)

In addition to the mandates specifically about education, the principles also cover areas that would be useful to teachers in presenting the rights of LGBTQ persons in the classroom. The principles include the right to the universal enjoyment of human rights, the rights to equality and non-discrimination, the right to freedom of opinion and expression and the right to participate in public, cultural and family life. These topics are currently disputed in the political arena in the United States and concern many young people. Broaching these topics will lead educators to fulfill some of the goals of the education mandates, such as teaching all students about a range of human rights, including the rights of persons of diverse sexualities and gender expressions.

Many countries already offer some protections for LGBTQ youth in schools. Recent surveys of students in the United States (and elsewhere globally) about heterosexism and bullying in their schools, however, revealed that what is being done in U.S. schools is not enough. The 2005 report, *From Teasing to Torment: School Climate in America*, shares the results from a survey and interview of 3,450 secondary students and 1,011 secondary teachers nationwide during January 2005 (GLSEN, 2005). This is the most comprehensive survey of school atmosphere on the topic of bullying and harassment. The researchers found that bullying in schools, whether on the basis of real or imagined characteristics of the bullied student, and even when not involving physical violence, interferes with a student's school performance and can create a less safe environment in the school for all students. The seriousness of the impact of harassment and bullying can be seen in the number of students that report being harassed, as well as the reason that they report for being targeted.

Students report feeling unsafe or harassed in schools most often due to their physical appearance. Sexist and homophobic remarks are the most often heard derogatory comments in schools, with 52% of students reporting hearing homophobic remarks very often or often and 51% of students reporting sexist remarks (GLSEN, 2005, pp. 12–13). These numbers are fairly consistent across race and class lines, with Latino and African American/Black students hearing slightly more of both types of comments than White students, but with no difference between students from families with different education levels (used to measure class difference). LGBT students heard more homophobic and sexist comments than non-LGBT students, perhaps due to those comments being directed at them. Also, girls were more likely to hear sexist remarks than were boys. One comment, "You're so gay" or "That's so gay," was heard very often or often by 69% of students, and 84% of LGBT students (GLSEN, 2005, p. 20). These types of verbal harassment are likely to be pervasive in a school, with most students, rather than a small group of bullies, using homophobic and sexist language. A quarter of both boys and girls also report being harassed for acting outside of constructed gender boundaries: girls acting too much "like a boy" or boys acting too much "like a girl" (p. 21). These strict binary gender codes keep all students in check, both heterosexual and homosexual, limiting the self-expression of boys and girls and restricting the possibilities for all students to grow and develop their identities.

Organizations working for LGBTQ rights have focused their efforts in the educational realm on protecting the safety of LGBTQ youth in schools and on comprehensive sex education curriculum. The Human Rights Campaign (HRC) and the National Gay and Lesbian Task Force (NGLTF) both have legislative campaigns to change the national policy requiring federal funds solely be used to support abstinence only until marriage sex education (HRC, 2007; Sklar, 2007). HRC has sponsored specific legislation, the Responsible Education About Life Act, S. 972/H.R. 1653, which promotes comprehensive sexuality education that includes non-heterosexual sexuality and gender variance (for an explanation of the bill see Planned Parenthood, 2007). Safety and safe access to schooling is promoted by Lambda Legal (http://www.lambdalegal.org), the Gay, Lesbian and Straight Education Network (http://www.glsen.org), and the National Education Association (NEA) Gay and Lesbian Caucus (http://www.nea-LGBTQc.org/training.html). These organizations all provide support to students, teachers and parents to promote tolerance education programs, such as the National Day of Silence and support organizations within schools to help change homophobic and heterosexist climates to ones more tolerant of difference. With the support of Lambda Legal, students have won court cases in which they charged their school districts with not protecting them from a hostile environment in schools which resulted in the student losing access to education (*L.W. v. Toms River Regional Schools, Board of Education*, 2007; *Nabozny v. Podlesny*, 1996). Schools, too, have been successful in keeping tolerance education content in the curriculum against parents' wishes (*Morrison v. Board of Education of Boyd County, Kentucky*, 2006).

There is no organized effort in the United States around curriculum content change, however. Curriculum changes were proposed in a California Senate bill sponsored by Senator Sheila Kuehl that passed the legislature but was vetoed by Governor Arnold Schwarzenegger. Kuehl wrote the legislation, SB 1437 (Equality California, 2006), which would require the inclusion of significant historical contributions of lesbian and gay historical figures. It would also eliminate any curriculum material that denigrated lesbian, gay, bisexual, and transgender people. Although other states have implemented mandatory treatment of non-heterosexual sexuality and gender variance into the health and sex education curriculum (e.g., the Massachusetts Safe Schools Program for Gay and Lesbian Students, http://www.doe.mass.edu/cnp/safe/ssch.html), no other state has included mandates about gay and lesbian (or bisexual or transgender) historical, literary, or contemporary figures into the curriculum, or mandated teaching about gender and sexual variability in biology classes. Proposals have been made by education scholars, however, that students need to learn about non-heterosexual sexuality and non-binary gender in sex education classes, and in other subjects, both for the benefit of LGBTQ students and heterosexual students.

Queering Education

Queer theory is useful for thinking of a sexuality justice education for the ways that it disrupts categories that assume the natural, biological basis of sexuality and gender, and proposes new ways of imagining relations between persons. Queer theory came to exist in response to some of the essentializing tendencies of lesbian and gay studies and earlier women's studies. It questions the categories of the subjects of its studies—even as it seeks to say something about those persons and about the material conditions of being viewed as belonging to a marginal category (Dilley, 1999). "Queer studies is largely a deconstructive enterprise, taking apart the view of a self defined by something at its core, be it sexual desire, race, gender, nation or class" (Gamson, 2000, p. 348). Based in the foundational work of Michel Foucault's analyses of sexuality and Judith Butler's analyses of gender, queer theory exposes the fluid, socially constructed and always contested boundaries of sexual and gender categories (Foucault, 1978; Butler, 1990).

Queer theory allows for complexity in understanding identity because of the ways that it interrupts assumptions about who belongs to a category. Homosexuality has often been used in institutional settings to subsume the specifics of the person under a universal definition of what it means to be non-heterosexual or gender variant. That is, in school policy and advocacy work, gender issues are about white girls, race issues are about people of color and queer issues are about white boys. These strategies ignore how a person may belong to more than one of these categories, and have interest in more than one of these issues. This categorization strips the individual of the complexity of class, race, gender and other differences. The lens of queer theory makes possible thinking about sexuality interrelated with other axes of identity—the intersectionality of identity (Loutzenheiser & MacIntosh, 2004).

A queer lens also facilitates the reframing of the languages that schools use to talk about sexuality. Schools often frame sexuality as private or inappropriate for classroom discussions (when it covers non-heterosexuality) and, at the same time, schools promote a heterosexist structure that forms bodies, relationships, and gender roles in a particular, heterosexual and gender binary form by defining differently the appropriate behavior for boys and girls. Queer theory can illuminate the ways that sexuality exists in schools—overwhelmingly in one form—and show that only certain kinds of sexuality are labeled as private or inappropriate (Epstein, O'Flynn, & Telford, 2000–2001; Loutzenheiser & MacIntosh, 2004). From there, educators can take the next step to broaden the discussions of sexuality in schools to be inclusive of the differences between individual and to include the silenced sexualities and genders.

Sexuality Justice in Education

Sexuality justice in education may seem like a distant goal to some, but educators have already been theorizing about how justice and sexuality can come together in the classroom. Students must be able to name their sexuality in schools, participate in public dialogues about sexuality without hiding that they are sexually different, and to voice their questions and concerns about justice for those named sexually (or otherwise) Other in school. They also must be free to pursue sexual and romantic relationships in school—as queer theory shows that heterosexually-identified students are able to—and express their gender preferences and be visible as their sexual and gendered selves.

In a sexually just education, sexuality would not be impelled to assimilate to heterosexist norms, nor would non-heterosexual students have to renounce sexual behaviors. LGBTQ student relationships would not necessarily have to follow the dating/relationship/prom model of their heterosexual peers. Trans students would not be required to subscribe to one or the other of the two binary genders, but would be allowed to fashion their gendered bodies as they felt they should. LGBTQ students would not become only gay or trans, to the exclusion of their racial, gender, ethnic, religious or class identities. A queer lens would advocate for an understanding of sexuality outside of the normative, romance-to-marriage-for-life paradigm. It would advocate an understanding of sexuality and gender expression as always contingent and in the process of forming, within relations with others. It would also disrupt the formal sexuality education model currently in place that frequently implicitly or explicitly positions girls as victims of sexual violence and boys as sexual conquerors (Fine & McClelland, 2006; Tolman, 2006). It would create possibilities for different sexual subjectivities regardless of one's sexual desires or partners.

This queered notion of sexuality offers an opportunity for all students to interact with others different from themselves, and with ideas that may be strange or unknown to them. It has been stated in educational policy and legal decisions about educational policies and practices that students should be entitled to an education that will prepare them for the "real world" (Russo, 2006). This preparation requires that students know about and be comfortable interacting with others with ideas, skin color, languages, customs, religions, political beliefs, sexualities, genders, abilities, and appearances (among other things) that are different from their own in a professional, collegial manner. Learning to talk about difference without resorting to hostility, to discuss disagreements or competing claims to legitimacy or truth without denying the humanity of others, are lessons of democracy that educators can model and students can learn in schools.

Beyond Safe Spaces and Tolerance

In seeking to meet the needs of and provide educational justice for queer students, many schools, districts, and states have opted to allow or encourage students to start Gay-Straight Alliances (GSA). GSAs are usually after-school clubs that design service projects for the members, sponsor activism days that promote tolerance of LGBTQ students and adults (such as the Day of Silence, or National Coming Out Day) and provide a safe space within which students can act and speak like "themselves". Bullying and silencing in schools make necessary the separate safe space of GSAs and similar clubs (Friend, 1993, 1998; MacGillivray, 2000; Quinlivan & Town, 1999; Sadowski, 2001). In the larger school environment queer students often feel silenced and/or they fear social or physical consequences for speaking out about, acting as or becoming legible (Butler, 1990), that is, visible and recognizable, as queer. Schools, however, claim to promote participation and access by all students. Students need to learn about their rights and responsibilities as citizens through their participation in schools. As mentioned in the previous section, although all students may be portrayed as citizens (and equal) by the school, their full participation in the daily life of school lessons and activities is limited by silencing of some of their knowledge, history, or experiences. GSAs make a space from which students can work for greater tolerance among their classmates and find solidarity and support for their ideas, experiences and inquiries.

Supporting separate spaces for LGBTQ youth and promoting tolerance among non-LGBTQ youth has been criticized by some as deflecting attention from the real problems and continuing to stigmatize LGBTQ youth (Leck, 2000; Rasmussen, 2004, 2006). Segregated spaces for queer youth locate the problems that queer youth experience in schools, such as bullying and harassment, in the queer student, who has to be removed from the other students because of the disruption that is caused. Not only does this relieve the harassers of any culpability, it also requires that the LGBTQ youth claim a status—gay student or straight ally—that he or she may not be ready to claim. In addition, a student who does claim that identity, but who does not experience social or physical consequences in school, or doesn't "behave" or "look" gay enough, may be unable to or unwilling to access the community that is provided by the GSA. It may exclude students on two fronts—those who are excluded from the larger community of school and made to seek shelter there, and those who would join and look for community there but feel unwelcome due to their inability to be seen as really queer, or queer enough.

Tolerance is a problematic goal for schools to work toward as well. Some social justice advocates assert that tolerance is just enduring differences at worst and celebrating differences at best (Nieto, 1996). Tolerance does not provide a lens through which the power differences between groups in society can be analyzed and reconceptualized. It leaves the superiority of heterosexuality and binary gender unchallenged, and the inferiority or moral marginalization of sexuality and gender differences in place (Birden, 2005). Tolerance is sometimes viewed as a paternalistic acceptance of difference that does not require seeing value or importance in others' ways of doing things. It is also criticized for picking and choosing the least offensive differences, those who best fit into the dominant structure, to focus on in education. In this way, teachers and students can avoid confronting differences that would directly challenge their fundamental beliefs. Social justice education inclusive of sexuality and gender variance should strive toward accepting, recognizing and affirming differences and the value of sexuality and gender expression to human happiness.

Queering the Curriculum: Interrupting Heteronormativity

Queering the curriculum, then, is not about adding famous homosexuals to the list of required authors, or acknowledging the broader spectrum of sexuality in the family life/sex education curriculum. It is about noticing and noting aloud the knowledge that appears in textbooks and on school booklists, and that which is omitted (Kumashiro, 2001). Queering recognizes heteronormative practices as the processes through which schools and educational policies reinforce the belief that human beings fall into two distinct sex/gender categories, male/man and female/woman. Queering the curriculum emphasizes the importance of developing critical analyses of heterosexism, heteronormativity, and normativity with the goal of helping students understand that binary categories are not givens, but rather social constructions we are often forced to perform (Butler, 1990). Bryson and De Castell (1993) used the term "queer pedagogy" and described it as "a radical form of praxis implemented deliberately to interfere with, to intervene in, the production of 'normalcy' in school subjects" (p. 286). We also consider queering the curriculum a form of pedagogy that deliberately interferes with the production of normalcy because it requires the teachers and student to interact with competing discourses about sexuality and gender. Spurlin's (2002) definition of queer pedagogy furthers this idea:

> In one sense, a "queer" pedagogy would imply not only an analysis of (sexual) difference(s) in the classroom but of interrelated, broad-based pedagogical commitments to free inquiry and expression, social equity, the development of more democratic institutional and pedagogical practices, and the broadening of dialogical spheres of public exchange within and beyond the classroom as sites for engaged analyses of social issues and collective struggles. (p. 10)

In order to access the transformative possibilities, queering the curriculum might involve talking with students about why history books and biographies often avoid mentioning the same-gender relationships of famous people or examining the construct of gender with a biology class and discovering together the prevalence of offspring born with indistinctly formed (according to binary gender standards) genitalia or that chromosomally humans can be many combinations of X and Y (Fausto-Sterling, 2000). The aim of these conversations, however, is not to simply add more points of view or give a finer-grained version of the truth (Kumashiro, 2001). The aim is to discuss with the class what was left out, how the story, or the science or the canon or the logics was constructed in order to support the current beliefs and worldview. This kind of queering can be done to show how heteronormativity and gender binaries have been constructed, but it can also be used at the intersections of identity to show how stereotypes of races, genders, sexualities, ethnicities, and classes are all socially constructed, and how each of us is more complex than the stereotype would suggest (Crenshaw, 1994; Loutzenheiser & MacIntosh, 2004).

In queering the curriculum, queer identity is not restricted to gays and lesbians, but open to anyone who feels marginalized. Rather than trying to find the limits of the category "queer" and to work for rights in schools only for that group, "queering" would require teachers and students to think about how to make the classroom a more inclusive and accepting environment all the time, at every turn, within every conversation. Queering the curriculum attempts to *not* socialize youth into a world that can be described by common sense. It hopes to help them understand they have choices and alternatives in how they learn to be adolescents or men/women and how they express their gendered and sexual identities through taking up or rejecting competing narratives of sexuality or gender in their lives.

Pedagogy, practices, and policies can also be queered. Teachers and administrators can examine the ways they interact with students that might be silencing to some and encouraging to others. Teachers can learn to recognize what characteristics they assign to the "good student" and vary their teaching styles to take advantage of the characteristics of other students in the class as well. Assignments can be varied so that students are allowed to interact with the material they are learning in ways that don't require them to show mastery or to recite back to the teacher the content exactly as it was presented (Kumashiro, 2001; Rofes, 2000). These alternative assignments will allow students to bring their own imaginations, knowledges, deductions, and conclusions to bear on the subject matter, and to create a space in the classroom where everyone is learning at the same time, where students are not expected to find the answer that the teacher already knows, but where they are interacting with information and creating knowledge together. The classroom would become a space in which the relations between the persons in the room and the materials were constantly being evaluated and renegotiated.

Similarly, practices and rituals in the school can be shown to support a certain kind of order, a certain regulation of students, teachers and administrators that works for certain purposes. In the case of heterosexism, the tradition of school dances can be historically situated in the era in which they emerged—a time when urban areas struggled to keep students in school longer, out of the workforce and unmarried. In order to appeal to more students, after-school sporting events and organized dating events were added to the academic curriculum (Lesko, 2001). The question can be posed about what types of after-school activities and events are appropriate for this age. It can be explicitly asked what role the school has in heterosexually socializing students in dating rituals and gendered roles such as cheerleading and homecoming kings and queens.

Finally, challenging practices and knowledge will cause ruptures and "crises" in the comfortable spaces that teachers and students and communities inhabit (Kumashiro, 2001). In order to introduce ideas that contradict the beliefs of members of the community, and that leave everyone in a complicit position with the oppression of someone, teachers, administrators, teacher educators, and district leaders should be prepared to anger and upset some people (probably most people) and to need time to talk through the issues (Rofes, 2000). In the case of sexuality, the precedent is not encouraging. Changes in schools' presentation of sexuality and other curriculum changes that have contradicted parents' knowledge have often led to Conservative and Religious Right-funded backlashes against the schools (Irvine, 2002; Lugg, 1998). These backlash efforts have been fairly successful so far at scaring parents and unseating educational leaders through electoral or appointment changes. Change will have to happen incrementally, and may be more effective if it is initiated by students with the support of teachers and parents. Many policy studies have advocated for curriculum and policy changes that will give greater safety and support to LGBTQ students, and the courts have supported these studies. Schools and teachers must work in these openings to expand the possibilities for sexuality and gender.

Living Safely in the Present Moment

Thich Nhat Hanh is a Buddhist scholar and spiritual leader who believes that spiritual practice should involve both solitary reflection and community and social action. His views on friendship, peace, and diversity are crucial to our approach to developing new standards for queering education and can take the field forward. Nhat Hahn's key teaching is that, through *mindfulness*, we can learn to dwell in the present moment in order to experience peace. Doing so demonstrates that practical concerns have practical effects where each of us takes a vested interest in promoting diversity. Instead of tolerating others, or from seeing individuals and groups who are "different" as adversaries, we believe that Hanh's approach to friendship and peace encourages us to act as allies for each other, including those we deem as different from ourselves. Doing so moves us away from shutting out and silencing individuals and groups to working through differences and conflict. Tolerance is inadequate because it implies a separation between groups, where one group lives in fear of another. Hanh (2002) asserts that people cannot live together if one person is "not capable of looking" (p. 12) at another with compassion. Seeing each other with compassion is the main taproot from which friendships can blossom and peace among members of community can occur.

To support our quest to engage in the community with a spirit of friendship and to become a responsible "ally" for others, Hanh urges us to build safety through our actions. By being mindful of our actions, we can take up practices that lead to peace in our lives, society and schools. While each tree in a forest may look different, as Hanh proclaims, each member of the forest, or community, must learn to understand the different perspectives of each other in order to live in peace. We believe that Hanh's metaphors of the trees and forests can help us to understand how to move beyond tolerance and into spaces of acceptances and harmony in education. His ethical guidelines, discussed below, shape our standards.

Hanh (2007) has translated the Buddhist ethical guidelines for laypersons (Five Precepts) as the Five Mindfulness Trainings in a way that takes into account current demands for healthy, friendly and safe living. These central guidelines serve as the basis for our standards of social justice. They are Respect for life, Generosity, Respect for sexual boundaries, Mindful speech, and Mindful consumption. The Five Mindfulness Trainings are guides on how to cultivate and practice good judgment so that individuals can discern the most beneficial action and thus conduct themselves with compassion and loving kindness. We believe these standards should be used in schools, and have the potential to alter human rights legislation, both domestic and international, traditionally applied to LGBTQ communities. If individuals use these standards as a basis to learn and work, we believe perspectives and policies will change. These are our social justice standards because they are experiential ways of living and working for peace and justice for people and the environment. Each standard has an *"I promise to"* component because social justice is a living practice that requires individuals to be committed to bring about a change not simply in how they think, but also in their perspectives and in their behaviors.

Five Standards for Living and Working for Peace and Justice

1. Cultivate Compassion and a Spirit of Friendship

Aware of the suffering caused by the destruction of living things, I promise to cultivate compassion and learn ways to protect the lives of people, animals, and the environment. I promise to engage in a spirit of friendship, allowing people from different social status, classes, genders, ethnicities, and sexualities to interact with one another and live peacefully. Thus, I am determined not to harm or let others harm, in actions or words, any living thing on the planet.

2. Work for the Well-Being of all Living Things

Aware of the suffering caused by exploitation, social injustice, misuse, oppression, and hatred, I promise to develop a loving kindness and learn ways to work for the well being of all people, animals and the environment. I promise to act as an ally and friend to all living things and to prevent others from profiting from the suffering/destruction of people, animals, and the environment.

3. Protect the Safety and Integrity of All Living Things

I promise to protect the safety and integrity of all people (even if they are different from me), animals and the environment. To protect the happiness of others and myself I am determined to respect my commitments and the commitments of others, even if their commitments or way of life is different than my own.

4. Promote Loving Speech and Deep Listening

Aware of the suffering caused by cruel speech and the inability to listen to others, I promise to promote loving speech and deep listening in order to bring joy and happiness to others and relieve their suffering. Knowing that words can create happiness or suffering, I promise to learn to speak in ways that do not harass, harm or hurt others. I am determined not to spread news that I do not know to be true and not to criticize or condemn things which I am not sure of or do not understand.

5. Practice Mindful Consumption

Aware of the suffering caused by unmindful consumption, I promise to lead a healthy life, by practicing mindful thinking, talking, eating, drinking, and consuming. I am determined not ingest or read/view items that contain toxins, such as certain TV programs, magazines, books, films, Web sites, and conversations. I understand that to damage my consciousness with these poisons is to betray my society and future generations.

We believe these standards apply to all educational institutions. Having standards for living and working for peace and justice is necessary as globalizing trends dislocate, marginalize and destroy entire communities of people and concurrently wreak havoc on the environment. These standards can readily be applied to K-12 students, schools and higher education institutions, and teacher educators because they are straightforward, uncomplicated, and not difficult to embrace. Yet, because of their simplicity, we have provided additional guidelines below with respect to students and individuals who might identify themselves as anything other than *heterosexual or normatively gendered*. As with the Yogyakarta Principles, these standards are practical goals that address the material conditions of students, teachers, and schools in dealing with differences and sensitive topics in ways that seek to offer protections to those who are most vulnerable, and guarantee a certain level of opportunity to everyone. In addition, those entrusted to educate need to promise to be mindful and live and work for peace and justice through their work as teachers, administrators, and teacher educators for all of their students regardless of who they are or who they are attracted to sexually.

Guidelines on Gender and Sexuality

In Schools, K-12 Students Seeking to Support Social Justice Should

1. Be introduced to the point of view that sexuality is historically contextual, and that what is "natural" has been seen very differently by humans in different time periods and cultures. Sexuality appears in a variety of iterations in other animals,
2. Understand that all people have a right to pleasure in their bodies,
3. Explore the queer social justice issues that appear in the media and in the context of national and international human rights struggles, including LGBTQ persons' rights to exist and have fully integrated lives in their communities,
4. Critically examine the structures of gender and explore the meanings they have in ones' life and the connection to selfhood. Explore the right to live gender as one feels it is appropriate for oneself,
5. Investigate and understand the connection between gender and sexuality norms and power imbalances between women and men, and between queer and straight persons,
6. Explore the possibilities for relationships between boys, between girls, and between boys and girls without stigma or coercion,
7. Explore and appreciate the lives, abilities, intelligences, uniqueness, personalities, emotions, and the inherent and independent value of people of all sexualities and genders,
8. Explore the connection between homophobia, sexism, racism, speciesism, ableism, ageism, and other forms of binary structures that portray some persons/beings as deficient or less worthy. Consider how these structures work to systematically privilege one class or group of persons more than others in society.

Schools and Higher Education Institutions Striving to Structure Their Practices in Accordance with the Principles of Sexuality Justice Should

1. Expose how the hetero/homo binary opposition is insufficient to fully encompass all dimensions of sexuality, pointing out this reduction fails to account for sexual desires and practices that may not be tied to the gender of object choice (Sedgwick, 1990),
2. Consider sexuality in relation to the pressures of other normalizing regimes pertaining to ethnicity, class, gender, citizenship, and social class,
3. Present queer theory as a mode of analysis (among many) and as an oppositional strategy that has the potential to disrupt normative and heteronormative discourses thereby challenging fixed identities as they manifest themselves through various discourses,
4. Promote critical pedagogies enabling present and future educators to critique the reproduction of knowledge that serves the interests of dominant social groups,
5. Include sexuality in the discrimination policies, including granting domestic partnership benefits to LGBTQ couples,
6. Prepare adults with the necessary tools to question, critique and disrupt identity categories in and across contexts through discourse-analytic approaches the challenge the habitual ways of reading/viewing and producing/designing texts,
7. Provide a safe space where students, faculty, and staff can engage in a community with a spirit of friendship, thereby becoming responsible "allies" for others,
8. Include gender and sexuality variance in the university mission statements,
9. Encourage scholarship that engages and challenges taken-for-granted views of gender and sexuality in the spirit of academic freedom.

Teacher Educators, Specifically those Involved in Teacher-Education Programs Striving to Teach in Accordance with the Principles of Sexuality Justice, Should

1. Prepare teachers to discuss sexuality in the public sphere,
2. Prepare teachers to let students use their sexuality and their desires as pedagogical assets rather than as liabilities,
3. Prepare teachers to utilize the history of LGBTQ persons and advocacy to empower and inform students in schools,
4. Prepare teachers to prevent bullying and hate-speech from occurring in schools,
5. Prepare teachers to use queer theory to challenge heteronormative practices (gender-sexuality) in schools; giving students the liberty to be who they wish,
6. Prepare teachers to utilize perspectivism to contest taken-for-granted texts, such as the literary canon and content textbooks,

7. Prepare teachers to serve as an ally to LGBTQ students, recognizing that each child has a right to an education, and that discrimination based on a student's sexuality denies a student access to that right,
8. Prepare teachers to understand that love and desire appear in a myriad of forms, and to use those forms as part of their teaching practices,
9. Prepare teachers that families and communities are not monolithic, but are diverse and plural, yet intricate parts of the child's education,
10. Prepare teachers to provide a safe classroom and school for every student,
11. Prepare teachers to set aside their personal biases to help educate each student.

Justice for ourselves and justice for others depends on not only a few people becoming mindful and responsible enough to follow the experiential standards and become allies or friends, but on everyone being aware of what it means to make a commitment to these standards. For our world to have a better future in this time of uncertainty, we could work to follow Hahn's basic guidelines and change our behaviors to protect others and ourselves from the violence that is everywhere. We need to join together and look deeply and seriously for ways to help people and society get "re-rooted." If we practice these and other standards discussed in this book—as a family, a community, a city, a nation, and a world—we will be able to identify the causes of all of our suffering and work collectively as friends to find solutions.

Notes

1. Lesbian, gay, bisexual, transgender, queer (and sometimes questioning), or LGBTQ, will be used interchangeably with queer in this chapter to denote the largest and most diverse group of persons who may experience a loss of rights, violence, persecution, or family, religious, or social isolation due to their sexual attractions or behaviors, the relationships they belong to, or their gender expression (whether they present as male or female or neither and whether that matches their physical sex characteristics).
2. Same-sex marriage is legal nationwide in five countries: the Netherlands, Belgium, Spain, Canada, and South Africa. Same-sex civil unions are legal in 16 countries: Denmark, Norway, Sweden, Greenland, Iceland, France, Germany, Portugal, Finland, Luxembourg, New Zealand, United Kingdom, Andorra, Czech Republic, Slovenia, and Switzerland.

References

Ahmed, A., Shafqat, S., Shemirani, K., & Toor, S. (2006). *Que(e)rying Islamophobia: Race, sexuality and imperialism*. Paper preseneted at (CLAGS) City University of New York Lesbian and Gay Studies Conference, October 19, New York.

Arondekar, A. (2005). Border/line sex: Queer postcolonialities, or how race matters outside the United States. *Interventions*, *7*(2), 236–250.

Birden, S. (2005). *Rethinking sexual identity in education*. Lanham, MD: Rowman & Littlefield.

Bryson, M. & De Castell, S. (1993). Queer pedagogy: praxis makes im/perfect. *Canadian Journal of Education, 18*(3), 285–305.

Butler, J. (1990). *Gender trouble: feminism and the subversion of identity.* New York: Routledge.

Butler, J. (1993). *Bodies that matter: On the discursive limits of "sex."* New York: Routledge.

Civil Union. (2007). Wikipedia. Retrieved August 6, 2007, from http://en.wikipedia.org/wiki/Civil_union

Crenshaw, K. (1994). Mapping the margins: Intersectionality, identity politics, and violence against women of color. In M. A. Fineman & R. Mykitiuk (Eds.), *The public nature of private violence* (pp. 93–120). New York: Routledge.

Dilley, P. (1999). Queer theory: Under construction. *Qualitative Studies in Education, 12*(5), 457–472.

Epstein, D., O'Flynn, S., & Telford, D. (2000–2001). "Othering" education: Sexualities, silences, and schooling. *Review of Research in Education, 25*, 127–179.

Equality California. (2006). Equality California-Sponsored Legislation: SB 1437: Bias-Free Curriculum Act. Retrieved August 28, 2007, from http://www.eqca.org/site/apps/nl/content2.asp?c=9oINKWMCF&b=1352277&ct=2120323

Fausto-Sterling, A. (2000). *Sexing the body: Gender politics and the construction of sexuality.* New York: Basic Books.

Fine, M., & McClelland, S. I. (2006). Sexuality education and desire: Still missing after all these years. *Harvard Educational Review, 76*(3), 297–338.

Foucault, M. (1978). *The history of sexuality: An introduction.* New York: Random House.

Friend, R. A. (1993). Choices, not closets: Heterosexism and homophobia in schools. In M. Fine & L. Weis (Eds.), *Beyond silenced voices: Class, race and gender in United States schools* (pp. 209–223). Albany: State University of New York.

Friend, R. A. (1998). Heterosexism, homophobia, and the culture of schooling. In S. Books (Ed.), *Invisible children in the society and its schools* (pp. 137–165). Mahwah: Erlbaum.

Gamson, J. (2000). Sexualities, queer theory, and qualitative research. In N. K. Denzin & Y. S. Lincoln (Eds.), *Handbook of Qualitative Research* (2nd ed., pp. 347–365). Thousand Oaks, CA: Sage.

Gay Lesbian and Straight Education Network. (2005). *From teasing to torment: School climate in America.* New York: GLSEN.

Hanh, T. N. (2002). *Friends on the path: Living spiritual communities.* Berkeley, CA: Parallax Press.

Hanh, T. N. (2007). *For a future to be possible: Buddhist ethics for everyday life.* Berkeley, CA: Parallax Press.

Human Rights Campaign. (2007). Responsible education about life act. Retrieved June 27, 2007, from http://www.hrc.org/Content/NavigationMenu/HRC/Get_Informed/Federal_Legislation/REAL_Act_110th_Factsheet/Responsible_Education_About_Life_Act.htm

Human Rights Watch. (2007). "Yogyakarta Principles" a milestone for lesbian, gay, bisexual, and transgender rights: Experts set out global standards for sexual rights and gender equity. Retrieved June 27, 2007, from http://hrw.org/english/docs/2007/03/26/global15546.htm

Irvine, J. M. (2002). *Talk about sex: The battles over sex education in the United States.* Berkeley: University of California Press.

King, C. (2002). Embracing diversity in the mindfulness, diversity, and social change

Sangha. In J. Lawler & T. N. Hanh (Eds.), *Friends on the path: Living spiritual communities* (pp. 215–224). Berkeley, CA: Parallax Press.

Kumashiro, K. (2001). "Posts" perspectives on anti-oppressive education in social studies, English, mathematics, and science classrooms. *Educational Researcher, 30*(3), 3–12.

L.W. v. Toms River Regional Schools, Board of Education, PQ07IE-02596 (New Jersey Supreme Court 2007).

Leck, G. M. (2000). Heterosexual or homosexual? Reconsidering binary narratives on sexual identities in urban schools. *Education and Urban Society, 32*(3), 324–348.

Lesko, N. (2001). *Act your age! A cultural construction of adolescence.* New York: Routledge Falmer.

Loutzenheiser, L. W., & MacIntosh, L. B. (2004). Citizenships, sexualities, and education. *Theory Into Practice, 43*(2), 151–158.

Lugg, C. A. (1998). The religious right and public education: The paranoid politics of homophobia. *Educational Policy, 12*(3), 267–283.

MacGillivray, I. (2000). Educational equity for gay, lesbian, bisexual, transgendered, and queer/questioning students: The demands of democracy and social justice for America's schools. *Education and Urban Society, 32*(3), 303–323.

Morrison v. Board of Education of Boyd County, Kentucky (United States District Court Eastern District of Kentucky 2006).

Murray, S., & Roscoe, W. (1998). *Boy-wives and female husbands: Studies in African homosexualities.* New York: Palgrave.

Nabozny v. Podlesny, 92 F.3d 446 (7th Circuit 1996).

Nieto, S. (1996). *Affirming diversity: The sociopolitical context of multicultural education* (2nd ed.). White Plains, NY: Longman.

Peplau, L. (2001). Rethinking women's sexual orientation: An interdisciplinary, relationship-focused approach. *Personal Relationships, 8*, 1–19.

Planned Parenthood. (2007). Support R.E.A.L. Sex Ed! Retrieved August 28, 2007, from http://www.plannedparenthood.org/news-articles-press/politics-policy-issues/teen-pregnancy-sex-education/support-real-15506.htm

Quinlivan, K., & Town, S. (1999). Queer pedagogy, educational practice and lesbian and gay youth. *Qualitative Studies in Education, 12*(5), 509–524.

Rasmussen, M. L. (2004). "That's so gay!" A study of the deployment of signifiers of sexual and gender identity in secondary school settings in Australia and the United States. *Social Semiotics, 14*(3), 289–308.

Rasmussen, M. L. (2006). *Becoming subjects: Sexualities and secondary schooling.* New York: Routledge.

Reese, W. J. (1986). *Power and the promise of school reform: grassroots movements during the Progressive era.* Boston: Routledge & Kegan Paul.

Rofes, E. (2000). Bound and gagged: Sexual silences, gender conformity and the gay male teacher. *Sexualities, 3*(4), 439–462.

Roshan, M., & Shemirani, K. (August 15, 2006). Perspective on the Iran Debate. *Dissident Voice.* Retrieved July 21, 2007, from http://www.dissidentvoice.org/Aug06/Roshan-Shemirani15.htm

Russo, R. G. (2006). The extent of public education nondiscrimination policy protections for lesbian, gay, bisexual, and transgender students: A national study. *Urban Education, 41*(2), 115–150.

Sadowski, M. (2001). Sexual minority students benefit from school-based support—where it exists. *Harvard Educational Letter, 17*(5), 1–5.

Sedgwick, E. K. (1990). *Epistemology of the closet.* Berkeley: University of California Press.

Sklar, R. (2007, June 22). Task Force denounces Congress' failure to halt heinous abstinence-only funding. Retrieved June 27, 2007, from http://www.thetaskforce.org/press/releases/pfMF_062207

Spurlin, W. J. (2002). Theorizing queer pedagogy in English studies after the 1990s. *College English*, *65*(1), 9–16.

Tolman, D. L. (2006). In a different position: Conceptualizing female adolescent sexuality development within compulosory heterosexuality. *New Directions for Child and Adolescent Development* (112), 71–89.

Vasagar, J., & Borger, J. (August 30, 2005). Bush accused of AIDS damage to Africa. *The Guardian*. Retrieved July 30, 2007, from http://www.guardian.co.uk/aids/story/0,1558903,00.html

Yogyakarta Principles on the Application of International Law in Relation to Issues of Sexual Orientation and Gender Identity. (2007). Retrieved August 6, 2007, from http://yogyakartaprinciples.org/index.php?item=25

Part IV

Themes, Challenges, and Potential of SJPEE Visions and Guidelines

Introduction

The final three chapters provide important tools and analysis for reflection, providing necessary conditions, further development, implementation, and synthesis of the social justice, peace, and environmental standards presented in the chapters throughout this book.

Marta Baltodano reviews and deepens an analysis of the historical development and theoretical analysis of social justice education in chapter 16. Using the United States as a prime example, she explores manipulations, obstacles, and reversals of social and environmental justice policies. She illustrates how the pursuit of social justice in the United States has been hindered by a lack of understanding of the philosophical principles of social justice and their deep connection to the global economy. She reveals how concepts like equality and impartiality can be used to maintain or increase injustice while implying the opposite. In contrast, she points to Young's clear and nuanced definition of oppression as a strong foundation for SJPEE and an examination of global human rights covenants.

While such documents as the Universal Declaration of Human Rights are powerful ingredients of international rights movements, Baltodano explains why civil and political rights must be accompanied by economic, social and cultural rights in order to be fully effective. Purporting that schooling has historically been used as a colonizing process to subjugate indigenous populations and minority groups, and, more recently, has played a pivotal role in the consolidation of the globalized economic order, Baltodano offers an emancipatory educational agenda grounded in the work of Paulo Freire, Iris Young, Antonia Darder, Peter McLaren, and other critical pedagogues, that essentially begins with a deschooling process: conscientization. She concludes by proposing a set of guidelines for teacher protections and freedoms for the workplace, the curriculum, and teacher education. Based on the International Covenant on Economic, Social and Cultural Rights (ICESCR), these rights are fundamental to implementing global justice, peace, and environmental education and they lay the groundwork for a potential formulation of a "Declaration of Teachers' Rights."

Robert Crafton's chapter 17 is included in this final section to show how professional education organizations, like the National Association for Multicultural Education (NAME), can be a catalyst for SJPEE through the development of standards and evaluative instruments, in ways similar to the Alaska Native Knowledge Network. Crafton iterates some of the potential pitfalls of such an enterprise: re-inventing another oppressive agenda, "turning education into indoctrination," reifying standards into orthodoxy, and setting a stage for endless controversy. However, in light of the imposition of state and federal educational mandates promoting the opposite of social justice, peace, and environmental education, he reveals the dangers of relinquishing this difficult task to others: imposition of a dominant perspective as universal, repression of critical and challenging views, and censorship of controversial and oppressive components.

Thus, as challenging as such a course might be, Crafton describes the process that NAME initiated and presents the criteria, in this case developed to evaluate state curriculum standards, as a powerful example of using standards for social justice, peace, and environmental education. The document adopted by NAME in 2001 considers five areas: inclusiveness, the representation of diverse perspectives, an understanding of the ways knowledge is socially constructed and a respect for alternative epistemologies, self-knowledge, and social justice. Crafton contends that SJPEE standard development must focus on process, embrace conflict, and assure dialogue across differences and disagreements.

In the final chapter, editors Julie Andrzejewski, Marta Baltodano, and Linda Symcox reflect with Ray Barnhardt on a collective vision for social justice, peace, and ecojustice that has been imagined and discussed in this volume. After coding the narrative and standards sections from each chapter, we found that the different contributions converged in agreement on a number of key areas on which to base social justice, peace and environmental education. Therefore, in this concluding chapter the editors lay out a set of *six common themes*, and a present a set of *five comprehensive standard areas*—standards for educators, students, educational institutions, teacher educators, and communities—that have been distilled from the work of all the authors in the book. These documents are presented as a beginning step toward a larger dialogue about positive standards, principles, guidelines, or queries to assist educators, students, educational institutions, and communities in taking action for a better world. As we examine the themes and challenges that have emerged from this book, we hope to inspire a vision for the future when social justice, peace, and environmental education will become part of the social and pedagogical experience of every student in the United States and beyond.

16 The Pursuit of Social Justice in the United States

Marta P. Baltodano

This chapter describes the historical and theoretical development of the concept of social justice in the United States. It proposes a set of guidelines for the teaching and learning of social and environmental justice, peace education, and teachers' rights.

In a research study conducted to assess teachers' beliefs about social justice, 100 pre-service and in-service teachers were interviewed using an open-ended questionnaire (Baltodano, 2006). Ninety five percent of the teachers expressed support for the infusion of social justice in teacher preparation programs, and their belief that social justice should be a mandatory topic in public school classrooms. Despite some skepticism, this is an indication that the people of the United States[1] hold the value of social justice very close to their hearts. A look at the history of this nation exhibits a tradition of engagement with social justice that is unknown to more recent generations, as stories of activism are not regularly taught in public schools. However, if the people of the United States, particularly teachers, have such a strong commitment to social justice, why is it that society and schools continue to reproduce social inequalities?

This chapter argues that in spite of such a commitment to social justice, its pursuit has been hindered by a lack of understanding of its philosophical principles and its deep connection to the global economy. Because the United States has deliberately rejected an engagement with political economy frameworks as a result of the Cold War, its society lacks the theoretical elements to visualize social justice beyond a charitable, distributive paradigm. When the teachers in the aforementioned study were asked to define social justice their understanding was limited to equality, fairness, equal opportunity, and fair treatment. These definitions were clearly anchored on the questionable assumption that providing equal access to goods, rights, and opportunities corrects social injustices (Rawls, 1971). At the root of this limited representation of social justice is the belief that 1) equal opportunities are possible in an advanced capitalist society like the United States, 2) that by simply redistributing resources justice is served, and, 3) that reproduction of inequalities and social justice violations are accidental rather than structural. These premises lack a theoretical engagement with the formative role of the economy in the creation and consolidation of social injustice in the United States.

This chapter deepens an understanding of the larger economic and structural context for social justice, provides recommendations to make the study of social justice a mandatory subject in K-16 education, and formulates a series of guidelines to infuse public school curricula with the basic tenets of United States history, political economy, international human rights, activism, and advocacy.

United States Historical Context

Early discussions on social justice go back to John Dewey (1916), the founding father of philosophy of education and one of the precursors of the Progressive Movement, also known as social liberalism, which lasted from the 1890s to the 1920s. Progressivism emerged in the United States as a reaction to the abuses of industrialization that had expanded considerably with the rise of urbanization and the massive influx of immigrants into the United States. Dewey, as one of its major exponents, opposed the laissez-faire liberalism of Adam Smith on the basis that the government must protect liberty and opportunity for all, and that every member of society should have access to basic social needs, among them education, economic opportunity, healthcare, and protection from forces outside their control. Dewey argued that society and its government had an obligation to provide protection and compensation for those less fortunate. Progressivism advocated restrictions on economic policies to protect workers' rights, among them minimum wage and anti-trust laws to control monopolies.

It was not until the 1929 stock market crash and the subsequent Great Depression, that President Franklin Delano Roosevelt decided to move away from laissez-faire capitalism and began instituting Keynesian[2] economic policies that advocated strong state intervention and participation of the private sector in the regulation of economy (Miroff, 1993). These measures advocated reduction of interest rates and government investment in infrastructure to reduce unemployment. Roosevelt's first and second New Deal set the foundations of the welfare state which changed the status of the United States industrial worker as the new economic policies instituted a minimum wage, protection of collective bargaining, low income housing projects, and Social Security.

Additional social justice legislation was approved during the Kennedy and Johnson administrations through the New Frontier and Great Society programs. Federal funding was allocated to education and medical insurance for the poor and elderly, Medicaid and Medicare, were instituted. Other important pieces of legislation during this period were the Civil Rights Act and the Immigration and Naturalization Act (prohibiting the use of racial quotas for immigration). The Elementary and Secondary Education Act, the Higher Education Act and the Bilingual Education Act provided money for low income schools, Head Start programs, student loans and scholarships for universities, and bilingual instruction for second-language learners. This was the time in the U.S. history when social justice was associated with the emergence of the welfare economy. It was the government's last attempt to create a more humanistic form of capitalism.

Social Justice in the Age of Globalization

In spite of the New Deal, the Great Society, the Civil Rights Movement of the 1960s, and liberal efforts to humanize capitalism through welfare policies and other social reforms, unbridled capitalism has continued its course and become revitalized by the demise of socialism in Europe. Major social legislation of the 1960s has been dismantled. The welfare state has disappeared.

To understand the current situation, it is necessary to grasp the complexity of the transformation of the economy in the last 40 years. One of the major goals of the welfare state was to compensate for the inequalities produced by capitalism. This intention to "humanize" capitalism is what conferred the welfare society its distributive orientation (Young, 1990, p. 67). That situation changed after Ronald Reagan took power and implemented his promises of a smaller government and drastic reduction in taxes, particularly for those with the highest incomes. "Reaganomics," as Reagan's economic policies were called, marked an 8-year period under which the United States economy moved away from a welfare nation to a *corporate wealthcare* nation. The Reagan presidency abandoned many of the regulations that the government had imposed on the financial and manufacturing industries to protect the common citizen.

The end of the Cold War created the conditions for a "revitalized global order built around the logic of the free market" (McLaren, 1998, p. 431). The "dangerous triumph of global capitalism brought about material shifts in cultural practices and the proliferation of new contradictions between capitalism and labor" (McLaren, p. 431). As anticipated by Marxist economic theory, capitalism had finally arrived at the *point of no return*. With global competition, profit began declining for companies in the United States. They could not continue operating under the same conditions as in the past. Corporations wanted to pay lower wages, lower taxes, and do away with protection laws. They sought subsidies, unregulated environmental activity, and support for outsourcing jobs. They were able to achieve all this by financing electoral campaigns and lobbying the government to assure legislation favoring their business interests.

These devastating effects of globalized capitalism in the United States have not been addressed by the media or government. On the contrary, free, unregulated market subventions to corporations, job outsourcing, breaking of the labor movement and military campaigns around the world, have been skillfully manipulated and constructed as symbols of democracy and patriotism. Many people in the United States remain unaware that the pursuit of the mythical *American Dream* for new generations has forever been deferred by this shift in the economy (McLaren & Rizvi, 2002). The dream of John Dewey, Myles Horton, and Martin Luther King to draw on education to consolidate democracy and eradicate poverty and racism is fading away.

The Illusion of Impartiality and the Myth of Equality

Young (1990, 2001) considers two of the major tenets of liberal theories of social justice incomplete to address all the modalities of oppression. They are impartiality and equality. Young argues that these very concepts are the greatest obstacles to the full achievement of social justice. These values, which are part of the ideology of the United States and represent the legacy of the liberal political philosophy that inspired its constitution, have remained unchallenged in spite of the drastic changes in the economy.

The concept of impartiality acquired a significant dimension with the rise of instrumental reason and the need to detach values and feelings in the interpretation of the world. The establishment of a *moral point of view* sought to create a platform for homogeneity, consensus and harmony that was essential for the creation of a social contract and the establishment of a dominant society. Most theories address social justice as fairness on the same premises: Equal members of society agree on a social contract to protect their liberties and wealth.

The idea of impartiality rests on the assumption that there is a universal system of beliefs, an absolute truth, and a standard vision of the world. It also assumes that there is such a thing as objectivity and that people and their institutions can be neutral. However, at stake in this conception is the question of whose interests are better served by the discourse that impartiality defends? Who defines the normative content of social justice? (Young, 1990, 2001). "Who frames the principles of justice? For whom are these principles framed?" (Nussbaum, 2006, p. 21). This is why Young (1990) argues that "the ideal of impartiality serves ideological functions. It masks the ways in which the particular perspectives of dominant groups claim universality and helps justify hierarchical decision-making structures" (p. 97). Young claims that the concept of impartiality is related to the notion of "universal citizenship" that has traditionally excluded women, gays, Blacks, Latinos, American Indians, people with disabilities, immigrants, poor people, non-Christians, and other culturally-distinct groups. The concept of impartiality "feeds cultural imperialism by allowing the particular experience and perspective of privileged groups to parade as universal. The conviction that bureaucrats and experts can exercise their decision making power in an impartial manner legitimates authoritarian hierarchy" (Young, 1990, p. 10). This notion of impartiality neutralizes difference and therefore, degrades the experiences, feelings, and knowledge of distinct groups creating the conditions for marginalization, violence and exploitation. In that sense, impartiality becomes one of the key values implicated in the reproduction of social injustices.

In the same manner, the concept of equality is problematic, and it was based on the doctrine of equal opportunity that evolved in the nineteenth century that argued that "everybody who would work hard could be somebody" (Young, 1990, p. 214). This premise is no longer valid in an economic system where social mobility is based on meritocracy, social Darwinism (Darder, 1991), and where the division of labor is informed by the sweeping principles of a globalized economy (McLaren, 1998). As Young argues, today the concept of equal opportunity means that everyone is allowed to fiercely compete for very few privileged jobs. The concept of equal opportunity assumes that race, gender, sexual orientation, language, ethnicity, and social class do not make any difference to people's rights and opportunities (p. 157). It assumes that society naturally provides full access to rights and material goods even in the midst of an unregulated capitalism.

Young (1990) argues that "this mechanical interpretation of equality also suppresses difference." She affirms that a commitment to social justice "sometimes implies overriding a principle of equal treatment with the principle that group differences should be acknowledged in public policy and in the policies and procedures of economic institutions, in order to reduce actual or potential oppression" (p. 11). This is what it is called equity.

An authentic social justice advocacy implies a reconceptualization of the concepts of impartiality and equality as they are values that support and sustain the efficient operation of an economic system that inherently oppresses and dominates social groups in order to subsist. These "assimilationist" ideals, as Young categorizes impartiality and equality, should be replaced by a preferential treatment of disadvantaged groups in order to overcome the organic obstacles that keep them subordinated.

What is Social Justice? Contending with the Roots of Oppression

According to Young (1990), an enabling definition of social justice implies a vision of what the concept is intending to address: oppression. Young deconstructs the large category of oppression into a set a conditions that are shared by people who "suffer some inhibition of their ability to develop and exercise their capacities and express their needs, thoughts, and feelings" (p. 40), including death, slavery, wage slavery, misery, life-long impoverishment, and so forth. She describes what she calls the five faces of oppression: 1) exploitation, 2) marginalization, 3) powerlessness, 4) cultural imperialism, and 5) violence.

1. ***Exploitation***—who works for whom—it is a direct outcome of the economic system that makes possible the unjust distribution of labor, the control of the means of production, and the profit that results from that relation (p. 49).
2. ***Marginalization***—who does not work—it refers to the status of people whose labor is not used by the economic system, such as senior people, single mothers and their children, unemployed, unskilled workers, mentally and physically disabled people, and Native Americans on reservations.
3. ***Powerlessness***—is how the content of the work defines one institutional position relative to others. It is also related to the division of labor and to the lack of participation in the political and economic decision-making process (e.g., immigrant workers, teachers).
4. ***Cultural Imperialism***—is the "universalization of a dominant group's experience and culture, and its establishment as the norm" (p. 59). The very notion of equality and impartially that appears to mitigate oppression is grounded on this concept of cultural imperialism.
5. ***Violence***— is the visible manifestation of dominance. Young affirms that violence is not just "direct victimization, but the daily knowledge shared by all members of oppressed groups that they are *more likely* to be subject to violation, solely on account of their group identity" (p. 62, emphasis added).

Young's views on oppression have clear implications for the advocacy of social justice as they primarily focus on the nature of the economic system. Since the United States society profits from the predatory nature of global capitalism, we need to be aware of the social responsibilities we all share in the injustices created to sustain a culture of privilege and abundance.

Educators, activists, students, parents, and community members have the opportunity to reclaim social justice, peace, and environmental education and ignite a process to return to all people the right to build a better life without exploitation or military occupation. Global citizens deserve the right to live under peaceful conditions without harming other members of the global village. Fortunately, an international human rights movement has been growing alongside these economic developments to address such as concerns.

International Human Rights Movement

Founded in 1945, 51 nations agreed to establish the United Nations to prevent another tragedy like the Second World War. The trauma of the holocaust convinced the international community of the need to create a supra-national institution that could be vigilant of human rights abuses committed by governments or other groups in power.

One of the first instruments that the United Nations prepared in 1947 was the *Universal Declaration of Human Rights*. Though it is not a binding treaty, the General Assembly adopted it as a set of standards to protect human rights. In order to make the protection of human rights compulsory and governments accountable, the United Nations drafted two new covenants later, reflecting what the international human rights community considered the promulgation of the first and second generation human rights[3]. In 1966, the International Covenant on Civil and Political Rights and the International Covenant on Economic, Social, and Cultural Rights were presented to the community of nations for ratification. The Covenant of Civil and Political Rights was signed by the United States almost 30 years later (1992) with so many reservations that its implementation is very limited. President Carter signed the Covenant of Economic, Social and Cultural Rights in 1979, but the U.S. Senate has never ratified it.

In the preamble of the International Covenant on Economic, Social and Cultural Rights (ICESCR), the United Nations declared that "the ideal of free human beings enjoying freedom from fear and want can only be achieved if conditions are created whereby everyone may enjoy economic, social and cultural rights, as well as civil and political rights and freedom." The rationale behind this covenant was that the United Nations Declaration of Human Rights and the Covenant of Civil and Political Rights were not enough to guarantee the "freedom" of humanity. People cannot live only on basic civil and political rights. The obligation of governments does not stop with the provision of civil liberties but it is necessary to provide citizens with access to decent jobs and wages, and possibilities to enhance their material conditions and pursue cultural and intellectual interests.

The United Nations covenants are binding legal instruments for the countries that have ratified them, but the United States and other governments have failed to fully authorize them, therefore their implementation is very limited at the domestic level.

Students should have the opportunity to learn the history of the international human rights movement and the reasons why the U.S. government has refused to fully ratify the most important treaties respecting the integrity of its citizens and protecting their social and environmental rights.

Teaching for Social Justice

Dewey was one of the first scholars in the early 20th century to address the need to infuse teachers' work with an agenda for social justice. His vision of a democratic society inspired other social thinkers, particularly members of the Pragmatic and Social Reconstructionist movements to develop a deeper understanding of social justice within the context of school, race relations and the formation of a democratic society (Brameld, 1936; Counts, 1932; Rugg, 1996; Dubois, 1935, 1996). Social reconstructionism, which developed in the United States during the 1920s, further advanced Dewey's formulation of social justice by arguing that schools and education should be structured to become vehicles for social change.

Brameld (1936) specifically believed that the curriculum of public schools should focus on real life problems as a way of addressing social injustices. Dubois, although not rigidly anchored in any of these philosophical movements, worked along the same vision of Dewey and Brameld to address the insurmountable problem of racism in the United States. He argued that education was the potential conduit for African American equality (Lummis, 2004). Later, social activists, educators, and philosophers inspired by Dewey, Dubois, and Brameld began implementing these visions to advance the pursuit of social justice, among them Myles Horton, "considered by some to be one of the sparks that ignited the civil rights movement" (Darder, Baltodano, & Torres, 2003, p. 3). He founded the Highlander Research and Education Center in Tennessee in 1927, an organization whose objective was to provide education first to White laborers then Blacks and Whites who were trained to use civil disobedience to oppose the segregationist laws of the time. For example, as a student of Highlander, Rosa Park's resistance to give up her seat at the front of a bus in Alabama was not an accident. It was the result of a firm and planned decision to engage in civil disobedience to further the anti-racist struggle of that time—and not the casual outcome of exhaustion as claimed in some history books (Darder et al., 2003, p. 3). Another educator, Herbert Kohl, provided the impetus for the development of the Open School Movement that created the conditions for a "striking a balance between the politics of teaching, teaching politically, and the craft of teaching" (Darder et al., p. 5).

During the 1970s, social and cultural reproduction theorists (Bowles & Gintis, 1976; Bourdieu & Passeron, 1977) contended that schools are spheres that reproduce social inequalities as they mirror the workplace and the injustices of the larger society. Contrary to the humanist tradition that visualizes education as the most egalitarian and democratic social institution, reproduction theorists assert that schools are driven by the needs of the market, and hence, they reproduce class stratification and allocate people to a hierarchically divided labor force. These theorists also argue that schools perform the function of validating the cultural capital[4] of the dominant society and impose a view of the social order consistent with the interests of the dominant elite. Schools are places where teachers and other professional educators innocently play the role of legitimizing establishment beliefs and values.

The Brazilian educator Paulo Freire, author of the classic book *Pedagogy of the Oppressed* (1970) explained how that reproduction of dominant values happens at schools. He strongly criticized the traditional banking approach to education in which teachers and other professional educators envision students as empty vessels and blank slates, and teachers believe themselves to be experts as certified by their university degrees. In that banking approach, the teacher deposits the legitimized knowledge (dominant values) into the students, and later students are tested to find out whether that knowledge penetrated their minds.

According to Freire, education viewed from this banking perspective becomes an instrument of alienation. Students are bored to death receiving a knowledge that is irrelevant to their lives, cultures, and experiences. The students become passive recipients of a subject matter that does not represent their realities or aspirations in life. The teacher becomes the only source of knowledge, and the process of teaching and learning becomes a dull, drilling experience that kills the passion and the joy of learning. The classroom becomes a place of obedience, compliance, repetition, and tedium.

Freire envisioned teaching as process of awareness and empowerment. He called his approach "problem posing pedagogy." In his view, education is an academic and political conversation in which students and teachers problematize the world. In order to solve social and environmental problems they question how these problems came into existence, examining their root causes. In problem posing pedagogy, students engage in stimulating and challenging academic activities in which their cultures and native languages are integrated to make sense of the new knowledge (Foster, 1997; Irvine, 1990; Ladson-Billings, 2002; Nieto, 2002).

What is the best way to create emancipatory experiences in the classroom? How can educators live their advocacy for social justice? Critical pedagogues (Anyon, 1980; Apple, 1972; Darder, 1991; Freire & Macedo, 1997; Giroux, 1981; McLaren, 1986; Shor, 1992) contend that good teachers never water down the curriculum when teaching working-class children, English language learners, or any students for that matter (Bartolomé, 1998; Delpit, 1995). Great educators teach a rigorous curriculum and keep their expectations high. They teach the cultural capital of the dominant society but they problematize that knowledge and bring the "funds of knowledge" of their students into the classroom (Gonzalez, Moll, & Amanti, 2005).

Critical pedagogy encourages educators to reflect on how their teaching practices, curriculum, teacher expectations, and administrative decisions are driven by the interests of the ruling classes rather than by social justice. Teachers, administrators, school psychologists, and counselors should strive to understand the role they might inadvertently be playing in the reproduction of social inequalities. For example, how might teachers address the tendency to create pathologies out of cultural differences and conflicts? How can administrators change their role as middle people in the process of social reproduction? Do educators see themselves as transformative and organic intellectuals or as apologists of the status quo?

Education for Social Justice: Transformative Principles for Learning and Teaching

The *transformative principles*[5] for social justice described subsequently provide a framework for the protection of social and environmental justice and the promotion of peace that is based on an understanding of the geo-political forces that shape the current globalized economic order. Adapted from the United Nations International Covenant on Economic, Social and Cultural Rights (ICESCR, 1976), they are applied here to the educational context, particularly to the work of teachers and teacher educators.

For the effective study and engagement with social justice these guidelines are divided into three major sections: 1) Protecting Teachers and their Work; 2) The Curriculum: Unpacking Hegemony; and 3) Beyond NCATE: Transforming the Preparation of Teachers.

To move away from education that reproduces oppression and inequalities, environmental destruction, and military expansionism, teachers must be free to provide emancipatory education for a better world. Teachers must have certain protections to do this.

A. *Protecting Teachers and Their Work*

Teachers must have the protection:

1. To freely choose where to work. This protection shall include technical and professional training programs to achieve steady and productive employment under conditions safeguarding fundamental political and economic freedoms (adapted from article 6 of ICESCR).
2. To learn and teach in safe, stress-free, and healthy working conditions, including sanitary facilities, well-equipped kitchens and cafeterias, healthy menus, safe playgrounds, transportation, medical office, and ventilated classrooms free of pesticides or other toxic substances.
3. To remuneration which provides (adapted from article 7 of ICESCR):
   a. Fair wages and equal remuneration for work of equal value without distinction of any kind. Women should be guaranteed equal pay for equal work and working conditions equal to those enjoyed by men.
   b. Equality in promotion, tenure, and all aspects of employment subject only to seniority and expertise. Student test scores, sexual orientation, disability, religious beliefs, or political values cannot be used for demotion, promotion, or tenure.
   c. Rest, leisure, reasonable work hours and periodic holidays with pay, as well as remuneration for overtime work.

   d. Class-sizes of 20 students per classroom to maximize differentiated instruction.
4. To form trade unions, join trade unions of their choice, and initiate grievance processes against those (union leaders as well as school leaders) who are not protecting the rights of teachers or are involved in corruption. (adapted from article 8 of ICESCR).
5. To strike (adapted from article 8 of ICESCR).
6. To social security and affordable health care (adapted from article 9 of ICESCR).
7. To protection and assistance for their families, particularly for the care and education of dependent children, spouses, same-sex partners, and living companions (adapted from article 10 of ICESCR).
8. To special protection before and after their birth of children or the adoption of a new family member with paid leave or adequate social security benefits for mothers and fathers. Under no circumstances should their jobs be jeopardized nor used as an excuse for transfers, demotions, or other veiled repercussions (adapted from article 10 of ICESCR).
9. To exercise academic freedom for research, creative activity, and dissemination of knowledge.
10. To be able to teach human rights, social and environmental justice and peace. School policies should reflect a particular concern with the right to be free from hunger, which means to teach and reflect on:
    a. Improving production, conservation, and distribution of food at the local level, promoting organic food, and supporting small, community-based producers.
    b. Examining the problems of both food-importing and food-exporting countries, to ensure an equitable distribution of world food supplies in relation to need.
    c. Examining the root causes of hunger and the primary people and institutions responsible (adapted from article 10 of ICESCR).
11. To create their own curriculum as long as it generally meets the benchmarks for grade level. No teacher should be forced to follow teacher-proof curricula, or be threatened, harassed or demoted for not implementing pre-packaged curricula.
12. To pursue additional educational degrees and licenses with adequate release time to accomplish these goals.

B. Unpacking Hegemony: The Curriculum

Teachers must have the protection:

1. To teach human rights; including an examination of the development of the major international treaties and a clear discussion and knowledge of the countries that have ratified them. Among them:
   a. United Nations Declaration of Human Rights.
   b. International Covenant of Civil and Political Rights.
   c. International Covenant on Economic, Social, and Cultural Rights.

   d. Declaration of the Granting of Independence to Colonial Countries and People.
   e. Convention Concerning Indigenous and Tribal Peoples in Independent Countries.
   f. Geneva Conventions and their Protocols.
   g. International Convention on the Elimination of All Forms of Racial Discrimination.
   h. Convention on the Elimination of All Forms of Discrimination against Women.
   i. Convention against Torture and other Cruel, Inhuman or Degrading Treatment.
   j. Convention on the Rights of the Child.
   k. International Convention on the Protection of the Rights of All Migrant Workers and Members of their Families.
   l. The Kyoto Protocol and the United Nations Framework Convention on Climate Change.
   m. The Convention on the Rights of Persons with Disabilities.
   n. The Convention on Biological Diversity.
   o. The Convention on the Rights of Indigenous Peoples.
2. To teach about peace, social justice, and environmental justice appropriately connected to the teaching of literacy, numeracy, social studies, science, arts, sport, and technology.
3. To plan their own curriculum including thematic units developmentally designed to address the following learning units (for example):
   a. The historical and contemporary struggles for social justice in the United States: anti-slavery, civil rights, and anti-racism movement; the history of the labor movement; the gay, suffragist, womens, and indigenous rights movements; global justice, environmental issues, animal rights, and voters' rights.
   b. Philosophies and values of peoples all over the world.
   c. Political geography and the U. S. foreign policy.
   d. Urban studies and the history of immigration.
   e. The roots of multilingualism in the United States.
   f. Civil society, social movements, global justice movement, organizing, advocacy, and virtual public spheres.
   g. Political processes and ballot initiatives.
   h. Welfare state and late capitalist societies.
   i. Poverty in first and third world countries, hunger, toxic waste, consumerism, overconsumption, the culture of abundance, and wealth.
   j. Neo-Liberalism: the World Bank, the International Monetary Fund, the G-7, and the World Trade Organization.
   k. Free Trade Agreements: NAFTA, CAFTA, GATT, the Multilateral Agreement on Free Trade and Investment (MAFTI), and so forth.
   l. Globalization, transnational financial markets, transnational capital flows, and the post-national production and distribution of goods and services (outsourcing).

m. *Maquiladoras*, immigrant workers, the sex trade, and child labor.
n. Global warming and the globalized economy; sustainable development, environmental justice, reduction of fuel consumption, rejection of genetic engineering and biopiracy of indigenous knowledge.
o. Human-animal relations and animal rights, the consequences of human activities on the lives of other animals and living beings and the cause of the sixth mass extinction, and actions to ameliorate these serious problems.

C. Beyond NCATE: Transforming the Preparation of Teachers

Teacher candidates must have the freedom:

1. To learn pedagogical skills and global political knowledge that will make them competent teachers and transformative intellectuals in the classroom. Their experiences shall prepare them to face the uncertainties and contradictions of school life in order to stay longer in the teaching profession.
2. To learn about political economy and to use an historical lens to engage in discussions of social justice, the connections between the economy and U.S. foreign policy, and the role of schools in reproducing the discourse of the dominant society.
3. To learn more social and cultural foundations of education as opposed to only psychological theories of learning.
4. To experience modeling of pedagogical models such as problem posing pedagogy, Socratic dialogues, questioning, feedback, authentic pre- and post-assessment, experiential learning, heterogeneous grouping, peer grouping, and so forth.
5. To discuss classroom management and respect without relying on bribery and punishment.
6. To learn about classroom environments that protect the integrity of all class members.
7. To discuss the pernicious effects of tracking and ability by group level.
8. To learn how to assign homework that takes into account the political economy of the community.
9. To experience a culture of inquiry. Foundations and methods courses should be infused with research components allowing students to become familiar with the inquiry process.
10. To experience a student-teaching experience before being formally inducted into the classroom.
11. To learn how to teach second language learners academic content and language development.
12. To learn critical literacy and how to design creative literacy curricula without being compelled to rely on pre-packaged, teacher-proof curricula.
13. To learn about authentic assessment and the value of naturalistic pre-and post-evaluation of students' learning.
14. To experience fieldwork and coursework assignments related to social justice, peace, and environmental education.

15. To learn a deconstructed vision of social justice (not the marketable version) including skills in activism, social movements, organizing, and advocacy.
16. To receive affordable tuition, adequate work-study opportunities, and autonomy from debilitating school loans.
17. To receive special financial, academic, and emotional support for their underrepresented peers who are pursuing degrees and credentials for the teaching profession.

Conclusion

Emancipatory education is vital for the development of a true democratic society. Schools should be places to engage in academic and political dialogues about the historical and economic foundations of the United States. Students should learn about democracy not only by reciting the Pledge of Allegiance, but by experiencing it daily in the classroom. The curriculum should be centered on real life issues and teaching and learning should be experienced using dialogue and problem posing pedagogy. By asking who benefits from a particular curriculum, who benefits from obsessive testing, who benefits from the exclusion of subjugated knowledge, and who benefits from the silencing of students and their teachers, students may learn lifelong democratic skills. This practice will induct them into social justice activism. It will allow them to recognize how the United States evolved into a powerful country at the expense of many disadvantaged nations. Students may become aware that the rights and privileges they experience and take for granted are possible thanks to the past struggles and sacrifices of many heroes and activists of social justice. One day they may even realize that the culture of abundance of this great nation is sustained by depleting other countries of their food and resources. An education for social justice is the only hope for the reestablishment of a democratic society that is founded in the vigorous civic engagement of all its members, particularly, the younger generations.

The pursuit of social justice starts in the classroom (Freire, 1993). Thus, educators must take the lead and continue the work of past social justice leaders. It must be their call to contribute to the reestablishment of U.S. democracy and advance the pursuit of social justice. Educators should keep in mind the words of the Father of the Common School, Horace Mann (1796–1859), who, in his farewell to a graduating class, told them "be ashamed to die until you have won some victory for humanity" (Mann, 1868, p. 575).

Notes

1. I have deliberately used the term *people of the United States* instead of Americans in recognition that Americans are people from all over the globe, not only the United States. This misappropriation is particularly offensive to Latin Americans who relate this usage to the imperialist doctrine of Manifest Destiny—historically invoked by the United States government to justify military expansionism in the area. This term is also a sad reminder of the declarations of some United States presidents who have stated that Latin America is the United States' backyard.

2. John Keynes is the father of macroeconomic theory that advocates strong state intervention and the use of fiscal and monetary measures to prevent catastrophic fluctuations of the market, among them depression, inflation, deflation and unemployment.
3. Human rights activists consider civil and political rights to be the first generation of protected human rights as opposed to the second generation that refers to newer protections of economic, social and cultural rights.
4. Bourdieu and Passeron developed the concept of cultural capital—"class interests and ideologies" (MacLeod, 1995, p. 13)—to explain how schools legitimate the cultural background of the dominant society manifested in the "knowledge, dispositions, and skills" that are vital for students' success and "are passed from one generation to the next" (MacLeod, 1995, p. 13). Cultural capital is inherited in upper-class households and refers to social codes, language, communication styles, social contacts, high culture, mannerisms, and ways of behaving of the dominant society.
5. This term was coined by Graham Smith (2004; see chapter 2, this volume).

References

Anyon, J. (1980). Social class and school knowledge. *Curriculum Inquiry, 11*(1), 3–42.

Apple, M. (1972). *Education and powe*r. Boston: Routledge.

Baltodano, M. (2006). The accreditation of schools of education and the appropriation of diversity. *Cultural Studies-Critical Methodologies Journal, 6*(1), 123–142.

Bartolomé, L. (1998). *The misteaching of academic discourses: The politics of language in the classroom*. Boulder, CO: Westview.

Bourdieu, P., & Passeron, J. C. (1977). *Reproduction in education, society, and culture.* Beverly Hills, CA: Sage

Bowles. S., & Gintis, H. (1976). *Schooling in capitalist America*. New York: Basic Books.

Brameld, T. (1936, Fall). American education and the social struggle. *Science and Society, 1,* 1–21.

Cho, S. (2000). Selflessness: Toward a Buddhist vision of social justice. *Journal of Buddhist Ethics, 7,* 76–85

Counts, G. (1932). Dare progressive education be progressive? *Progressive Education, 9,* 257–263,

Darder, A. (1991). *Culture and power in the classroom.* New York: Bergin & Garvey.

Darder, A., Baltodano, M., & Torres, R. (2003). *The critical pedagogy reader.* New York: Routledge.

Delpit, L. (1995). *Other peoples' children: Cutural conflict in the classroom.* New York: The New Press.

Dewey, J. (1916). *Democracy and education.* New York: McMillan

Dubois, W. E. B. (1996). *The souls of black folk.* Eric J. Sundquist (Ed.) Oxford: Oxford University Press. (Originally published 1903)

Dubois, W. E. B. (1935, July). Does the Negro Need Separate Schools? *Journal of Negro Education,* 328–335.

Foster, M. (1997). *Black teachers on teaching.* New York: New Press.

Freire, P. (1970). *Pedagogy of the Oppressed.* New York: Seabury Press

Freire, P., & Macedo, D. (1997). *Literacy: Reading the word and the world.* South Hadley, MA: Bergin & Garvey

Gonzalez, N., Moll, L., & Amanti, C. (2005). *Funds of knowledge: Theorizing practice in households, communities, and classrooms*. Mahwah, NJ: Erlbaum.
Giroux, H. (1981). *Ideology, culture and the process of schooling*. Philadelphia: Temple University Press.
Irvine, J. J. (1990). *Black students and school failure: Policies, practices, and prescriptions*. New York: Praeger.
Ladson-Billings, G. (2002). Fighting for our lives: Preparing teachers to teach African American students. *Journal of Teacher Education, 51*(3), 206–214.
Lummis, K. (2004). *Educating to Change the World: John Dewey, Jane Addams, and W.E.B. Du Bois in Turn-of-the-Century America*. Unpublished thesis, Boston College, Massachusetts.
MacLeod, J. (1995). *Ain't no makin'it. Aspirations and attainment in a low-income neighborhood*. Boulder, CO: Westview.
Mann, M. (1868). *Life and works of Horace Mann*. New York: Boston, Lee & Shepard.
McLaren, P. (1986). *Schooling as ritual performance*. Boston: Routledge & Kegan Paul.
McLaren, P. (1998). Revolutionary pedagogy in post-revolutionary times: Rethinking the political economy of critical education. *Educational Theory, 48*(4), 431–462.
McLaren, P., & Rizvi, M. (2002). *Educating for social justice and liberation*. Retrieved October 22, 2006, from http://www.zmag.org/content/print_article.cfm?itemID=2229§ionID=36
Miroff, B. (1993). *Icons of democracy*. Lawrence: Kansas University Press.
Nieto, S. (2002). Bringing bilingual education out of the basement and other imperatives for teacher education. In S. Nieto (Ed.), *Language, culture, and teaching* (pp. 205–226). Mahwah, NJ: Erlbaum.
Nussbaum, M. (2006). *Frontiers of justice. Disability, nationality and species membership*. Cambridge, MA: Harvard University Press.
Rawls, J. (1971). *A theory of justice*. Cambridge: Harvard University Press.
Rugg, H. (1996). Reconstructing the curriculum. An open letter to Professor Henry Johnson commenting on committee procedure as illustrated by the report of the joint committee on history and education for citizenship. In W. Parker (Ed.), *Educating the democratic mind* (pp. 45–60). New York: State University of New York Press.
Shor, I. (1992). *Empowering education: critical teaching for social change*. Chicago: University of Chicago Press.
Smith, A. (1776). *An inquiry into the nature and causes of the wealth of nation*. December 14, 2008, from http://www.econlib.org/library/Smith/smWN.html
Smith, G. (2004). Mai i te Maramatanga, ki te Putanga Mai o te Tahuritanga: From conscientization to transformation. Educational perspectives. *Indigenous Education, 37*(1), 46–52.
United Nations. (1996). *International covenant on economic, social and cultural rights* Retrieved April 15, 2003, from http://www.hrweb.org/legal/escr.html
Young, I. M. (1990). *Justice and the politics of difference*. Princeton, NJ: Princeton University Press.
Young, I. M. (2001). Equality of whom? Social groups and judgments of injustice. *The Journal of Political Philosophy, 9*(1), 1–18.

17 Developing Social Justice Standards

A Multicultural Perspective

Robert E. Crafton

> The responsibilities of all citizens in a democratic society are inseparable from the responsibility to promote human rights. To flourish, both democracy and human rights require people's active participation. Human rights education includes learning the skills of advocacy—to speak and act everyday in the name of human rights. (Flowers & Rudelius-Palmer, 1998)

> Human rights are both inspirational and practical. Human rights principles hold up the vision of a free, just, and peaceful world and set minimum standards for how individuals and institutions everywhere should treat people. Human rights also empower people with a framework for action when those minimum standards are not met, for people still have human rights even if the laws or those in power do not recognize them. (Costain, 1998)

Standard Deviation: Whose Politics Do Curriculum Standards Reflect?

Let's face it: The attempt to set curriculum standards governing public education has always been something of a problem. At its core is a question of what lessons we will teach and how we will teach these lessons, questions which became critical following the integration of the public schools in the 1960s and 1970s. Education in the 1950s, still conducted in segregated classrooms, was meant to foster "American" values, a unified and unifying belief in the democratic traditions of our country, of the rule of popular opinion and the curiously exclusionary effects of a democratic culture so conceived. *Brown v. Board* acknowledged the baleful effects of this segregated educational system and initiated, if nothing else, a rising self-consciousness that would, in time, succeed in "novelizing" the romance of America's master narrative, as Bakhtin might say, opening at least a little space for diverse voices and points of view. The legacy of the *Brown* decision, the attention it paid to segregation and the attempts to dismantle segregation or ameliorate its effects, is a long and complicated story which is still unfolding. The creation of more diverse classroom populations following *Brown* can be tied, in one way or another, to a number of disparate effects: to the development of "learning styles theory" and theories of multiple intelligences introduced to account for the perceived differences in the abilities and achievements of different groups of students; to the declines of education's effectiveness noted in *A Nation at Risk*, which the current No Child Left Behind legislation is still attempting to solve; to the development of "more inclusive" multicultural curricula, on the one hand, and the English-only/anti-bilingual language initiatives pushed forward in California, Arizona, and Massachusetts, on the other; to the culture wars, in general, and the specific battles waged over curriculum standards for the teaching of U.S. history; to outcomes-based education and the attempts, often through the use of standardized tests, to assess the effectiveness of instruction.

In this climate, the promulgation of educational "standards," often in the form of national and state curriculum guidelines, tends to favor a normative or nationalistic agenda, to prescribe the "essential" or "core" knowledge every student needs in order to participate effectively in American society, that is, to teach students what it means to be an "American." Education is a civic enterprise, its (purported) goal to create an educated citizenry. The question, of course, is just what kind of society we are talking about and how education can best serve the interests of that conception of society. What are the core values we are seeking to reproduce?

While this sounds like a simple question, the answer is not as simple as it seems. The April, 2004, issue of *PS: Political Science and Politics*, for instance, raised this question in a symposium on civic education. The focus of these six articles is on the teaching of civics *per se*, courses relating to United States history and detailing the structure and functioning of the government, that is, instruction devoted directly to imparting the knowledge and skills citizenship depends on. Insofar as all education is civic education, their discussion can be taken as one part of a more general consideration of the purposes of public education. And more specifically, if, as Flowers and Rudelius-Palmer (1998) contend, promoting human rights is the central responsibility of all citizens, then the key question will be how social and environmental justice are factored into civics instruction.

The problem is that no clear consensus exists as to what the goals of a civic education are, beyond the need—at least in theory—to create an effective, engaged, and educated citizenry. What it means to be a citizen, however, and how we can most effectively engage students in the important work of government remains a matter of debate, a debate that *seems* to pit "patriotism" against "politics." (The distinction is really a false one, as we will see, dependent on narrow definitions of these terms.) In the first case, civic education, as Joel Westheimer (2004) describes it in his introduction to the symposium, is conceived of as "primarily a means of conveying knowledge of important historical facts and a sense of civic unity, duty, and national pride to the Nation's youth and young adults" (p. 231). This is a 1950's conception of civics, a view still very much alive in many places, that "Americans, while representing diverse backgrounds and cultures, are all part of a unified American creed or a common set of beliefs, and that these beliefs are easily identifiable" (p. 232). For such people, "what it means to be an American," Westheimer writes, "is more answer than question" (p. 231), something somehow self-evident. We can imagine that, in this scenario, the United States will be portrayed historically as defending civil rights and social justice. We can also imagine that this attempt to present certain elements of the "American experience" as somehow self-evident will foster a party-line politics in direct conflict with the educational mission of civics instruction, turning education into indoctrination.

While students will come away from such a course of study imbued with a general sense of the United States' democratic spirit, they may not, on the other hand, be very well prepared by such instruction to act as social justice advocates. Moreover, insofar as such instruction aims at defining the "essential" character of the American people, it is conceived of as being beyond politics, at least where politics is defined by partisan or narrowly personal interests. By contrast, those educators supporting more political constructions of civic education see politics as "the process by which citizens with varied interests and opinions negotiate differences and clarify places where values conflict" (Westheimer, 2004, p. 231). Civics courses should therefore "teach the critical and deliberative skills necessary to participate effectively in contentious public debates" (p. 231), a model of citizenship that "recognizes ambiguity and conflict, that sees human conditions and aspirations as complex and contested, and that embraces debate and deliberation as a cornerstone of democratic societies" (p. 231). E. Wayne Ross (2004) echoes these points in his contribution to the symposium:

> The primary (and overlapping) tensions that have energized the field while simultaneously threatening its existence include: (1) the relative emphasis on the cultural heritage of the dominant society versus the development of critical thought; and (2) conflicting conceptions of citizenship, that is citizenship for social reproduction or social reconstruction. (p. 249)

Rather than seeing one form of civic education as political and the other as apolitical, we need, as Westheimer (2004) suggests, to ask "whose politics do civic education programs reflect and why?" (p. 233). This political perspective seems to lay a more effective basis for advocacy and for reform than the so-called apolitical model, but it can, potentially, prove divisive. What are we trying to accomplish in the classroom? How can we best prepare students to become citizens? The debate goes on.

Precedent Cases: The Human Rights Educational Mandate

If there is anything surprising in this discussion of education's purpose, it is that we are still asking and trying to answer the most basic of questions, questions, for instance, that arose in the drafting of the United Nation's 1948 Universal Declaration of Human Rights. The Universal Declaration includes education in its list of inalienable rights to be extended to all peoples. Article 26 of the Declaration contains three clauses:

1. Everyone has the right to education. Education shall be free, at least in the elementary and fundamental stages. Elementary education shall be compulsory. Technical and professional education shall be made generally available and higher education shall be equally accessible to all on the basis of merit.
2. Education shall be directed to the full development of the human personality and to strengthening of respect for human rights and fundamental freedoms. It shall promote understanding, tolerance and friendship among all nations, racial or religious groups, and shall further the activities of the United Nations for the maintenance of peace.
3. Parents have a prior right to choose the kind of education that shall be given to their children.

In the opening chapter of *The Universal Right to Education*, Spring (2000) considers the challenges the framers of this document faced and their problems, among other things, defining *education*. As Spring notes, "education meant different things to a Buddhist and to a Stalinist" (p. 16). Nevertheless, while saying what constitutes an education is difficult, I. E. Kandel, in his contribution to the UNESCO symposium which led to the drafting of Article 26, specified what an education would *not* do. According to Kandel, an appropriate education "(1) was *not* unequal; (2) did *not* practice racial and cultural segregation; (3) was *not* nationalistic; (4) did *not* indoctrinate; (5) did *not* control teacher and student learning through a system of national examinations; (6) did *not* prescribe methods of instruction; (7) did *not* deny teachers freedom of speech and inquiry" (cited in Spring, 2000, p. 18). While the United States Congress failed to ratify the Universal Declaration, just as the United States has frequently failed to ratify other international human rights and environmental accords, the general right to a free and appropriate education, one that does not violate, at least according to our constitution, the First and Fourteenth Amendment rights of its citizens, seems incontrovertible.

Coming at the end of World War II, the discussions which led to the drafting of the Universal Declaration of Human Rights provide a historical context for considering educational standards and the challenges we face as United States citizens in promoting standards that will foster social and environmental justice in our schools. Broadly defined, education can serve two distinct and opposing ends, working either as a tool of social control/indoctrination or as a means of fostering self-realization/self-determination. Given the immediate past history of World War II, the Universal Declaration clearly favors self-realization over social control and open enquiry over indoctrination, a position, in general, which U. S. Supreme Court rulings have traditionally upheld. In *West Virginia v. Barnette* (1943), for instance, a World War II-era ruling which struck down a West Virginia law requiring school students to recite the Pledge of Allegiance on a daily basis, the court argued that "If there is any fixed star in our constitutional constellation, it is that no official, high or petty, can prescribe what shall be orthodox in politics, nationalism, religion, or other matters of opinion or force citizens to confess by word or act their faith therein."

There is, it seems, an unresolvable tension at the center of the debate, an attempt to balance the centripetal and centrifugal forces at work in society. On one level, the question may be whether we can promulgate standards at all. The use of *standards*, the word itself, suggests both an orthodoxy and a means of measuring deviations from the core concerns defining the center. On another level, legislative and educational policies challenging the underlying principles of the Universal Declaration (which are, like our Supreme Court decisions, a kind of standard) demonstrate the need to establish some basic educational standards. State laws mandating the daily recitation of the Pledge of Allegiance; federal and state programs that tie educational assessment (and consequently, local curricular decisions) to standardized test scores; state laws forbidding the use of certain pedagogical methods (e.g., bilingual language instruction)—not to mention the wide differences in school funding which continue to perpetuate patterns of privilege and poverty in the United States—all of these points, when considered in light of these earlier discussions, both argue the critical need to make social justice a central goal of education and demonstrate how far we are from providing a just and equitable educational system in the United States today. Teaching students, as Flowers and Rudelius-Palmer (1998) put it, that "The responsibilities of all citizens in a democratic society are inseparable from the responsibility to promote human rights," in an educational system that provides unequal opportunities, legislates patriotic observances, controls student and teacher learning through systems of examinations, prescribes methods of instruction—that is, in school systems that fail to promote fundamental educational rights—may seem quixotic, at best. Still, these challenges, if anything, suggest how crucial developing minimum standards for fostering social and environmental justice is. For educators devoted specifically to multicultural concerns, the stakes are even higher.

Developing Criteria for Evaluating Curriculum Standards: A Multicultural Perspective

In the fall of 1999, at its ninth annual convention, held that year in San Diego, the National Association of Multicultural Education (NAME) included a series of open meetings the purpose of which was to gauge interest in the creation of committees developing the work of the association. The committee structure was conceived by then-president Donna Gollnick, and among the possible committees was one on "educational standards." The initial questions turned on the possible focus of this committee's effort—what educational standards the committee might consider—and on the possible relevance of this investigation to NAME's mission. In response to these initial discussions, a committee was formed. It focused on the standards of learning/curriculum guidelines, either already in place or still being developed in each state, which set out the curricular goals and objectives for instruction in that state's public schools. The initial task was to consider how responsive such guidelines were to multicultural interests and concerns, and to establish a set of guidelines describing the tenets of a sound multicultural education. This work, conducted via e-mail by a small and shifting group of committee members, resulted in a draft document presented at the business meeting of the organization's 12th annual convention, held in 2002 in Washington, D.C.

As might be expected, multicultural interests are unevenly represented in state curriculum guidelines, especially those devoted, for instance, to the study of U.S. history. The Virginia Standards of Learning as they appeared on the department of education's website in 1999 are a case in point. In general, these standards are "content-rich" standards, setting out in specific terms the content of the study and not, as some other states do, simply setting out a broad array of skills students should acquire. The standards name names and cite dates, giving these guidelines an objective appearance. Following the debacle surrounding the national history standards project, the standards were cited as a possible model, apparently apolitical, arguably objective, beyond partisan politics. The problem, of course, comes in the selection and arrangement of materials, a selection that offers a view of U.S. history that tends to homogenize heterogeneous experiences, to downplay debate, to eliminate the controversial and sometimes ugly elements in our past. These standards cited no Native Americans, Asian Americans, or Latino/a figures by name. Of the African Americans cited, the list was clearly one-sided, citing Booker T. Washington and Martin Luther King, but not W.E.B. Dubois or Malcolm X; Arthur Ashe, born in Richmond, was included. The standards made no mention of Trail of Tears, the Sand Creek Massacre, Wounded Knee, or the internment of Japanese Americans during the Second World War. The phrase "manifest destiny" appears nowhere, and on the rare occasions when racial conflict is considered, it is considered in the past tense as a conflict already resolved. Students are prompted in places to consider the material and economic effects of Native American beliefs, a form of analysis Christianity is not subjected to. In short, this truncated view of U.S. history omits discussion of those events that defined the experiences of the indigenous peoples and of people of African, Asian, and Spanish descent in this country. And in doing so, it makes it equally impossible for students of European descent to know themselves.

In might be argued that, given the controversy that surrounded the national history standards project, the Virginia Standards were designed to avoid controversy, to include, as a sort of lowest common denominator, only those people and events that everyone would agree on. Even so, the effect of such a curriculum is clear. Such a study does not record the experiences and contributions of the diverse peoples who compose this country, nor does it, in any meaningful way, allow students to consider, for good and bad, how their identities have been constructed by the historical and cultural conditions we live within. In avoiding conflict, these standards fail to do justice, in every sense of the word, to the study of U.S. history. Simply put, questions of social and environmental justice are ill-served in such a curriculum.

The guidelines that developed from this discussion emerged in two movements, the main body of the text—the opening paragraph and five principle points—receiving the bulk of our initial time and attention, with the final paragraph emerging separately, following the completion of this initial work. The final paragraph, in particular, was informed by the roundtable discussion devoted to social and environmental education standards held at the American Education Research Association's 2002 annual convention, a discussion which considered whether social and environmental justice education should be evaluated by guidelines or standards. The draft guidelines were reviewed both by interested members of NAME's Board of Directors and the document posted on the association's website for consideration by the membership.

Two basic premises guided the drafting of the initial document, that the population of the United States is multicultural in composition and that sound educational practices recognize and respond to the multiethnic, multicultural nature of that population. In short, a good education is a multicultural education. Based on this premise, five principle points emerged: (1) A sound education would be inclusive, representing the contributions and concerns of all those peoples composing U.S. society; (2) it would respect diverse perspectives and opinions; (3) it would recognize the ways in which knowledge is socially constructed and accommodate alternative ways of knowing and being in the world; (4) it would foster a sense of self-knowledge, of the ways individual identity is constructed; and, finally, (5) it would emphasize questions of social justice. Under each of these five headings, four points appear, carrying the student through an increasingly complex analysis of that element, building a knowledge base first—e.g., recognizing the elements that constitute our multicultural society—and thereafter considering the causes and effects, both good and bad, that have emerged from that condition. The intent, in keeping with the tenets of a critical multiculturalism, is not to reproduce patterns of experience but to provide a basis for understanding them, and in understanding them, to provide a basis for action.

Criteria for Evaluating State Curriculum Standards

The population of the United States of America has been multicultural since its inception. Moreover, the longstanding status of this nation as an economic world power draws persons from across the globe who contribute further to its multicultural character. This historical and contemporary diversity has considerable implications for the work of educators in the nation's schools. Specifically, state curriculum standards designed to guide public education need to include the particular contributions, distinct heritages and values, as well as the multiple ways of knowing that represent our diverse population. Curricula should be designed to facilitate the development of individuals who appreciate the complexity of the human condition and who can effectively negotiate the diverse cultural contexts of U.S. society. Such individuals must acquire critical understanding and appreciation of their own cultural heritage as well as the cultural heritages of the diverse groups that are represented in our collective national identity. Similarly, through curricula and school-based experiences individuals should become critically engaged with the principles of social justice for all people. Ultimately, curriculum standards must do far more than simply stress the multicultural composition of the United States. Rather they must also outline classroom practices that help educators impart the knowledge, skills, and dispositions necessary for individuals to participate fully and meaningfully in our multiethnic and multiracial society. To this end, the National Association for Multicultural Education has established curriculum guidelines that respond to five key concerns:

NAME Curriculum Guidelines

I. Inclusiveness

Inclusive curriculum guidelines will

a. Represent the broad range of experiences and peoples that compose the population of the United States;
b. Acknowledge the ways multicultural experiences have contributed to the knowledge base, value systems, and ways of thinking within disciplines;
c. Provide an integrated understanding of human experience in its many varieties and complexities by attending to the exceptional as well as the ordinary;
d. Promote understanding of the interdependence of groups and the reciprocal ways, both historic and contemporary, in which our collective experiences shape the lives of the diverse peoples in the United States.

II. Diverse Perspectives

Curriculum guidelines emphasizing diverse perspectives will

a. Represent the multiple constituencies and points of view in the United States;
b. Encourage students to entertain competing constructions and understandings of social, historical, and natural phenomena;
c. Recognize the ways these constructions are rooted in the cultural and historical experiences of the people who espouse them;
d. Facilitate independent, contextual, and critical thinking among students about what they are being taught in schools.

III. Accommodating Alternative Epistemologies/ Social Construction of Knowledge

To provide students with the means to understand the ways knowledge is socially constructed, curriculum guidelines will

a. Recognize that alternative cultural constructions entail distinct ways of thinking;
b. Provide a basis for appreciating the differences in traditional ways of knowing, both the content of knowledge and the forms of evidence advanced to support it;
c. Set out the paradigms and logic that structure knowledge within a community;
d. Provide the analytic tools students need to evaluate both the causes and the effects of traditional and alternative belief systems.

IV. Self-Knowledge

In order to foster a sense in students of how their own identities have been constructed by the complex interplay of historical, social, political, economic, and even geographic factors, curriculum guidelines will

a. Provide a structure that allows students to investigate their own cultural and ethnic identities and to examine the origins and consequences of their attitudes and behaviors toward other groups;
b. Lead students to a critical understanding and appreciation of their own cultural and ethnic identities, including both their strengths and weaknesses;
c. Recognize that identity is based on multiple factors, including the diverse and sometimes contradictory realities of membership in multiple groups;
d. Foster in students an understanding that identity is dynamic and therefore, that change is possible.

V. Social Justice

Curriculum guidelines fostering the goals of social justice will

a. Emphasize the constitutional rights accorded all members of our society and the responsibilities entailed by citizenship in our multicultural society;
b. Recognize and uphold the statutes set forth by the *Universal Declaration of Human Rights* adopted by the United Nations in 1948, in particular Article 26.2, that "Education shall be directed to the full development of the human personality and the strengthening of respect for human rights and fundamental freedoms. It shall promote understanding, tolerance and friendship among all nations, racial or religious groups, and shall further the activities of the United Nations for the maintenance of peace";
c. Prepare students to "think globally and act locally" by fostering a critical understanding of the ways local knowledge and actions are situated within and have an impact on global contexts;
d. Provide students opportunities to evaluate the results of personal, organizational, corporate, and governmental decisions and to develop a critical understanding of how such decisions may benefit some groups while negatively impacting others;
e. Promote social action, creating an engaged, active, and responsible citizenry committed to eradicating bigotry and to developing a fair, just, democratic society responsive to the needs of all our people regardless of race, class, gender, age, sexual orientation, physical appearance, ability or disability, national origin, ethnicity, religious belief or lack thereof.

The value in articulating curriculum standards at the state level is really two-fold: First, setting standards represents each state's commitment to hold all students to equally high standards for performance while providing the instructional programs and support functions necessary for all students to meet these standards. All students deserve a quality education; curriculum standards define the core knowledge and skills we expect all students to master while providing an impetus for programs that facilitate the processes of learning and instruction. Second, the process of setting state standards itself represents a crucial step in our school systems' attempts to acknowledge the multiple constituencies composing each state's population and by extension, the United States' multiethnic, multicultural nature. For the process to be meaningful, it must itself be open and inclusive, the standards representing a consensus of opinion reflecting and respecting the broad range of needs, interests, and bodies of expertise that students, parents, educators, representatives of numerous professional organizations, politicians, and our elders bring to the discussion. To be fully effective, such negotiations should acknowledge the international, national and local initiatives adopted by educational and professional organizations which represent the most fully developed understanding of educational purposes and pedagogical practices currently available. Examples of specific statements include, but are not limited to, the United Nations' Universal Declaration of Human Rights; "The Standards for English Language Arts" developed jointly by the National Council of Teachers of English and the International Reading Association; "Principles and Standards for School Mathematics" developed by the National Council of Teachers of Mathematics; "National Science Education Standards" developed by the National Research Council in consultation with the American Association for the Advancement of Science and the National Science Teachers Association; the National Council for Social Studies' "Curriculum Guidelines for Multicultural Education"; Alaska Standards for Culturally Responsive Schools adopted by the Assembly of Alaska Native Educators; the American Speech and Hearing Association's position paper "Social Dialects and Implications of the Position on Social Dialects." In order to respond to the changing realities of life in our academic disciplines and in our schools, state standards need to be open to regular review and revision. Moreover, the standards movement will prove most valuable insofar as it fosters the on-going discussion of what we teach and how and why we teach these things to our students (NAME, 2002).

***

The logic behind NAME's five major points, and the reasons why standards like those for the study of U.S. history in Virginia are deficient, should be clear. A curriculum which is not inclusive will be incapable of representing diverse views and ways of knowing, which in turn, will not provide the necessary knowledge base which will allow students to understand how knowledge and identity are socially constructed. The students are required only to reproduce the terms of this master narrative, not to enter into dialogue with it and with one another. Such an education cannot serve the ends of social justice. The NAME guidelines, by contrast, recognize, at the most general level, the need (1) to provide students with an understanding of human rights; (2) to foster in the student an understanding of democratic culture, of both its progressive and its regressive elements; (3) to develop in the student a sense of obligation to protect the rights of all people, and (4) to provide the student with the tools to do so.

Moreover, the final paragraph of the document attempts to address some of the central concerns the whole movement toward academic standards raises. On one level, having standards is not necessarily a bad thing, if, by that, we mean offering an equally rigorous education to all students, if it includes the expectation that all students are equally capable of learning, and if it also includes some provisions guaranteeing that all schools will receive the resources they need to provide the programs their students need to meet these standards. Unfortunately, the impulse behind standards, as noted above, has been too often to prescribe those core or essential concepts students should know, the mastery of which can then be tested, typically by machine-scored multiple-choice tests. Such standards tend to be imposed from the top down, the goal to dictate, to indoctrinate, not to encourage an active and critical understanding of complex materials. They undercut real learning. Hence the question asked by the 2002 AERA panel: Should social and environmental justice education be evaluated by guidelines or standards? To develop yet another set of "standards," however well intended and however critical they might be of prevailing standards, risked legitimizing the standards movement, not liberating education from its baleful effects. Were we, in the end, simply imposing one more set of standards on education, one more hoop or hurdle to jump through, one more line to toe?

The critical concern here is how we conceptualize standards, what possible good they do, and how we go about generating these standards. In this case, the standards need to practice what they preach, to be as open to and accepting of multiple constituencies and points of views as we hope and believe public-school curricula should be. In theory, setting standards suggests that all students are capable of learning and that all students should and can be held to the same high standards. We are all too familiar with the inequitable distribution of educational resources in this country, with the fact that all schools are not created equal, and with the racist and/or classist assumptions of low expectations. Students in inner-city and rural schools should have the same opportunities and resources that students in affluent neighborhoods and schools have access to. This, at least, is the underlying reason for setting standards in the first place.

Beyond that initial assumption, however, the setting of standards needs to engage the multiple constituencies that make up the educational community and to respect the needs and alternate ways of knowing within that community. Process here is product. To that end, the final paragraph recognizes the importance of foundation documents like the Universal Declaration of Human Rights and of the discipline-specific contributions of professional organizations like the National Council of Teachers of English or the American Speech and Hearing Association. These organizations have entertained the questions we confront in forming educational practices and policies; their deliberated positions often represent the "best practices" within that discipline, at least as they are currently understood. Our deliberations need to be informed by their findings, on the one hand, just as, on the other, we need to see that our deliberations are open-ended and on-going. The operative phrase here is "at least as they are currently understood." All standards are provisional, the product of particular conditions, and, as such, subject to reevaluation and revision as these conditions change.

Unifying Principles

The attempt to articulate standards, whether for the teaching of U.S. history or for a curriculum responsive to multicultural concerns or for social and environmental justice education, will always be, to some extent, problematic. How problematic has been made clear, especially in the case of social and environmental justice standards, by the discussions that have taken place at the annual AERA conventions over the past years, from 2002 to 2004. The participating parties, representing a wide range of special interest groups, not unlike those parties involved in the drafting of the Universal Declaration of Human Rights, have brought a wide variety of concerns to the table, each approaching the project (or resisting it) from a different angle. As in the preliminary discussions of the Universal Declaration, our draft standards have cited an equally broad range of background experiences, from Buddhist to Marxist. In spite of these differences, however—differences which, can, at times, even extend to what we mean by "social justice" or "standards" (just as defining "education" and "right" proved difficult for the drafters of the Universal Declaration)—some key points do seem to emerge from these initial drafts. We all seem to share three points: (1) A commitment to social justice, that is, a general understanding that the end of education is to promote a just society, that good education is social justice education; (2) A recognition of the value of diversity, at all levels; (3) A belief in the transformative power of education, especially (though perhaps not exclusively) through the exercise of critical thought. All education is civic education, its end to produce an educated, engaged, effective citizenry. At its core is a commitment to social justice rooted in a "deep democracy," not the superficial and exclusionary reign of popular opinion, but a deep and abiding belief in the integrity of the individual person.

This much, it seems, everyone might agree to, but, again, problems immediately appear, and a debate begins similar to that over civic education. Everyone might agree with the general goal of fostering social justice and then differ on just what that means and on how we can best achieve that goal. The answers produced by the special interest groups have been various, ranging from those like the NAME guidelines cited above that articulate a finite set of aims and principles, to others who believe the territory so conflicted or opinion on the matter so disparate, even within their interest group, that they altogether resist the effort as inherently flawed. Even in this response, however, some common ground seems to appear, the discussion turning on the nature of the conflict, the value of the product versus the process through which that product is achieved, and the need for dialogue.

Embracing the Conflict

The territory is conflicted. In this case, we need to own the conflict. The discussions over civic education provide something of a model here. Civic education seems to be conceptualized along two distinctly different lines, a dichotomy between patriotism and politics, between social control and self-realization, between social reproduction and social reform, between perpetuating the traditions of the dominant culture and negotiating the differences within a pluralistic population. This is, however, something of a false dichotomy. The United States was founded through an act of political dissent; this revolutionary spirit and the honoring of an individual's right to determine matters of conscience for him- or herself stands at the center of our political structure. Our solutions have always been political. Or, risking the obvious cliché, we have always agreed to disagree. And this is the case here. If we were all in agreement as to what social justice is and how we might best achieve it within our schools, we wouldn't be engaged in this enterprise in the first place. That we do disagree only underlines the importance of the discussion. The field is subject to competing forces, centripetal and centrifugal. We need to own the dynamic nature of these competing forces and work to balance them. The biggest mistake we can make here is refusing to enter the dialogue.

Process, Not Product

The dynamic nature of the field, that the lines of force are constantly shifting, means that any solutions are bound to be temporary, tentative, provisional. Social justice is a work in progress, as is the attempt to articulate standards for educational systems that will foster social and environmental justice. As a participant in the drafting of the NAME curriculum standards document, I do believe we have produced a useful product, not because it sets out once and for all time the standards by which state curriculum guidelines can be judged, but because this document will provide the basis for future conversation. Clearly, these standards are subject to revision. Meanwhile, they give everyone with a stake in education—which is, quite literally, everyone—a way of thinking about what we are teaching and how we teach that material in our schools, which is something worth talking about. The process required by the drafting, review and adoption of these standards may be more valuable in the end than the document itself. It certainly proved useful to me. If it proves useful in furthering the discussion, then it will have fulfilled its function.

Dialogue

Drafting these guidelines required us to talk to one another, and, as always, the NAME document was stronger for the input it received from the people who participated in its writing and review. Once written, these guidelines have the potential to sponsor further conversations. That these guidelines are the result of dialogue and the occasion for further dialogue is the important point. In this regard, The Alaska Native Knowledge Network's Standards for Culturally Responsible Schools provides an important example, most impressive in the ways it has succeeded in organizing the discussion, discussions that began in the communities, moving from the "bottom" up, and which brought so many people to the table.

In the end, the differences in form and opinion recorded in the various special interest group documents seem less important than the insights that they share.

The points that emerge—the commitment to social justice, the perceived value of diversity, the critical importance of dialogue to the process—while probably not profound, do seem to perform the functions Costain (1998) describes: First, they provide a vision which is both inspirational and practical. The goal of a public education is to promote social justice. Second, they provide "minimum standards for how individuals and institutions everywhere should treat people." The dialogue does need to be open and inclusive, respecting the diverse experiences and positions represented by all members of the community. These few shared ideas do provide a point of departure, certainly a good place to begin, not end, the discussion.

References

Alaska Native Knowledge Network. (1998). *Alaska standards for culturally responsive schools.* Fairbanks: University of Alaska Fairbanks.

American Educational Research Association. (2002, April). *Social and environmental justice: Should it be evaluated by guidelines or standards?* Panel presentation at AERA Annual Meeting, New Orleans, LA.

Costain, P. (1998). What are human rights? In N. Flowers (Ed.), *Human rights here and now.* Retrieved December 12, 2008, from http://www1.umn.edu/humanrts//edumat/hreduseries/hereandnow/Part-1/whatare.htm

Flowers, N., & Rudelius-Palmer, K. (1998). The right to know your rights. In N. Flowers (Ed.), *Human rights here and now.* Retrieved December 12, 2008, from http://www1.umn.edu/humanrts//edumat/hreduseries/hereandnow/Part-1/whatare.htm

National Association of Multicultural Education Standards Committee. (2002) Criteria for evaluating state curriculum standards. Retrieved December 12, 2008, from http://www.nameorg.org

Ross, E. W. (2004, April). Negotiating the politics of citizenship education. *PS: Political Science and Politics, 37*(2), 249–251. Retrieved December 12, 2008, from http://www.apsanet.org

Spring, J. (2000). *The universal right to education: Justification, definition, and guidelines.* Mahwah, NJ: Erlbaum.

Virginia Department of Education. (1995). *Standards of Learning.* Retrieved December 12, 2008, from http://www.doe.virginia.gov/VDOE/Superintendent/Sols/home.shtml

Westheimer, J. (2004, April). Introduction: The politics of civic education. *PS: Political Science and Politics, 37*(2), 231–235. Retrieved December 12, 2008, from Jstor database: http://www.jstor.org/stable/4488811

West Virginia State Board of Educ. v. Barnette, 319 U.S. 624 (1943).

18 Towards a Collective Vision for Social Justice, Peace, and Environmental Education

Julie Andrzejewski, Marta P. Baltodano, Ray Barnhardt, and Linda Symcox

This book offers a forum in which progressive educators and activists have described their vision for a better world, seeking to initiate a conversation on how educators and educational institutions can foster the principles of social justice, peace, and environmental education in their daily practice. Each author presents a vision of how their particular area of concern intersects with the overarching issues of social justice, peace and the environment. They do this by globalizing their perspective, and by looking for ways in which their particular concern is related to the others. This proved to be a very challenging task because the authors were asked to research and think beyond the traditional boundaries of their respective disciplines. Reading through all these chapters, it seemed possible to discern a common set of themes that had emerged from the six-year process of discussions, negotiations, and writing that produced this collection of essays. It also seemed possible to produce a tentative set of common standards that would synthesize the specific points laid out in each chapter. While they will not have the specificity of those in each chapter, a comprehensive set might assist educators in taking the next steps.

After coding the narrative sections and the standards sections from each chapter, we found that all the various contributions converged to create an initial vision on which to base social justice, peace, and environmental education. Therefore, in this concluding chapter we lay out a set of *six common themes*, and a set of *five comprehensive standards*—standards for educators, students, educational institutions, teacher educators, and communities—that we have distilled form the work of all the authors in the book.

Six Common Themes

Through a coding process, these themes or strands emerged fairly consistently throughout the book. Here we highlight their convergences and suggest ways in which they can be used by educators and activists who wish to foster social justice, peace, and environmental justice.

Theme One

Neoliberal economic policies and globalization are antithetical to social justice,

peace, and environmental sustainability, and we must therefore imagine a new economy grounded in social and environmental responsibility.

Because neoliberal economic policies are based on deregulation and the short-term maximization of profit, they run counter to the goals of social and environmental justice, which require regulation, based on a vision of the common good, and a consciousness of the long-term implications of global economic development. Increased poverty, greenhouse gases, social inequality, and the erosion of traditional cultures are the byproducts of the economic transformations related to neoliberal globalization. Furthermore, critics of neoliberal economic policies argue, as we do, that these developments are not occurring in a cultural and political vacuum, but that they fuel ethnic, religious, and factional tensions that lead to wars and breed terrorism. Not only has the U.S. government contributed to and often led these global trends, but over the past 25 years it has also retreated from its own social justice policies that were envisioned and created during the New Deal, New Frontier, and Great Society. One could argue that we have returned to the Gilded Age of the 1890s, but now with a new twist: this new Gilded Age is now global, not national. Globalization is free trade as conceptualized by the classical economists Adam Smith and David Ricardo, stripped of the localized and state-based economic, social and political constraints that for two centuries had kept Ricardo's "iron law of wages" from becoming a reality. Perhaps Adam Smith's "invisible hand" is now larger and more invisible than ever as capital and labor flow freely and imperceptibly across national borders. Since neoliberal globalization makes it possible to move capital, technology, ideas and jobs across borders in search of maximum profits and minimal labor costs, it is easy for governments and corporations to evade social justice and environmental issues with a fancy shell game.

The authors of this book believe that the arguments for neoliberal economic policy must be challenged through education and activism; that we teach a new economic vision in opposition to the neoliberal model of globalization, laying the groundwork for a new business bottom line that factors in the human and environmental costs of doing business. It is time now to begin teaching this type of economic thinking because free market economic policies have clearly failed on their own terms. With the collapse of corporations such as Enron, Worldcom, and the sub-prime mortgage meltdown, and with increasing millions of Americans denied access to basic health care, it has become more and more obvious that the free market is incapable of regulating its own excesses. The time is ripe to teach students to imagine a world in which economic policies are grounded on social responsibility and concerns for peace and the environment. This book provides practical guidelines and support for educators who want to do this.

Theme Two

Social justice, peace, and environmental justice are indivisible, mutually dependent, and mutually reinforcing.

We believe that social and environmental justice and peace education are indivisible: each one is unachievable without considering its interrelationship to all the others. First, we see global capitalism as the systemic and common denominator which has formed and exacerbated human oppression: militarism, invasions, wars, and the destruction of the global environment. Since none of these phenomena is taking place in a vacuum, we investigate their interconnections in each chapter. Second, we move beyond essentialism within and among identity and issue-based groups by embracing the complexities of subjugation and emancipation. Third, we propose an educational vision that challenges the idea that one issue is more important than another, and that recognizes that issues of social justice, peace, and eco-justice are indivisible, mutually dependent and mutually reinforcing. Fourth, each author goes beyond a restatement of current theory and practice in their respective disciplines by exploring previously unrecognized or infrequently considered topics in the literature, such as global perspectives on local issues, and vice versa. By invoking international proposals, treaties, and actions of international bodies we have been able to convey these global and integrated perspectives. Fifth, we strive to bridge the mythical divides between the local, regional, national, and global. We highlight the connections between local and global, between personal well-being and the well-being of others and of the earth.

Theme Three

Educators must challenge the Standards movement and redirect the educational discourse from exclusively academic accountability to a broader definition of accountability that embraces social justice, peace, and environmental justice.

This book challenges the traditional view of schools as democratic institutions that promote social mobility. It contends that schools impose a view of the world that represents the ideology of the dominant society, and thus assimilates different cultural groups into the logic of the prevailing social order. Overt and hidden curricula are used to reproduce and legitimize stereotypes that create different forms of control under the guise of impartial and universal knowledge: conservative discourses on excellence and accountability represent sophisticated mechanisms that efficiently align the school curriculum to the interests of the global economy. This book challenges the hegemonic normativity that is transmitted in schools. It invites educators and activists to use formal and non-formal education as democratic spaces where people participate in collective forms of conscientization through dialogue; where the curriculum represents the lived experiences of the participants, and real life issues and social justice matters become the focus of the lessons. In the tradition of Paulo Freire, this book proposes not only the practice of naming the invisible and unmasking oppression, but it goes on to envision how we can transform the world.

Theme Four

To change the status quo, colleges of education must reform teacher education as we know it. Colleges of education can become pivots of transformative change.

Teacher education is another important focus of this book. The transmission of stereotypes and hegemonic values does not only occur in P-12 settings. Teacher preparation programs are another link in the chain of ideological transmission because they prepare teachers to transmit legitimized forms of knowledge and practices for culturally diverse students. Through No Child Left Behind and accreditation requirements, teacher education has been aligned to the needs of the global economy. Teacher education programs draw upon the same conservative discourses of academic excellence and accountability to impose hegemonic values through their training programs. This book claims that one sector of the struggle for social justice, peace and environmental education must focus on changing this critical educational institution. Colleges of education must change their curriculum by moving away from a view of teachers as technicians to a vision of teachers as transformative intellectuals. This means infusing the teacher education curriculum with foundation courses, problematizing traditional pedagogical practices that allocate students to a hierarchically divided labor force, and teaching through culture and globally recognized ancient and shared values. This book offers concrete guidelines to reclaim colleges of teacher education as public spheres in order to reignite our dreams for an authentic democracy where our privilege does not rely on the oppression of others.

Theme Five

We must create and sustain a positive vision for social justice, peace, and environmental justice education rather than dwelling only on the negative.

Several challenges faced the participants in the Social Justice, Peace, and Environmental Education (SJPEE) project. First, educators and scholars who teach and work in SJPEE areas may be more accustomed to being outside critics rather than actualizers of major institutional changes. Our scholarship and activism has increased our consciousness. We have used a variety of theoretical tools, including postmodernism and postructuralism, to "deconstruct" and analyze what is wrong with theories, research, models, processes, institutions, and systems. This work has been instrumental in developing the foundations of social justice education.

However, as Freire (2000) invites us to develop a pedagogy of hope, we must be able to articulate and implement positive visions for the education we believe will help forge a better world. Many educators are working to bridge this gap by developing curricula, programs, organizations, and working in many spheres of influence. The authors in this project attempt to aid in this effort by supporting positive educational guidelines that integrate social justice, peace, and environmental issues. Our inspiration, the Alaska Native Knowledge Network's Cultural Standards for Alaskan Natives, is an example of this desired vision of education presented in wholly positive terms.

In this book we presented a summary of the history and process of oppression, the roots of war, or the environmental problems exposed by social movements to help readers understand the need for the development of this framework. At first, we found ourselves writing lengthy critiques, rather than prescribing strategies for positive change. Our challenge was to conceive and write about how we could envision a better world, and what were the changes we needed in order to achieve what appeared a distant and unattainable dream. Drawing upon international agreements and documents, authors rose to the challenge and balanced diagnoses of the problems with positive and specific ideas for how education might prepare students to have greater appreciation and care for the natural environment and all living beings, to be skilled in seeking peace, withdrawing support for hatred, greed, violence and war, and forging creative economic arrangements for a more just society.

Theme Six

Global perspectives expand the horizons of thought and extend the possibilities for action.

The transformative guidelines for social and environmental justice and peace education presented in this book invite readers to move beyond localized and national contexts to examine the interconnections with the plight of peoples and forms of oppression in other countries. While understanding that the history of oppression and social justice in the United States should be a mandatory topic in public education, new insights about other oppressed populations in different parts of the world are crucial for conceptualizing social justice, peace, and environmental education within the framework of globalized capitalist practices. Studying the effects of colonialism, neocolonialism, and neoliberal globalization policies on people, animals, and the environment reveals patterns that are difficult to apprehend if the view is limited by national, provincial, or state borders. Examining which nations or regions consume most of the world's resources, where the resources come from, and how the people, animals, and environments of those regions are affected by the production and consumption of these resources provides a depth of understanding unattainable without a global perspective.

Global social movements and documents emerging from grassroots organizations and non-profits around the world remain largely untapped resources for education. Many chapters endorse some version of the concept "Think Globally, Act Locally." Through global activism and education, we can realize that our individual actions (what we eat, what we buy, what we do with our time and money) have a profound impact, for good or bad, on people, animals, and environments across the world. If we understand the benefits of acting, consuming, and buying in support of local, organic/non-genetically modified, fair trade, cruelty-free, environmentally conscious, peaceful living, we will develop a strong motivation to support these movements. Similarly, if we understand that the actions and policies of governments and corporations that harm people, animals, and the environment in places far away are also creating harm for ourselves, we will be motivated to monitor these activities and take civic action to halt, prevent, or repair the consequences of these activities. Thus, we contend that global education for social justice, peace, and the environment means "Thinking Globally, Acting Locally and Globally."

Five Comprehensive Standards:

Standards for Educators, Students, Educational Institutions, Teacher Educators, and Communities

The following five comprehensive standards represent an attempt to create a synthesis of key aspects of social and environmental justice as distilled from the ideas presented in each of the preceding chapters. The comprehensive standards are organized by the five main constituencies most interested in improving education: educators, students, educational institutions, teacher educators, and communities. Though such a synthesis does not fully represent the richness of all the points presented in the individual chapters, we believe it is a useful exercise to map out the major themes for SJPEE standards as presented in the chapters so that a discussion can begin. Throughout this entire process, we have adopted a key qualifier of the Alaska Standards for Culturally Responsive Schools for the standards we present in this book and concluding chapter: "The standards outlined in this document are not intended to be inclusive, exclusive, or conclusive, and thus should be reviewed and adapted to fit local needs" (Assembly of Alaska Native Educators, 1998, p. 3). Any individual or group planning to make use of the SJPEE standards should consider which of these standards are appropriate and which are not, and when necessary, develop additional SJPEE standards to accommodate local circumstances. These "standards" are not intended to produce standardization, but rather to provide some general principles and guidelines for how we can effectively nurture social and environmental justice for an equitable and sustainable future.

Standards for Educators, Students, Educational Institutions, Teacher Educators, and Communities

I. Educators Can Advance Social Justice, Peace, and Environmental Sustainability

1. Engaging in ongoing personal and professional development for self-knowledge, competence, and confidence to integrate SJPEE into all educational spheres.
2. Committing to practice and model just, peaceful, and environmentally principled actions.
3. Supporting the right to basic education that fosters the full educational potential for all children, youth and adults around the world.
4. Providing safe and healthy learning environments, including reasonable class sizes and safe work conditions.
5 Assuring professional and community participation in shaping curriculum and pedagogical practices.
6. Working closely with parents and communities in all aspects of the educational process.
7. Promoting academic freedom to incorporate transformative practices in the teaching of social and environmental justice including:

A. Examining accords, mandates, conventions, treaties, declarations, and other socio-political documents associated with the exercise of basic human rights.
B. Integrating diverse perspectives on SJPEE drawing on multiple ways of knowing, learning, interpreting, and relating to the world around us.
C. Addressing the historical and contemporary impacts of social, political, and economic policies and practices on the human and natural environment.
D. Helping students research individual and collective actions, social movements, and historical policies related to SJPEE.

8. Creating and maintaining effective learning environments that embody the principles and concepts of human rights and environmental sustainability, including:
   A. Developing holistic student understanding through participatory, experiential, accessible, and activist pedagogical practices.
   B. Incorporating local knowledge and ways of knowing through the study of 'place' in all its diverse forms.
   C. Fostering respect for the rights and empowerment of all children and youth.
   D. Building linguistically, culturally and ecologically responsive and accessible learning environments.
   E. Instilling competence, promise, and success for all students, including those experiencing socially constructed marginality.
   F. Providing avenues for societal transformation by promoting universal values, including selflessness, kindness, generosity, cooperation, compassion, and nonviolence.
   G. Cultivating a web of relationships that encompass all elements and creatures that make up the natural world in which we live.
   H. Developing multiple and varied forms of assessment to measure and achieve social justice, peace, and environmental education objectives.

II. Students Can Exercise Social and Environmental Responsibility as Global Citizens

1. Recognizing that humanity is an inseparable part of the web of life in an interdependent socio-cultural and bio-physical universe.
2. Knowing how to investigate and critically analyze the social impact of dominant ideologies, media and technologies, and recognize the influences of propaganda and censorship, including:
   A. Identifying cultural and institutional norms, structures, and practices that exclude and marginalize some groups while favoring others.
   B. Understanding the dynamics linking local and global, as well as personal and collective actions.
   C. Comprehending how personal decisions and actions influence and are influenced by institutional, corporate, and governmental policies and practices.

3. Studying diverse worldviews, knowledge systems, and epistemologies as reflected in varied cultural traditions.
4. Connecting prior knowledge and life experiences to local and global rights and responsibilities, including:
   A. Practicing the principle of "do no harm" in relation to people, other living beings, and the environment.
   B. Understanding how personal and collective identities are dynamic and constructed by the complex interplay of historical, social, political, economic, and geographic factors.
   C. Enacting a politics of identity that is non-essentialist and differentiated to encompass the ironies and contradictions of everyday existence.
   D. Exercising mindfulness of self and others in interacting with the sentient world in which we are situated.
5. Assuming responsibility for the well-being of the cultural and ecological community in which we live, and making sustainable choices by considering the long-term consequences of individual actions.
6. Restoring and protecting the safety and integrity of all peoples, lands, and life forms.
7. Developing analytical, social, and political skills for exercising civic engagement, including:
   A. Practicing the values of love, mutuality, honesty, respect, compassion, and interdependence in everyday affairs.
   B. Taking actions to counteract violence and reduce social/environmental injustices in the community, region, and world.
   C Building bridges and alliances between diverse interests to increase actions to address social and environmental justice issues.
   D. Using land and resources responsibly to sustain the planet for all species.
   E. Thinking globally and locally while acting locally and globally.

III. Educational Institutions (Schools, Higher Education Institutions, Accrediting Bodies) Can Foster Social Justice, Peace, and Environmental Principles

1. Integrating social and environmental justice principles into a collective vision/philosophy/mission statement and accreditation requirements.
2. Hiring a diverse faculty, staff, administration, and security personnel with SJPEE credentials who operate with vigorous fairness and set the standard for respectful treatment of faculty, staff, and students.
3. Incorporating cultural practices that emphasize collective responsibilities and obligations and foster a sense of community.
4. Encouraging student, community, and educator participation in examining and clarifying policies and practices with regard to implementing SJPEE standards.
5. Allocating safe spaces where students, faculty, and staff can engage in a community with a spirit of friendship and mutual support.

6. Ensuring safe, violence-free, pollution-free, energy-efficient, and environmentally friendly facilities.
7. Providing healthy, environmentally conscious, locally produced food and safe clean water.
8. Establishing links with external community, health, medical, and social agencies to provide support for students dealing with issues of safety and well-being.
9. Implementing institutional support systems, incentives, and awards for students, faculty, staff, and administrators who enact SJPEE-friendly practices.
10. Instituting remediation for elements of institutions that fail to meet SJPEE standards.

IV. Teacher Educators Can Support Social Justice, Peace, and Environmental Education

1. Critically analyzing and transforming the culture and curriculum of teacher education to include SJPEE issues that engage citizens and policymakers in understanding, identifying, and ameliorating disabling social structures and relationships in schools and communities.
2. Offering specific instruction on social and environmental justice issues in preparation for implementing the SJPEE standards.
3. Preparing educators to prevent bullying, violence, and hate-speech, providing a safe classroom and school for every student.
4. Providing teacher education students with opportunities to practice habits of respect, compassion, nonviolence, justice, and environmental conservation that model and foster considerate behaviors in students.
5. Preparing educators to collaborate with others and serve as allies to oppressed or marginalized students based on any actual, perceived, or socially constructed characteristic.

V. Communities Can Support Social Justice, Peace, and Environmental Education

1. Working to assure the safety and well-being of all children, youth, and families, including:
   A. Pursuing resolution to conflicts by peaceful and diplomatic means.
   B. Protecting children and families from homelessness, hunger, destitution, child labor, slavery, sexual abuse, violence, and unsafe air, food, and water.
   C. Providing adequate and accessible health care regardless of ability to pay.
   D. Providing child-friendly environments and life experiences for belonging, participation, pride, joy, and self-determination.
2. Increasing self-determination by insuring parent involvement with SJPEE decision-making in schools.

3. Validating and legitimating cultural aspirations and identity through comparative study and support for heritage languages, knowledge, culture, and values.
4. Sharing expertise with students, faculty, and other school personnel from a broad representation of SJPEE community organizations and cultural groups.
5. Involving children and youth in civil society through direct participation in monitoring problems, setting policies, and implementing solutions.

Closing Thoughts

In closing, we invite readers to join us in this dialogue and build upon it. We would like this book to offer a point of departure from which progressive educators and activists can develop a more sophisticated vision for a better society. Our book offers an alternative view to the prevailing neoliberal orthodoxy on education, a new discourse, propelled by a sense of urgency for change, for integrating social justice and environmental sustainability into the formal academic curriculum. Since many of the devastating social and ecological problems we face today stem from the currently dominant patterns of development, production and consumption that are validated and reinforced by the current educational system, we hope to broaden the debate so that the issues covered in this book will eventually be incorporated into the curriculum of every single school.

As the public demands that educational policymakers embrace social justice, peace, and environmental justice education, there must be animated public debate around these issues in schools, communities, states, and nations. While we acknowledge the dire need to put political pressure on governments, policymakers, and educational institutions to return education back to the public sphere, we realize that bureaucratic systems are resistant to change. To move this agenda forward with some urgency, we therefore advocate building a grass-roots social movement among teachers, teacher educators, administrators, parents, and students, in the traditions of the indigenous movements for educational self-determination or the social reconstructionist movement of the 1930s in which schools were seen as primary venues for societal transformation. This book urges a new dialogue as the starting-point for this new social movement. The guidelines offered here expand the current educational discourse of accountability to include social justice, peace and environmental sustainability as a framework to evaluate social and governmental institutions. Taking our cue from the indigenous theory and guidelines set out by Ray Barnhardt and Graham Smith in chapters 2 and 3 of this volume, we assert that it is time for all of us to transcend "the new formations of colonization embedded in the neoliberal restructuring of education" that we have all experienced over the past few decades (Smith, p. 21, this volume). It is time for us to reclaim the public sphere through a grassroots educational movement and to build a better, freer, more just, and more sustainable world.

References

Assembly of Alaska Native Educators. (1998). *Alaska standards for culturally-responsive schools.* Fairbanks: Alaska Native Knowledge Network.

Freire, P. (2000). *Pedagogy of the oppressed* (M. Ramos, Trans.). New York: Continuum.

Contributors

Julie Andrzejewski (St. Cloud State University) is a professor in the Department of Human Relations and Multicultural Education at St. Cloud State University in Minnesota. She is co-founder and co-director of the Master's degree program in Social Responsibility and has authored numerous articles on social justice issues, media, animal rights, activism, and global citizenship. She is the editor of *Oppression and Social Justice: Critical Frameworks* (1996), and co-author of *Why Can't Sharon Kowalski Come Home* (1988) which received a Lambda Literary Award. In 2003, she was nominated as the CASE Professor of the Year from SCSU. In 2000, she initiated the Social Justice, Peace, Environmental, and Interspecies Education Project and chaired American Educational Research Association sessions on various aspects of the project for six years. In addition to her scholarly work, she has worked on local, state, and national activist projects, and directed several university-wide curriculum transformation grant projects. Further, she created the first Animal Rights course at SCSU, is the author of "Teaching Animal Rights at the University: Philosophy and Practice" (www.cala-online.org), and serves on the Board of Directors for the Institute for Critical Animals Studies.

Marta P. Baltodano (Loyola Marymount University), PhD, is an Associate Professor of Education at the School of Education of Loyola Marymount University in Los Angeles. She is originally from Nicaragua where she worked as a human rights attorney for 13 years. Her current research focuses on interracial conflicts between Latinos and African American students in Los Angeles. She has also examined teachers' beliefs about social justice and has investigated the impact of the anti-bilingual legislation in the process of identity formation of second language learners in California. Her teaching includes issues of critical educational theory, globalization, social justice, and ethnographic research for classroom teachers and doctoral students. She is a founding member of the California Consortium for Critical Educators (CCCE); a founding member and past chair of the Special Interest Group: Critical Educators for Social Justice (CESJ) of AERA; past chair of Committee #1, Anthropological Studies of Schools and Culture, of the American Anthropological Association (AAA); a former member of the Dissertation Award Committee of the Council of Anthropology and Education (CAE) of AAA, and the 2005–2007 Contributing Editor of the Council of Anthropology of Education to *Anthropology News*. She is currently the co-chair of the Mission Committee of the Council of Anthropology and Education and the 2008–2009 program co-chair of Division G (Social Context of Education) of the American Educational Research Association. She co-edited the book *The Critical Pedagogy Reader* (Darder, Baltodano, & Torres, 2003, 2008) and has published several articles in peer-refereed journals. She is currently working on a book that unveils the role of teacher preparation programs in the process of social reproduction.

Ray Barnhardt (University of Alaska Fairbanks), is a professor of cross-cultural studies at the University of Alaska Fairbanks, where he has been involved in teaching and research related to Native education issues since 1970. He has served as co-director of the Alaska Rural Systemic Initiative for the past 10 years. Over the past 35 years, he has also served as the director of the Cross-Cultural Education Development (X-CED) Program, the Small High Schools Project, the Center for Cross-Cultural Studies, and the Alaska Native Knowledge Network. His research interests include Indigenous knowledge systems, Native teacher education, distance/distributed/higher education, small school curriculum, and institutional adaptations to rural and cross-cultural settings. His experiences in education beyond Alaska range from teaching mathematics in Baltimore, Maryland, to research in Canada, Iceland, India, Malawi, and New Zealand.

Nola Butler Byrd (California State University, San Diego), PhD, is an African American scholar and assistant professor in the Community-Based Block (CBB) Program in the Department of Counseling and School Psychology, College of Education at San Diego State University. CBB is a non-traditional MA-level multicultural counselor preparation program. Her research interests are: African-centered education and philosophy, experiential multicultural education and counseling for social justice, indigenous healing and world view, somatic body work, multicultural identity development, and multi-ethnic faculty retention.

David Lee Carlson (Arizona State University) is an assistant professor in secondary education at Arizona State University. His research focuses on methods that prepare teachers to teach literature and multiple forms of writing in secondary urban schools. He completed a genealogy of portfolio assessment for his dissertation, pursuing an interest in how the post-modern methodologies of Michel Foucault can influence English education. David earned his EdD in English Education from Teachers College, Columbia University. He taught in urban schools in Washington, D.C. and New York City, where he was awarded Teacher of the Year for his school and where he served as coordinator of the English department and dean of students.

Robert E. Crafton (Slippery Rock University) is an associate professor of English at Slippery Rock University, Slippery Rock, Pennsylvania. He holds a PhD from Washington University, St. Louis, Missouri, in English Language and Literature. A member of a number of professional organizations, Professor Crafton chaired NAME's Academic Standards Committee, which was responsible for developing criteria for evaluating the responsiveness of state curriculum standards to multicultural interests. He is currently the chair of the National Council of Teachers of English Standing Committee Against Censorship and serves as an elected officer on the board of Sigma Tau Delta, the International English Honor Society. His publications and conference presentations cover a variety of topics, including school censorship issues, the neuro-cognitive mapping of language structures in the brain, the representation of minority interests and histories in American history texts and state history standards, the representation of racial, ethnic, and minority experiences in contemporary crime fiction.

Antonia Darder (University of Illinois at Urbana-Champaign) is Distinguished Professor of Educational Policy Studies and Latina/Latino Studies at the University of Illinois Urbana-Champaign. She is author of *Culture and Power in the Classroom, Reinventing Paulo Freire,* and *After Race: Racism after Multiculturalism*; and co-editor of the *Critical Pedagogy Reader* and the *Latino Studies Reader.* Darder is involved in the independent media movement as a journalist for the community newspaper the *Public i* and producer of Liberacion!, a public affairs radio program on WEFT 909.1 FM that focuses on politics, art, and struggle.

Deborah Gallagher (University of Northern Iowa) is professor of education at the University of Northern Iowa, Cedar Falls. Her research interests center on the philosophy of science as it pertains to research, pedagogy, and policy in education. This work focuses on how choices of methodological and conceptual frameworks affect the possibilities of achieving equitable and inclusive schooling for students labeled as having disabilities. Among other recent publications, she is lead author of *Challenging Orthodoxy in Special Education: Dissenting Voices* (Love Publishing) with co-authors Lous Heshusius, Richard Iano, and Thomas Skrtic. In 2006, this book was selected as one of three Key Texts for the Inclusion Strand of the European Educational Research Association.

David A. Greenwood (formerly Gruenewald) (Washington State University) is an associate professor in the Department of Teaching and Learning at Washington State University, Spokane. A lifelong lover of the outdoors, David's current research, teaching, and community work revolve around place and sustainability studies. He has authored many papers on these themes in general education journals such as the *Harvard Educational Review*, the *American Educational Research Journal, Curriculum Inquiry, Educational Studies, Educational Administration Quarterly,* and *Educational Researcher.* With Gregory Smith, he is co-editor of *Place-Based Education in the Global Age: Local Diversity* (2007). These works invite making connections between the ecological and cultural contexts of living and learning. At WSU, David currently teaches Cultural and Community Contexts of Education; Environment, Culture and Education; and Action Research. In the Honors College at WSU, he team teaches the interdisciplinary course, The Science and Culture of Place, with environmental science faculty.

Menan Jangu (University of Michigan, Ann Arbor) is a PhD candidate at the University of Michigan, Ann Arbor. His research focuses on the knowledge of indigenous African peoples with a specific interest in traditional medicine practitioners. He has a background in global environmental and social justice issues. He has written numerous reports on environmental conditions in Tanzania.

Todd Jennings (California State University, San Bernardino), PhD, is a developmental and educational psychologist who teaches in the College of Education at California State University, San Bernardino. His research focuses on human rights education and topics related to the preparation of teachers who affirm diversity and see their work as related to social justice advocacy. Dr. Jennings is a volunteer with Amnesty International, supporting their efforts to promote human rights education in schools and communities.

Yvette V. Lapayese (Loyola Marymount University, Los Angeles) is assistant professor in the School of Education at Loyola Marymount University. She received her PhD from the University of California, Los Angeles. She formerly served as a bilingual elementary school teacher and is extensively involved in research on critical educators in the classroom. Professor Lapayese's other research interests include race and feminist methodologies and critical theory and practice as it relates to teachers and students of color.

Darla Linville (City University of New York) is a doctoral candidate in the Urban Education Program at the Graduate Center of the City University of New York. Her work focuses on issues of sexuality and gender equity for young people, and on making institutions more responsive to their needs. Her dissertation, "Resisting Regulation: Teens and Discourses of Sexuality and Gender in High Schools," asks about the current discursive climate in schools in which LGBTQ young people are creating their sexuality and gendered identities. She seeks to understand how students accept or resist discourses as they create their own sexual subjectivities. Her publications include "Race, Sexuality and Schools: A quantitative assessment of intersectionality," co-authored with Juan Battle and published in *Race, Gender & Class*, and "Queer Theory and Teen Sexuality: Unclear lines," forthcoming in a collection she co-authored with Jean Anyon, Michael Dumas, Kathleen Nolan, Madeline Perez, Eve Tuck, and Jen Weiss.

Bob O. Manteaw (Eastern Washington University) is an assistant professor at Eastern Washington University. Bob is originally from Ghana, and has lived, worked, and studied in England and the United States. His cross-cultural experiences and understanding of sustainable development thinking and practices continue to impact and direct his works, which have mainly been in education, both formal and non-formal. His current research focuses on the discourse of sustainability in education with a particular interest in multisector learning and action partnerships for sustainable development in different sociocultural settings. Currently, he teaches a course to pre-service teachers in Family, School, and Community Collaboration, and makes issues of sustainability, place-conscious education, and alternative pedagogies a central focus. Bob has also worked in different capacities for the World Bank and UNICEF on Development Education programs and social change. He is a member of the Education and Communication Commission of the World Conservation Union (IUCN) based in Gland, Switzerland.

Renée Jeanne Martin (University of Toledo), PhD, is a full professor in the Department of Educational Foundations and Leadership in The Judith Herb College of Education at The University of Toledo, Ohio. She has edited three books and published articles in numerous prominent educational journals. Among Dr. Martin's interests is the mentoring of graduate students into the profession. With her students, she has developed and created numerous readers' theater presentations about the lives of women in higher education. The focus of her scholarly research is on issues of social justice and the creation and development of critical pedagogical approaches to equity at all educational strata. Her other interests include theater, choreography, golf, and interior design. Dr. Martin is the recipient of two National Women Educators' awards; the University of Toledo Outstanding Woman Award; the University of Toledo's Eberly Center for Women Outstanding Woman Award; and the University of Toledo's Outstanding Teacher Award.

Leigh M. O'Brien (State University of New York – Geneseo) is Associate Professor of Education at State University of New York – Geneseo. She is a national and international presenter, author of numerous articles and chapters, and co-editor, with Beth Swadener, of *Writing the Motherline: Mothers, Daughters, and Education.* Her research interests include teacher preparation for a democratic society, women and education, and early childhood special education policies and practices.

Glenn Omatsu (University of California, Los Angeles) is a Lecturer in Asian American Studies and the Educational Opportunity Program at California State University, Northridge (CSUN) and also teaches classes at Pasadena City College and UCLA. At CSUN, he is coordinator of the Faculty Mentor Program. He is co-editor (with Steve Louie) of *Asian Americans: The Movement and Moment* and co-editor (with Edith Chen) of *Teaching about Asian Pacific Americans: Effective Strategies, Activities, and Assignments for Classrooms and Communities.* He also has written articles on Freedom Schooling, immigrant labor struggles, and other social movements for justice.

Valerie Owen (National-Louis University), PhD, an associate professor at National-Louis University, is the Director of the Disability and Equity in Education Doctoral Program, and teaches in a graduate special education program preparing "change of career adults" to become teachers. She began her career 30 years ago as a classroom teacher of children with autism as well as those considered the most significantly disabled. In addition to being a founding member and former officer in the Disability Studies in Education Special Interest Group of the American Educational Research Association, she a founder of the Second City Disability Studies and Education Conference. As such, she works to support a community of education scholars who critically examines the interplay of disability and various aspects of society and culture through research, practice, teacher education and activism. Her scholarship and publications focus on re-imaging teaching, assuring progress in the general education curriculum for all students, and critical perspectives of professional teaching standards.

Helena Pedersen (Uppsala University, Sweden), PhD in Education, is a researcher at the Centre for Gender Research, Uppsala University in 2008/09. Her primary research interests are species-inclusive critical pedagogies and intersectionality studies. Recent and forthcoming works appear in the volumes *Farewell to Noah: Transforming Animal Encounter in the Twilight of the Zoo* (Lexington Books, 2009), *Global Harms. Ecological Crime and Speciesism* (Nova Science Publishers, 2009), and *Values and Democracy in Education for Sustainable Development* (Liber, 2008). Helena Pedersen received the American Sociological Association's Award for Distinguished Graduate Student Scholarship (the Animals and Society Section) in 2006.

Thomas M. Skrtic (University of Kansas), PhD, is Gene A. Budig Teaching Professor of Special Education at the University of Kansas, Kansas City. He coordinates the program in special education policy and leadership and teaches courses in public policy, professional ethics, and organization and administration of special education. His 2005 text, *Special Education Policy and Practice: Accountability, Instruction, and Social Challenges* (with co-editors Karen Harris and James Shriner) is a compilation of research on the conditions of practice under standards-based reform. His academic interests are critical social theory, American pragmatism, and democratic reform, which inform several of his published works, including *Behind Special Education: A Critical Analysis of Professional Culture and School Organization* (1991) and *Disability and Democracy: Reconstructing (Special) Education for Post-modernity* (1995). He has lectured and consulted on these topics and special education reform throughout North America, and in Europe, Asia, Australia, and Russia.

Graham H. Smith (Te Whare Wananga o Awanuiarangi, Aotearoa) (Mgati Porou, Ngati Apa) is currently Distinguished Professor and Chief Executive Officer at Te Whare Wananga o Awanuiarangi, a Maori university in Aotearoa (New Zealand). Smith's academic work focuses on issues related to transforming Maori educational and schooling circumstances in New Zealand. He has researched and published in areas related to indigenous theorizing, language revitalization, and alternative schooling; educational policy, politics, curriculum, pedagogy, and political economy; and higher education with regard to the knowledge economy and institutional transformation.

Gregory A. Smith (Lewis & Clark College) is a professor in the Graduate School of Education and Counseling at Lewis & Clark College, Portland, Oregon. A former high school English teacher, he has devoted much of his career to strengthening the relationship between schools and the communities they serve. He is one of the early proponents of place- or community-based education, an approach to curriculum development that incorporates local knowledge and issues into students' school experiences. Greg serves on the board of the Rural School and Community Trust, a national organization devoted to strengthening the role of schools and students as agents of community transformation. He is the author, co-author, editor, or co-editor of the following books: *Reducing the Risk: Schools as Communities of Support* (1989), *Education and the Environment: Learning to Live with Limits* (1992), *Public Schools That Work: Creating Community* (1993), *Ecological Education in Action: On Weaving Education, Culture, and the Environment* (1999), and *Place-Based Education in the Global Age: Local Diversity* (forthcoming). Greg earned his BA at the University of Oregon in 1970, MA from Southern Oregon University in 1976, and PhD from the University of Wisconsin-Madison in 1989.

Robin M. Smith (State University of New York – New Paltz), PhD, is an Associate Professor of Special Education at the State University of New York at New Paltz. She has been a disability rights activist for 20 years, dealing with such issues as accessible mass transit and consumer directed personal care assistance. Her longstanding interest in promoting positive attitudes and images in media and society has surfaced in her academic publications, her activist conference presentations, and her classes as she seeks to promote competence oriented imagery and teaching practices. She has presented at conferences on competence oriented imagery and practice as well as the impact of disability humor on attitude. Areas of expertise are inclusion, academic engagement of students with severe disabilities, multiple intelligences in inclusive classrooms, classroom environments and supports for diverse populations. She has published refereed articles and given presentations on inclusion, the social construction of disability, disability awareness and self-advocacy, academic engagements of non-speaking students, and multiple intelligences.

Beth Blue Swadener (Arizona State University) is Professor of Early Childhood Education and Policy Studies at Arizona State University. Her research focuses on social policy, professional development, dual-language programs, and child and family issues in Africa. She has published seven books, including *Decolonizing Research in Cross-Cultural Context* and *Power and Voice in Research with Children* and numerous articles and chapters. She is also active in a number of social justice and child advocacy projects.

Linda Symcox (California State University, Long Beach), PhD, is a Professor of Teacher Education at California State University, Long Beach, (CSULB), director of the Curriculum & Instruction Masters Program, and co-director of the CSULB Urban Teaching Academy. Dr. Symcox serves as the lead history education scholar for several Teaching American History Grants in Southern California, and as lead education scholar for the groundbreaking KCET "Participation Nation" multimedia project. Dr. Symcox was formerly the associate director of the National Center for History in the Schools at UCLA (1989–1996), where she served as Assistant Director of the National History Standards Project. Symcox also served as a lead consultant developing curriculum standards for the Middle Eastern State of Qatar. Symcox's scholarly research examines the interplay between curriculum theory, policy, and reform, and she teaches courses in educational history, curriculum theory, curriculum policy, school reform, and social studies education. Professor Symcox is author of *Whose History? The Struggle for National Standards in American Classrooms* (Teachers College Press, 2002), and she has published numerous articles, book chapters, and curricula in the field of history education and teacher development. She is co-editor of *National History Standards: The Problem of the Canon and the Future of Teaching History* (Information Age Publishing, 2009).

Christopher Walsh (Deakin University, Melbourne, Australia), PhD, is currently working as a lecturer in language and literacy at Deakin University in Melbourne Australia. He relocated to Australia after working as a TESOL consultant for UNICEF in Kabul, Afghanistan working at the Ministry of Education to co-author two English language textbooks and train teachers. Through a Spencer Foundation grant, he researched and co-designed a transdisciplinary multiliteracies curriculum drawing on semiotics, visual grammars and systemic functional linguistics. His current research funded by the Australian Research Council (ARC), investigates literacy in the digital world of the twenty-first century and learning from computer games. The project aims to help teachers better understand and teach ICT-enabled forms of text and literacy, drawing on insights from young people's actual engagement with digital culture in their leisure hours. The project will help strengthen young Australians' capacity to critically evaluate and use ICTs for effective learning and communication.

Freeman Wicklund (Mercy for Animals) received his Bachelor of Science in nutrition from the University of Minnesota. He founded two environmental and animal protection nonprofits as well as the Twin Cities-based humane education program, Bridges of Respect. He worked at Bridges of Respect as a humane educator for 5 years at providing presentations to students in grades 6 through college. For 2 years, he worked for PETA's humane education program TeachKind, helping to create curriculum for educators. He currently is a volunteer coordinator for Mercy for Animals.

Index

Page numbers in italic refer to Figures or Tables.